# Secularism and Muslim Democracy in Turkey

In 2002 the Islamist Justice and Development Party (AKP) swept to power in Turkey. Since then it has shied away from a hard-line ideological stance in favor of a more conservative and democratic approach. M. Hakan Yavuz, a premier scholar of Turkey, negotiates this ambivalence, asking whether it is possible for a political party with a deeply religious ideology to liberalize and entertain democracy or whether, as he contends, radical religious groups moderate their practices and ideologies when forced to negotiate a competitive and rule-based political system. While the author explores the thesis through an analysis of the rise and evolution of the AKP and its more recent 2007 election victory, his conclusion – that everyday political realities ultimately override ideology and dogma – can be comparatively applied to other Muslim countries facing similar challenges. The book, which tackles a number of important issues including political participation, economics, internal security, the Kurdish question and Turkey's bid to enter the European Union, provides a masterful survey of modern Turkish and Islamic politics, which will be of interest to a broad range of readers from students to professionals and policymakers.

M. Hakan Yavuz is Associate Professor in the Department of Political Science and Center for Middle East Studies at the University of Utah. His recent publications include *The Emergence of a New Turkey: Democracy and AK Parti* (2006) and *Islamic Political Identity in Turkey* (2005).

*Cambridge Middle East Studies 28*

*Editorial Board*

Charles Tripp (general editor)
Julia Clancy-Smith
F. Gregory Gause
Yezid Sayigh
Avi Shlaim
Judith E. Tucker

**Cambridge Middle East Studies** has been established to publish books on the nineteenth- to twenty-first-century Middle East and North Africa. The aim of the series is to provide new and original interpretations of aspects of Middle Eastern societies and their histories. To achieve disciplinary diversity, books will be solicited from authors writing in a wide range of fields including history, sociology, anthropology, political science and political economy. The emphasis will be on producing books offering an original approach along theoretical and empirical lines. The series is intended for students and academics, but the more accessible and wide-ranging studies will also appeal to the interested general reader.

*A list of books in the series can be found after the index*

# Secularism and Muslim Democracy in Turkey

M. Hakan Yavuz

*University of Utah*

CAMBRIDGE UNIVERSITY PRESS
Cambridge, New York, Melbourne, Madrid, Cape Town, Singapore, São Paulo,
Delhi

Cambridge University Press
The Edinburgh Building, Cambridge CB2 8RU, UK

Published in the United States of America by Cambridge University Press,
New York

www.cambridge.org
Information on this title: www.cambridge.org/9780521717328

First published 2009

Printed in the United Kingdom at the University Press, Cambridge

*A catalogue record for this publication is available from the British Library*

*Library of Congress Cataloguing in Publication data*
Yavuz, M. Hakan.
Secularism and Muslim democracy in Turkey / M. Hakan Yavuz.
   p.   cm. – (Cambridge Middle East studies; 28)
Includes bibliographical references and index.
ISBN 978-0-521-88878-3
1. Turkey – Politics and government – 1980–   2. AK Parti (Turkey)   3. Islam
and politics – Turkey.   4. Islam and state – Turkey.   5. Secularism – Turkey –
21st century.   I. Title.   II. Series.
DR603.Y375   2008
324.2561′04–dc22

                                                                2008026923

ISBN 978-0-521-88878-3 hardback
ISBN 978-0-521-71732-8 paperback

To Tevhide, Neşe, Yasemen and Handan

Indeed, God does not change the condition of a people until they change what is in themselves. (Qur'an, 13:11)

I am like a compass. With one foot I stand securely on the foundation of my faith, with the other foot I wander throughout the seventy-two nations of the world. (M. J. Rumi (1207–1273))

# Contents

# Preface

This book examines the principal puzzle that confronts many Muslim and non-Muslim countries: is it possible for religiously inspired (Islamic) political movements to become agents of democratization and even of liberalization? Or is the adaptation of secular ideas (ideology) and institutions through a process of internal reform and secularization necessary to establish a liberal and democratic system in Muslim societies? In other words this puzzle is closely related to one central question that has been of primary concern to social scientists: what is the connection between religious movements and democracy, on the one hand, and democracy and secularism, on the other? Do prevailing Islamic ideas and norms pose an obstacle to the transition to democracy, as most prominently argued by Daniel Lerner, Bernard Lewis and Samuel Huntington?

My general contention is that radical religious groups moderate their practices and ideologies when they enter into a competitive and rule-based participatory political system. The political openness characterizing this kind of system leads to reflexivity and a gradual moderation of the interpretation of the religious dogma and of political platforms on the part of religious groups. This process, in turn, allows the log-jam between polarized secular and religious forces to be broken discursively, as each side is now able to engage directly with the other along multiple channels of interaction in political and public spheres, eroding monolithic and homogeneous socio-political blocs. Moreover, a peaceful transition to pluralist and democratic politics is facilitated if two conditions exist: a functioning tax-based liberal economic market, and a porous public sphere that allows for the cross-fertilization of contending values and identities.

Such a development has taken place in some Muslim countries, including Turkey, Malaysia and Indonesia, where major Islamic political movements have eschewed radical ideologies and now embrace democratic platforms. This book examines how and why this substantial transformation in the outlook of Islamist movements has happened. Earlier studies attempting to explain the absence of democratization have focused exclusively either on structural factors or on a monolithic and unchanging view of Islamic beliefs and textual understanding. This study seeks to bring structure (socio-political context) and agency (religious leaders and believers) together to explain why and how religious movements can contribute to the processes of democratization and pluralism in Muslim majority states through a dynamic reinterpretation of the religious tradition. The focus of this study will be on the ability of religious actors to reconstruct the meaning of religious texts through hermeneutical approaches, rather than using established religious dogma, in explaining political behavior in the public sphere. The book develops an interactive model of interplay between structural factors such as the type of political system and economic conditions and the ability of believers to reread the religious traditions to respond to new challenges. To this end, the book first identifies structural conditions for the emergence of a liberal religious discourse and then examines the interpretive abilities of embedded religious leaders. The book explains the evolution of liberal political attitudes as a result of the convergence between political convictions, religious hermeneutics, textual exegesis and political/strategic interactions.

In undertaking such a textual- and discourse-oriented humanistic approach, I hope to enhance and move beyond more conventional social science approaches, which focus on socio-economic and structural factors to explain Islamic socio-political movements. In addition to these structural factors, it is important to study the discursive practices of Islamic movements, because Islamic idioms still remain the most potent force of political mobilization in different Muslim countries, due to the lack of a process of secularization as has occurred in the West. This dominant religious discourse not only defines the spiritual and moral understanding of believers, but it also provides guidance to Muslims in different aspects of their private and public life, including politics. Historically, Islam has been among the most visible public religions in terms of its politicization; it has made itself readily available to reformers – and even to revolutionaries – calling for drastic cultural, social and political transformations, as well as to conservatives skeptical of any change in the customs and traditions of their countries. As a result, while Islamic movements in various guises have functioned as the vehicle of democratization in several Muslim countries, depending on the textual, historical, cultural and hermeneutical traditions, they have also emerged as the main obstacle to democratic reforms in many others.

Islamic movements reflect competing visions of community, authority, legitimacy and identity. The Islamization of Turkish political language in the 1980s and 1990s has had a significant implication for the struggle to redefine the nation and the meaning of the good life. Islamic ideas are injected into the debates over the meaning of nation and political life. Islam with the new media-saturated age became more significant in terms of its ability to provide symbols, networks, myths and identities, to be mobilized for or against real or imagined enemies. At the heart of the Islamic challenge in modern Turkey has been the continuing debate over how to define the public sphere, secularism and the political community. The conflict is between those who want a society based upon a Jacobin secular vision of social and political order – defined by the disestablishment of Islam in the public sphere – and those who embrace an Islamic conception of society and moral order. While the former affirm that the solution for Turkey's problem is modernity without Islam, the latter argue for modernity with Islam.

Islam as the most powerful source of solidarity helps to redefine who is a member of a given community; it offers shared moral values that regulate social order.[1] Thus, Islam, just like other religions, simultaneously homogenizes and differentiates. My study examines the manner in which religious ideas are deployed by social and political groups to enhance their interests, and the subsequent implications these have had for Islam, politics and social order. Since religion and politics are closely engaged in the same issues of normative order, collective identity and legitimate authority, they cannot be separated, as some militant secularists wish for. Indeed, Islamic pronouncements provide a licence to a specific political agenda, and identify it in the best interests of the community to be realized through mass mobilization. Thus, Islam affects the core identity of the ruling AKP and its conceptions of politics and identity.

This study will identify the contextual conditions under which Islamists prefer moderation over confrontation by utilizing the experience of Turkish Islamic groups. The case of Turkey is particularly important due to Turkey's recent experience of co-existence and co-evolution in the matter of the transformation of Islamic movements and the democratization and liberalization of political and economic systems. In Turkey, a group of committed liberal-democrats has emerged from within the ranks of an ostracized Islamic political movement, which has successfully formed a broad democratic platform appealing to a wide range of sectarian, ethnic, social and political forces hitherto marginalized by the Kemalist state. By utilizing the case study of Turkey, I reject an essentialist approach to understanding the politics of Muslim countries. On the contrary, I argue that the transformation of Islamic movements toward a

---

[1] Robert Wuthnow defines moral order as "values and norms that regulate and legitimate social institutions." Wuthnow, *Meaning and Moral Order: Explorations in Cultural Analysis* (Berkeley: University of California Press, 1987), p. 1.

genuine Muslim democratic orientation is a vindication of the need for abandoning essentialism, and the outcome of several contextual variables: the ongoing process of liberalization creating competitive political and economic spaces, the growing role of the Muslim bourgeoisie, the expanding public sphere and the inclusion of new intellectuals into the movement. The most important factor in the evolution of a Muslim democratic movement is the rising bourgeoisie and its continued commitment to democratic values as expressed in its support for cultural exchanges and new intellectuals' projects.

The book consists of three sections. In the first section, the introduction raises a number of theoretical questions about the definition and evolution of Islamic parties. It also seeks to explore the conditions under which an Islamic political movement ceases to be Islamic and becomes non- or post-Islamic. I argue that due to three structural factors (political participation, neo-liberal economic policies and the expansion of the market), the Turkish Islamic political movement has evolved to a point that it has ceased to be Islamic. The first chapter examines the context within which the AKP emerged, by focusing on the impact of history and economy on contemporary Turkish politics. This section examines five critical stages of modern Turkish history to understand the connection between democracy and development. It also examines the role of the state and economic policies in the constitution of the Turkish Islamic landscape.

The second section starts with chapter 2 and examines the socio-political origins of the AKP movement. It traces the trajectory of the Islamic political movement, starting from the establishment of the NOM until its culmination as the AKP. It also closely examines the political and social origins of the AKP's split from the VP, marking the historical transformation of the movement into a liberal-democratic force, abandoning its earlier discourse. It also analyzes the conditions that prepared the ground for the AKP's victory in the 2002 elections. The third chapter looks at identity, ideology and leadership issues within the AKP. The fourth chapter examines two prominent leaders of the AKP, Recep Tayyip Erdoğan and Abdullah Gül, and their role in the evolution of the AKP's identity.

The third section consists of 3 chapters. Chapter 5 analyzes the socio-political impact of the AKP government on Turkey's domestic politics, and the new political challenges it has faced during its term in government. It also examines the dynamic interaction between the AKP's policies and its supporters. The main questions to be addressed are: will the AKP convert its electoral majority into a durable electoral base? How will the AKP cope with poverty, secularism and the headscarf issue without confronting the powerful secular forces within the establishment? The sixth chapter focuses on the most controversial domestic and foreign policy issue: the Kurdish question and the AKP's policies in this field. Chapter 7 examines continuity and change in the making and implementation of Turkish foreign policy. It analyses the EU membership process, the Cyprus issue and US–Turkey relations within the context of Iraq. What guides the foreign policy of the AKP? Is it national/party identity or national/party interests? Is the confusing and fragmented foreign policy of the AKP a reflection of its syncretic identity? Chapter 8 analyzes the causes and political consequences of the 2007 national elections. The book's conclusion reflects the major shift of political grammar in Turkey in terms of ending "two track governments" (the power sharing between the unelected military and the elected politicians) and of stressing human rights discourse.

In short, I call the contemporary transformation in Turkey a conservative revolution for two reasons: the current revolution is led and shaped by civil society; and societal and economic changes have preceded political change. The conservative revolution is a bottom-up transformation in terms of the institutionalization of "politically correct" creole language and new actors. Thus, this is a bottom-up and gradual revolution in society to control the political language and society; and eventually the state.[2] The Islamic groups already control the political society and seek to control the state. With the AKP government, Islam has become the undisputed identity referent of Turkey. The agents of this conservative revolution launched an impressive and multifaceted challenge to the Kemalist status quo by capturing civil society organizations and associations. In short, Sheri Berman is partially right to argue that civil society has become an "incubator for illiberal radicalism."[3] Contrary to the dominant literature on civil society in the Middle East, civil society is not an inherently liberal and tolerant space in which people and associations interact in order to achieve democracy and reform. In the case of Turkey, some illiberal and conservative voices are rooted and fed by civil society associations.

The questions I address in this book have engaged me since 1998. I have addressed some of them before, principally in *Islamic Political Identity in Turkey* (2003) and *The Emergence of a New Turkey* (2006). I revisit some of the questions here, because my views have continued to develop and

---

[2] Asef Bayat, "Revolution without Movement, Movement without Revolution: Comparing Islamic Activism in Iran and Egypt," *Comparative Studies in Society and History*, 40:1 (January 1998), 136–169.

[3] Sheri Berman, "Islamism, Revolution and Civil Society," *Perspectives on Politics*, 1 (June 2003), 257.

even to change. What I say in this book is continuous with my previous writings on Islam and politics. However, there are a number of chapters that represent a break with my previous work. I owe this intellectual development to a number of friends here and abroad. During the writing of this book, I visited Turkey five times and carried out a series of interviews. I would like to thank Mujeeb R. Khan, Atilla Yayla, Mustafa Erdoğan, Ali Carkaoğlu, Nihat Ali Özcan, Edibe Sözen, Frederick Quinn, Yasin Aktay, İhsan Dağı, Şaban Kardaş, Uli Schamioğlu, Umut Azer, Fatih Balcı, Ali Yacıoğlu and Uygar Aktan. A special note of appreciation is due to the two readers of this text – Peter Sluglett and Eric Hooglund – and the two anonymous readers from Cambridge University Press. Thanks also go to Judd King, Halil İbrahim Yenigün, Ergun Yıldırım, Hasan Kösebalaban, Ahmet Kuru, Nader Hashemi, Mark Button, Asma Afsaruddin, Etga Uğur and K. Haluk Yavuz, who helped in a number of ways to complete the project. Throughout the writing of this book, I have benefited from several opportunities to present my chapters as they were evolving and have received feedback from my colleagues in America and abroad. These included a workshop organized by Mehmet Ümit Necef at the Southern Denmark University in September 2006; a professional presentation at Carleton University (Ottawa) in December 2004; and an invited lecture at a conference on Turkish politics at Baku State University in April 2007. Finally, I would like to thank Özay Mehmet, Adil Bagirov and Elin Suleymanov for their helpful comments.

# Abbreviations

| | |
|---|---|
| AKP | Justice and Development Party (*Adalet ve Kalkınma Partisi*) |
| ANAP | Motherland Party (*Anavatan Partisi*) |
| AP | Justice Party (*Adalet Partisi*) |
| BBP | Greater Unity Party (*Büyük Birlik Partisi*) |
| CHP | Republican People's Party (*Cumhuriyet Halk Partisi*) |
| DEHAP | Democratic People's Party (*Demokratik Halk Partisi*) |
| DP | Democrat Party (*Demokrat Parti*) |
| DRA | Directorate of Religious Affairs (*Diyanet İşleri Baskanlığı*) |
| DSP | Democratic Left Party (*Demokratik Sol Parti*) |
| DTP | Democratic Society Party (*Demokratik Toplum Partisi*) |
| DYP | True Path Party (*Doğru Yol Partisi*) |
| ECHR | European Court of Human Rights |
| FP | Virtue Party (*Fazilet Partisi*) |
| HADEP | People's Democracy Party (*Halkın Demokrasi Partisi*) |
| HEP | People's Work Party (*Halkın Emek Partisi*) |
| MÇP | Nationalist Work Party (*Milliyetçi Calışma Partisi*) |
| MHP | Nationalist Action Party (*Milliyetçi Hareket Partisi*) |
| MNP | National Order Party (*Milli Nizam Partisi*) |
| MSP | National Salvation Party (*Milli Selamet Partisi*) |
| MÜSİAD | Independent Industrialists' and Businessmen's Association (*Müstakil Sanayici ve İşadamları Derneği*) |
| NOM | National Outlook Movement (*Milli Görüş Hareketi*) |
| PKK | Kurdistan Workers' Party (*Partiya Karkeren Kurdistan*) |
| RP | Welfare Party (*Refah Partisi*) |
| RTÜK | The Supreme Board of Radio and Television (*Radyo ve Televizyon Yüksek Kurulu*) |
| SP | Felicity Party (*Saadet Partisi*) |
| TİP | Turkish Workers' Party (*Türkiye İşçi Partisi*) |
| TOBB | Turkish Union of Chambers and Stocks (*Türkiye Odalar ve Borsalar Birliği*) |
| TSK | The Turkish Armed Forces (*Türk Silahlı Kuvvetleri*) |
| TÜSİAD | Association of Turkish Industrialists and Businessmen (*Türk İş Adamları ve Sanayiciler Derneği*) |

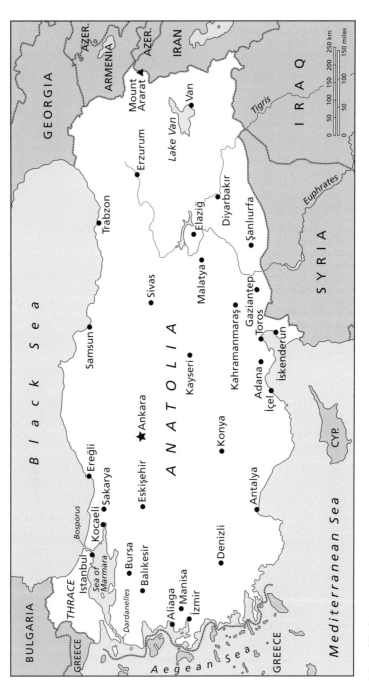

Map of Turkey

# Introduction: what is an Islamic party? Is the AKP an Islamic party?

In November 2002 and July 2007 the Turkish electorate voted decisively for the *Adalet ve Kalkınma Partisi* (AK Parti) – hereafter referred to by its Turkish acronym of AKP, demonstrating that it was willing to take a risk for broad political change.[1] The voters swept away a generation of established politicians to give Recep Tayyip Erdoğan's AKP enough seats in Parliament to form a government on its own.[2] The election posed a dramatic challenge, that of whether a modern democratic party with deep roots in political Islam was capable of expanding civil liberties and maintaining the democratic system. Before the November 2002 election, many in the Western media had described the AKP as a "fundamentalist party." After the election, the same journalists used the phrase "Islamist or Islamic party"; and when the party started to adopt the EU's Copenhagen criteria, they referred to it as a "party with Islamic roots."[3] Two years later, when parliament had passed several major reform packages, the AKP was characterized as a "reformed Islamist party."[4] Later, during parliamentary consideration of new legislation on adultery, the European media once again used the adjective "Islamist" or "Islamic" to describe the AKP.

---

[1] The "*Adalet ve Kalkınma Partisi*" is usually translated into English as the "Justice and Development Party" and is sometimes abbreviated to "AKP." The Party has declared that the official shorthand for its name is "*AK Parti*," so in English it is also referred to as the "AK Party." However, the use of this term is controversial since "ak" in Turkish means light, pure, white, clean and uncontaminated. The AK Party has the connotation of the "party of light" and its party symbol is a light bulb. Scholars who have a critical distance from the party do not use "AK Parti" or "Ak Party" but its Turkish or English abbreviation AKP, since "Ak Party" carries with it too much of a positive connotation. Therefore, the "neutral" and uncontroversial shorthand for the party is "AKP" in both Turkish and English.

[2] Emmanuel Sivan, "The Clash within Islam," *Survival* 45:1 (Spring 2003), 30. Sivan treats the electoral victory of the AKP as the rise and consolidation of Islamism in Turkey. His sweeping generalizations reflect a rather limited understanding of Turkish politics and this leads him to a number of ideologically tinged conclusions.

[3] Graham Fuller's writings were critical in the depiction of the AKP as an Islamic party. "Freedom and Security: Necessary Conditions for Moderation," *American Journal of Islamic Social Sciences*, 22:3 (Summer 2005), 23–24.

[4] *The Economist*, November 27, 2004.

1

movements are likely to facilitate democracy if they perceive it as the optimal solution to existing socio-political problems. Commitment to democracy is very important for a movement to facilitate the democratization process.

Religious identities, institutions and networks are important in the constitution of social capital and movement formation. Religious identities and ideologies help to protect marginalized groups from the dominant classes and provide a conceptual tool to challenge an oppressive government in the name of justice.[15] Moreover, in this context, religious movements can represent excluded groups and work for a more inclusive boundary between state and society via democratization. Studies on Christian Democratic parties in Europe and Latin America indicate that the secularization of the party's discourse stresses basic freedoms for the religious electorate. In order to appeal to the broadest possible electorate, confessional parties distanced their discourse and party organization from religious institutions and became more pragmatic. The result has been the evolution of a secular Catholic political identity. In addition to this electoral pressure for moderation, the parameters of the regime also play an important role in the transformation of religious parties.

1996); John Esposito and François Burgat (eds.), *Modernizing Islam: Religion in the Public Sphere in Europe and the Middle East* (New Brunswick, NJ: Rutgers University Press, 2003); Joel Beinin and Joe Stork (eds.), *Political Islam: Essays from Middle East Report* (Berkeley and Los Angeles: University of California Press, 1997); Seyyed Vali Reza Nasr, *Mawdudi and the Making of Islamic Revivalism* (New York: Oxford University Press, 1996); Charles Kurzman, "Bin Laden and Other Thoroughly Modern Muslims," *Contexts*, 1 (Fall/Winter 2002), 13–20.

[15] With respect to the proto-modern character of both Puritanism and Islamism Goldberg argues that:

Calvinism and the contemporary Islamist Sunni movements in Egypt are discourses on the nature of authority in society. Historically both movements arose as central state authorities made absolutist claims to political power and, in the process, sought to dominate transformed agrarian societies in new ways. Ideologically, both movements asserted that the claims of sweeping power by nominally religious secular central authorities were blasphemous egotism when contrasted with the claims of God on the consciences of believers. Socially, both movements transferred religious authority away from the officially sanctioned individuals who interpret texts to ordinary citizens. Institutionally, both movements create communities of voluntary, highly motivated and self-policing believers that yield greater degrees of internal cohesion and compliance than the absolutist authority can achieve, and they therefore can become the basis of postabsolutist political authority in an authoritarian and antidemocratic fashion. (195)

Ellis Goldberg, "Smashing Idols and the State: The Protestant Ethic and Egyptian Sunni Radicalism," in Juan R. I. Cole (ed.), *Comparing Muslim Societies: Knowledge and the State in a World Civilization* (Ann Arbor, MI: University of Michigan Press, 1992), p. 195.

## What is an Islamic party?

Definitional problems inevitably arise in any discussion of religious parties. For instance, is the AKP an Islamic party? How does one define a religious party? How should one differentiate religious parties/politics and secular parties/politics? I define a religious party as one whose ideology is derived from or shaped by religious ideas and which mobilizes the grass-roots on the basis of shared religious identity. Such parties seek *regime change* by implementing their religious worldviews; in the case of the Muslim world, the Islamization of the state and society is their main goal. Religious parties seek to overcome class and ethnic divisions on the basis of a shared religious affiliation.[16]

Religious parties not only focus on religious norms and issues but their platforms incorporate secular as well as religious appeals, issues and themes. This makes the task of disentangling the reasons why voters support these parties difficult.[17] Do voters choose these parties because they seek to bring religion back into the public sphere, or do they vote for them because these parties are seen as less corrupt and more committed to social justice, or because they provide a political opportunity to marginalized sectors of the population to take part in the political process? Religious parties may gradually moderate and secularize their agenda in response to electoral and non-electoral factors. Thus, the study of religious parties must focus on their ability to meld religious and secular agendas, on their electoral success or failure and especially on their protean nature, evolution and oscillation between religious and secular concerns and compromises. A closer study of Christian Democratic parties indicates that the evolution of these parties is the result of domestic and international transformations. The European Christian Democratic parties were often influenced by the ideas of the French Thomist philosopher Jacques Maritain. In *Integral Humanism*, he argued for an "integral democracy" that consisted of "pluralist," "personalistic" and "communitarian" conceptions of politics.[18] His major contribution was to develop an argument that theism provides a better basis for democracy than liberalism. He defended personalism over egotistic individualism; moral communal responsibility over self-interest; sharing over the profit motive. Moreover, Maritain regarded democracy as the most important framework for bringing Christian values into the public domain and for

---

[16] Scott Mainwaring and Timothy R. Scully (eds.), *Christian Democracy in Latin America: Electoral Competition and Regime Change* (Stanford: Stanford University Press, 2003).

[17] Vali Nasr, "The Rise of 'Muslim Democracy'," *Journal of Democracy*, 16:2 (April 2005), 13–27.

[18] Jacques Maritain, *Integral Humanism* (New York: Scribner's, 1938).

enhancing communities. He argued that democracy requires full religious freedoms for the socialization of faith into everyday life.[19]

It is important to differentiate religious (Islamic) parties from religious (Islamic) politics. A party might not be Islamic, such as the case of the Democrat Party under Adnan Menderes, the Justice Party under Süleyman Demirel and the Motherland Party under Turgut Özal, but could pursue "Islamic politics" by acting in conformity with the religious demands and concerns of the people. By Islamic politics I mean the competition and contest to define the meaning of life, identity and community via Islamic values. Islamic arguments are public statements or speech acts that are grounded in a religious tradition. On the basis of this definition, the AKP cannot be considered a religious party because it does not seek the *religious transformation of state and society*. Rather it seeks to maximize its seats in parliament to enhance its political power, but it does not seek to institute Islamic law in the political and social sphere or make political claims on the basis of religion. The AKP is, however, deeply involved in Islamic social ethics and cultural norms, and stresses the religious values and interests of its pious electorate. Just like the BJP in India, it has deep religious roots, but it has evolved to the point that one can no longer easily consider it as simply a religious party. The AKP's political activism demonstrates a deep interest in religious rights in terms of defending the freedoms of those who care about issues such as the headscarf, the imam-hatip schools where students receive a religious as well as a secular education, and optional Qur'anic study courses for students of high school age. The AKP toned down its Islamic identity and agenda after it came to power due to pressure from the Kemalist military and bureaucracy. The party has to adhere to strict secular regime guidelines for exercising power in order to maintain its legal status. The secular character of the regime in Turkey has been protected by the military through military coups in 1960, 1971, 1980 and 1997. The Kemalist elite have always remained suspicious about the activities of religious groups and parties, seeing them as reacting against the modernizing and secularizing mission of Kemalism.

In addition to the constraints set by the secular regime, Turkey's international engagements with NATO, the European Council and the EU force Islamic parties towards accommodation. In some cases, domestic legitimacy is guaranteed by international, especially US, support. In recent years, EU support has been essential for the democratic and

---

[19] More on the ideas of Maritain, see Paul Sigmund, "Maritain on Politics," in Deal Hudson and Matthew Mancini (eds.), *Understanding Maritain* (Macon: Mercer University Press, 1987), pp. 153–170.

economic transformation of the country. Hence AKP leaders became pragmatic and used opportunities to demonstrate their commitment to the Europeanization project and consciously avoided issues that could be viewed as overtly Islamic. They used Islamic language during the elections in dealing with emotionally charged issues, but largely in order to convert Islamic sentiments into votes. While its roots are Islamic and outwardly religious, as a political party the AKP leadership has compromised on its religio-political convictions and objectives. However, has the AKP actually reconsidered its ideology or even abandoned the Islamic vision so central to the movement's leadership and followers? Or is it more accurate to say that the AKP has in fact transformed itself into a typical political party, accepting the secular framework of the state while it functions within the confines of the Turkish polity. If this is the case, then what developments led to such a dramatic shift in ideology and goals? While it would be premature to suggest that Islamic objectives have been forgotten, it appears at least that they have been temporarily set aside in favor of more pragmatic goals. For now, it seems that a stable and more powerful Turkish democracy will suffice, with the AKP as the dominant political party. In the transformation of the movement, opportunity spaces played the most critical role. Eventually, the shortcomings of the February 28 coup in 1997 offered a tantalizing opportunity behind which new ideas of civil society and a democratic polity were promoted by a new leadership.

This book sheds light on the nature of the incentives that tend to lead policy makers to change their worldview, and also examines the conditions which facilitate socio-political transformation. The post-February 28, 1997 process was a critical juncture when a major change took place in the EU accession process. In the transformation of Islamic parties, we have to examine the facilitating and inhibiting factors, along with the recognition of windows of opportunity.

### When and how does an Islamic Party cease to be Islamic?

Recent literature on the growing moderation of Islamic movements/parties argues that the parties moderate themselves as a result of a number of factors.[20] I tend to differentiate those factors associated with the opposition

---

[20] For more on Islamic movements and democracy, see Vali Nasr, "The Rise of 'Muslim Democracy'," *Journal of Democracy*, 16:2 (2005), 13–27; Njorn Olav Utvik, "*Hizb al-Wasat* and the Potential for Change in Egyptian Islamism," *Critique: Critical Middle Eastern Studies*, 14:3 (2005), 293–306. For Indonesia, Robert W. Hefner, *Remaking Muslim Politics: Pluralism, Contestation, Democratization* (Princeton: Princeton University

from those associated with the government.[21] When Islamic parties are in opposition, they utilize strategic calculations to maximize electoral support. When there is a chance of coming to power or joining coalition governments, they moderate their position to win the centrist votes. In the emergence and evolution of the AKP, state oppression and the electoral strategies to receive more votes played crucial roles. In order to survive, the AKP expanded its electoral base, and to avoid state oppression, it internalized its adherence to democratic norms. When the party was voted into office in 2002, it even took unexpected steps to compromise with the Kemalist establishment to maintain its domestic and international legitimacy. In the case of Islamic parties in Turkey, one can argue that the conditions of moderation before and after the parties come to power are not the same. Before an Islamic party can come to power, state repression, electoral strategies of expanding its base and the ability of the system to reward the change by allowing it to govern are necessary conditions or factors for moderation to occur. State repression leads to splits within the Islamic movement due to new opportunities for more moderate groups. However, repression by itself is not a sufficient condition for an Islamic party to adopt moderation. A splinter group must be given the opportunity to participate and, if elected, to rule. When the party is in government, it must avoid confrontation and seek further moderation in order to maintain its domestic legitimacy.

Moreover, in parliament or in government, Islamic parties become more moderate as a result of learning and internalizing democratic values and norms. In order to end authoritarian state repression, Islamic parties begin to realize the virtue of democracy and pluralism. However, sections of the party, rather than the whole, are more prone to democratic conversion. Why are some party members more prone than others to democratic conversion? It appears that those members who were directly targeted by state repression, those who experienced more harassment, jailing or even torture when in the legal or underground opposition, are less likely to adopt the democratic conversion process when in power. Yet, there is a way of shaping one's conduct through setting examples as well.

There is a trade-off between the AKP's participation and remaining in the government and the moderation of its ideology and tactics. Political

Press, 2005). For Turkey, M. Hakan Yavuz, *Islamic Political Identity in Turkey* (Oxford: Oxford University Press, 2003). For Morocco, Isabelle Werenfels, "Between Integration and Repression," *SWP Research Paper*, S 39 (December 2005).

[21] Stathis N. Kalyvas, "Commitment Problems in Emerging Democracies: The Case of Religious Parties," *Comparative Politics*, 22 (July 2000), 379–397; John Waterbury, "Fortuitous By-Products," *Comparative Politics*, 29 (April 1997), 383–402; Nancy Bermeo, "Myths of Moderation: Confrontation and Conflict during Democratic Transitions," *Comparative Politics*, 29 (April 1997), 305–322.

participation of all Islamic voices in competitive electoral politics as legitimate parties tends to moderate their discourses and tactics. During and after the 1995 elections, for example, one witnessed a major trade-off between ideology and vote maximization by the Refah Partisi (RP). After the closure of the RP, the Saadet Partisi (SP) emerged as the continuation of the RP, and its single goal was avoiding the oppression and closure of the party organization. Thus, both vote- and legitimacy-seeking behaviors constrained the conduct of the SP. In other words, in order to establish a democratic system the leaders do not need to be committed democrats. By complying with democratic rules, these parties have gradually moderated their positions and tactics. Hence the moderation of radical voices who seek regime change takes place more as a result of self-interest than of ideological change. In other words, behavioral moderation precedes ideological moderation. When the younger generation of the RP realized that their just-order ideology was not in tune with the practical realities of Turkey, they gave it up and adopted a neo-liberal framework instead.

Even though I agree with those scholars who stress (a) strategic calculation, (b) state repression and reward and (c) political learning as key variables in the moderation of Islamic parties, I stress the role of structural factors, which are: (a) economic opportunity spaces, normally accompanied with the public sphere and (b) legal protection to allow the opportunity of governance if they are to be elected. In the case of Turkey and the AKP, the rise of the Anatolian Muslim bourgeoisie has been at the center of the "silent revolution", and the democratization and liberalization of Islamic actors has been very much achieved by this bourgeoisie. Özalian neo-liberal economic policies helped to create a new middle class that became the agent of a "historic compromise" between secularism and Islam, and between Kemalism and democracy. When in government, Islamic parties are constrained by the systemic constraints of the constitution, laws regulating political parties, the military establishment and the requirements of international organizations. In some cases moderation takes place while the party is in government. This is the case with the AKP, even though it was not particularly radical during the elections.

In addition to economic opportunity spaces and the evolution of a new Anatolian conservative bourgeoisie, one also needs to stress the role of political institutions in this ongoing contestation over the new "settlement" between religion and politics. Islamic politics in Turkey is not a zero-sum game between the Kemalist secularists and the religious groups that the secular regime is gradually losing. One needs to examine how the secular and Islamic confrontations shape each other and the political landscape of the country. Did the Islamic political agenda become more secular as it moved into parliament and government? What is the impact of contact with the state institutions? In the case of Turkey, the boundary between religious and secular is becoming fluid and blurred. The Turkish state pursued a number of strategies towards the Islamic opposition: co-optation, repression and power sharing. This interaction between the Islamic opposition and state institutions led to a mutual transformation and the emergence of a *modus vivendi*. Yet, there is still an ongoing tension between religious and secular ideas and forces concerning legitimate life styles and the nature of state and society. The tension is not between the state and its religious challengers, as is the case in many Muslim states, but within Turkish society itself. This tension is not uniform and varies according to the changing economic, cultural and political context within which Islamic movements and the state policies are rooted.

Although the state's modernizing policies have largely been recognized as a contributing factor in the evolution of a political Islamic opposition, in recent years economic and political opportunity spaces have provided the necessary context for the formation of an Islamic modernity. Moreover, some states tend to legitimize their policies in terms of Islamic idioms and symbols. The relationship between state secularism and the institutions of official Islam have been challenged by societal secularization and society-centric Islamism as well. Thus, the religious field consists of official state Islam, traditional Sufi networks, the neo-Nur movement of Fethullah Gülen, as well as a small but deadly Kurdish-Hizbullah. In the case of Turkey, the religious field has been a contested zone among "religious specialists" who seek to administer the "means of salvation." Competition over the meaning and role of Islam constitutes a new form of political discourse. Politics is deeply rooted in the lifestyles expressed in diverse religio-secular symbols. For instance, the headscarf is a symbol which points to certain values and lifestyles. Eickelman and Piscatori rightly argue that the language and use of symbols are "signs that point to values."[22] Eickelman and Piscatori's definition of politics is helpful in our attempt to understand contemporary Turkish politics. They define politics as "competition and struggle over the meanings of symbols ... and control of the institutions that define and articulate social values."[23] The politics of Turkey has become the conflict and competition over different lifestyle and value systems.

This transformation of Turkey's Islamic movement could be called a conservative revolution because it seeks to maintain Turkey's generally

---

[22] Dale F. Eickelman and James Piscatori, *Muslim Politics* (Princeton: Princeton University Press, 1996), p. 9.
[23] Eickelman and Piscatori, *Muslim Politics*, p. 9.

conservative traditions and bring local-level norms and identities to the national level; it is a normative revolution in that it seeks to moralize the political institutions and networks. By "conservative revolution" I mean not advocating wholesale change or an abrupt transformation, but rather creating new cognitive spaces for different imaginings of the past and the reconstruction of the present.[24] This conservative revolution is very much based on the Ottoman imperial dream of becoming "bigger" and "better" by overcoming the rigid nation-state ideology. This imagining is not carried out by the intelligentsia. It is a bottom-up imagining of those who feel excluded and dissatisfied with the prevailing socio-political conditions of Turkey. In its conception of a new Turkey, the AKP leadership has looked towards reconfiguring alliances and redistributing political power; it has sought ways to create new institutions and new values; and more importantly it has attempted to overthrow the ingrained Kemalist mode or pattern of "progressive" and elitist thinking. The main goal is to level society so that top and bottom are not widely separated. In short, the AKP's dream is to re-shape politics along the identity and needs of civil society. However, the party's dream of putting power firmly into the hands of people has failed to materialize fully, due to the authoritarian temptations of Erdoğan and the structural problems of modern Turkey.

[24] Bjorn Olav Utvik, "The Modernizing Force of Islam," in John Esposito and François Burgat (eds.), *Modernizing Islam: Religion in the Public Sphere in Europe and the Middle East* (New Brunswick, NJ: Rutgers University Press, 2003), pp. 43–68.

# 1    Historical and ideological background

Sometimes major revolutions take place quietly, their importance obscured by the hubbub of more dramatic events. Only with time does the shift become perceptible. Turkey has changed, but not because of a war or a major crisis; it has changed because of the emerging Anatolian bourgeoisie with its EU ambitions. The catalysts for this change have been the February 28 coup of 1997, the 2001 economic crisis and the Copenhagen criteria for EU membership. The EU process has played an important role in the speed and focus of the political reforms since 1999. However, the impact of the process is very much conditioned by the dynamics of Turkish domestic politics, especially the commitments of the major civil society organizations, as well as the governing party's commitment to the EU process.[1] Although many scholars tend to explain the current wave of democratization in terms of the Copenhagen criteria, I tend to treat external factors as facilitators rather than direct causes of this ongoing democratization of the state and society in Turkey, and I stress the role of opportunity spaces in the constitution of a greater democratic and more civic consciousness in Turkey.[2] This book also explains the mechanism through which and under what conditions the EU process has shaped Turkish domestic politics.

The current transformation of Turkish politics is an outcome of the interplay between internal and external events. It is the product of a bizarre blend of Islamic tradition and EU norms, acting on local and

---

[1] Societal groups such as as the Turkish Industrialists' and Businessmen's Association (TÜSİAD), the Economic and Development Foundation (IKV) and the Turkish Economic and Social Studies Foundation (TESEV) played a major role persuading the skeptical bureaucracy and the media.

[2] On those who stress external factors more than domestic, see E. Fuat Keyman and Ziya Öniş, "Helsinki, Copenhagen and Beyond: Challenges to the New Europe and the Turkish State," in Mehmet Uğur and Nergis Canefe (eds.), *Turkey and European Integration: Accession Prospects and Issues* (London: Routledge, 2004), pp. 173–193; Ziya Öniş, "Turkish Modernization and Challenges for the New Europe," *Perceptions*, (Autumn 2004), 5–28.

global policies. The framework for this transformation is, of course, the EU membership process. This process has a number of social and political implications. Politically Turkey is becoming more open, diversified and syncretic, and the AKP is both an outcome of this transformation and the agent of the new wave of change in Turkey.

Although some scholars explain the revolution of the AKP as a result of its search for security and legitimacy vis-à-vis the Kemalist establishment, I stress structural, social and economic factors. İhsan Dağı presents the AKP's adoption of human rights and democracy as a discursive shield and the building of a "liberal-democratic coalition with modern/secular sectors that recognize the AKP as a legitimate actor." Yet the 1997 military–civilian coup against the democratically elected Erbakan government revealed the weaknesses of domestic political forces and forced Turkey's Muslim groups to search for international support against the military's pervasive political power. The leadership of the AKP realizes that in order to foster democratization and the expansion of human rights, they need the safeguards of the EU. I would argue that this reliance on the EU is not simply tactical but rather an effort to deepen civil society and democracy. The biggest breakdown of the center-right alignment came as a result of the February 28 military–civilian coup. Before this, the Turkish electorate was divided between the left (twenty-five per cent) and right (seventy per cent). The right was dominated by two ideologies: Islamism and Turkish nationalism. These two forms of identity, like overlapping circles, have a constant circulation of people between nationalism and Islamism. The Islamic circle also has some overlap with Kurdish nationalism as well. In a way, Islamic identity functions as a link, although not a bridge, between Turkish and Kurdish nationalism. Yet Islamic identity has more dominant Ottoman and Turkish colors than Kurdish ones, since the dominant Islamic identity is largely constituted by and derived from the Ottoman legacy. Islamic identity in itself failed to address the Kurdish question, but it prevents radicalization between the two ethnic groups.

Since the February 28 coup, these circles have become more autonomous and less overlapping. Historically, the overlap between Islamism and Turkish nationalism established the ideological language of the center-right as pro-state and communitarian. It sought to protect itself against the left and foreign forces by taking refuge under the authority of the state. The center-right Islamic groups stress the significance of community over egoistic individualism. This center-right, along with Islamic groups, has come to regard freedom from the authority of the state as the first goal. By targeting the presence of Islamic values in the public sphere, the February 28 coup attacked the traditional base of the center-right by harassing the Nakşibendi and Nurcu groups. For the first time, these pro-state, center-right Muslim groups asked hard questions about the legitimacy of the Turkish military. The conservative and Islamic sectors of the population turned against the self-declared mission of the military and sought to free the state and their own liberties from the hegemony of the military by supporting the EU process. As a result, the biggest loser of the February 28 coup has been the military itself. It succeeded in removing the democratically elected government, but it has never regained its former credibility in the eyes of the center-right.

The shattering outcome of this conservative revolution was the 2002 general election, which cannot be fully understood unless we take into account the Özal revolution of the 1980s. Turgut Özal initiated Turkey's economic, social and political liberalization. Özal's reform policy was aimed at expanding the political sphere and opening new opportunities in education, economy and law. It was a revolution of new spaces and a new dynamism. From the sudden death of Özal in 1993 until 2002, the country was governed by a group of corrupt politicians, businessmen and media barons. They used the military whenever necessary to undermine the "radical Islamic" opposition.

I want to examine current events within the framework of Turkey's two centuries of Westernization, without ignoring the role of social movements that resisted some structural change. In the absence of a powerful national bourgeoisie, the Turkish bureaucracy, especially the military, had full responsibility for carrying out this Westernization project and building a new state and nation.

Turkish history after 1960 reflects the conflict between the emerging bourgeoisie and the hegemonic civilian–military bureaucracy over the definition and speed of the process of modernization, as opposed to Westernization. In this regard, class structure and the structure of political alliances went through a radical change during the Özal period as the influence of the military–civilian bureaucracy waned and the new Anatolian business class, along with Istanbul-based industrialists, increased its power. This process has created new economic opportunities, a participatory, secular political system and new forms of communication networks, and has emphasized the language of human rights. The AKP is the product of the conflict between vernacularized modernity and Westernization, highlighted by two key events: the 1997 coup and the 2001 economic crisis. It came to power to restore the process, and even accelerate it, by fulfilling the Copenhagen criteria for Turkey's membership of the EU. Thus, the AKP should not be treated as a "rebellion" against either modernity or even Europeanization, but rather against rigid Kemalism and the events tied up with the coup and the economic crisis.

## The facilitating factors of secularism: *hizmet* and *kanun*

The historical approach is important for understanding whether the Turkish experiment of modernity and democracy could become a model for emulation by other Muslim countries. Here I pay close attention to the five stages of Turkey's transformation.[3] Before I examine these stages, it is important to provide a brief background of the Ottoman state and society and the role of Islam within them.

With the establishment of the Ottoman state, the Turks rendered their service (*hizmet*) to the expansion of Islam, and Islam reached its greatest might under the Ottomans. The Turks built the strongest and most stable polity ever known in the region. Coming from the steppes of Central Asia and establishing a number of dynastic states in Anatolia, the Ottomans expanded in three continents: Asia, Europe and Africa. In the seventeenth century, the Ottoman state reached the apex of its territorial expansion. As a result of its flexibility, diversity and organizational skills, as well as the weaknesses of its enemies, it stretched from the gates of Vienna to Azerbaijan, from Crimea to Sudan.

Islam provided the source of legitimacy, the unity of state and religion, and a source of identity. Islam was not only the basis of the state; it symbolized the unity of Turkish society, provided a cognitive map of action and meaning, a repository of memory and also a sense of authority. Both state and society had a deep religious content and evolved together. However, the Islam of Anatolia has always been shaped by the tension between the *medrese* (seminaries where clergy are educated) of orthodox Islam and the *tekke* (Sufi lodges) of heterodox Islam. This dichotomy is very useful in understanding the evolution of Islamic practices and institutions in contemporary Turkey. In the Ottoman empire, Sunni–Hanafi Islam became the religion of the central authority in major urban centers, with its own education networks, whereas the oral-culture-based heterodox Islam of Sufi lodges remained the religion of marginalized and persecuted groups and could always be utilized as an oppositional identity vis-à-vis the central authority. Moreover, Sunni Islam developed a well-defined written theology on the basis of the Qur'an and Sunna, whereas heterodox Islam is unsystematic, largely syncretic and based on oral transmission.[4]

---

[3] The Tanzimat period (1839–1923); the Republican period (1924–1950); Multi-party period and the Cold War (1950–1983); the neo-liberal revolution (1984–1999); the Europeanization, i.e. the implementation of the Copenhagen criteria, period (1999–present).

[4] Halil İnalcık, "Turkey," in Robert E. Ward and Dankwart Rustow (eds.), *Political Modernization in Japan and Turkey* (Princeton: Princeton University Press, 1964), pp. 42–63; Serif Mardin, "Ideology and Religion in the Turkish Revolution," *International Journal of Middle East Studies*, 2 (1971), 197–211.

The formulation of *gaza* ideology, *din-ü-devlet* (unity of religion and state) and the caliphate in the nineteenth century all illustrate the Islamic sources of the Ottoman state and society.[5] The tradition of *gaza* wars, or waging wars in the name of the expansion of Islam, constituted the main source of Ottoman military activities.[6] Today, this *gaza* ideology still remains, especially for the supporters of the center-right, and is an important component of the self-imagination of the Turkish military. The conquest of Mecca and Medina and the victory over the Mamluks of Egypt in 1517 helped the Ottoman rulers to shift from *gaza* ideology to the "principal defenders of Islam," since Sultans inherited the title "Custodian of the Two Holy Precincts" (possessors of the holy cities of Mecca and Medina). In the late nineteenth century, Sultan Abdulhamid II (1876–1908) stressed the concept of the caliphate to enhance his legitimacy and empower the state against European encroachment. The institution of the caliphate was popularized with the weakening of the Ottoman state, and it was first utilized in the Treaty of Kaynarca, signed in 1774 by the Ottoman and Russian states. Halil İnalcık argues that the Ottoman rulers always paid close attention to Islamic law in terms of justifying their conducts and decisions.[7] In the Ottoman Empire, the ruler issues the *kanun*, the body of written secular law, which is in full conformity with Islamic law. The *kanun* has roots in the Turko-Mongol tradition that stresses the role of state law issued by the ruler for the maintenance of law and order and the public good.[8]

In the Ottoman state, the *ulema*, the body of the learned men who are trained in Islamic jurisprudence, was responsible for teaching (*tedris*), interpreting (*ifta*) and enforcing (*kada*) Islamic law. Although the *ulema* never constituted a church-like institution, it was centralized and structured by the Ottoman rulers, especially after the sixteenth century. In other words, the *ulema* were fully integrated into the state bureaucracy in terms of appointments and salaries. The *kadis* (judges in Islamic courts) had a number of functions in the provinces to maintain order and dispense the public good of justice. They even collected taxes and controlled pious foundations. Through the integration of the *ulema* into the Ottoman bureaucracy, the state established the most effective control. Thus, the

---

[5] Niyazi Berkes, *The Development of Secularism in Turkey* (London: Routledge, 1999).
[6] A number of prominent Ottoman historians, such as Colin Imber, Rudi Paul Lindner, Gyula Kaldy-Nagy, Ronald C. Jennings and Colin Heywood, argue that there is not enough historical evidence to prove the *gaza* thesis. See Heath W. Lowry, *The Nature of the Early Ottoman State* (Albany: State University of New York Press, 2003); Colin Imber, "The Ottoman Dynastic Myth," *Turcica*, 19 (1987), 7–27. Imber's interpretation has been challenged by Camal Kafadar, *Between Two Worlds: The Construction of the Ottoman State* (Berkeley: University of California Press, 1995), p. 152.
[7] Halil İnalcık, "Islam in the Ottoman Empire," *Turcica*, 5–6 (1968–70), 23–25.
[8] İnalcık, "Islam in the Ottoman Empire," 20–21.

"control of religion" was the main function of the Ottoman system, and this institutional tradition has been continued in Republican Turkey, where Islam has always been subordinated to the needs of the state. One of the key facilitating factors in the secularization of modern Turkey is closely related to this Ottoman legacy of institutionalized control of religion by the state and by the role of the *kanun*.

Following the concept of *hizmet* as a sense of rendering one's service to the state, the second most important concept one needs to register in order to understand the Ottoman contributions to Turkish secularism is the *kanun*, or edicts issued by the Sultan in areas not covered by Islamic law. The administrative law of the Sultan, or "Sultan Prerogative," directly covered the workings of bureaucracy and bureaucrats. They were trained in the palace schools and relinquished the protection of Islamic law; they remained at the mercy of the Sultan and were judged in terms of their service to the state. Thus, the *kanun* helped to create a secular domain outside the religious law and this, in turn, had a major impact on the secularization of the Ottoman system in the twentieth century. Although the *ulema* (Muslim scholars who have been trained in the religious sciences) could annul any *kanun* if it was believed to be contrary to Islamic law, they rarely did so, since they were also employees of the state. In short, in the Ottoman system, the role of Islam was defined by the power of the *kanun* as an instrument of protecting the state. Thus, this separation between Islamic law and the *kanun* shifted the control to public administration, and the state was perceived as an independent entity. The Ottoman state never became an Islamic theocracy, due to the power of the *kanun* and the expansive role of the bureaucracy. The religious institutions were tightly controlled by the state.

In order to confront the decline of the state, the Sultan – with the inherent legitimacy of the *kanun* – issued the Tanzimat (Reform) Edicts, a series of legal acts to restructure the state and its relations with society. The Tanzimat era (1830–1860) sought to modernize the state and society through centralization, to improve administrative participation by stressing the role of education and to develop a new value-structure by reforming the existing one.

The challenges on both the war front and within Ottoman society encouraged officials to reform the bureaucracy, education and legal systems, and to create a new sense of Ottoman identity. This defensive reform of Tanzimat debate culminated in the establishment of the 1876 Constitution and the introduction of the first Ottoman parliament.[9]

---

[9] For the Tanzimat era, see *Tanzimat I* (Istanbul: Devlet Basımevi, 1940); İlber Ortaylı, *İmparatorluğun En Uzun Yüzyılı* (Istanbul: Hil Yayınları, 1995).

However, these reforms did not seek to undermine Islam, but rather to establish a parallel secular system, and some reforms were even justified on the basis of Islam or presented as Islamic. The Tanzimat, therefore, did not challenge the Islam-based normative system as the founding principle of the Ottoman state, and Islam remained a source of legitimacy.

The Tanzimat bureaucrats also used this liberal era to consolidate the power of the state, especially the bureaucracy. The new education system, outside the control of religious institutions, helped to mold a new class of bureaucrats that would lead the constitutional movement in the Empire. Some students were sent to France and Germany for education and they returned with Western ideals gleaned from journalism and novels and helped to construct proto-nationalistic feelings around the state and homeland, or *vatan*. This group, to be known as the "Young Turks," included Ibrahim Sinasi Efendi (1824–1871), Namık Kemal Bey (1840–1888) and Ziya Pasa (1830–1880), all of whom were instrumental in vernacularizing European concepts of liberty, citizenship, public opinion, natural rights, nation, fatherland and constitutional government. It was Sinasi Efendi, after his education in Paris, who used *millet* in the sense of "nation" and also debated the power of constitutional government.[10] Namık Kemal was crucial in redefining the role of the state as an instrument to defend the rights of its citizens, and introduced the idea of sovereignty of the people that could be used by the government according to the rule of law. He wanted to rethink Islamic concepts within the framework of constitutionalism and a new sense of identity: *millet* (nation). Namık Kemal became the key theoretician of Ottomanism. He popularized the concept of *vatan* (homeland) as a framework of loyalty and allegiance for all Ottomans, regardless of faith and ethnicity.[11] He also associated the concept of *vatan* with popular sovereignty, and he argued that the love of the fatherland requires people to acknowledge the sovereignty of that fatherland. Yet, Namık Kemal sought to justify his concepts within the framework of Islam and never challenged the Islamic normative system. The debates of these intellectuals formed the backdrop for the 1876 Constitution, which was prepared by Namık Kemal and put into practice by Mithat Pasa (1822–1884) with the opening of the first

---

[10] Berkes, *The Development*, pp. 197–198.
[11] Şerif Mardin, *The Genesis of Young Ottoman Thought: A Study in the Modernization of Turkish Political Ideas* (Princeton: Princeton University Press, 1962); Şerif Mardin, *Jön Türklerinin Siyasi Fikirleri, 1895–1908* (1964, 2nd edn., Istanbul: İletişim, 1983); David Kushner, *The Rise of Turkish Nationalism, 1876–1908* (London: Cass, 1977). See also Masami Arai, "Jön Türk Dönemi Türk Milliyetçiliği," in Mehmet Ö. Alkan (ed.), *Tanzimat ve Meşrutiyet'in Birikimi: Cumhuriyet'e Devreden Düşünce Mirası* (Istanbul: İletişim, 2001), pp. 180–195.

Ottoman parliament on March 19, 1877. As a result of European encroachment, defeats in the Balkans and chaos inside the country, Sultan Abdulhamid II closed down the parliament in 1878, but reopened it in 1908. The Abdulhamid II period was defined by its reaction to the Young Turks, with the Sultan trying to consolidate state power by stressing the role of Islam. His experiment, however, failed to prevent the defeats in the Balkans. Moreover, many intellectuals took more secular and positivist approaches to the governance and rebuilding of society along the lines of Turkish nationalism.

The later Young Turks, unlike the generation of Namık Kemal, demanded the total transformation of Ottoman society via political power. They considered themselves a "knowledge elite" and, heavily influenced by positivism, sought to restructure society along scientific principles. The positivist motto "Order and Progress" shaped not only the thinking of the Young Turks but also the name of their organization, "Union and Progress." They kept "progress" and replaced "order" with "union."[12] However, in order to disseminate their ideas and also get the support of society against Abdulhamid II, the Young Turks never hesitated to utilize Islam, since Islam remained the dominant source of legitimacy.

After the removal of Abdulhamid II in 1909, a number of intellectual groups formed to address problems of state and society. Some intellectuals, such as the sociologist and political activist Ziya Gökalp, regarded Islam as the key element of Turkish national identity. Gökalp fully recognized the power of nationalism and argued that it was time to make a necessary cognitive shift from *ümmet* (community of believers, religiously defined community) to nation to join the "new life" (*yeni hayat*) by creating a new social, political and moral order on the basis of national identity and solidarity.[13] Gökalp developed a new framework for reconstructing society and polity. He differentiated culture (national) from civilization (international) and asked the Turks to participate in civilization by critiquing their tradition. He also took a very rational view of Islam as a social glue and a source of morality, and defended the secularization of public administration. His ideas shaped the modernization reforms of the Young Turks between 1913 and 1918. Under the Committee of Union and Progress, the Young Turks enacted a new secular Code of Family

---

[12] One of the best analyses of Turkish nationalism is Yusuf Sarınay, *Türk Milliyetçiliğinin Tarihi Gelişimi ve Türk Ocakları (1912–1931)* (Istanbul: Ötüken Neşriyat, 2004); Şükrü Hanioğlu, *The Young Turks in Opposition* (New York: Oxford University Press), p. 204.

[13] The journal *Yeni Felsefe Mecmuası* (The Journal of New Philosophy) was published in 1911 to disseminate the ideas of the group of the new life (*yeni hayat*).

Law, secularized the education system and subordinated religious courts to secular ones. Unlike most Young Turks, Gökalp did not attack religion and did not treat religion as an obstacle to science and progress. Some of the Young Turks who supported the ideas of *yeni hayat* and its journal *Yeni Felsefe Mecmuası* sharply criticized Islam and regarded it as the source of backwardness and a "problem to be solved," and this brand of militant secularism remained more powerful and vocal than the ideas of Gökalp among the founders of the modern Republic.[14] Abdullah Cevdet, a fierce militant secularist, argued that Islam could not be reconciled with science and the needs of the modern age.[15] Cevdet was one of the most zealous of the Young Turks in criticizing Islam and defending the project of a positivist social revolution to end the role of religion in society. Gökalp's concept of national identity is based on his nuanced reading of culture (*hars*) and civilization (*medeniyet*). He integrated Islam as the critical factor of Turkish culture. Culture, for Gökalp, contained the shared values, beliefs and ideals that help to form a nation. He defined civilization as non-religious and the product of shared humanity.[16] Thus, for Gökalp, the Turks could become part of Western civilization, since it was not defined by Christianity.

### The mission of the DRA: enlightened Islam

The nineteenth-century reform project of the Ottoman Empire was qualitatively different from the reform project of the twentieth-century Republic. The former aimed at protecting the multi-ethnic state with a set of reforms to enable it to compete with Europe. The goal of these reforms was not the exclusion of an Islamic worldview or creating a "reformed Islam"; rather, Islamic terms were utilized to legitimate the

---

[14] Ziya Gökalp, *Türkçülüğün Esasları* (Istanbul: Toker Yayınevi, 1999); Gökalp, *Türkleşmek, İslamlaşmak, Muasırlaşmak* (Istanbul: Toker Yayınevi, 1999); Mehmet Ö. Alkan, "Laik Bir İdeolojinin Doğusu ya da II. Meşrutiyet'te Türkçülüğün Toplumsal İdeolojisi: Yeni Hayat ve Yeni Felsefe Mecmuası," *Tarık Zafer Tunaya'ya Armağan* (Istanbul: Istanbul Barosu Yayını, 1992), p. 378.

[15] The defeats in the Balkans and World War I had a major and traumatic impact on the Ottoman elite. This deep sense of humiliation before European states turned the Turkish elite against Islam; they identified Islam and the Ottoman past as the causes of this humiliation and the loss of dignity. In order to restore dignity and self-confidence, the Republican elite used all means to create a new sense of identity and solidarity free of religion and a society shaped by science. The Republican elite established the DRA to control Islam and prevent its regressive role.

[16] Selim Deringil, "From Ottoman to Turk: Self-Image and Social Engineering in Turkey," in D. Gladney (ed.), *Making Majorities: Constituting the Nation in Japan, Korea, China, Malaysia, Fiji, Turkey and the United States* (Stanford: Stanford University Press, 1998), pp. 217–226.

new institutions and practices to strengthen the state. It was modernization *with* Islam rather than *against* or *without* Islam. The Republic did not
pursue this mode of Islamically legitimated modernization; instead, it
adopted a new policy of disestablishing Islam in the public sphere and, if
necessary, creating a "reformed Islam" that would facilitate the secularization program. The shift from the nineteenth-century reforms *with* Islam
to the Republican reforms *against* Islam represents a major rupture that
would eventually turn Islam into an oppositional identity.[17]

During the War of Independence, some of the *ulema* did not obey the
Caliph and supported the initiatives of Atatürk.[18] These nationalist *ulema*
closely identified with the national struggle, and they supported the secularism of Atatürk to carve out a more prestigious position for religion in
terms of serving the advancement of the nation. For instance, Ahmet H.
Akseki, then the director of the Diyanet İşleri Başkanlığı (DRA), argued
that a good Muslim was also a good Turkish citizen. He tried to stress the
role of religion in maintaining the well-being of the Turkish nation, and
defended religious values to consolidate civic duty. There was a genuine
effort to create a national religion. Akseki also stressed the social utility of
Islam in the building of a civil society. These efforts might be read as a way
of creating a "civil religion," that is, a religion devoid of dogmas and
rituals but with principles to promote morality and a sense of civic duty,
to enhance social order in society. The Turkish Republic tried to create its
own "modernist Islam" through the DRA.[19] Since 1924, the DRA has
been in charge of religious affairs and the interpretation of Islam through
(a) controlling the content of Friday religious sermons and religious
opinions in order to prevent the formation of anti-Republican ideas;
and (b) formulating a "modern Islam" in accordance with the needs of
the state.[20] The state owns the mosques and appoints the religious officials
as state employees with regular salaries. These religious officials are

---

[17] Halil Ibrahim Yenigün, "Islamism and Nationalism in Turkey: An Uneasy Relationship,"
paper read at 2nd Annual Graduate Student Conference of the Department of Politics,
March 28, 2005 at the University of Virginia, Charlottesville. <www.virginia.edu/politics/
grad_program/print/wwdop-2006-paper-yenigun.pdf>

[18] Paul Dumont, "Hojas for the Revolution: The Religious Strategy of Mustafa Kemal
Atatürk," *Journal of the American Institute for the Study of Middle Eastern Civilization*, 1
(1980–1981), 17–32.

[19] Kamil Kaya, *Türkiye'de Din-Devlet İlişkileri ve Diyanet İşleri Başkanlığı* (Istanbul, 1998),
pp. 188–189.

[20] There are very few studies on the DRA, which was created on March 3, 1924 after the
dissolution of the caliphate and the Ministry of Religious and Charitable Foundations.
The head of the DRA is appointed by the president on the advice of the prime minister.
İştar Gözaydin's legal study of the DRA is the best study on the organization. The first
comprehensive policy-oriented study was carried out by TESEV, a social-democrat
think-tank in Istanbul, which includes a number of analytical articles as well. See İştar

educated in Imam Hatip schools under the supervision of the Ministry of Education.

The mission of the DRA has been expanded from simply supervising faith and worship under the 1924 Constitution to "taking necessary steps to secure the loyalty of Muslims to the national ideas" of the Republic. Law 633 of 1963 redefined the task of the DRA in terms of "conducting the affairs of belief, worship and enlightening society on religious matters and the moral aspects of the Islamic religion." The new law added the concepts of morality and "enlightening society" on religious issues. In other words, the state sought to create a moral order based on Islamic values. The 1982 constitution went even further and asked the DRA to "carry out its mission within the framework of the principle of secularism and with the goal of achieving national solidarity and integration." In short, the DRA has three functions today. Its first mission is to control and administer worship and the places of worship through its own bureaucracy. Second, the DRA is expected to control and administer the study of Qur'anic courses under the Ministry of Education. Third, the DRA is in charge of enlightening the public on religious subjects by answering believers' questions; organizing conferences and workshops; publishing religious materials to enlighten Muslims; and providing Friday sermons (hutbes) to promote the values of family and national unity. The main function of the DRA has been to stress the social utility of Islam in the wellbeing of the state and nation.

In Turkey, the Kemalist revolution not only attacked Islamic institutions but also Islamic practices. During Ottoman times, all state institutions and laws were linked with Islam, which meant that the new state and society required another source of legitimacy. Being Turk still meant being a Muslim. The main task of Mustafa Kemal was the transformation of society in terms of "reaching the level of contemporary civilization." This "contemporary civilization" (muasır medeniyet) meant constructing a new society on the European model. This could and in fact also did mean the exclusion of Islam from the new construction. Islam was deliberately excluded from the building of the new identity and institutions. In short, the Kemalist reforms ignored the writings of Gökalp and utilized the ideas of Abdullah Cevdet by rejecting the Islamic–Ottoman past and aiming to imitate Western institutions and practices. Through secularizing reforms, the regime tried to construct a new Turkish identity and integrate into European civilization.

Tarhanlı-Gözaydın, *Müslüman Toplum, "Laik" Devlet, Türkiye'de Diyanet İşleri Başkanlığı* (Istanbul: Afa, 1993); Ruşen Çakır and Irfan Bozan, *Sivil, Şeffaf Ve Demokratik Bir Diyanet İşleri Başkanlığı Mümkün Mü?* (Istanbul: TESEV, 2005).

## The five stages of Turkish political development

The first stage of political development in the twentieth century was provoked by the demise of the Ottoman Empire.[21] In order to save the state from collapse, Ottoman intellectuals raised a set of questions about the form and content of modernizing reforms in education, the judiciary and the military, which were needed to consolidate and reassert state power.[22] They also sought to undermine the power of religious institutions and religious authority. The Tanzimat reforms promoted the centralization of the bureaucracy, with the goal of incorporating society into the state. The state became the key mechanism for transforming and modernizing society.[23] The state changed the social, cultural and political landscape of Turkey through top-down reform policies. Similarly, the history of the early Turkish Republic was the story of the expanding role of the state over society. Ottoman and Republican bureaucrats and intellectuals pursued Westernization not for the sake of democracy, the nation or being Western, but rather to protect and empower the Turkish state.[24] Thus, there is a close tie between Westernization and the consolidation of state power.

With the establishment of the Republic in 1923, the state defined its interests in terms of secularizing and crafting a new Turkish nation out of diverse ethnic and religious groups. The Kemalist state, indeed, is a missionary state. Its goal has been to create a Turkish nation and elevate this nation to the level of European civilization. After 1923 Mustafa Kemal, its founder, implemented a series of reforms to create a homogeneous nation-state by subordinating ethnic and religious identities into a state-determined and -regimented Turkish nationalism. These reforms, known as Kemalism, sought to control religion to create a new secular society. The twin pillars of Kemalist ideology, Turkish nationalism and secularism, are the main sources of the current crises in Turkey. Secularism has not meant simply a formal separation between religious and political authority and institutions, but rather a positivist state ideology to engineer a homogeneous and stratified society. Secularism in Turkey derives from the Jacobin–Statist and positivist French tradition of the Third Republic (1871–1942) and differs thus markedly from the Anglo-Saxon understanding of secularism. Instead of a state that is

---

[21] Stanford J. Shaw and Ezel Kural Shaw, *History of the Ottoman Empire and Modern Turkey* (New York: Cambridge University Press, 1977).
[22] Eric Zürcher, *Turkey: A Modern History* (New York: I. B. Tauris, 1997).
[23] Yusuf Oğuzoğlu, *Osmanlı Devlet Anlayışı* (Istanbul: Eren, 2000).
[24] Şerif Mardin, "Center and Periphery Relations: A Key to Turkish Politics?" *Daedalus*, 102 (1973), 169–190.

neutral on the question of the religious practices and beliefs of its citizenry, the secularist state, with its origin in the Jacobin tradition, seeks to remove all manifestations of religion from the public sphere and put religion under the strict control of the state. As an intellectual and political project in Turkey, it has a long history of differentiating, marginalizing and excluding large sectors of Turkish society.[25] The secularization of law and education are the two instruments of the Kemalist conception of secularism.[26] In examining Islamic political forces in Turkey today, one needs to take this exclusionary history of secularism into account.

The Kemalist project has developed an elaborate system of secularism for the purpose of "controlling" religion and reducing it to the faith of the individual. Turkish secularism, therefore, can be understood only in the context of a modern nation-building project. Islam as a religion does not separate state and religion; it seeks to regulate public life with its own conception of the law and provides an alternative sense of loyalty, identity and community. These ideological and historical aspects informed the Kemalist understanding of secularism and the heightened sensitivity toward any form of Islam-based claims.

As a result of Mustafa Kemal's secularizing reforms, Islamic institutions and ideas no longer functioned as the sources of legitimacy in political life. In particular, the educational system was carefully separated from any form of religious influence or interference. Moreover, the Islamic presence in the cultural and social spheres was undermined through the new alphabet, dress, calendar and official rest days. In short, the Republic introduced a new set of symbols to mark the shift from Islamic to Western civilization. Turkish secularism maintained the Ottoman legacy of state control over religion due to the comprehensive claims of Islam, especially in the political sphere. Thus, Turkish secularism was radical in terms of its symbolic, political and social disestablishment of religion and the strict control of religious knowledge by the state. Binnaz Toprak regards the Turkish form of secularism as a "semi-secular" state, since it was not based on the separation but rather on the tight

---

[25] In the decisions of the Turkish Constitutional Court, only the secular public sphere is assumed to offer peace by removing any form of difference rooted in ethnicity or religion. The state wants to make sure that the Turkish public sphere is homogeneous and unified, without any religious marking. In other words, religiously derived claims in the public sphere are treated as divisive and dangerous for the tranquility of society. Secularism as defined in Turkey has thus tended to be an authoritarian state ideology to stamp out religious and ethnic differences in the name of Enlightenment values and homogenization.

[26] Berkes, *The Development*, pp. 467–468.

control of religion.[27] Bülent Daver also regards this form of secularism as different from that in France by arguing that Turkish secularism is "narrow." It separates religion from state policies but keeps state control over religious affairs.[28] On the basis of the Constitutional Court's interpretations of the principles of secularism, Istar Tarhanlı argues that Turkish secularism is a "comprehensive ideology" that seeks to organize every aspect of social and political life.[29] In short, there are two major characteristics of Turkish secularism: it is based on the principle of the control of religion by the state due to the nature of Islam, the Ottoman legacy and the radical reforms of Mustafa Kemal, and it seeks to create its own version of "modern Islam" to enhance the reforms of the nation-state.

After the establishment of the Republic of Turkey, the dominant issue was how to consolidate the secular–nationalist Kemalist regime. In order to carry out this project (stage two), the state first created its own ideologically guided (Kemalist) bureaucracy to maintain its autonomy from society.[30] Kemalism is an ideology which aims at state autonomy from domestic and international forces with the goal of creating a modern (that is, secular) and homogeneous (Turkish) nation-state. The Kemalist guardians of the state, the Turkish military, also became the guardians of the nation and its modernization. They never hesitated to protect the state from societal forces, if necessary by seizing power.[31] Of course, Mustafa Kemal is not only an historical figure, but is enmeshed in the tattered web of legitimacy on which the Republic of Turkey rests. He is part of the founding mythology of the Turkish revolution that wished Turkey to become European, which is why his portrait hangs in every school and his statue is found in every public square. Even among ordinary Turks, Atatürk retains a hold on their imaginations, and some urban Turks regard him as the embodiment of contemporary Turkey. I think Atatürk's ruthlessness in such things as language reform was a catastrophe at the time, but there is more to the story. He helped lay the groundwork

---

[27] Binnaz Toprak, *Islam and Political Development in Turkey* (Leiden: E. J. Brill, 1981); Binnaz Sayarı, "Türkiye'de Dinin Denetim İşlevi," *A.U. Siyasal Bilgiler Fakültesi Dergisi*, 33 (March–June 1978), 176.

[28] Bülent Daver, *Türkiye Cumhuriyetinde Layiklik* (Ankara: Son Havadis Marbası, 1955), p. 234; Halide Edip, "Dictatorship and Reform in Turkey," *The Yale Review*, 19 (1929), 38.

[29] Istar Tarhanlı, *Müliiman Toplum ve "Laik" Devlet* (Istanbul: Afa, 1993), p. 164.

[30] For an account of this social engineering carried out by the Kemalist elite, see Jeremy Salt, *A Fez of the Heart* (Washington, PA: Harvest Books, 1996).

[31] One of the key characteristics of the 1961 and 1982 constitutions is the expansion of the "reserved domains" of power and authority for the military and civilian bureaucracies that are not directly accountable to the electorate.

for the rebirth and rise of modern Turkey after two centuries of chaos and decline.[32]

After World War II, a new international system pressured Turkey to ally itself with the West against the communist threat. The Cold War thrust a spotlight on Turkey's security needs, and to address them Ankara joined NATO. During this third stage of political development (1950–1983), Turkey adopted the multi-party system in order to take its position among the Western democracies. The dominant issues of the day were: *how to defend the country* (against the Soviet Union) *and regime* (against Islamic assertiveness) and *how to become a developed nation*. The defense of the regime (Kemalism) became the priority of the military in the multi-party system, since the Republican People's Party (CHP) did not have enough popular support to maintain its Kemalist hegemony. Under the multi-party system, there has been a constant tension between elected officials and the unelected military and civilian guardians of the regime. Political parties have had to play the electoral and regime games simultaneously. In the electoral game, parties seek to maximize their votes and seats vis-à-vis other opposition parties, whereas in the regime game they seek to reform the existing regime. Thus, almost all conservative center-right parties such as the DP, AP and ANAP, now the AKP, have played this dual game simultaneously. Whenever the pro-regime CHP realizes that it may not come to power through the electoral game, it evokes a regime crisis and seeks to delegitimize these center-right parties. The present strategy of the CHP is to delegitimize the AKP by accusing it of being an anti-regime party that seeks to change the secular regime. Thus, the AKP has developed an electoral game vis-à-vis other competing center-right and religious parties to maximize its votes – and to compete with regime actors such as the military, the judiciary and the universities in showing that it is not an anti-regime party. The authoritarian regime actors, especially the military, have always been powerful enough to veto government policies that amount to regime change by a variety of pressures and practices. These actors allow free and fair elections, and also allow any elected party to govern the country as long as it does not seek regime change. Although the multi-party system empowered Turkish democracy, the Cold War conditions enhanced the power and regime role of the military.

After World War II, Turkey was extremely poor and had limited resources to invest in either development or defense. However, with

[32] Vamik Volkan and Norman Itzkowitz, *The Immortal Atatürk* (Chicago: University of Chicago Press, 1984); Andrew Mango, *Atatürk: The Biography of the Founder of Modern Turkey* (Woodstock, NY: Overlook Press, 2000).

United States aid, the Turkish Armed Forces (TSK) became the second largest military establishment within NATO, and Turkey's international political role was improved. Although Turkey joined NATO in order to be able to divert more resources to education, transportation and economic development, it had to increase spending on national defense and quickly became dependent on the United States. This, in turn, consolidated the power of the military and made the TSK the most trusted agent of United States policy in Turkey. The major political implication of this over-powerment of the military was the emergence of a kind of "dual sovereignty": an unelected military and civilian bureaucracy versus an elected government. During this period, the multi-party system, the new liberal constitution of 1961 and the ideological polarization of society in the 1970s all intensified state–society interaction.[33] In spite of limited public funds, the state managed to improve education, the economy, urban conditions and transportation. These changes facilitated societal penetration into the state. The state not only transformed society, but was transformed in the process.[34] However, Cold War conditions helped Turkey to freeze centrifugal ethnic and religious identities in the name of national security and the fight against international communism. When the Alevi and Kurdish groups tried to carve out a space for themselves within leftist ideology, they in fact limited their freedom of action and became targets of the state's anti-leftist campaign.[35]

The fourth stage of Turkish history (1983–1999) was dominated by the politics of identity and the search for individual wealth, along with the introduction of a new political language about privatization, human rights and civil society.[36] Neo-liberal economic policies were fostered, and a new Anatolian bourgeoisie emerged. Kurdish, Islamic and Alevi groups gained confidence and posed the question: "How can I bring my privatized Kurdish, Islamic or Alevi identity into the public sphere?" Although these groups first sought to come out as collective entities, democratic and market forces individualized, personalized and in time fragmented their identities. As a result of the neo-liberal economic policies adopted in the mid-1980s, people have become focused on "individual" and

[33] Walter F. Weiker, *The Turkish Revolution: 1960–1961* (Washington, DC: Brookings Institution, 1963).

[34] Robert Bianchi, *Interest Groups and Political Development in Turkey* (Princeton: Princeton University Press, 1984).

[35] Elisabeth Özdalga, et al., *Alevi Identity* (Istanbul: Swedish Research Institute in Istanbul, 1998); Yasin Aktay, *Türk Dininin Sosyolojik İmkanı* (Istanbul: İletişim Yayınevi, 2006).

[36] Nilüfer Göle, *The Forbidden Modern: Civilization and Veiling* (Ann Arbor: University of Michigan Press, 1997).

"self-oriented" issues. Economics, not politics, has come to determine the orientation of Turkish society. By neo-liberalism, I mean the subordination of state and politics to market forces and individual choice.[37] Neo-liberalism means privatization, decentralization and citizen participation. Privatization assumes that state enterprises are rendered ineffective by the lack of information and of incentives that can be provided only by the market; thus, privatization becomes the goal for economic efficiency. Decentralization is presented as the democratization of governance and as public accountability to the electorate at the local level. It assumes the privatization of certain public services such as health care, education and even security. Citizen participation becomes the means of privatization and decentralization. Neo-liberalism in Turkey has gone further than in any other country of the region, and has altered the cognitive map through which people think about society and state. It opposes state intervention in the economy and the public sphere and stresses an entrepreneurial mentality in politics. The state is redefined in entrepreneurial terms as an institution providing service to consumers (citizens). Prime Minister Erdoğan calls this entrepreneurial mentality "*tüccar zihniyeti*" in Turkish, and he wants to generalize it to government, party and all other social interactions.[38] By entrepreneurial politics, Erdoğan means politics with results, without getting bogged down in bureaucratic rules and institutions; consequences rather than means or rules are what matter for the new politics. It means the expansion of the entrepreneurial form to politics. Indeed, there is a potent change taking place in Turkey's domestic and foreign policy, driven by the new bourgeoisie's political prowess and its role in projecting its power in domestic and foreign policy.

---

[37] David Harvey, *A Brief History of Neoliberalism* (New York: Oxford University Press, 2005), pp. 2–3.

[38] Erdoğan argues that "During the debate over the budget, I used the term 'entrepreneurial politics (*tüccar siyaset*).' One opposition MP, who speaks only by and in terms of books, said this was the first time 'I hear this term.' He has a lot to learn! Their life is always structured according to books. They build their career by reading books someone put in front of them. They thought this is all about the life. They never reconciled theory with practice. Never forget that life is not about theory; life is practice itself. If you do not know practice, you cannot govern societies." R. T. Erdoğan, "Türkiye'nin İmkanları ve Kaynaklarıyla Türkiye'yi kaldıracağız, April 1, 2003", in *Konuşmalar* (Ankara: AK Party, 2004), p. 130. The governing party (AKP)'s platform is about "reform" and "change" in terms of a privatization and a decentralization that treat citizens as consumers and customers. Erdoğan argues that "Kitapta ne yazıyorsa o. Bunun dışına asla çıkmayacaksınız; hayır çıkacaksınız. Onun için tüccar siyaset diyoruz. 'Siyaset literatüründe bu yok' diyorlar; bu da girsin." See also Erdoğan's speech, "Diyarbakir'a Giden Neden Erzurum'a Rize'ye Gitmiyor," *Yeni Şafak*, December 25, 2004.

When the state attempted to exclude Islamic identity by criminalizing it, it failed in the face of society's determination to shape and redefine the state. Society rebuffed state efforts at penetration and actually succeeded in subjugating the state to its own character.[39] I have examined the fifth stage of Turkish political development in my *Islamic Political Identity in Turkey*, a book that considers the restructuring of state–society relations after the December 1999 Helsinki decision, which provided a clear compass for Turkey for the next several decades. It would be difficult to capture the revolutionary involvement of all the components of Turkish society in this historic transformation. By comparison, it is easy to build a coherent narrative of this transformation. However, this coherence is obtained only by eliminating the jagged edges, where much of the vitality of the people is to be found. In this book, I focus on only one critical actor, the AKP, within the larger international and domestic context.

At the core of this Turkish experiment are several formative factors that dominate the political landscape. Turkey has the most powerful state tradition and state-centric political culture among Muslim countries. Historically, the Ottoman imperial system was not in conflict with Islam, but rather Islam was subordinated to the interests of the state.[40] There was no profound legacy of colonialism or confrontation with the West. Consequently, Turkish political thought (secular or Islamic) was not suffused with anti-European ideas.[41]

The Turkish military is the founding institution of the Republic and has a clear doctrine of modernization and a secularizing mission. It has never collaborated with outside forces and never allowed any ideological clique to hijack its project. The military, the self-declared guardian of the secular regime, still remains a more prestigious and respected institution than any religious organization. The first key parameter of Turkish politics is the state-centric political culture perpetuated by Kemalism, which defines politics as "administering a modern society" in terms of implementing the principles of secularism and nationalism. The second key is the popular legitimacy of democracy. These two deeply rooted parameters are in regular tension and occasional cooperation with the religious

---

[39] Jenny B. White, *Islamist Mobilization in Turkey: A Study in Vernacular Politics* (Seattle: University Washington Press, 2003); M. Hakan Yavuz, *Islamic Political Identity in Turkey* (Oxford: Oxford University Press, 2003).

[40] Carter Vaughn Findley, *The Turks in World History* (New York: Oxford University Press, 2004).

[41] M. Hakan Yavuz, "Islam and Europeanization in Turkish–Muslim Socio-Political Movements," in Peter J. Katzenstein and Timothy A. Byrnes (eds.), *Religion in an Expanding Europe* (Cambridge: Cambridge University Press, 2006), pp. 225–255.

opposition. The source of the contemporary crises in Turkey is rooted in the Kemalist ideology, which aims at modernizing society through the instruments of the state. This Turkish version of modernity seeks to engineer a new "secular Turkish citizen" with a specific lifestyle, identity and duty. The educational system, tasked with creating this new, secular Turkish being, has been the main instrument in the pursuit of this goal. Those who resist this engineering or insist on their ethnic or religious identities are considered "enemies" of the state and of its founding ideology.

In fact, the state allows leftist and rightist parties to function as long as they remain within the parameters of state ideology and work towards the integration of society according to the Kemalist doctrine. The state uses all means to get the parties to translate peripheral voices into the language of nation-building or become the mechanisms that control and transform centrifugal forces. Thus, democracy in Turkey allows peripheral identities to flourish only in the private domain; they exist in the public domains only as long as they are excluded from the zones of the state or give up their claims to particular ethnic or religious identity. It is the state that draws the borders of the politics, not the other way around.

The tension between secularism (Western lifestyle) and the Turko-Islamic lifestyle is the root of political cleavage in the electoral system. In Turkey, it is the personal characteristics of the leaders, their lifestyles and positions on daily issues that shape the voting decisions of the people, rather than party ideology. Yet, in recent years, especially at the local level, people have cast their vote on the basis of regional identities and interests. Increasingly, identity issues and lifestyles, rather than class divisions, are what shape electoral behavior. Moral issues, religious education, the wearing of the headscarf at universities, Kurdish secession and relations with the EU (over Cyprus and Turkey's membership) and the United States (over Iraq) kept religio-cultural issues at the top of the electoral agenda in the 1995, 1999 and 2002 elections. One's worldview and ethnic origin, more than class issues, still dominate the polarization of society. Politics in Turkey is about a clash of lifestyles and values that perpetuates competing lifestyles. With the expansion of the opportunity spaces Islamic and Kurdish identities seek to expand their lifestyles. This, in turn, leads to a clash of worldviews and prevents the emergence of a shared collective language. Thus, a social cleavage in terms of the lifestyles and values of the Republic (secularism, state-nationalism, centralism) versus the lifestyles and values of the larger Muslim society (religious morality, traditional values, decentralization, the free market) still dominates voting behavior and partisan alignment. In addition to this religious versus secular, Sunni versus Alevi cleavage, ethnic origin is becoming an increasingly important factor in voter alignment. Many Turks still identify terrorist attacks by the PKK as the most important threat to the unity of the nation and the security of the state. For instance, electoral support for the Kurdish parties (HADEP, DEHAP) is totally concentrated in the Kurdish-populated region of the southeast. These parties do not have much appeal outside this region. Yet, these ethnic and religious parties reflect the segmented nature of political culture in Turkey, which is riddled with divisions: Turks vs. Kurds; Sunni Muslims vs. Alevi Muslims; secularists vs. Islamic groups; and socio-economic distinctions. The politics of Turkey is still heavily based on the first three cultural cleavages as the sources of political mobilization. Islam plays a dual role: it provides both a shared language of national unity as well as a source for disagreement and conflict.

In addition to this constant political tension, Turkey is not a rentier economy, but rather a tax-based market economy with a growing middle class. Islam has been the transmission belt between state and nation, and the diversified economy has provided the necessary context for the pluralization of Islamic movements. Decades of rigid application of secularism failed to confront the fact that Turks are religious beings and that Islamic mores are the building blocks of their personal evolution and everyday life. In order to live a meaningful life in the Turkish context, one needs to have a cognitive map that is rooted in Turko-Islamic civilization.

In conclusion, the history of modern Turkey is the story of the tensions between the state's attempts to "modernize" and the peripheral forces seeking to redefine the state. The parameters of the state are still more influential than the emerging impacts of the neo-liberal economic policies of Özal in terms of creating a new political configuration of alliances between Islamic groups and big industrialists. The pro-statist industrialists have gradually moved away from rigid Kemalism to a more liberal (EU) outlook.

### The triple helix of the statist discourse: Turkish ideology: nationalism, conservatism and Islamism

SÜLEYMAN DEMİREL: The state is a magnificent institution. If the subject is the state, we should not talk lightly. Whatever the issue, go ahead and investigate. But do not nibble at the state.

YEKTA GÜNGÖR ÖZDEN: The state is grand, august, and sublime. I never accuse the state. Only persons are responsible if proven, but never the state.[42]

---

[42] Quoted in Mithat Sancar, *Devlet Aklı Kıskacında Hukuk Devleti* (Istanbul: İletişim, 2000), p. 64.

In Turkey, there is very little connection between abstract thought and politics, or theory and practice. With the Kemalist reforms, politics was reduced to administration. The administration always aimed to empower and maintain the state. Political thought always evolved around the defense or control of the state, and there was no powerful class in Turkey to challenge the state-initiated radical transformation.

In the Turkish case, even though nationalism, Islamism and Kemalism provide competing images of society and identity, they are always mixed with each other; this in-between ideological space has always been identified as conservatism. One of the key characteristics of Turkish conservatism is the protection and strengthening of the state. The state and nation are regarded as one organic whole, and ethnic or religious diversity is barely accepted. As long as the state acts to protect the values of the nation, it has the sole right to determine the national interest as well. In this mode of thinking, diversity disappears, society becomes a homogeneous nation, and the nation is equivalent to the state. Whoever dissents against the state and its ideology is regarded as a rebel and is de-legitimized. The state, in the context of Turkish history, always resisted the emergence of new social centers outside its control and never encouraged political pluralism. The main problem in Turkey, which is also the problem of Kemalism, is coming to terms with what has become a diverse, multi-ethnic and multi-religious sense of nationhood. The state still fears any differentiation or communalization (*cemaatleşme*) of the nation. State institutions, especially the military, regard as undesirable the politicization of any identity outside Turkish nationalism or its Kemalist version (citizenship and patriotism as the sources of Turkishness).[43] The viewpoint that the state is the highest authority is dominant among AKP voters, even if it is not shared by the party leadership. Such conservatism lies at the center of state–society relations in Turkey and helps to create a transcendental vision of the state as omnipotent and omnipresent. Many societal groups help to produce this image and reify it as a force that shapes their own conservatism.

---

[43] Turkish nationalism is a contested zone among three different conceptions of Turkishness: ethno-religious, which sees Islam as the definer of Turkishness; ethnic Turkish nationalism, which stresses ethnicity and language; and the civic Turkish nationalism of Mustafa Kemal, known as *Atatürk milliyetçiliği*, which stresses loyalty to the state and its progressive secularist agenda.

## A comparison of nationalist, conservative and Islamist in Turkey[44]

|  | Nationalist | Conservative | Islamist |
|---|---|---|---|
| **Ideology** | Nationalism | Turkish–Islamic synthesis | Islamic |
| **Identity** | An ethno-linguistic, Turkish first and Muslim–Ottoman identity. Citizens constitute organic body of Turkish nation. The main task is loyalty and service to the Turkish state. The identity is based on internal and external (especially neighbor) "others." Not comfortable with globalization. Obsessed with territory. | An ethno-religious identity. Turkish–Muslim identity defined by traditional Anatolian values. Pro-state and in favor of expanding a civil society that consists of *cemaats* and neighborhood. Service to national and spiritual values is welcomed and cherished as the ultimate mission. | Islam and Islamic loyalty first, nation and national loyalty second. National identity is defined by Islamic values and the Islamic history of the Turkish people in the service of Islam. Emphasis on the Islamic past of the Seljuk and Ottoman states. Service to community, *umma* and Muslim state is praised. Has an anti-imperialist flavor. |
| **State** | State is regarded as the most sacred entity to fight and kill for. Unconditional love of and loyalty to the state is required and perpetuated. | State is obeyed and respected; defined as the guardian of national and traditional values. State is regarded as a "father" figure. | State is respected as long as it protects religious values and memory. State is criticized if it restricts religious freedoms and rights. The goal is to Islamicize the state. The state must perpetuate religious values. |
| **Secularism** | Religion is a private matter and an important component of national culture. Headscarf could be managed according to the needs of the public order. It is not the most important right. | Religion is a communal and private issue and the state system should be free from religious influences – but the state could interfere in the preservation and perpetuation of religious values. Secularism is a matter of state affairs, and citizens are not expected to be secular. | System does not differentiate public and private; stresses the presence of Islamic values in the public sphere. Religious demands must shape political landscape. Headscarf is a religious duty and must be allowed in all places and services. Has obsession about Islamizing everything it meets in modern life. |

[44] This comparison is derived from the following three volume studies: Conservatism (*Muhafazakarlık*), Islamism (*İslamcılık*), and Nationalism (*Milliyetcilik*) (Istanbul: İletişim, 2004).

|  | Nationalist | Conservative | Islamist |
|---|---|---|---|
| **Kurdish Problem** | Against any form of compromise and supports the criminalization of Kurdish political activism. | Territorial integrity and national unity are the highest principles. Kurdish identity is a sub-national identity and could survive at the communal and private level. Against any political concession to Kurdish secessionism. Trusts the long period of sharing the same culture with Kurds. | Supports religiously defined "national unity" and regards Islamic identity and loyalty as a solution to Kurdish secessionism; supports cultural rights of education, public broadcasting, and religious education in Kurdish. |
| **Foreign policy** | In favor of the existing relations with NATO. Gives priority to relations with neighboring Turkic nations and groups. Critical of US hegemony and supports Turkish–Israeli relations. | In favor of NATO and Turkey's European orientation; seeks closer ties with Turkic and Muslim countries. In favor of close relations with the US and Israel. In short, very pragmatic. | Not enthusiastic about Turkey's relations with NATO. Supports closer ties with Muslim countries; in favor of pan-Islamic solidarity; opposes US role in the Middle East and is very critical of Turkish–Israeli relations. Inspired by the Ottoman past, assumes a leading role for Turkey among other Muslim countries. |

If the state is the first pillar of Turkish conservatism, the second is the Islamic ethos of community: communitarian values shape the daily life of Turks.[45] In this mix, secularism plays a contradictory role – both weakening the Islamic ethos and empowering the state. Turkish secularism offered a controlled space for Islamic activism and never allowed it any space to change the secular character of the state.[46] One of the essential principles of the Turkish constitutions of 1961 and 1982 is the state's commitment to establish and protect the secular aspect of the polity and

---

[45] Şerif Mardin, *Religion and Social Change in Modern Turkey: The Case of Bediüzzaman Said Nursi* (Albany: State University of New York, 1989); Şerif Mardin (ed.), *Cultural Transitions in the Middle East* (Leiden: E. J. Brill, 1994); Şerif Mardin, "The Nakshibendi Order of Turkey," in Martin E. Marty (ed.), *Fundamentalisms and Society* (Chicago: University of Chicago Press, 1993), pp. 204–233.

[46] M. Hakan Yavuz, "The Case of Turkey," *Daedalus*, 132:3 (Summer 2003), 59–62.

society. The institutional parameters of Turkey prevented any party from making an explicit statement that it was either an Islamic party or in any way challenging the secular nature of the state. The regime rules forced Islamic groups to work within the center-right parties, which created a closer affinity between Islamic groups, conservatives and some Turkish nationalists. Thus, *mukaddesatcı* (sacred-centered conservative identity) became a surrogate identity for Islamic groups. This close affinity between conservatives (who stress morality and loyalty to homeland and the state) and Islamists (who stress Islam as a blueprint to be implemented in social and political life and seek the unity of the Muslim community) constitutes the skeleton of the center-right parties. Conservatives define their task as preserving the national, traditional and spiritual values of the nation.[47] They regard Islam as the social cement of society and as a key element of national culture.

Islamic groups always searched for an opportunity to change the character of the regime through center-right parties; whereas conservatives, who controlled center-right parties, used the discourse of spiritual (Islamic) values (*manevi değerler*) and religious symbols to expand their electoral base and to contain the demands of the religious groups within the secular system. The focal point became change *in* the regime rather than change *of* the regime. Nuray Mert argues that the major cleavage between the Islamists and the conservatives is the way in which they define their political discourses: the Islamic movement defines itself in opposition to the regime and seeks regime change, whereas the conservatives stress the discourse of power and accommodation.[48] In spite of these differences, center-right conservative parties became the protector of Islamic groups against militant secularism. The center-right parties such as the DP, AP and ANAP have always been successful in winning the support of a large segment of religious voters. This historical affinity between Islamism and conservatism played a facilitating role in the transformation of Islamic discourse and organizations. It was easier for ex-Islamic groups to frame themselves as conservative due to this legacy.

### Nationalism and Islamism

Turkish secularism means "taking religion out of politics while keeping the state involved in religious affairs."[49] Secularism in the Turkish context

---

[47] Nazim İrem, "Turkish Conservative Modernism: Birth of a Nationalist Quest for Cultural Renewal," *International Journal of Middle East Studies*, 34 (2002), 87–112.

[48] Nuray Mert, *Hep Muhalif Olmak* (Istanbul: İletişim, 2001), p. 238.

[49] Turhan Feyzioğlu, "Türk İnkılabının Temel Taşı: laiklik," in Ethem Ruhi Fığlalı (ed.), *Atatürkçü Düşüncesinde Din ve Laiklik* (Ankara: ATAM, 1999), pp. 137–198: this edited

is a tool to establish and control the boundaries of Islam. Although Turkish secularism might seem radical and progressive, it is in fact authoritarian and regressive. The main goal of Mustafa Kemal was not to disestablish religion but rather to create a set of institutions and a legal system to "control," "use" and "reinvent" Islam, if necessary, for the furtherance of national and state interests. The state banned any parties or social groups, such as the Sufi orders, that were based on religious identity or established to promote religious interests. Moreover, no Islamic symbols or language were tolerated in the political sphere, which was also structured by the state. The task of the state was to organize and shape the religious needs of the people in accordance with the state's own secular nature. There was an elaborate military–legal constraint against the politicization of Islam. Yet the state also maintained an open, competitive political system as long as parties worked within the bounds of Kemalist doctrine.

Turkish scholars who were raised in Turkey, obsessed with emulating the West and transforming the country into a European society, always interpreted Islamic voices critical of Westernization as rebelling against their version of modernity.[50] Similarly, scholars of Turkish politics outside Turkey tend to read the Islamic movement as being in opposition to the state rather than focusing on the symbiotic and subordinate relationship between the two.[51] This custom of assuming an inevitable clash of Kemalist and Islamic ideologies ignored the more nuanced evolution and mutual transformation of state and society. One of the logical outcomes of this reading is to see the rise of political Islam as the failure of Kemalism or the demise of Islamism as the rise of Kemalism. This mutually exclusive analysis has become one of the dominant modes in contemporary Turkish studies.

Mustafa Kemal's reforms and Özal's economic liberalization facilitated the formation of opportunity spaces, which, in turn, became nuclei for the reconstitution of Islam. Because Kemalist secularism is perceived as anti-religious, almost all scholars see the reconciliation of the 1980 coup with Islam and Islamic activism as the cause of post-1980 Islamism in Turkey. This reading ignores the complex and multifaceted relationship between Islam and the state. It exaggerates the secular character of the state and ignores the fact that the branches of state institutions in the

volume provides the best essays on the official version of Turkish secularism; Reşat Genç, *Türkiye'yi Laikleştiren Yasalar 3 Mart 1924 Tarihli Meclis Müzakereleri ve Kararları* (Ankara: Atatürk Araştırma Merkezi, 2005).

[50] Tarık Zafer Tunaya, *İslamcılık Akımı* (Istanbul: Simavi Yayınları, 1991).

[51] Feroz Ahmad, *The Making of Modern Turkey* (New York: Routledge, 1993); Bernard Lewis, *The Emergence of Modern Turkey*, 2nd edn. (London: Oxford University Press, 1969).

provinces behave very differently from their parent bodies in Ankara. The main source of the legitimacy of the Turkish state has always been Islam, as well as the state's close ties to Islamic groups. Islam and Republican secularism are not separate worlds in conflict, but symbiotic parts of the same historical development. Berkes, Tunaya and Lewis all misread the relationship between Islam and the state when they presented this relationship in terms of an inevitable clash between two ideologies and life-styles,[52] since it has been more diverse and ambivalent than some orthodox secularist scholars want us to believe. Turkish nationalism, the logic underlying the population exchanges with the Balkan countries and the discriminatory taxation policies implemented during World War II all reflect the deep religious roots of the state. Neither Islam nor Turkish Islamism but rather uncontrolled Islamism or Arab Islamism is regarded as an ideological "other" of the Turkish state.

In the Turkish context, state institutions as well as the Turkish version of nationalism have played a moderating and assertive role in the constitution of Islamic movements. Islamic activism, or Islamism, has been contained and shaped within the framework of Turkish nationalism. Turkish Islam, always state-centric, was utilized as a national ideology and form of identity in the nation-building process.[53] The constant flux between nationalism and Islamism helped to entrench conservatism in the political domain. During the Cold War, Islamic activism was identified with the anti-communist center-right conservative parties. Islam *with* nationalism formed a conservative ideology against liberalism and the left-leaning parties.[54] Nationalism became the framework for imagining possible and acceptable Islamism in Turkey. Historically, late-nineteenth-century Ottoman intellectuals, who were influenced by nationalist ideas, sought to construct a nation on the basis of Islamic bonds and loyalties. These intellectuals imagined the religiously defined community (*ümmet*) as the nation, and Islamism as nationalism. Şerif Mardin examined the politicization of Islam as a proto-nation-building process and described how Turkish nationalism evolved out of the Islamism of the nineteenth century.[55] In the Turkish context, this conceptual kinship between Islamism and Turkish nationalism blurred the usual boundaries.[56]

---

[52] Niyazi Berkes, *Teokrasi ve Laiklik* (Istanbul: Adam, 1997).
[53] M. Hakan Yavuz, "Is there a Turkish Islam? The Emergence of Convergence and Consensus," *Journal of Muslim Minority Affairs*, 24:2 (2004), 1–22.
[54] Howard A. Reed, "Revival of Islam in Secular Turkey," *The Middle East Journal*, 8:3 (1954), 267–282.
[55] Şerif Mardin, *Türkiye'de Din ve Siyaset* (Istanbul: İletişim, 1991), p. 56.
[56] M. Hakan Yavuz, "Nationalism and Islam: Yusuf Akçura, 'Üç Tarz-i Siyaset,'" *Oxford Journal of Islamic Studies*, 4:2 (1993), 175–207.

Turkish identity is inextricably intertwined with Islam, and the Turkish service for the perpetuation of Islamic doctrine is praised. Thus, one cannot be a Turk unless one is a Muslim. A non-Muslim Greek, Armenian or Jew can be a Turkish citizen but not a Turk.[57] For those ethno-religious Turkish nationalists, the Turkish nation was considered as the Muslim nation with a special mission within and for Islam. They treated the state as the best defender of Islam against Christianity.

During the heyday of Kemalism, especially after the 1930 Menemen rebellion against the reforms of Mustafa Kemal, state institutions stressed the secular notion of nationalism and used all means to eliminate Islam from the public domain. With the advent of the multi-party system in the 1950s, the masses generally reacted against this policy and allied themselves with the opposition Democrat Party.

During the Cold War, Islamism and Islamically oriented political activism were organized around the latent Sufi orders. This period witnessed a dual process: the nationalization of Islam and the Islamization of nationalism against rising leftist activism in Turkey. The neo-Sufi Nur movement developed a close affinity with nationalism, and the Naksibendi tradition stresses the authority of the state. Also, anti-colonial sentiments had fostered their involvement in the War of Independence under Mustafa Kemal.

In the 1960s, Necip Fazıl Kısakürek (1904–1983) and Osman Yüksel Serdengecti (1917–1983) defined Turkish nationalism within the framework of Islam; they played a formative role in the construction of Turkish Islamism-with-nationalism. During this period, Islamic opposition was based on nationalism, and Kısakürek and Serdengecti framed their Islamic criticism of the Kemalist system in nationalist terms. As a result, for many Turks, "love for religion and love for nation is intermingled, even unified."[58] Meanwhile Arab, Persian and Pakistani Islamists such as Qutb (1906–1966), Shariati (1933–1977) and Mawlana Mawdudi (1903–1979) promoted a new form of radical Islamism, with the goal of freeing Islam from local culture and developing an Islamic state. Turkish Muslim intellectuals, such as Necip Fazıl and Nurettin Topcu (1909–1975), and Sufi groups rejected the influence of these "foreign" radical writers and defined Islam as a basic component of Turkish culture. While radical Islamists sought to transform society and the state, these Sufi-oriented traditional intellectuals stressed conserving the state and the cultural values of Turkey. Thus, AKP conservatism is very much rooted in a

---

[57] M. Çağatay Okutan, *Tek Parti Döneminde Azınlık Polikaları* (Istanbul: Bilgi Universitesi, 2004).
[58] Tunaya, *Islamcılık Akımı*, p. 202.

Turkish Islam that has been tested and vernacularized with the goal of conserving *Turkish-Muslim* values. Some aspects of Turkish nationalism functioned as a surrogate for Islamic identity and also as an intellectual space in which religious values could be brought into the public domain.

## The Islamic landscape: domestication via incentives and punishment

Thus, the history of the Islamic movement is the story of the synergy of new social, political and cultural networks. The networks became movements; the movements hardened into political parties; and the parties played an important role in the advancement of an alternative modernity. Islamically informed debates are always going forward; these debates cannot be represented comprehensively by any party or clearly encapsulate the past or the present. To this end, Muslims refer to Islam to address the three problems of globalization: identity, justice and morality. The Islamic debate, therefore, must be viewed as a process; it does not end the conversation or say the last word but rather offers a common ground for discussion. Islamic debate allows ordinary people to participate in a process with the familiar language of society: Islamic concepts and moral discourse.

The Islamic movement evolved and was defined very much as a result of its interactions with the state. Yet the interactions between the state and Islamic movements are not about a bipolar clash of identities and ideologies, but rather occasional co-optation, confrontation or symbiotic interaction. Three key factors in this contest have been the internal competition over resources, the interpretation of the Qur'an within the various Islamic movements, and the concept of *hizmet* (rendering service to the state and society) in Turko-Islamic culture.[59] Almost all Islamic political movements derive their popular legitimacy by framing their activities as *hizmet*; Islamic activities have their own internal reference point (serving people for the sake of God) but similarly must legitimize their presence in terms of secular language as well.

The internal diversity and institutionalized competition among diverse Islamic movements have a dynamic and domesticating impact. The Turkish religious landscape includes four actors: political Islam; the social Islam of the widespread (neo-)Sufi groups; the state Islam of the

---

[59] For more on the concept of *hizmet*, see M. Hakan Yavuz, "The Gülen Movement: The Turkish Puritans," in M. Hakan Yavuz and John Esposito (eds.), *Turkish Islam and the Secular State: The Gülen Movement* (Syracuse: Syracuse University Press, 2003), p. 26.

Directorate of Religious Affairs (DRA); and the radical Islamic groups.[60] There is a struggle taking place for the soul of Islam, and in this intramural contest the radical groups such as Kurdish Hizbullah are no longer empowered, since the relatively open political system has generated a dynamic discussion and prevents any group from dictating the meaning of Islam (see chapter 6).

The presence of an Islamic party in local and national politics is very important in domesticating the excesses of Islamic claims and "learning" to articulate religious interests and claims in the secular idiom of politics. With the advent of the multi-party system in the 1950s, it was the center-right Democrat Party that first brought Islamic claims to the political sphere, in terms of human rights and respect for culture.[61] The DP utilized religious issues to challenge the oppressive policies of the CHP. Almost all politicians from the center-right, beginning with Adnan Menderes, have included religious language in their public addresses. They all stress the unifying role of Islam and the obligation of the state to protect the values of the Turkish people. Scholars have labeled such discourse as "civil religion," in which political leaders emphasize religious symbols and transcendent principles to engender a sense of unity and shared national identity. However, political Islamists have differed from the center-right by seeking to convince their supporters that it is a religious duty to support their political platform.

After the closure of the DP in 1960, the Justice Party (AP) of Süleyman Demirel stressed Islamic issues and religious liberties in its election campaigns, and most Sufi groups, especially the Nur movement, supported his political agenda. To foster national industries, Demirel pursued import-substitution economic policies through three interrelated programs: (a) import restrictions and high tariffs to protect home-grown industries; (b) fixed exchange rates to keep the Turkish lira artificially high and to encourage Turkish companies to borrow dollars from the state to import raw materials; (c) subsidies for farmers and above-market-value wages for industrial labor. These policies worked against the petty

---

[60] The DRA is one of the largest Turkish institutions, with its own budget and branches both inside and outside Turkey. It has the second largest representation outside Turkey after the Ministry of Foreign Affairs. It owns more than 120 mosques and employs several hundred people in various European states. The DRA licenses mosques, appoints all prayer leaders (imams), pays their salaries and controls all the activities and speeches of prayer leaders. The education of the personnel of religious institutions is carried out by the Ministry of Education and the autonomous Council of Higher Education, known as YÖK. Education and religious services and the meaning of Islam are tightly controlled in Turkey. This state Islam regularly contains and contests diverse interpretations of Islam.

[61] Cem Eroğlu, *Demokrat Parti: Tarihi ve Ideolojisi* (Ankara: İmge, 1998).

bourgeoisie – artisans, craftsmen and small businessmen – who became
the major base for a separate political Islamic movement under the leadership of Necmettin Erbakan, the chairman of the Turkish Chambers of
Stock Exchange and Commerce.[62] Moreover, conservative–nationalist
politicians (Professor Osman Turan and Yüksel Serdengecti) grew very
dissatisfied with the cultural policies of the center-right AP and decided
to support the new political formation under Necmettin Erbakan. Most
of the founders of the Milli Görüş movement were ex-members of the
AP.[63] The Milli Nizam Partisi (MNP) was established in 1970, after
Erbakan was elected as an independent from Konya province in 1969.
On October 11, 1972, the elite of the MNP established the Milli Selamet
Partisi (MSP).

### Conclusion

There was some expectation that the Kemalist modernization project
would end with a modern and secular society. None of this expectation
has been borne out by recent events in Turkey, especially the rise of
political Islam. Secularism and consumerism are spreading to every corner of life, but at varying speeds and with diverse implications. Turkey is
becoming more modern with Islamic networks and an assertive Muslim
identity. These processes, especially those unleashed by the neo-liberal
policies of Özal, are producing hybrid forms of life and identities rather
than homogeneous secularism. The Kemalist modernization project left
much of everyday life untouched until the 1980s. However, with the
advance of neo-liberal economic policies, consumer patterns and images
have been drastically transformed.

   The old Turkey that is defined in terms of Kemalist ideology still calls
itself "modern," though it is in fact senile, if not in decline. A new Turkey
with a new understanding of the state, nation and politics is being born.
The demise of the old Turkey and the emergence of a new one appears to
some as revolutionary and to others as reactionary. The shift to moderation is being led by a new configuration of social actors, especially Islamic
groups and the emerging bourgeoisie.

   As of 2008, Islamic groups in Turkey are adopting a different agenda.
They do not seek an Islamic polity but rather the freeing of religion from
state control and the removal of obstacles to living a religious life. At the

---

[62] Binnaz Toprak, *Islam and Political Development in Turkey* (Leiden: E. J. Brill, 1981); Ali
Yaşar Sarıbay, *Türkiye'de Modernleşme Din ve Parti Politikası: "MSP Örnek Olayı"*
(Istanbul: Alan Yayıncılık, 1985).
[63] Süleyman Akif Emre, *Siyasette 35 Yıl* (3 Vols.) (Ankara: Keşif Yayınları, 1991), pp. 130, 163.

same time, they want the state to: protect the moral values of society, which they believe are derived from Islam and its sense of the good life; strengthen solidarity with Muslim countries and communities; and represent Islamic civilization – in all its economic, cultural and scientific dimensions – in the world. As these moderate sentiments evolve, the EU's requirements for membership stand as the most powerful incentive for the consolidation of democracy.

The Turkish Republic was created through revolution, and its founding principles cannot be easily altered through democracy. This does not mean that democracy is all about management within the framework of the Kemalist regime. Yet, in the case of Turkey – and also that of Iran – one needs to pay close attention to the distinction between permissibility (*makbuliyet*) and legitimacy (*meşruiyet*). One should expect a gradual transformation of politics through a carefully structured modus vivendi agreed between the guardians of the revolution and those who seek to alter it through popular participation.

# 2 Political and economic origins of the AKP: opportunity spaces and the backlash of February 28, 1997

> Not ideas, but material and ideal interests, directly govern men's conduct. Yet very frequently the 'world images' that have been created by 'ideas' have, like switchmen, determined the tracks along which action has been pushed by the dynamic of interest[1].

In the analysis of the transformation of the pro-Islamic parties in Turkey, there are three competing explanations: the effect of repression, EU conditionality within the framework of the Copenhagen criteria, and the emergence of a new generation. Even though these "effects" played important facilitating and restraining roles, none of them were the causes of this deep transformation. I explain the transformation in terms of the emergence of new economic opportunity spaces and the evolution of a new set of actors.

This chapter argues that the main reasons for the evolution of a liberal Islamic movement in Turkey are the domestic changes that took place during the premiership of Turgut Özal, between 1983 and 1993. These changes have been consolidated by external factors, especially Turkey's desire to join the European Union. Thus, I argue, *the origins of this transformation are rooted in Turkey's neo-liberal economic history, but the movement towards democratization has been consolidated by the EU process.* The chapter will address the following questions. What are the political and social origins of the split of the AKP from the National Outlook Movement (NOM) of Necmettin Erbakan? What is the role played by Islamic entrepreneurs in the emergence of a pro-European, pro-market and pro-liberal Islamic movement in Turkey? Lastly, what accounts for this transformation?

Turkey presents a new way of thinking about the transformation of Islamic activism and the interaction between Islam and democracy. To understand the transformation of political Islam in Turkey, one needs to

---

[1] Max Weber, "Social Psychology of the World Religions," in H. H. Gerth and C. W. Mills (eds.), *From Max Weber: Essays in Sociology* (New York: Oxford University Press, 1958), p. 280.

45

focus on internal and external structural factors. There are three factors: (1) "Opportunity spaces" in the market, media and politics that have played a *formative* role in the integration and pluralization of Islamic actors[2]. (2) The constitutional prerogatives that have directed the orientation of political change by banning anti-system Islamic parties and some key politicians from the political arena. These bans, in turn, have opened new opportunities for a younger and reformist generation of conservative Muslim politicians and facilitated the political learning process of the political elite. (3) Turkey's unquestioned commitment to becoming European by joining the EU, a process which has become a major factor in the transformation of the Islamic movement. While I will examine in detail the impact of the EU process in chapter 7, it is important to notice that after the Helsinki summit in 1999 in which the EU recognized Turkey as a candidate for full membership, a "grand compromise" between business, the military and the politicians was created for a number of political reforms.

At the Copenhagen Council summit in 1993, the criteria for future membership of the EU were determined. These criteria were: (1) the stability of institutions guaranteeing democracy, the rule of law, human rights, and the protection of minority rights; (2) the existence of a functioning market economy, as well as the capacity to cope with competitive market forces within the EU; and (3) the ability to shoulder the obligations of membership, such as adherence to the goals of political, economic and monetary union. The first set of criteria are known as "political criteria" and candidate countries are expected to meet all of them before they start accession negotiations. Each year, the EU commission is expected to prepare a progress report in respect of these criteria. On the basis of this report, the EU Council decides whether a candidate country can start accession negotiations.[3] For membership to take place, the approval of the EU Parliament is required as well as that of the national parliaments. Some countries also want to hold a referendum to decide on new member states. Since the "Copenhagen criteria" require candidate countries to fulfill a number of democratizing reforms, along with the recognition of the rights of cultural groups, Turkey pursued major legal reforms which would transform state–society relations at the expense of state power. Under the Copenhagen criteria, the EU developed an effective instrument to transform the political, societal and economic structures of candidate countries by providing material incentives and legal support for domestic actors to transform their societies and polities from the bottom up. Thus,

---

[2] For more on the opportunity spaces, see Yavuz, *Islamic Political Identity*, pp. 22–23.
[3] See Copenhagen European Council, Presidency Conclusions, June 1993.

the EU provides a powerful opportunity structure for reformist elements in Turkey. The Copenhagen criteria have become the watchwords for the AKP to consolidate democracy and empower civil society.

In this chapter, I will show that the transformation of Islamic movements in Turkey is an outcome of a combination of an ongoing liberalization process of creating competitive political spaces, the growing power of the Anatolian Muslim bourgeoisie, the expanding public sphere and the inclusion of new intellectuals in the movement. The most important factor in the evolution of this Muslim democratic movement is the rising bourgeoisie and its commitment to democratic values through supporting various cultural and political activities. Expanded political participation has been the most important factor in moderating religious radicalism. Political participation provides a variety of flexible learning opportunities for religious actors to make trade-offs between their ideology and vote-maximization. In order to exist as a legal party and acquire genuine popular support, religious parties must engage in coalition building and pragmatic compromises. In addition to avoiding repression, in order to gain political power religious parties have to trade off between the desire for ideological purity on the one hand and the maximization of votes on the other by paying close attention to public opinion. Moreover, competitive and honest political competition and legal guarantees for those who play according to the rules help consolidate this transition to moderation and political pluralism. In order to gain and sustain electoral success the political leadership of religiously inspired parties had to expand their electoral strategies beyond purely confessional appeals and also to moderate their ideology. Islamic parties entered into a series of coalition governments, an experience of power-sharing which was crucial in consolidating moderation in the political system.

Ironically, in the long run, while the Islamic parties have generally not managed to "Islamicize society," the ballot box has tended to liberalize the Islamic parties. In an open public sphere where media outlets are not fully under state control, diverse ideas and contestation amongst religious parties and entrepreneurs will prevent the hegemony of any single authoritarian voice. Religious actors will bring their religious sensitivities and arguments to the public sphere by translating them into a secular language or framework that has broad public appeal. In Turkey, Muslim democrats have learned how to compromise, backtrack and discuss and frame religious issues through secular concepts that have broad public appeal even among segments of society that are not particularly devout.

By taking these three factors into account, this book offers an embedded constructivist approach to understanding the ongoing transformation of Turkey's Islamic movements. Although structural conditions are crucial in the evolution of the movement, the political learning process of the new economic and political leadership has helped to form a moderate and more democratically oriented movement. This learning process is based on the twin pillars of punishment and incentives. In order to explain the way in which the twin processes work, I will first examine the political, legal, communication and economic opportunity spaces as the social context of the learning process by focusing on the macro socio-historical factors of secularism and nationalism.

The second part of this chapter analyzes the legal and political constraints that led to the closure of Islamic parties, especially the impact of legal decisions on the evolution of political Islam within the context of punishment and reward. I will then examine the implications of the coup of February 28, 1997 for the Islamic movement, and its fragmentation into two competing groups:[4] The Saadet Partisi of Erbakan and the AKP of Tayyip Erdoğan. The third part will focus on the political consequences of the EU membership criteria on the internalization of democratic values by the AKP.

### Political space: becoming a party

By utilizing competitive political opportunity spaces with the country's multi-party system, the Islamic movement established its own party in 1970. The process of "partification" and acting in a coalition government fostered the independence of the Islamic party and the socialization of the party within the system. Moreover, being a part of several coalition governments made the Islamic Milli Selamet Partisi (MSP) act responsibly and distance itself from radical fringe groups.

In the early 1970s, under the leadership of Necmettin Erbakan, the symbolically and politically more Islam-oriented *Milli Nizam Partisi* (MNP) was established and Erbakan became the spokesperson for the petty bourgeoisie and artisans who were denied state support.[5] After the

---

[4] This military-led "soft" coup forced Erbakan to resign in June 1997. The Constitutional Court closed the Refah Party on the basis of its anti-secular activities. Erbakan was consequently banned from political activity for five years. The Fazilet Party (FP) was formed under the leadership of Recai Kutan, a close confidant of Erbakan, who tried to maintain Erbakan's legacy. Due to pressure from younger and reformist members of the party, the 1999 election platform declared entry into the EU to be the primary goal of Turkey's foreign policy. However, in June 2001 the Court closed the FP also due to its anti-secular activities, leading to further division and the transformation of the political Islamic leadership.

[5] Sevket Kazan, *Refah Partisi Gerceği* (Ankara: Keşif Yayınları, 2002); Yavuz, "Political Islam and the Welfare (Refah) Party in Turkey," *Comparative Politics*, 30:1 (October 1997), 63–82.

1971 military coup, the Constitutional Court dissolved the MNP on the basis that the party's program sought to "establish a theocratic state" and violated the prohibition against the use of religion for political purposes.[6] Erbakan took refuge in Switzerland, later returning to Turkey to establish the *Milli Selamet Partisi* (MSP), which stressed the role of public morals and virtues (*ahlak ve fazilet*) to differentiate itself from other parties. The National Outlook Movement (NOM) of Erbakan had a petty bourgeois class base, which changed as Erbakan's MSP became a partner in a series of coalition governments in the 1970s. Erbakan's constituency included the homogeneous Sunni-Muslim base of farmers and the conservative petty bourgeoisie of shopkeepers, small merchants and artisans from provincial towns and cities. The NOM's discourse was based on the underdevelopment of Anatolia and the economic marginalization of the provincial bourgeoisie by the pro-Kemalist Istanbul-based capitalists. This gap was articulated in terms of the secularist–Kemalist policies of the other political parties that resulted in the marginalization of the "children of Anatolia." In other words, the NOM constituted a class-based rebellion against the policies of the secularist–Kemalist state. For Erbakan, this "system" was alien and alienating since it lacked the moral values of the Anatolian bourgeoisie. Thus, the NOM was not only a critique of Kemalist cultural policies but also of Kemalist economic policies, but the criticism was never anti-modern or anti-free market. It aimed at conservative modernization, that is, becoming modern *with* Islam. By modern, Erbakan meant industrialization, better health care, more technology and better living conditions through the incorporation of Turko-Islamic values. Erbakan's economic project was based on national industrialization, but was opposed to big Istanbul-based industrialists, and had close ties to what was then the European Common Market.

The party program of Erbakan included two key targets: the national production of heavy machinery by state-owned enterprises, and more generous economic credit and machinery support to small and middle-size companies. These policies aimed to reduce the Western penetration into the Turkish economy that took place through joint ventures between Istanbul-based big corporations and Western companies, which resulted in the undeserved competitive advantage of big corporations. The small size businesses also complained that the credit policy of large banks favored big business over the less profitable small businesses. As far as the cultural sphere was concerned, Erbakan highlighted Islamic and Ottoman social and moral values in opposition to the imported and

---

[6] Binnaz Toprak, *Islam and Political Development in Turkey* (Leiden: E. J. Brill, 1981), pp. 98–99.

elite-forced European values of the Kemalist elite. The leaders of the current AKP received their political education under the leadership of Erbakan.

Erbakan was pragmatic and politically successful enough to hold the key to the formation of a number of coalition governments throughout the 1970s, including one with Bülent Ecevit's center-left Republican People's Party in 1974, and one with Demirel's center-right Justice Party (*Adalet Partisi*; AP) between 1975 and 1977. Due to Turkey's rigid secularism, heavily influenced by Atatürk's political thought, Erbakan and the people around him began to discuss Islamic claims and identity politics without using specifically religious language. Thus, Erbakan's *milli görüş* ("national outlook") ideology viewed other political parties as simply mimicking the West, and he presented his movement as an anti-system party while, ironically, working within the system.[7] He stressed the role of the state in the economic and spiritual development of the nation, emphasized a conservative approach to family and championed state-led religious education to create a new generation of *Muslim* Turks. Due to the rising polarization of society and the fragmentation of the state structure, the military intervened in 1980 and closed the MSP, along with nearly all other parties. The economic decline in the 1970s had led to the polarization of society along the axes of left vs. right, Islamic vs. secularist, Kurd vs. Turk, and Alevi vs. Sunni. Moreover, the 1979 Islamic Revolution of Iran and the Soviet invasion of Afghanistan later that same year created a deep sense of insecurity within the Turkish military, which some have labeled as the main reason behind the 1980 military coup (while the Afghan invasion itself was likely a reaction to the Iranian Revolution, and the Iranian Revolution an overdue reaction to the 1953 CIA-sponsored coup in Iran). In 1980, the Turkish military sought to restructure the political landscape by introducing a Turkish–Islamic synthesis as a new national glue to combat or pacify divisive ethnic and religious forces. The military used the Ministry of Education, the Directorate of Religious Affairs and the State Planning Organization to carry out what amounted to a socio-political project.

With the transition to democracy and a multi-party system, the Refah Partisi (RP) was founded in 1983 but failed to make major gains in the shadow of the Motherland Party of Turgut Özal, who had very close ties to influential Nakşibendi and Nurcu groups. During the 1980s, Özal carried out a radical economic transformation project by introducing neo-liberal policies that, among other things, resulted in the rise of new Islamic

---

[7] Necmettin Erbakan, *Milli Görüş* (İstanbul: Dergah, 1975).

entrepreneurs. The multi-party system and joining a series of coalitions not only integrated Islamic voices into the political system, but also encouraged the socialization of democratic rules by Islamic groups. This learning process and inclusion prevented the radicalization or use of force by Islam-oriented parties in Turkey.

## Economic opportunity space

In order to understand the origins and policies of the AKP, one has to explore not only the social and political context of the new Muslim actors, the Islamic Anatolian bourgeoisie, the most significant force in the evolution of Turkish Islamic movements, but also their identity, politics and relationship to other Islamic political groups. It is very important to study the role of these particular actors because it is this Anatolian bourgeoisie that provided the financial means to foster the development of diverse Islamic movements and discourses through its charities, television stations, radio stations and newspapers. Who are these actors? What are their identity and politics? How have they shaped the orientation of the AKP? What is the role of the Islamic bourgeoisie in the fragmentation, and even in the possible end, of fundamentalist Islamism in Turkish politics? It is important to note that Islamic movements in Turkey are not shaped in the many shanty towns surrounding major cities but rather by rising social groups through their wealth and education. Indeed, it has been these rising social groups, especially the Islamic bourgeoisie, which have become the engine of the Islamization of consumer patterns and the vanguard of Turkey's recent democratization. In the hands of these new Islamic entrepreneurs, religious symbols and practices are woven into upper-middle-class life-styles. Yet this Islamic moralizing has been limited to rhetoric and not necessarily expanded towards a just and fair treatment of workers.

The most crucial period for modern Turkey occurred in the years 1983–1987, a period punctuated by the ideas and personality of Turgut Özal, a man with deep religious beliefs, yet with a strong commitment to capitalism and the market economy. He unleashed and coalesced the economic and religious forces of Anatolia to create a "new form" of bourgeoisie, which eventually provided fertile ground for the political and cultural transformation of the second political revolution of Erdoğan. Özal's neo-liberal economic policies enabled a major expansion of opportunity spaces in politics, economics, education and the media. By opportunity spaces, I mean "an arena of social interaction that creates new possibilities for augmenting networks of shared meaning and associational life." Such arenas include civic and political forums, electronic and print media, cyberspace and the free market. Opportunity spaces are not simply mobilizing structures, because the manner by which they adhere is through social interactions and expressive space rather than through formal or informal organizational structures. The key opportunity space remains the market since economic prosperity allows one to become plugged into broader cultural and political processes of social change. Opportunity spaces give one the ability to pick and choose one's definition of personal identity; to resist the policies of the state or the market; and, more importantly, to change the meaning of everyday life. Opportunity spaces undermine state-based or society-based attempts to generate a hegemonic ideology and to mix private and public spheres. Opportunity spaces free diverse voices and transform religiously shaped stocks of knowledge into a *project* of shared rules of cooperation and competition. In these spaces, not only are individuals and collective actions blurred, but the boundary between the public and private is constantly redrawn.

### New actor: the Islamic bourgeoisie

The Islamic bourgeoisie of Turkey evolved out of the state's neo-liberal economic policies, which created conducive economic conditions and emerging transnational financial networks as a result of deregulation and the opening of the economy. The Islamic bourgeoisie has also benefited from the local government successes of the *Refah Partisi* (RP), especially after the 1994 municipal elections. Since the symbiotic relationship between the state and the large Istanbul-based capitalists was based on an agreement over secularism and the Kemalist ideology, the RP represented a class-based ideological challenge to this powerful secularist coalition.

The emergence of an Anatolian-based Islamic bourgeoisie was a counter process to the existing economic and cultural alliance between the state and Istanbul-based capitalists. This new actor is both a cause and an effect of the neo-liberal economic policies championed by Özal. The majority of Islamic entrepreneurs are first-generation college graduates and often part of the Anatolian-based petty bourgeoisie who benefited from Özal's neo-liberal economic policies, which increased social mobility and allowed them to establish their own middle- and small-size businesses. They are the first generation of an urbanizing economic elite who still maintain strong ties to the small towns and villages of Anatolia.

Because they were first introduced to Islamic values at a young age in their towns and villages and then spent several years in university dormitories, mostly run by Nurcu or Naksibendi Sufi orders, they learned to objectify Islam as an alternative project and became conscious (*şuurlu*)

Muslims who had a clear notion of Islamic identity.[8] By conscious Muslims, I mean those believers who seek to differentiate themselves through their deeds from others who are Muslim by name or by custom. These self-conscious believers seek to live as "real" Muslims who define the good life as that of abiding by the broader teachings of Islam. According to Yasin Aktay, a Turkish sociologist and scholar of Islam, these believers think they are *conscious* Muslims because they choose to work, live and think according to what they regard as the Islamic worldview.[9] They regard themselves as knowledgeable about the teachings of Islam and tackle the challenges of modern life by interpreting Islamic principles in accordance with modern conditions.[10] With the disestablishment of the religious authorities (*ulema*) there have emerged new Muslim actors who interpret Islam independently, to guide a meaningful life. Thus, a close study indicates that most of the members of Turkey's pro-Islamic business group, MÜSİAD (Independent Industrialists' and Businessmen's Association), came from a conservative Muslim social environment with a history of anti-establishment discontent.[11] They were critical of the state subsidies received by the Istanbul-based business class and were disgruntled with the status quo, that is, with the doings of the state–big business axis.

The Anatolian-based petty bourgeoisie were mostly excluded and marginalized by the state policy of import-substitution, a policy which always favored the secular-oriented, big city bourgeoisie. This former group was thus co-opted and designated as the government's vehicle for its modernization projects and the model of its life-styles as well. Most of the new, Anatolian, urbanizing economic elite were involved in fast-growing textile and construction businesses. Eventually, services, transportation and tourism became important fields of economic activity as well.[12] Most of these small and medium firms are family owned and maintain traditional family structures characterized by conservative religious values.

---

[8] After the coup in 1997, conscious Muslims stopped defining themselves as Muslims opposed to the West or Western practices. One can see the evolution of Euro-Islamic ways of life as mixed and heterogeneous.

[9] Interview with Yasin Aktay, June 23, 2006, Konya.

[10] Interview with mayor of Konya, Tahir Akyürek, June 23, 2006, Konya.

[11] Şennur Özdemir, *MÜSİAD: Anadolu Sermayesinin Dönüşümü ve Türk Modernleşmesinin Derinleşmesi* (Ankara: Vadi, 2006); Ayşe Buğra, *State and Business in Modern Turkey: A Comparative Study* (Albany: State University of New York, 1994); Buğra, "Class, Culture, and State: An Analysis of Interest Representation by Two Turkish Business Associations," *International Journal of Middle East Studies*, 30:4 (1998), 521–539.

[12] Abdullah Topçuoğlu, *Akrabalık ve Hemşehrilik İlişkilerinni Toplumsal Sermaye Değeri* (Konya: Çizgi Kitabevi, 2003).

the same groups by diverse identities and concerns. This undermines the Muslim image of a homogeneous Islam and Muslim *umma* (community), and rather highlights diversity. New Muslim actors compete simultaneously with secular circles and among themselves. These actors create their own Islamicly shaped public spheres and networks to shape and benefit from new political and economic forces. New opportunity spaces in the market have allowed Muslim actors to carve their own space, among other things through their own movies, novels, poetry, music, fashion shows, entertainment, magazines, restaurants and hotels. New hybrid nationalistic–Islamic, modern–traditional identities and roles are under construction. Although Turkish Islamic movements still seek to control and manipulate the public sphere, they are also eventually being forced to deal with everyday life issues and "open up" private domains to public scrutiny.

The term public sphere might become more useful if we appropriate the term as spaces of communication. These new spaces, which emerged as a result of the neo-liberal economic policies of Özal, opened "public debate" on many issues, including Kurdish and Alevi rights. These topics all challenged the authoritarian Kemalist framing of socio-political goals. Previously, "public debate" in Turkey had only been allowed within the framework of the Kemalist conception of a "good society." However, even though the public sphere often comes into being outside the control of the state, this was not the case with Turkey. State policies played an important role. Moreover, though the Muslim "public" stood outside the state, it also struggled to find a dominant discourse with the support of the state.

In conclusion, Özalian neo-liberal economic policies led not only to the decline of radical Islamism but also to the revival and transformation of Turkish Islam. With its free-market policies and the expansion of the public sphere, a number of Islamic companies started to punctuate the Anatolian economic landscape with their Islamic financial institutions, Islamic media and Islamic educational system. This renaissance of Islamic activism became possible through the expansion of opportunity spaces. This new economic base also facilitated the emergence of new Muslim intellectuals who remained outside the control of the state and who were funded by Islamic entrepreneurs.

### The commodification and associationalization of Muslim activism

Until the mid-1990s, Islamic movements remained very much a cross-class coalition of diverse forces. With the neo-liberal economic policies, "winners" and "losers" started to reimagine Islam on the basis of their own experience. With the 1989 elections, Islamicly inclined voters began to migrate to the RP, especially those who had not benefited from Özal's neo-liberal economic policies. Thus, as a result of the new economic situation of the 1980s, the RP had a different social base from that of the MSP in the 1970s. It managed to expand its traditional constituency by reaching out to the urban poor, new upwardly mobile middle class professionals and especially to emerging Islamic urban entrepreneurs. This was a coalition made up of the "marginalized" and "excluded" sectors of Turkish society as a result of the bankruptcy of the now defunct state ideology of Kemalist secularism. It was the new entrepreneurs in particular who benefited from the educational system and new policies of Özal. Having accumulated some wealth they then sought to be fully included as conscious Muslims into the Turkish political and cultural systems. Their exclusion from the ranks of the dominant elite due simply to their life-style and articulated Islamic identity led them to undertake a major struggle for recognition and power. This struggle is at the root of the current conservative revolution in Turkey.

With the victory of the RP in the municipal election in 1994, the ties between Islamic entrepreneurs and politicians created a new symbiosis with the twin goals of transferring public (municipal) funds to the newly emerging bourgeoisie and also of utilizing these established networks to shape the practices and ideas of an Islamic movement. Yet, the political discourse of Erbakan very much dominated the economic discourse of MÜSİAD and its anti-EU policy as well. However, this subordinate position started to change in the late 1990s, especially after the 1997 coup. How did these new actors become the shapers of a new generation of Islamism in Turkey? Islamic entrepreneurs played an important role in supporting and promoting the development of "print Islam" or "media Islam" in new television and radio stations and newspapers.

Since neo-liberal economic policies led to the drawing back of state institutions and a cut in welfare subsidies, religious groups and new Islamic entrepreneurs filled this gap by supporting education, healthcare and new welfare services for the urban poor and dormitories for students. This turned the new bourgeoisie into the principal actor in the maintenance and promotion of Islamic discourse. Another impact of the new bourgeoisie was on the party-political level in terms of funding candidates, campaigns and also supporting grassroots organizations. These groups defined emancipation as not from God but from the interventionist state, which meant the marriage of the market and religion, where religion became the lubricant facilitating the working of market institutions. In conclusion, as a result of new opportunity spaces in the national and global markets, the conservative petty bourgeoisie of Anatolia has been transformed into medium and large size business owners with more ambitious strategies and with a new Islamic identity that promotes work ethics and communal responsibility in order to create better economic conditions.

One of the major impacts of neo-liberal economic policies has been the development and autonomization of diverse interest groups and the eventual split of the Islamic movement between pro-market and anti-market forces. The glue of Islam under the leadership of Erbakan was not enough to keep these divergent Islamic interest groups together. The major tensions were between the Islamic bourgeoisie of MÜSİAD and the urban poor of the Hak-İş[18] (an Islamic trade union) and articulated in terms of two opposing images of Islam. These class distinctions were played out in the domain of consumerism and the life-styles of the Anatolian nouveaux riches. With the Islamization of consumer patterns and the emergence of entrepreneurial Islam, Islamic businesses created their own niche in the market. With this economic wealth, one sees the development of "Islamic taste," "Islamic elegance," "Islamic products" and "Islamic vocation." Some firms have consciously chosen key Islamic and Arabic names such as *Tevhid* (unity of God), *Ittifak* (alliance), *Ihlas* (sincerity) and *Tekbir* (calling God's name). This process of "going Islamic in the market" increased the already tangible tension between Islamic market forces and the hegemonic secularist taste and mode of consumerism.

Islamic social movements represent the "coming out" of private Muslim identity in public spaces. It is not only a struggle for recognition of identity but also a mode of "going public" through private identities. In these public spaces, identities and life-styles are performed, contested and implemented. This "coming out" has had three major effects. It financed the religious public sphere in terms of journals, newspapers, books, television and radio stations and by creating and funding foundations to work on history and intellectual activities; it supported an independent economic base to further the evolution of new Muslim intellectuals; and finally this economic expansionism led to the emergence of new Muslim business actors and facilitated their increasing involvement in social and political life. As a result of these three effects, ways of life, ways of reasoning and the working norms of Turkish society have been transformed. For instance, the expansion of the public sphere has resulted in the re-imagining of Islam and Islamic practices within the context of a

---

[18] Hak-İş is an Islamically oriented trade union. Even though it was founded in 1976 by a pro-National Outlook Movement group, it became the third largest union in Turkey with 350,000 members by the end of 1980s. Hak-İş has always supported pro-Islamic parties. Yüksel Işık, *Siyasal Islam ve Sendikalar* (Ankara: Öteki Yayınevi, 1996), pp. 219–231.

liberal–secular state and the re-imagining of Europe as no longer the "other" of Islam.

This period, between 1983 and 1987, was dominated by economic revolution and the release of society from the chains of a state obsessed with security. It was a period of normalization for Turkey. The expansion of opportunity spaces took place during the reign of self-defined conservative politicians whose "conservative revolutions" involved a legal and cultural struggle colored by conflicting loyalties of identity, rebellion and a determination to redefine the meaning and the role of the state, previously the master and purveyor of the "correct" concept of Turkish culture. The significance of these dramatic changes and events of the 1980s is quite different from the EU-led AKP transformation of 2000s. One of the key differences between the Motherland Party of Özal and the AKP of Erdoğan is that Özal was rooted at the center right of the system and his party was regarded as the establishment party. As the party of the center, it was seeking to control the language of the periphery. The AKP is the party of the periphery and seeks to restore the center of politics by stressing the "enduring values" of the society. However, the AKP has now accommodated its language and policies to become the party of the center.

## The Welfare Party (*Refah Partisi*) (RP)

| *Milli Görüş Hareketi* (National Outlook Movement) | Leader | Period | Reason for Closure |
| --- | --- | --- | --- |
| *Milli Nizam Partisi* (MNP) | Necmettin Erbakan | 1970–71 | Constitutional Court |
| *Milli Selamet Partisi* (MSP) | Necmettin Erbakan | 1972–80 | Military coup |
| *Refah Partisi* (RP) | Ahmet Tekdal | 1983–87 | |
| *Refah Partisi* (RP) | Necmettin Erbakan | 1987–97 | Constitutional Court |
| *Fazilet Partisi* (FP) | Recai Kutan | 1997–2001 | Constitutional Court |
| *Saadet Partisi* (SP) | Recai Kutan | 2001–present | |
| *Adalet ve Kalkınma Partisi* (AKP) | Recep T. Erdoğan | 2001–present | |

After the 1987 referendum that allowed for increased political pluralism and political involvement, Necmettin Erbakan managed to re-emerge with the RP in 1987.[19] The clear political identity of the RP made it easier for its followers to display their identity and distance themselves from other

---

[19] M. Hakan Yavuz, "Political Islam and the Welfare (Refah) Party in Turkey," *Comparative Politics*, 30:1 (October 1997), 63–82; Birol Yesilada, "The Virtue Party," *Turkish Studies*, 3:1 (Spring, 2002), 62–81; Haldun Günalp, "Globalization and Political Islam: The Social Bases of Turkey's Welfare Party," *International Journal of Middle East Studies*, 33 (2001), 433–448.

Islamic groups. Özal's death in 1993 and the failure of Mesut Yılmaz, then the chairman of Motherland Party, to keep conservative forces within the party and the RP's focus on worsening economic conditions, corruption and genocide in Bosnia provided new opportunities for Erbakan. The turning point for the Islamic politics of Erbakan was the 1994 municipal elections in which the RP received close to one-fifth (19%) of the popular vote as a result of effective neighborhood organizations and networks, along with activated hometown (*hemşerilik*) associations, and social welfare programs among the poor and the new rural-urban immigrants in major cities.[20] The party projected itself as anti-system, and differentiated itself from other parties which were classified as "representative of the oppressive system" and loyal to the status quo. Its populist slogans targeted the "rentier" circles of big business and the media who had close ties with the state. Its economic program, known as "just order," was populist and appealed to Turkey's expanding shanty-town poor, the newly emerging middle class, Kurds and some rural voters by stressing "the distributive role" of the state in the economy. Yet, as class distinctions became clear so did the political fault lines within the party. The rising middle class of the RP supported more moderate and conciliatory policies, whereas the hardliners demanded more state intervention in the economy.

This victory at the local municipal level made people willing to experiment with and watch the activities and programs of the RP. The municipalities governed by the RP offered a different sense of politics by stressing both cooperation and competition among decentralized administrative units. These horizontally linked organizations included voluntary, non-profit and private organizations and services. The party had great success in fighting against corruption, introducing new social services, improving existing ones and opening new public spaces for the middle and lower-middle classes, including the opening of new public parks. The major engine of change in Turkey was the municipalities which introduced money, consumerism and fashion to conservative Muslims. The 1994 election was an important turning point for the Turkish Islamic movement in terms of its integration into the market and the public sphere.

### The philosophy of RP municipalities

The philosophy of RP local governments, known as *milli görüş belediyeciliği* ("local government municipalities"), emerged when the RP won 19% of the vote that resulted in their controlling 329 municipalities (mayorships) in

---

[20] A. Cengizhan Köse, "Yöresel Dayanışma Örgütlerinin Kentlileşme Sürecindeki Rolü" (unpublished thesis), Selcuk University, Konya, 1996.

the 1994 elections, including the municipalities of Istanbul and Ankara.[21] The RP demonstrated a new way of playing local politics by defining politics as the ways and means to provide urban services and by building an urban consensus to address the main issues of urban areas. Having won the election, Erdoğan became the new mayor of the Greater Istanbul municipality, along with sixteen other districts, and implemented a successful plan to give Istanbul a new and functioning infrastructure. During this period of the 1990s, the RP also invented the concept of the "social municipality" (sosyal belediyecilik) to deal with poverty by creating horizontal networks of aid to the needy. With the "white table" (beyaz masa), the municipalities linked citizens to the city administration and responded to the pressing questions and inquiries of ordinary folk. With "people's assemblies" (halk meclisleri), the RP managed to bring people to participate in the polical re-making of the municipalities and created an institution of urban consensus building. During this period, the municipalities organized many national and international conferences, workshops, panels and conventions to define the political culture and political orientation of the country. This was the period in which the municipalities used their considerable political and financial means to construct a new historical memory that would resonate in the public sphere. During this period the municipalities opened new public parks, restaurants and beach resorts, but banned the sale of alcoholic beverages, thus making these areas more family-friendly and Islamic.

The municipalities played an important transformative role in the reconfiguration of the practices and ideology of the RP. As the RP grew and won municipalities, it was forced to confront new demands requiring pragmatic approaches to problem-solving and faced greater pressure to deal with the daily needs of the people. Moderates within the party realized that they could also win national elections if they lowered their ideological commitments and stressed pragmatic policy solutions. This is the period when the current AKP elite of Turkey first tested their ideas and began constructing networks. (The municipal experience of the AKP politicians was very important for the maturation of the party leadership. It taught them how to build and utilize dense neighborhood networks, how to translate local political issues to national politics and how to develop close ties with ordinary people.)

The remarkable success of the RP in the municipalities translated into a major victory in the December 1995 national elections, making the RP the largest party in parliament with over 21% of the popular vote. The two

---

[21] Kenan Camurcu, Ak Parti'nin Stratejik Meseleleri (Istanbul: Şehir Yayınları, 2006), pp. 118–120.

center right parties of Çiller and Yılmaz formed a coalition government to exclude the RP and to prevent what was perceived by some as the political Islamization of the state. Due to corruption charges brought against Yılmaz and Çiller, however, the coalition government fell apart and Çiller, ironically, formed a coalition with Erbakan as Prime Minister. When Erbakan started to listen to the hardliners who then formed the core constituency of the RP in domestic and foreign policy, the party alienated many moderate groups and Erbakan became vulnerable to military pressure. The reason for Erbakan's decision to embrace the position of the hardliners had to do with his failure to implement the RP's populist economic policy. Since Turkey's economy and international financial standing was under the strong influence of the IMF and the World Bank, it was not possible to pursue any significant policy outside the program imposed by these institutions and this, in turn, encouraged Erbakan to focus on foreign rather than domestic policy and impose his own cultural agenda to differentiate it from other parties. In other words, neo-liberal economic policies and Turkey's dependence on international credit and institutions restricted individual parties from implementing their own particular economic policies. Thus, the RP tried to differentiate itself from other parties and previous governments through new and controversial foreign policy initiatives, such as visiting Libya and Iran and directly organizing the Jerusalem Night (*Kudus Gecesi*) programs to critique the policies of the state of Israel. Erbakan also pursued an Islamization policy of cultural spaces by attempting to build a mosque in Istanbul's Taksim Square, by seeking to change holidays, by encouraging the wearing of the headscarf and by establishing close ties with Sufi networks, inviting Sufi leaders to the Prime Minister's official residence for a Ramadan dinner. These initiatives angered Turkey's Republican establishment and eventually resulted in the "soft" military coup of February 28, 1997.[22]

### The February 28 process and the constitutional prerogatives

When the state failed to cope proactively with these new actors, it sought to criminalize them through the February 28 process.[23] The events of February 28, 1997 are known as the "soft coup" because the military

---

[22] The National Security Council asked the government to implement a policy of "cleansing Islam from the public sphere" by implementing an eight year compulsory educational system, which led to the closure of the religious education schools – Imam Hatip Middle Schools.

[23] M. Hakan Yavuz, "Cleansing Islam from the Public Sphere and the February 28 Process," *Journal of International Affairs*, 54:1 (Fall 2000), 21–42.

mobilized major business associations, media cartels, university rectors and a judiciary long subservient to its commands to engineer an anti-RP drive to force the recently elected Erbakan government to resign. Behind this public campaign was the unmistakable message that Erbakan's government should resign "voluntarily" or be forced out by the generals. The coup viewed Islamic identity as a national threat and proposed a number of directives to cleanse the Islamic presence from public spaces even where it had been present even in the most reactionary period of Kemalist zeal. This "soft coup" is also known as the "February 28 process" because the coup was not only limited to the removal of the RP-led government but was also a process for the state establishment, mainly the military and civilian bureaucracy, to monitor, control and criminalize all Islamic activism as a security threat and institutionalize a permanent legal framework for ostracizing devout and/or active Turkish Muslims from the market, educational and political spheres. Furthermore, the "securitization" of Kurdish and Islamic identity claims was increasingly politicizing society. Securitization is hereby referred to as a concept articulated by Barry Buzan and Ole Waever whereby the state brands certain religious, ethnic, class or ideological groups and movements as a national security or even "existential" threat, thus justifying coercive and often extra-judicial measures against them.[24] Assertive Kurdish and Islamic identity claims have reinforced the "securitization" of domestic politics in Turkey and the institutionalization of a national security state, in which the military has expanded its overseer role to include such civilian areas as the judiciary, the economy, education and foreign policy. In accordance with its endowing ideology of Kemalism, the Turkish military regards the acknowledgement of ethnic or religious diversity as a potential threat and a precursor of disunity. In the 1990s, this fear of ethnic and religious assertiveness and its potential to undermine the political and ideological hegemony of the Kemalist establishment underpinned the state policy of denying individuals and groups the right to articulate their religious and ethnic identity claims outside very narrow and officially sanctioned spaces.

## Legal Restraints

The military in Turkey has always considered itself as the guardian of Kemalism and secularism, and the protector of the state against the

---

[24] Carsten Bagge Laustsen and Ole Waever, "In Defence of Religion: Sacred Referent Objects for Securitization," *Millennium: Journal of International Studies*, 29:3 (2000), 705–739; Ole Waever, "Securitization and Desecuritization," in Ronnie D. Lipschutz (ed.), *On Security* (New York: Columbia University Press, 1995), pp. 46–86.

internal and external enemies of ethnic nationalism and Islamic extremism (known as *irtica*). In recent years, the Constitutional Court of Turkey (CCT) became as militant as the military in the defense of secularism and the Kemalist legacy.[25] Indeed, the CCT is not part of the human rights revolution in Turkey because of the history of secular nation-building and its dealings with Kurdish and Islamic resistance groups and individuals. Thus, in the founding ideology of the Turkish Republic there have been two "others" – or enemies: the Kurdish and the Islamic movements. Without the unpacking of the historical context of the process of nation-building in Turkey, one cannot understand the statist attitude of the Turkish judiciary. Some scholars, such as Mustafa Erdoğan, have argued that the CCT hinders the liberalization of the Turkish democratic transition. The judges of the CCT are not insulated actors. They all go through the state process of legal socialization and the highly indoctrinatory high school and university educational system. The law schools of Turkey especially inculcate the same Kemalist values of nation-building. This shared cognitive map plays an important role in the formation of alliances among the CCT judges, with other state institutions, and also with some sectors of civil society. The judges of the CCT are part of the Kemalist alliance. The military and the judiciary both regard themselves as the guardian of the Republican project and have developed a strong collective identity – (*esprit de corps*) – in opposition to the elected and populist politicians. This alliance is deeply rooted in the Turkish state tradition and cannot be understood outside the collective memory of the collapse of the Ottoman Empire and the founding philosophy of the Republic. The CCT has been very activist in defending the autonomy of professors, civil servants and judges against the government and even against citizens.

The hegemonic ruling Kemalist elite wants to preserve its power against elected officials and their decision-making areas by empowering the CCT. The CCT is a powerful institution for protecting Kemalist doctrine and its guardians such as the military and the universities who benefit the most from the status quo. The logic in the establishment of the CCT in the 1961 constitution, along with other autonomous institutions, was to protect certain areas from the power of elected officials. The main concern of the framers of the 1961 constitution was not the government's power over the citizens but over the Republican institutions and state organs.

---

[25] Dicle Koğacıoğlu, "Dissolution of political parties by the constitutional court in Turkey: Judicial delimitation of the political domain," *International Sociology*, 18:1 (2003), 258–276; Koğacıoğlu, "Progress, Unity, and Democracy: Dissolving Political Parties in Turkey," *Law & Society*, 38:3 (2004), 433–462; Mustafa Erdoğan, "Fazilet Partisi'nin Kapatma Kararı Işığında Türkiye'nin Anayasa Mahkemesi Sorunu," *Liberal Düşünce*, 23 (Summer 2001), 36–40.

A number of entities from universities to public broadcasting companies were regarded as autonomous enclaves outside the control of elected officials. The goal was to protect certain areas during the nation-building process from the majoritarian democracy that had been practiced by the DP in the 1950s. The CCT decisions on protecting secularism at the expense of religious liberties were even upheld by the European Court of Human Rights. The CCT became more conservative in the 1990s due to the challenges the state and the republican ideology faced from Kurdish nationalists and Islamists.

As a part of the February 28 process, several Refah Party mayors became the target of intensive investigation, including the mayor of Kayseri. The mayor of Sincan was jailed because he allowed a rally against Israel in which a number of religious speeches were made – he was sentenced to a prison term for "inciting religious hatred." The court also went after Erdoğan. Prosecutors filed a number of charges against him, charging him with "inciting religious hatred" and calling for the "overthrow of the government" on the basis of reading out a poem in 1997 that it was claimed stirred up religious feeling in the south-eastern city of Siirt:

> The mosques are our barracks
> The domes our helmets
> The minarets our bayonets
> And the faithful our soldiers.

On the basis of the reading out of this poem, on April 21, 1998 Erdoğan was convicted by the state security court.[26] The court decision ended his office as mayor, convicted him to a ten-month prison term, and barred him from standing for elected office. Contrary to the Kemalists' intentions, however, Erdoğan's ten-month imprisonment was not the end of his political career, it was a new beginning. The prison term enhanced his popularity, and in the absence of another credible political force and with a worsening economic situation as a result of the 2001 economic crisis, Erdoğan's party, the AKP, became the only viable option in the minds of the electorate. Furthermore, Ecevit's weakening health caused many Turks to worry about the political stability of the country.

The February 28 process had a number of impacts on the political landscape of the country. For instance, the governing AKP now acts as if it fears a similar coup taking place at any time. The shadow of the 1997 coup still dominates and orients the Party's policies. As the AKP lives in fear of a repeat of the February 28 coup, the secularist establishment lives with the paranoia of an extremist Islamist take-over, known as the rule of

---

[26] Faik Işık, *Recep Tayyip Erdoğan Davası, No. 1998/36 Esas* (Istanbul: Keskin, 1998).

*seriat.*[27] The AKP rides on the railroads of the previous government and has no intention of changing its political direction or adding new road-maps. Among other things, the AKP leadership has been forced to inter-nalize the EU process. In essence, the AKP has no special "mission or a distinct vision to lead the country."[28] Deputy Prime Minister Abdullah Gül argues that through the February 28 process "we all changed and learned a great deal. We gained new experiences. Some of our friends were imprisoned and later released. Some of us occupied very sensitive positions in the state. We are trying to do our utmost to derive good lessons from these experiences."[29] Bülent Arınç, the speaker of the parlia-ment, told a reporter that the February 28 coup was a critical turning point in his political worldview. He says:

We used to have a different understanding of the state; the leviathan, with a scowl, that reminded one of the gendarmerie and the police. We came to the conclusion [after the coup of February 28] that we need a new conception of the state that rejects the sacredness of the state and protects the individual and delivers better services to the individual. What is important is the individual; and the individual's welfare, his or her peace of mind. If the state fulfils these functions, it is in the service of the individual. This is how we came to believe in the EU goal.[30]

The coup also taught Erdoğan to realize the parameters of democracy and the power of the secularist establishment, and forced him to become a moderate and a democrat. Moreover, by barring Erbakan from politics, the February 28 process created new "opportunities" for younger politi-cians like Gül. Under pressure from the military, the CCT closed the RP and banned six politicians, including Erbakan, from politics for five years.[31] The Court dissolved the RP as a "center of activities contrary to the principle of secularism." The Court defined "secularism" as

a civilized way of life which tears down the dogmatism of the Middle Ages and constitutes the cornerstone of rationalism, science, improving the concept of freedom and democracy, becoming one nation, independence, national sover-eignty and the ideal of humanity. ... Although it is defined as separation of state and religious affairs in a narrow sense and interpreted in different manners, the opinion that secularism is, in fact, the final phase of the philosophical and organ-izational evolution of societies is also being shared in theory. ... Secularism has accelerated modernization by preventing religion from replacing science in state affairs. Secularism cannot be narrowed to the separation of religion and state. ... In

---

[27] Author interview with Ersin Gürdoğan, January 15, 2005.
[28] Author interview with Ersin Gürdoğan, January 16, 2005.
[29] Gül's interview in *Vatan*, September 28, 2003.
[30] Murat Yetkin, "Beni 28 Şubat AB'ci Yaptı," *Radikal*, June 5, 2005.
[31] Two of the Turkish Constitutional Court judges dissented on the basis of the European Convention for the Protection of Human Rights and Fundamental Freedoms.

a secular state, sacred religious belief should never be mixed with politics, civil affairs and legal regulations which shall be formulated according to needs of individuals and the whole society by using scientific data.[32]

After the closure of Erbakan's RP, the leadership of the party took their case to the European Court of Human Rights in the hope of having the ruling overturned, but the court in Europe upheld the Turkish court's decision to close the party on the basis of the RP's desire to establish legal pluralism, introduce Islamic law (which according to the Court was fundamentally at odds with the Convention), and its suggesting the use of jihad and political violence.[33] The European Court stated that

the principle of secularism is certainly one of the fundamental principles of the State which are in harmony with the rule of law and respect for human rights and democracy. An attitude which fails to respect that principle will not necessarily be accepted as being covered by the freedom to manifest one's religion.[34]

The key lesson of the RP experiment was the realization that parties would be rewarded and allowed to participate in politics as long as they stayed within the constitutional boundaries. If any party decides to challenge the constitutional system – the secular orientation of the country – that party will have to confront the powerful military in the form of a possible coup, and the judiciary would then ban that party or civil association, with significant support from business groups and civic associations committed to the ideals of Kemalism. These three institutional constraints are important, but they do not explain the internal dynamics of this transformation: the role of the new bourgeoisie and intellectuals in the constitution of a new democratic cognitive map of politics.

Since 1994, Erbakan's National Outlook Movement (NOM) had been going through major internal transformations by stressing competition and

[32] "Relevant parts of the Constitutional Court's decision on the dissolution of the Welfare Party" (hereafter *TCC Decision*). This translation was submitted to the ECHR by the lawyers of the RP, pp. 21–23.

[33] Christian Moe, "Refah Partisi (The Welfare Party) and Others v. Turkey," *The International Journal of Not-for-Profit Law* 6(1): 2003. European Court of Human Rights (ECHR), Refah Partisi and Others vs. Turkey (No. 41340/98). On July 10, 2001, a Chamber of the Court, by four votes to three, upheld the ban on the Welfare Party. The decision was appealed before the Grand Chamber of the Court. In February 2002, the 17 judges of the Grand Chamber agreed with the judgment. The Chamber majority opines, "a political party whose actions seem to be aimed at introducing sharia in a State party to the Convention can hardly be regarded as an association complying with the democratic ideal that underlies the whole of the Convention." Özlem Denli Harvey, *Islam and the Freedom of Religion or Belief: Perspectives from Contemporary Turkey*, Human Rights Report No. 1/2000 (Oslo: Norwegian Institute of Human Rights, 2000).

[34] *Refah Partisi (The Welfare Party) and Others vs. Turkey*, Judgment, Strasbourg, February 13, 2003 (includes a concurring opinion of Judges Ress and Rozakis and a concurring opinion by Judge Kovler).

the free market over the welfare state and distributive economic policies, individual rights over communal values, decentralization and empowerment of local municipalities over centralization, and European values over conservative Turkish–Islamic ones. The RP was evolving from an anti-system (anti-Kemalist) party to a more pro-system and democratic party. As a result of this transformation, the RP came to power in 1996. During its eleven months' governance, the RP tried very hard to shed its anti-system policies and views. Eventually, however, it could not transform itself as fast as the system required. In addition, the pro-status quo forces, primarily the military, did not want this transformation and used all their means to end the government. After the coup of February 1997, the government resigned and the process of the transformation of the NOM was intensified, and resulted in a full identification with the pro-European worldview.

While the securitization of domestic politics was going on, the military helped to bring Ecevit into the government, which carried out the wishes of the military. The turning point for Ecevit was in 1999 when Turkish special forces, with the help of the American CIA, and possibly the Israeli MOSSAD, captured the Kurdish leader Abdullah Öcalan in Nairobi, Kenya, and brought him back to Turkey. This event helped to turn Ecevit into a national hero – at least in the eyes of most ethnic Turks. He was consequently voted into office in the April 1999 elections. His DSP received 22% of the popular vote and became the largest party, forging a coalition government with the MHP and ANAP. Popular confidence in Ecevit's government, however, was shattered by a natural disaster: the August 1999 earthquake. The government was slow to respond to the ensuing human suffering, which resulted in the loss of 25,000 lives. Many saw the government's unpreparedness as a sign of incompetence. Yet the quake drew unexpected sympathy from Turkey's long rival and neighbor, Greece, as well as the EU. This international – European – sympathy translated into the decision at the Helsinki summit in December 1999 to give EU candidate status to Turkey. The decision raised hopes and expectations in the Ecevit government to restore a new compass of political change within the Copenhagen criteria. Within these high hopes in the restoration of the rule of law, Ahmet Necdet Sezer, the chief justice, became the president of Turkey in May 2000, replacing the person who had become the symbol of corruption, Süleyman Demirel.

Contestation between the new president and the government resulted in the February 2001 economic crisis, which was akin to a financial earthquake. It led to the collapse of Turkey's banking sector, with the national currency, the lira, losing 54% of its value; interest rates skyrocketed, resulting in the shrinking of GDP by 10%, and the loss of 3 million jobs in 2001. Under such a scenario of economic bankruptcy, the government asked Kemal Derviş, then a vice president at the World Bank (currently the head of the UN Development Programme), to "fix and restructure" the Turkish economy. Derviş, with the support of the US, persuaded the IMF and the World Bank to provide $10 billion in additional loans to the Turkish government for a total package of $17.5 billion. With this new line of credit to help stabilize the economy, Derviş shifted to the management of the Turkish economy, now increasingly dependent on international financial institutions. While the economic stability operations were going on, a number of corruption charges led to a series of resignations within the DSP, which included the resignation of Derviş. These events also led Ismail Cem, then foreign minister, to create a new social democrat party. This resignation encouraged Devlet Bahceli, the leader of the MHP and then deputy prime minister, to push for early elections in 2002, even though opinion polls showed a near total collapse of public confidence in all existing parties. A newly formed party, the untried AKP of Erdoğan, became the most popular party in the public mind. Angered over the government's mishandling of the country and its economy, large numbers of people from the marginalized and the middle-class voted for the AKP in the 2002 elections. However, the AKP did not originate with the February 2001 crisis. While the crisis may have fueled the bonfire of social discontent and provided the necessary impetus for its electoral victory, the leadership of the AKP and its political platform also played important roles.

### An apolitical party: the Virtue Party (*Fazilet Partisi*) (FP)

With the closure of the RP, the pro-Islamic parliamentarians formed the Fazilet Partisi (Virtue Party; FP) in 1997, which entered the 1999 national elections, received about 15.5% of the popular vote, and entered Parliament as the third largest party.[35] People hesitated to vote for the FP in the 1999 elections because they did not want an ongoing crisis between the state (the military) and the government (Islamic parties). Before the 1999 elections, the military and its allies in the media made it clear that the FP would not be given a chance to govern the country. The military had already intimated that even if the FP emerged victorious in the April 1999 elections, it would not be allowed to form a government. This pre-election statement was aimed at pre-empting a possible worst case scenario: a formal military takeover. Moreover,

---

[35] For a discussion on the Virtue Party, see Birol A. Yesilada, "The Virtue Party," *Turkish Studies*, 3:1 (2002), 62–82.

Erbakan's opportunist policies angered many within the FP, and its share of the vote dropped from 21% to 15% in the 1999 elections. Erbakan's decision to support the disgruntled parliamentarians who were trying to cancel the elections was seen as an opportunist attempt to avoid election.[36] However, the party did extremely well in the elections at the municipal level.

The fear of being closed down was the main context of politics for the FP, and it adopted a much more moderate program by stressing market forces and privatization more than the distributive role of the state, as well as individual and human rights. It also made no explicit reference to Islam or Islamic values, emphasized the delegation of authority to municipalities, and committed itself to Turkey's European (pro-EU) foreign policy. The FP constituted the largest bloc in the parliament and had undergone significant transformation since its days as the RP.[37] It abandoned the public use of Erbakan-style "anti-Western and faintly anti-Semitic" rhetoric. The core leadership, which included nationalist-conservatives such as Cemil Çiçek, Ali Coskun, Nevzat Yalcintaş and Nazlı Ilıcak supervised this transformation. This new leadership was socially conservative, culturally nationalistic, free market-oriented, not reflexively anti-Western, and was seeking to reinvent a centrist image for the FP. Moreover, it adopted new practices by changing its decision-making structure and allowing greater participation by university faculty both in the central committee and the consultative council, where they were allocated 15 seats. The younger generation argued that the RP had made mistakes in the past when they failed to go far enough to allay the fears of secularists or centrists that they had no intention of forcing their religious views upon them.

For example, Bülent Arınç, then an active member of the FP and the former speaker of the parliament, argued that the FP needed to further the democratization process as opposed to focusing on purely religious matters, as well as create more spaces for women, who have been vital to the movement. This was not a shift from rhetorical politics to dialectical politics, but rather one from a counter-hegemonic worldview to national–conservative centrism. The policy of the FP was the consummation

---

[36] Yavuz Selim, *Yol Ayrımı: Milli Görüş Hareketindeki Ayrışmanın Perde Arkası* (Ankara: Hiler, 2002); Karaman, "İlkeli mi Faydacı mı?" *Yeni Şafak*, March 21, 1999; Taşgetiren, "Fazilet Yara Alıyor Farkında mısınız?" *Yeni Şafak*, March 11, 1999.

[37] Mehmet Bekaroğlu, a prominent Muslim democrat, has written the best study on the evolution of the AKP and its leadership: see M. Bekaroğlu, *"Adil Düzen"den "Dünya Gerçeklerine": Siyasetin Sonu* (Ankara: Elips, 2007). This lengthy yet detailed work provides deep sociological and psychological insights into the roots of the AKP.

Table 2.1 *Comparison of RP, FP and AKP*

|  | Refah Partisi (Welfare Party) RP | Fazilet Partisi (Virtue Party) FP | Adalet ve Kalkınma Partisi (Justice and Development Party) AKP |
|---|---|---|---|
| **Economic Role of the State** | The role of the state is important in the distribution of resources and creating a just society. The role of the state is as important as privatization. | The role of the state is de-emphasized and privatization is treated as the way of overcoming economic inequalities. | The market is treated as the new cure to all social and economic problems. Improve efficiency and productivity. Privatization is supported and the role of the state in the economy is criticized. |
| **Democratization** | Communitarian conception of democracy; not individualism but rather personalism. Communal and religious rights are stressed. The leader-based party system and no sense of pluralism and homogenization via Islam are the goal of the political process. | The human rights discourse is fully integrated and the EU process is welcomed to improve the human rights situation. Religious freedoms are treated as the core to human rights discourse | The European Union process is fully embraced as a project of democratization. Leader-based and majoritarian democracy. Not much intra-party participation and shift between nationalism and communal democracy. |
| **Nationalism** | Turko-Ottoman nationalism. Turkishness is defined by Islam and the Ottoman legacy and Turkey as the leader of the Islamic civilization. Islamo-imperialism. | No time to discuss these issues. | Constitutional patriotism. Redefinition of Turkishness on the basis of ethnicity to recognize and integrate the Kurds on the basis of their identity. Unclear and confused discourse on nationalism and statism. |
| **Sources of Values** | Religious values as didactic system to become a "moral person." Islamic values must be incorporated into the political system in order to create a just society. Not much room for secular values. | Moral values are stressed but secular human rights discourse is also treated as an additional source of values. | Religious values are recognized as important but not a value system to shape public debate. Human rights discourse is utilized to create a new value system. God is not part of the value debate. Individual responsibility, success and competition are stressed. |

Table 2.1 (*cont.*)

| | Refah Partisi (Welfare Party) RP | Fazilet Partisi (Virtue Party) FP | Adalet ve Kalkınma Partisi (Justice and Development Party) AKP |
|---|---|---|---|
| **Centralization versus Local Government** | Active role for the central government to bring justice and achieve development. | Stress on decentralization and empowerment of local municipalities. | Privatization and decentralization as the "only game in town." Attempt to empower local municipalities and weaken the power of Ankara. |
| **Foreign Policy Orientation** | Starts with very anti-Western and anti-EU bias but gradually softens its position. Favors close ties with Islamic countries and pan-Islamism is the key to its foreign policy rhetoric. In government, it pursues the traditional foreign policy of Turkey. | More pro-EU and pro-West to expand its legitimacy. No stress on Islamic identity as a source of foreign policy conduct. | Pro-EU in order to overcome charges of Islamism and to enhance democracy and weaken the military power within the system. EU seen as a way of creating an alternative to US-centric foreign policy. EU seen as the market and civilizational pull of Turkish transformation. Not much stress on Islamic issues and loyalties. |

of the center-right version of Kemalist ideology rather than the offering of new ideas and strategies for the formation of a new social contract. Instead of redefining its vague terminology of just order and social justice, the FP was seeking to give up its revolutionary image and adopt a "mainstream" image which was to gradually shift the state and society toward its positions. In order to exist in the Turkish political arena, the FP decided not to define itself directly against other parties and the Kemalist system. In the light of the military's closure of the RP, some feel that the FP attempted to accommodate to the Kemalist establishment and thus inflamed its authoritarian impulses. The FP never tried to become an agent of change but rather a subject of change. The party did not aim to reform the political system, but rather preferred to be changed in accordance with state ideology. Avoiding being closed down became the main concern of the FP and prevented it from functioning as a normal political party.

Furthermore, Recai Kutan, the leader of the FP, adopted a conciliatory approach towards the provocations by the military by stating that they might have a legitimate right to interfere in civilian affairs. The FP clearly hoped that by presenting this moderate face it could avoid further confrontation. However, such an approach encouraged Kemalist excesses while fueling growing popular anger against the failure of civilian politicians to stand up to the unpopular generals.

However, the case of Merve Kavakcı, a newly elected female FP member of parliament who wore a headscarf and refused to remove it while being sworn into office, led to huge protests in the parliament. Both the president and the prime minister called her an "agent provocateur." The court, in turn, stripped Kavakcı of her citizenship and denied her deputy status, ostensibly due to her failure to inform the authorities about her acquired US citizenship.[38] Furthermore, Vural Savas, the Supreme Prosecutor of the Court of Appeals, demanded the closure of the FP by accusing it of being "a malignant tumor that has metastasized."[39] The Kavakcı case in the Constitutional Court ended the FP's political life in June 2001.

A younger generation of FP politicians did not like Erbakan's authoritarian decision-making and became very critical of FP leader Recai Kutan's policies. For the first time in the history of the movement, two powerful candidates ran against each other at the first convention of the

---

[38] Merve Safa Kavakcı, *Başörtüsüz Demokrasi* (Istanbul: Timaş, 2004). Kavakcı provides first-hand information about her ordeal in this passionately written book.
[39] *Sabah*, January 19, 2000.

party. Gül,[40] the candidate of the younger generation, received 521 votes even though he lost the election to Kutan (633 votes), a close friend of Erbakan.[41] This was the first major political earthquake in the NOM and the first open rebellion against the political hegemony of Erbakan. Thus, the NOM could not immunize itself against democratic ideas and practices. After the first FP convention, Gül argued that:

> Even though [the] FP is a political party, it would not be [a] mistake to say that the FP encountered first time with politics on Sunday with the party convention. The party convention was dynamic and active because it went to election with two different candidate[s] for the party leadership. ... [For the] first time in its history, the FP critiqued itself before the public opinion.[42]

After this convention, the old guard of the party began an internal war against Gül and his associates, further undermining the unity of the party.

With the closure of the FP, two splinter groups emerged and these groups established separate parties. The old guard under Erbakan's direction formed the *Saadet Partisi* (SP) in July 2001, which was led by Erbakan's close associate Recai Kutan. Because some of the most liberal politicians had left the party, the SP revived its old Islamic discourse. Yet even the SP made a major change in its party program by arguing that Turkish–EU relations are "important for the implementation and realization of human rights and democratic norms and the further development of Turkey through closer ties with Europe."[43] In the breakdown of the *milli görüş* movement, ideological, generational and class differences played critical roles. The newly emerging Anatolian provincial bourgeoisie fully supported the reformist group, who promoted a more accommodationist policy as opposed to Erbakan and his coterie. These economically and politically vulnerable provincial businessmen did not support a confrontational policy with the state and decided to support Gül's economically liberal and socially conservative agenda. The fragmentation of the class coalition and the division of the party leadership were outcomes of the formation of an influential bourgeoisie within the Islamic movement and also of military–legal pressures to act within the rules of the constitutional system. During the FP period, as a result of both internal and external factors, the shift from anti-system to pro-system and a more

---

[40] Gül was born in 1950 in Kayseri and worked as an economist at the Islamic development bank in Jeddah (1983–1991). He was elected in 1991 from the RP list in Kayseri province. In 1996–97 he was a minister. Gül is known for his "bland and self-effacing style." Jim Bodgener, *Briefings*, No. 1420 (Nov. 2002).

[41] On the convention, see *Milliyet*, May 15, 2000. On Gül's ideas and background, see Yavuz Selim, *Gül'ün Adı* (Ankara: Kim Yayınları, 2002).

[42] Abdullah Gül, "Fazilet Kongresi," *Milliyet*, May 17, 2000.

[43] For the party program, see www.saadet.org.tr.

democratic party was completed. Many leaders of the FP realized that Turkey's policy options were conditioned by international norms and institutions. The EU's Copenhagen norms of human rights, cultural rights and the consolidation of the rule of law, for example, became the reference points for change and a source of protection against the excesses of the state.[44]

The decision of the Constitutional Court to ban the FP created new opportunities for younger and moderate Muslim politicians from the now outlawed FP. Not only was a new party, the SP, created in August 2001, in addition the more moderate members of the FP formed the AKP under Erdoğan's leadership. There remain a number of questions about the origins, intentions and goals of the AKP. People wonder whether the newly founded AKP is a cloned version of the previous pro-Islamic parties or whether it is truly a new political entity on the Turkish political scene. If it is a new party, what does its "newness" entail?

### Conclusion

Özal's reforms in the 1980s helped to create the so-called "Anatolian tigers," a new autonomous force in Turkish history, outside the control of the state, who acted to redefine Turkey by supporting a neo-liberal economic transformation, along with a conservative religious culture. One can find the origins of the current transformation in the ideas of this new merchant class and the new Muslim intellectuals, who were very critical of the Kemalist conceptualization of modernity, which they perceived as heavily laced with anti-Islamic sentiments.

In addition to their anti-Kemalist stance, these two groups – Islamic merchants and intellectuals – placed the attainment of happiness not in the afterlife but in the here and now. They were involved in a number of projects to realize their goal. For them, not unlike the Christian Protestant Calvinists of the sixteenth century, happiness is defined in terms of profit and the struggle to get ahead, and by creating large physical spaces for personal enjoyment. This philosophy has become the new dream of Turkey: to earn and succeed in the market and utilize new economic and scientific means to further the individual and society. Inherent in the triumph of the market economy over the statism of Kemalism, the introduction of private education, the spread of new media networks, the

---

[44] Saban Kardas, "Human Rights and Democracy Promotion: The Case of Turkey-EU Relations," *Alternatives: Turkish Journal of International Relations*, 1:3 (2002), 136–150; Hasan Kösebalaban, "Turkey's EU membership: a clash of security cultures," *Middle East Policy*, 9 (June 2002), 130–146.

expansion of the public sphere, and new forms of abstract reasoning, came the moment of the redefinition of the place of the state and secularism in society, and also the question of what it means to be a Turk and a Turkish citizen. Özal introduced the idiom of "rights" and civil society into the political discourse of Turkey. The AKP is an outcome of the transformation of liberal Islam, directed by four socio-political factors: the new Anatolian bourgeoisie, the expansion of the public sphere and the new Muslim intellectuals, the Copenhagen criteria, and the February 28 soft coup.

Can the Turkish experiment of liberal Islamism and the AKP be exported? Şerif Mardin, the Turkish sociologist, treats the AKP as the outcome of four Republican legacies: the attempt to reinterpret Islam resulting in a modernized and vibrant Islam, the shift from *umma* to citizenship, the new economic opportunities, and the encouragement of critical thinking with the new educational system.[45] Mardin identifies informal network building as the most important strength of the AKP. Mardin raises questions, however, about the ability of the AKP to create and work with more formal networks. Mardin has doubts about the exportability of the Turkish experience (the shift from Islamism to democracy) to other Muslim countries because of others' lack of the Kemalist experiment.[46] In the following chapter, I will examine the policies and identity of the AKP.

---

[45] My interview with Mardin, Istanbul, April 1, 2005; for Şerif Mardin's interview, "AKP's victory should be seen as the success of Kemalism," see *Vatan*, September 30, 2003.
[46] *Vatan*, September 30, 2003.

# 3    Ideology, leadership and organization

In August 2001, the reformist and younger sector of the FP, led by Abdullah Gül, formed the AKP with the support of the rising Anatolian bourgeoisie. *Adalet ve Kalkınma Partisi* (Justice and Development Party) is also called *Ak Parti* meaning the "pure" or "uncontaminated" party to differentiate itself from the other political parties, which were allegedly involved in widespread corruption before the 2002 elections.[1] The party committed itself not to use Islam for political purposes and ended its confrontational policies. To the surprise of many observers, although the AKP emerged out of the Islamic political movement, it is pro-European and tolerant of diversity. Due to the collapse of the government in 2002, the newly formed AKP found itself in the midst of an election on November 3 of the same year. A little more than a year after its foundation, the party received 34% of the votes and won 363 seats out of a total of 550 parliamentary seats – a near two-thirds majority of seats.[2] Kutan's *Saadet Partisi* (SP) (Felicity Party) received a mere 3% of the votes in the same election.[3]

The 2002 election victory of the AKP can be explained by a convergence of factors.[4] Widespread popular dissatisfaction with the economy and political parties encouraged many people either not to vote or to vote against the existing parties and try the untested AKP instead. Thus, the

---

[1] Similar complaints of corruption and nepotism have been raised against the AKP. Fahrettin Altun, "AKP ve Muhafazakar Demokrasi," *Anlayış*, March 2004, 32–34.

[2] In the 2002 elections, 8.6 million voters (20.9% of the total) did not cast their vote. Moreover, 1.2 million (3%) votes were discarded. This voter antipathy was the outcome of the decline of hope in politics due to the 2001 economic crisis and the decline of trust in coalition governments. Corruption and cronyism were endemic within all governing coalition parties. Many questioned the party leaders whose entourages were tied in a web of business connections.

[3] Fulya Atacan, "Explaining Religious Politics at the Crossroad: AKP-SP," *Turkish Studies*, 6:4 (September 2005), 187–199.

[4] Ali Carkoğlu, "Turkey's November 2002 Elections: A New Beginning," *MERIA e-Journal*, 6:4 (December 2002) (http://www.biu.ac.il).

Table 3.1

| Party | total votes | % |
|---|---|---|
| Democratic Left Party (DSP) | 384,009 | 1.2 |
| Democratic People's Party (DEHAP) | 1,960,660 | 6.2 |
| Country Party (YP) | 294,909 | 0.9 |
| Nationalistic Action Party (MHP) | 2,635,787 | 8.4 |
| True Path Party (DYP) | 3,008,942 | 9.5 |
| Nation Party (MP) | 68,271 | 0.2 |
| Greater Unity Party (BBP) | 322,093 | 1.0 |
| Motherland Party (ANAP) | 1,618,465 | 5.1 |
| Liberal Democrat Party (LDP) | 89,331 | 0.3 |
| Felicity Party (SP) | 785,489 | 2.5 |
| Independent Turkey Party (BTP) | 150,482 | 0.5 |
| Freedom and Solidarity Party (ÖDP) | 106,023 | 0.3 |
| Communist Party of Turkey (TKP) | 59,180 | 0.2 |
| Young Party (GP) | 2,285,598 | 7.3 |
| Worker Party (İP) | 159,843 | 0.5 |
| Republican People's Party (CHP) | 6,113,352 | 19.4 |
| Justice and Development Party (AKP) | 10,808,229 | 34.3 |
| New Turkey Party (YTP) | 363,869 | 1.15 |
| Independents | 314,251 | 1.0 |

*Source:* Yüksek Seçim Kurulu (2002).

effects of the 10% threshold and the high percentage of non-voters (46.3% of voter turnout) translated into a major parliamentary victory for the AKP. The elections created a major debate since 21% of eligible voters (8, 671, 982 people) did not use their vote, and 3.9% of the used votes (1, 262, 671 votes) were invalid. In addition to this, 46% of voters' choice was not reflected in the parliament due to the 10% threshold. In short, 25 million voters were not represented in parliament.

In retrospect, the AKP's victory is not surprising. The Turkish electorate usually votes to punish the past rather than to govern the future. Thus, the victory of the AKP in the 2002 elections was more an outcome of the voters' decision to punish, even eliminate, the existing "corrupt" party system, than a vote for the AKP and its leader, Recep T. Erdoğan. The voters rightly blamed the governing coalition of the three parties (DSP, MHP and ANAP) for the 2001 economic collapse and the DYP for the 1997 soft coup. Not surprisingly, the DSP dropped from 22% in the 1999 elections to 1.2% in 2002 (see table 3.1). The economic recession of 2000–2001, coupled with high inflation and increasing unemployment, had forced a large sector of society to live either below or on the margin of poverty. While the economy was collapsing, the political parties were ineffective in addressing the problems of the country, and were also involved in a number of corruption scandals.

This search for "hope" and the desire to get rid of the existing political party leadership created the necessary incentive to vote for change. During the November 2002 elections, in the AKP many voters saw the only new face with a clean reputation capable of raising the hopes of the people by addressing the deepening socio-economic crisis. The party's leadership became the symbol for the Turkish electorate that wanted new faces and a different way of conducting politics. The people were disgusted with the business-as-usual style of politics and hungry for a fresh approach. Although past experiences and a shared socio-cultural language were instrumental in the victory of the AKP, voters shared a view of the same future and the same ideal for Turkey: a capitalist, democratic and pluralist entity in which secularism would not be an ideology protected by the state, but rather an outgrowth of socio-economic conditions. Thus, the AKP represented the new Turkey and the new voices.

Moreover, the ongoing legal persecution of Erdoğan made him more popular, even a "hero" of hope and change. His charisma today is largely based on the perception by the public of his unfair treatment, his having become a *mazlum* ("one who is wronged") in addition to having been a successful mayor of Istanbul with an honest public life free of major corruption. Those who voted for Erdoğan saw their own biography in him and their desire to succeed as much as him. For his part, Erdoğan enjoys public rallies wherein he ignites hopes and raises the people's expectations and emotions, helping the average man believe that he can succeed in life.[5]

Despite his popularity, Erdoğan was left out of the parliament because of a prior ban on his political activities dating from his time as mayor of Istanbul. Thus, president Ahmet Necdet Sezer asked Gül to form the 58th Turkish government, one to be dominated by the AKP. When the Higher Electoral Council invalidated the election results in the south-eastern Siirt region, a province of mixed Kurdish, Arab and Turkish ethnicities, on the grounds that at least one village had not been able to vote, a new election was scheduled for March 9, 2003. The parliament thus had acquired time to make the necessary legal changes to make Erdoğan eligible for the election. Erdoğan, along with another AKP candidate, won the March 9 election and the AKP's seats in parliament rose to 365, giving it yet another clear majority, and making it strong enough to make some

---

[5] He is not very convincing in one-and-one interviews where people can question his comments. Thus, one would argue that Erdoğan is a man of mass rallies rather than deliberative democracy.

changes in the constitution. Such a wide margin of victory was a political feat that had not been achieved by any party in Turkey in at least fifteen years. The critical factor in the victory of the AKP was not the party's program, but the determination of the voters to get rid of the previous political parties whom they considered as being heavily tainted with corruption. This open political space allowed the emergence of the AKP with little resistance from other political actors.

### Identity and ideology of the AKP: conservative without tradition

Erdoğan's earlier experience as mayor of Istanbul shaped his understanding of politics and gave him the idea that people expect service (*hizmet*), not ideology or big ideas. Thus, politics for Erdoğan has not been *an instrument to impose a life-style but rather to create better living conditions for diverse life-styles to co-exist*. Erdoğan's conception of politics is about providing "services" to the people and even the name of the party, "justice" and "development," reflects this mode of thinking. In his first parliamentary group meeting in the Bilkent Hotel on November 11, 2002, Erdoğan used the term *hizmet* at least eight times to explain the mission of the party as that of economic development and democratization.[6] His conceptualization of politics as offering service has also shaped his understanding of the state and bureaucracy. Erdoğan's understanding of politics is very much informed by his perception of the functions of the state. Like Özal, Erdoğan treats the state as an instrument of public service to improve daily life. For Erdoğan the state is not a sacred institution that knows the interests of the nation and is above reason:

The AKP represents the feelings of our cherished nation in the government of Turkey. This is our mission as a party. Values which constitute these feelings have become and shall continue to be the fundamental values to form policies. We have achieved a great convergence by opening our door to everyone who embraces the aspirations of the nation. A sulky and burdensome state shall be eliminated, and will be replaced by a smiling and capable state. The concept of *a nation for the state* will not be imposed any longer, and the concept of *a state for the nation* shall flourish

---

[6] A closer content analysis of his first published speeches reveals the constant use of *hizmet*, people (*halk*), nation (*millet*; but not Turkish nation), country (*memleket*), state (never Turkish state), Turkey (*Türkiye*) and civilization as far as Turkey's EU membership is concerned. Erdoğan's speeches indicate that he delivers his speeches in declarative form without much analysis or explanation. He is not a man of nuances or heavy thinking but rather a charismatic personality with good oral skills. He argues that EU membership is a civilizational project. Recep Tayyip Erdoğan, *Konuşmalar* (Ankara: Ak Parti, 2004). This book includes Erdoğan's speeches in parliament November 10, 2002–July 28, 2003.

instead. The state shall be prevented from becoming fetters around the legs of the nation which prevents its progress.[7]

Erdoğan has always argued that the state exists to serve the people and its primary task is to remove obstacles to the realization of individual potential. He argues that "the basic value is the human being and the task of the state is to serve for this human being."[8] He seeks to maintain the Özalian philosophy of public management in terms of shifting the bureaucratic culture from the mission of civilization to serving the people and improving their daily lives.[9] He argues that:

The first task and fundamental duty of those who use state authority, namely bureaucracy, is to serve the people. According to us, bureaucracy [*memuriyet*] should not be the position of privilege and immunity. A bureaucrat should not look down on society, should not make things difficult but rather should be a "civil servant" as it is defined in the West, namely serving the public interests.[10]

Moreover, the dominant culture of public management, which was based on the state's suspicion and distrust of the people, was undermined and new rules of public management were introduced for acquiring one's driver's licence, passport and other such things. The idea of the state being suspicious of its subjects and treating its citizens as potential threats was ended. This helped to narrow the distance between the state and citizens. Erdoğan wanted to pursue this transformation of bureaucracy by presenting it as a necessity for the Turkish nation-state to become "European."

It is important to understand that the concept of conservatism has a particular history and meaning in Turkey. The Turkish version of conservatism was never against modernity or modernization, but was critical of the state-imposed life-style in the name of Westernization. The concept of conservatism cannot be fully comprehended without understanding the master concept of *hizmet* ("rendering social services" in the name of Islam) in the political language of Turks.[11] Conservatism, for Erdoğan, is a political identity that stresses morality, family and orderly change. Since there are different versions of conservatism, the dominant version for the AKP is fideistic conservatism, which stresses the role of religion in

---

[7] The speech was translated by the party itself. Available at www.akparti.org.tr.

[8] Erdoğan, *Konuşmalar*, p. 194; speech at the TBMM, May 6, 2003.

[9] He argues that the bureaucracy should be the "civil servant" as service provider to people. Erdoğan, *Konuşmalar*, p. 194; speech at the TBMM, May 6, 2003.

[10] Erdoğan, *Konuşmalar*, pp. 193–194; speech at the TBMM, May 6, 2003.

[11] The Seljuk and the Ottoman Turkish Empires were very pragmatic and less ideological, with the goal of maintaining order, justice and peace. This pragmatism has remained as one of the key aspects of Turkish political culture.

defining the good life.[12] The AKP conservatives stress the role of Ottoman history and Islam more than abstract contract or imagined political order. They define meaningful life in terms of tested historical arrangements and the meanings of the public good in terms of the shared moral understanding that is derived from Islam. They seek to redefine the good society on the basis of faith and a history-centric consensus. The concept of *hizmet* brings all these ideas together. In other words, *hizmet* requires openness to change and the utilization of technology to create better economic conditions. Major economic changes in Turkey took place during the conservative governments of prime ministers Adnan Menderes (1950–60) and Turgut Özal (1983–91). The center-right parties, or those critical of the state-led modernization project of Kemalism, supported economic development but stressed cultural conservatism on the basis of Islam, tradition and nationalism. Due to its stress on politics as a way of providing "services," the AKP's main ideological principle has thus been pragmatism. The AKP's evolving identity is thus very much dominated by pragmatism, with only some vague hints of conservatism on social issues and liberalism on economic issues.

The AKP is a party that seeks to provide services and performance rather than ideology. This characteristic has been in tune with the electorate, since in the 2002 and 2007 elections the people did not vote for ideology or identity. Rather, they voted *against* what they saw as the corruption of other parties instead of voting specifically *for* Erdoğan. In some ways, therefore, Erdoğan was the "anti-candidate." Still, his image, leadership and ability to represent the interests of the nation more than any ideology played a role in the AKP's victory at the polls. Erdoğan's popularity has always been ahead of his party or the cabinet. Thus, the identity or ideology of the party has been an issue secondary to the charismatic personality of Erdoğan.[13]

In a conversation in the conservative southern town of Konya, a group of people argued that "we voted for the AK Party but we are not necessarily AK Party [members]." (*AK partiye oy verdik ama AK partili değiliz.*) Among the electorate in the same study, no one claimed to be an active member of the AK party, rather they simply responded "we voted for it." The identity of the AKP does not stick on people. It provides them with a

---

[12] There are rationalist conservatives who stress eternal and absolute laws and skeptical conservatives. Fideism stresses reliance on faith and the negation of reason.

[13] For instance, in ANAR polling results, 73% of the respondents were positive about the performance of Erdoğan and over 62% about the performance of the cabinet. See "İşte Son Anket!," *Dünyaonline*, 4.5.2004 (www.dunyaonline.com/143964.asp). In short, first there was *Tayyip*, then the emergence of the AKP around *Tayyip*, then government under the leadership of *Tayyip*, and then the search to create an identity for the AKP.

flexible framework to move in and out under different conditions. One might see the voters of the AKP as new "political tourists" who are constantly moving to explore new sites and new ways of experiencing and influencing the national politics. Thus, because the AKP is not an ideological or identity party, few voters want to identify themselves with it, however much they continue to support it. Many claim that they voted because "the party leaders lived just like us." This corresponds well with the idea that in today's Turkey, people expect social services and improvements in their daily lives, not necessarily an ideology or an identity. Abdullah Gül, the first prime minister of the AKP, has argued that "we [the AKP] do not hide our identity. Our life-style is open and we are in the public. Is there anything that the prime minister is hiding? His wife and his children are under the public eyes."[14] This is an identity with life-style or identity by action rather than ideologization of identity.

Hüseyin Besli, a close associate of Erdoğan and an MP, has argued that the AKP:

has no identity or ideology. This is necessary in order to allow it to become a leader-centered party and, as such, the leader can shape it as he likes. If the party has an established identity and ideology, it cannot survive due to the presence of too many diverse groups within the party. Moreover, party ideology could limit its actions. Yet, I also believe that having a party without identity demonstrates the maturity of Turkish society. The people do not need identity or ideology but rather a leader who will provide *hizmet* [social services] and *iş* [getting things done]. In other words, the AKP has no identity. But its members and activists have their own identities. The task of the party is not to assimilate or dissolve these identities. ... The second most important characteristic of the party is the determinant role of informal networks [*resmi olmayan ilişkiler ağı*] in the choosing of appointments and promotions within the government and the party."[15]

In electing the AKP, did the people of Turkey vote against identity and ideology? Had they grown sick of repeated failures to assert their different identities on the national level and as a result abandoned the notion of identity-based parties in favor of more broadly-based parties, which promise major changes in their lives? Does the election of the AKP translate into an end to identity-driven politics in Turkey, or is it mainly a temporary convergence of the interests of a few groups? If it is the former, what

[14] Ruşen Çakır's interview with Gül, *Vatan*, September 28, 2003. In this interview Gül, unlike other AKP politicians, offers a richer and more nuanced conceptualization of conservatism as "a set of values derived from history, culture and religion. ...We demand religious freedoms as they are practiced in European countries."

[15] My interview with Hüseyin Besli in Istanbul, October 23, 2004. Şerif Mardin also regards the AKP's major strength as its ability to create and use informal networks: *Vatan*, September 30, 2003. Indeed many policemen in Istanbul complain about the role of Murat Aksu, the son of the minister of Interior, in the appointments of security officials.

specific events have brought about such a great change in Turkish politics? Is this perhaps a sign that Turkey has now moved to a more issue-based (à la Europe) sort of democracy? By this, I mean a European-style democracy like that of France or Germany, where there are no dominant, specific identity-based parties, but rather issue-based parties which contain people from the full spectrum of society. That asked, does the AKP need an articulated identity? Indeed, the AKP does not have a positive, but a negative identity. It defines itself as an "oppositional party" to the pre-2002 crises and the policies of Kemalism.[16] This "oppositionalism" is what unifies the party, even though its constituents all have different reasons to be in opposition. It is the center of opposing groups and voices. These groups are mobilized for different reasons, some economic and some cultural. The main goal has been to end this ongoing exclusion and create a new framework of social contract. It is important not to reduce political and cultural demands to economic demands in Turkey even though some of these demands are utilized for economic needs. Indeed, the AKP consists of a series of separate ethnic, regional and religious communities: Turkish, Kurdish and Sunni "oppositional" identities. It is not purely liberal because its building blocks are these ethnic, religious and regional communities. In order to contain the politics of identity, the AKP, for Dengir Mir Mehmet Fırat, the vice chairman of the party, has three red lines that cannot be crossed: "No regionalism, no ethnic-nationalism, and no religious politics."[17] Fırat argues that the AKP is a democratic party and seeks to expand democracy, the public debate over human rights and the nature of the state and its policies.

In addition to this ethno-social cleavage, there is also an economic cleavage at the grass-roots level in terms of an economically marginalized sector of the electorate, which wants to see more state intervention in the economy, and the new rising bourgeoisie, which seeks the institutionalization of the free-market policies of the international financial institutions, namely the IMF and the World Bank. The party's program and policies are economically liberal but it has no other option given the current international economic structure. Thus, it seeks to differentiate itself by stressing cultural and ideological issues since it cannot develop and implement its own economic policies. This "culturalism" is the key reason for its self-declared "conservatism" as well. The AKP thus upholds a certain "communitarian conservatism," with communally defined values being the guiding principles of its politics.

---

[16] M. Hakan Yavuz, "AK parti ve sorunları," in *Uluslarası Muhafazakarlık ve Demokrasi Sempozyumu* (Istanbul: Alfa, 2004), pp. 202–208.

[17] My interview with Dengir Mir Mehmet Fırat on July 8, 2004 in Ankara.

## Conservative democracy

To begin with, one must separate Turkish conservatism as a political movement, a broad coalition of forces that defend the integrity of the nation-state as an organic whole, from the radical Kemalist project of "inventing new memory and identity" with the goal of creating a Western society. Turkish conservatism is not anti-statist but rather pro-nation, pro-state and especially pro-Ottoman-Islam. Its main goal has been to mesh and meld together the notions of the nation, state and religion. Its Ottoman and Islamic origins are communitarian and often less libertarian. Despite an occasional nod to Peyami Safa or Kemal Tahir, most Turkish conservatives actively engaged in political life are singularly uninterested in attaining clarity about the character of conservatism as an intellectual movement.

In order to exist and to govern the country, the AKP had to disguise or change its language to accommodate the neo-liberal requirements of globalization. It has shed its Islamism, the rhetoric of excluded sectors of Turkish society and become pro-EU. The major problem of the AKP during its establishment was legitimacy. Due to its Islamic origins and the shadow of the February 28 process, the party sought to overcome suspicion by adopting conservative democracy as its identity and the Copenhagen criteria as its sole political compass of governance.[18]

The need to have an identity is at the same time a way of communicating with the bureaucratic state, some intellectuals, and also suspicious foreign powers, especially Europe and the USA, about the "real"

---

[18] Ali Bayramoğlu, "AK Parti makineleri stop etti." *Radikal*, March 21, 2005. This interview reflects the deep-seated Orientalism of Turkish intellectuals. Bayramoğlu's understanding of Turkish democracy and the social sources of power reflects this intellectual poverty on the part of this journalist. According to Ali Bayramoğlu, the only source of power of the AKP is not its electoral victory but its ability to carry out the EU-required reforms. This tactical decision to carry out the EU project empowered the AKP and enhanced its legitimacy in the eyes of Turkey's powerful media and business groups. Bayramoğlu demonstrates a high degree of elitism and lack of faith in the people's decision. This Orientalist perspective does not see Muslims as agents with their own sources of legitimacy and projects of modernity but rather subjects that can only be allowed to play the script of the powerful. This denial of agency to the Turkish people in general and to Islamic groups in particular is very problematic. He says, even though the AKP came to power with the support of the periphery, that the center allows it to rule as long as it accepts the Copenhagen criteria as the ultimate compass of governance. In other words, one sees from Bayramoğlu's thinking that the source of legitimacy is not the people but rather the powerful coalition of the establishment. His understanding of democracy is about the civilization of the power of the military and the exclusion of the military from the system. Democracy means faith in people and accepting the electoral process as the expression of the will of the people and the rule of law. His notion of democracy is defined in opposition to the military. He regards the Turkish military as the source of all problems and the reason for Turkey's weak civil society.

intentions of the AKP. There are functional uses of conservative democracy.[19] The party defines itself as an agent of change rather than an agent of conserving a particular socio-economic structure. This contradiction between "change" and "conservation" is the outcome of Turkey's political landscape. For pragmatic reasons, the party leadership prefers to bill itself as part of "conservative democracy": it accepts the cultural and religious roots of the Turkish identity and value system. Taşgetiren, a prominent Islamist journalist who was fired from a pro-Erdoğan newspaper for his criticism of the AKP government, argues that "the concept of conservative democracy was formulated within the context of the February 28 process and the search for external legitimacy for the AKP. The content of the concept is filled by the personalities of the Party leadership."[20] For Taşgetiren, the AKP is expected to transform not only itself but also its popular base towards a more secular democracy. Taşgetiren argues that this "mission" of transformation is the cost that the

---

[19] It was Mustafa Erdoğan who first suggested that Tayyip Erdoğan could become the leader of a "conservative democratic" movement due to his background. Erdoğan, *Radikal*, July 10, 2001. The AKP refuses to promote the previous Islamic political claims of the just order, i.e. Islamic unity, headscarf, Imam Hatip schools, Islamic courses in public schools, interest-free banking system, anti-Western language and anti-Americanism. In other words, it has managed to distance itself from almost all Islamic claims. The AKP regularly prefers the language of "dialog of civilizations" to "the clash of civilizations" to overcome suspicion in the United States. For a critique of this identity, see Alev Alatlı, "Pişmiş Aşa Su katmak," *Zaman*, April 4, 2004; Eyup Can, "AK parti neyi Muhafaza Ediyor?," *Zaman*, August 27, 2004; Muhsin Öztürk, "Muhafazakar mı Reformist mi?," *Aksiyon*, (no. 476) January 23, 2004. Yalçın Akdoğan, an advisor to Tayyip Erdoğan, wrote the first booklet about conservative democracy, which was published and printed by the AKP as its political manifesto: Akdoğan, *Muhafazakar Demokrasi* (Ankara: Ak Parti, 2003). This book, which is published by the party itself, is incoherent and has no clearly articulated ideas; rather a "cut and paste" type of reasoning punctuates the book. Its second version is a little bit better and is printed by a private publisher. It is filled with comments and remarks by diverse intellectuals and journalists about the concept of conservative democracy (Akdoğan, *Ak Parti ve Muhafazakar Demokrasi* (İstanbul: Alfa, 2004). But again, there is not much deep thought in it. The main goal of the second version is to demonstrate the rupture between the Islamism of the National Outlook Movement and the conservative democracy of the AK Party. After defining the National Outlook Movement as a moderate, modernist and democratic Islamic movement, Akdoğan argues that even though the leadership of the AKP came from the NOM, they were the reformist branch of the Refah Party and the agent of change within the Refah Party. Yet, the AKP decided to make a clean break with the past and adopted conservative democracy to distance itself from the legacy of the National Outlook Movement, and defines Islamism as the "other" of conservative democracy (Akdoğan, 2004, pp. 104–113). A close reading of the book demonstrates that neither the party nor its intellectuals are clear about the concept or the history of intellectual thought in Turkey. The parliamentarians, for Akdoğan, "are in intellectual poverty" and "no one deals with ideas, except myself."

[20] Ahmet Taşgetiren, "Muhafazakar Demokrasinin içi yeterince dolu değil," *Anlayış*, (December 2005), 55–57.

AKP is forced to pay in order to be in government. Indeed, the party has been more successful in transforming its conservative–Muslim base than the state. Ahmet Yıldız, a political scientist who leads the research office of the Turkish parliament, argues that "because the AK Party's identity is very much formulated by its narrow leadership and excludes its parliamentary group, organization and its public supporters in the making of its identity, its democratic aspect has been undermined. ... Thus, this identity has not been fully internalized."[21] This identity protects the party against the charges of Islamism; it allows it to identify itself simultaneously with Islam and democracy by stressing the supposed values of the ideal Turkish society. Moreover, the party's conservative democracy is very much like a "space" where people with diverse identities and interests meet to express their desire for a change in the status quo. Erol Kaya, the mayor of Pendik, argues that the AKP is a "supermarket" where people come to meet their needs and as such, by itself, "it has not formed an identity." Its claimed identity of conservative democracy does not necessarily reflect in all its policies but rather is an identity tool for external legitimacy. Ahmet Yıldız argues that the AKP's conservative democracy does not seek to lead or guide its party policies but it is a means of overcoming the suspicions of outside countries and entities, especially the US and the European Union states. The party's image of conservative democracy, according to Yıldız, also carves a space in the center-right spectrum of Turkish politics to overcome secularist suspicions and seeks to connect with the Islamist-oriented masses. In short, Yıldız is right to conclude that the AKP's conservative democracy tries to define the party for others rather than serving as a guiding ideology by itself.

The AKP also recognizes the role of religion in the public sphere to be one of multiple voices without becoming a source of justification of any particular public policy. By presenting itself as a proponent of "conservative democracy," the AKP rejects any attribution of being an Islamic or Muslim party, per se.[22] The main reason the AKP wants to be known as a conservative party has to do with its difficulty in translating its cultural, Muslim roots and identity into political ones. In order to overcome its legitimacy and insecurity problems, the AKP has thus adopted the

---

[21] "AK Partinin 'Yeni Muhafazakar Demokratlığı': Türkiye Siyasetinde Adlandırma Problemi," *Liberal Düşünce*, 34 (Spring 2004), 44; Yıldız, "Muhafazakarlığın Yerlileştirilmesi ya da AKP'nin Yeni Muhafazakar Demokratlığı," *Karizma*, 5 (January–March 2004), 53–56.

[22] Y. Akdoğan, *Ak Parti ve Muhafazakar Demokrasi*. Although Akdoğan uses all his persuasive power to fill the concept of "conservative democracy," it raises more questions. The main goal of this concept is to create new imagined political roots with Menderes and Özal and to distance itself from its "actual" roots with Necmettin Erbakan.

concept and ideal of "conservative democracy."[23] By declaring itself the heir to the legacy of Menderes and Özal, it wants to distance itself from its Islamic roots and Erbakan by providing new historical roots. The AKP leadership, especially Erdoğan, want to locate their roots in the Democrat Party (DP) of Menderes,[24] hence there is an attempt to re-root the AKP outside the legacy of Erbakan. The party wants to distance itself from the legacy of Erbakan by defining itself as the center-right party with close ties to the legacy of Adnan Menderes and Turgut Özal to overcome the fear of Islamism in Turkey. However, both the social origins and ways of living of the AKP leadership separate it from the legacy of the DP. The leadership of the DP came from the Republican People's Party (CHP) and were part of the establishment. The DP leadership split from the CHP due to intra-party debate. The DP leadership was committed to the Kemalist ethos of nation-building and secularism, and Menderes, Fuat Köprülü (former foreign minister) and Celal Bayar (former president) all came from elite families and were part of the establishment. The AKP leadership, however, came from provincial towns and lower-middle-class families, and emerged from a different socio-political milieu. It is thus a "counter-elite" with a different life-style from the leadership of the DP.

As far as the ideology of the DP was concerned, it was pro-Kemalist, pro-NATO, and pro-American. It regarded the foreign policy of Turkey as the extension of Turkey–NATO relations. The Cold War shaped the way in which it understood the leftist and communist movements as threats to national security and the state, and defined its identity in opposition to the "communist other" or what is commonly known as *Moskof usağı* ("servants of Moscow"). The leadership of the DP allowed a degree of freedom to religious groups as long as they were anti-communist and pro-NATO. Neither civil society nor human rights were at the top of the

---

[23] Conservative movements are usually derived from fear of the uncertainty of the future more than fear of the past. They seek to manage this fear of uncertainty. In the case of Turkey, fear of the past is more important. Opportunities of the future and difficulties of the past force the AKP to stress the future and control these new opportunities. Its goal is not to preserve the past but rather increase its share in the future opportunity structure. Thus, the AKP is not conservative but rather liberal in terms of its political and economic program to carry out the EU process. The AKP defines itself with the future more than the past. The politics of the AKP is about social services. It is the politics of municipalities, not about opening a debate over a social contract or developing a vision of a new polity and civilization. They do not have a vision of Turkey or a vision of the Muslim world but rather one of controlling bureaucracies and constructing the legal framework as the EU wants. Their main goal is to get commissions from their privatization projects and get richer. It is a party without vision and a mission, but it articulates networks of receiving commissions and kick-backs.

[24] "Erdoğan: Milli Görüş' ün Değil Demokrat Parti'nin Devamıyız," *Zaman*, May 17, 2003.

DP agenda. Its primary goal was to defeat communism in Turkey. On the contrary, the leadership of the AKP does not define itself against the left, and in fact has developed close ties with post-Cold War Russia.

Thus due to both international and domestic factors, the AKP decided to settle with a "conservative" identity rather than a Muslim one in the political domain. Although conservatism does not have much resonance at the grass-roots level, the party leadership seeks to define the concept as Muslim, traditional and even liberal. Thus, cultural identity does not necessarily overlap with political identity, but at times the two are at odds with one another. In his Istanbul speech on January 10, 2004, for instance, Erdoğan argued that the AKP's philosophy and politics are rooted in the "social and cultural traditions" of Turkey and "represent a deeply rooted vernacular value system." Thus, vernacular/local value systems, they argue, very much represent the identity of the party.[25] By democracy, the AKP means the "process" of determining the majority opinion which is very much a majoritarian democracy. Erdoğan argues that:

One day, nobody will take the rostrum to tell the nation what to do. On that day, the state will live for the nation in Turkey, and sovereignty will belong to all people unconditionally. On that day, nobody will assume one group's supremacy over the other based on pretexts ... Our nation should know that those who are today trying to make Turkey a country full of suspicions are unable to accept the fact that sovereignty belongs to the nation unconditionally.[26]

The AKP differentiates the state from government and is inclined toward majoritarian democracy. When AKP leaders talk about "limited political power" they are referring to "state power." The party still defines itself against the state and sees it as the main opposition. According to the AKP leadership, the state must be defined, shaped and controlled by its citizens. Their conception of multiculturalism means connecting the local with the global and the means by which a cross-fertilization of diverse

---

[25] Atilla Yayla, a co-founder of the Turkish Liberal Society, argues that "the AKP is also our product. We provided the necessary legitimacy to them in the early days; we helped them to overcome their isolation to become more radical; we always worked together with them and helped them to internalize the language of rights and liberties. We made it very clear to them that Muslimhood could not become a political position and they have to search for a secular position to participate and transform the politics and political language in Turkey. We encouraged them to become liberal in order to protect their own ways of life. We are the ones who taught the virtues of conservative thinking to the AKP leadership. For instance, Yalçın Akdoğan 'borrowed' and derived his argument of *Conservative Democracy* from Berat Özipek's work which was published by Liberal Düşünce." Yayla stresses the role of liberal thought in the evolution of the AKP. Interview with Yayla, January 18, 2005.

[26] Erdoğan speech; see *The New Anatolian*, April 26, 2006.

ideas is possible. Yet the party wants to preserve local values by renewing its meaning and role in society. Erdoğan argues, for example, that:

A significant part of Turkish society desires to adopt a concept of modernity that does not reject tradition, a belief in universalism that accepts localism, an understanding of rationalism that does not disregard the spiritual meaning of life, and a choice for change that is not fundamentalist. The concept of conservative democracy is, in fact, an answer to this desire.

However, regardless of the party's self-definition of itself, its identity is still determined by outsiders, especially at the grass-roots level, with the AKP's identity emerging in practice in terms of the party's policies.

Political Islam has always aimed to redefine the center in terms of Islamic norms and networks, whereas the AKP wants to "become a center-right party" with the goal of sharing the benefits of the center. It seeks to get its economic share from the state. In other words, the AKP does not want to transform the center but rather wants to be assimilated to the center. Before the party tries to transform the center, however, it has to transform itself in terms of liberal, conservative and democratic values within a specifically Turkish context.

On January 10–11, 2004, the AKP organized an international symposium in Istanbul to discuss the concept of conservative democracy.[27] During the symposium, almost all scholars critiqued the concept of conservative democracy as an "invention," with little or no social and intellectual origin.[28] Many liberals, by rejecting a co-existence between

---

[27] For the papers of the symposium, *Uluslararası Muhafazakarlık ve Demokrasi Sempozyumu* (Ankara: AK Parti, 2004). I was one of 22 scholars, along with 7 Turkish journalists, who presented a paper at the symposium.

[28] Before and during the conference, three criticisms were raised against the concept: (1) The concept of "conservative democracy" does not exist in the political science literature and the concept is problematic because democracy cannot be defined by conservatism. Although this view was first expressed by Yayla, he changed his view after the symposium. See Atilla Yayla, "Muhafazakar Demokrasi ve Muhafazakar Demokratlar," http://liberal-dt.org.tr/guncel/Yayla/ay_muhafazakar%20demokrasi.htm. However, Ali Y. Sarıbay and Ali Bayramoğlu sharply attacked the concept (*Uluslararası Muhafazakar ve Demokrasi Sempozyumu*, 2004). (2) It is an opportunist or "only-available" concept in terms of covering "Islamic" or "Muslim democracy", because of the existing legal restrictions in Turkey and international conditions. For instance, Ahmet Taşgetiren, the most respected consciously Muslim journalist in Turkey, argues that conservative democracy is the only available concept covering the realities of Turkey and the international system (Taşgetiren, "At Üstünde Durmak," *Yeni Safak*, August 16, 2003). Also see Etyen Mahcupyan, "Muhafazakar bir Tür Mekez mi?," *Zaman*, August 25, 2003. Ahmet Yıldız argues that the AKP did the right thing by not using "Islamic" or "Muslim" to save Islam from political contestation. He argues that "conservative democracy has three addresses: first one is the Turkish electorate who has local concerns. Second address is the outside, especially the West, to find legitimacy with conservatism. Finally, with the conservative democracy, the AKP want to assure the Kemalist establishment that it has

democracy and conservatism, or the use of conservative as an adjective, fail to understand that democracy is not about content, but rather about the process and form of governance. Indeed, terms such as conservative, social, socialist, liberal and radical democracy have been used and put into practice by diverse political movements. So, one could easily talk and debate the notion of conservative democracy as well, since it is a form of democracy rooted in local norms and culture. As such, the criticism of liberal scholars about the non-existence of conservative democracy is rather weak.

The ideology and identity of the AKP is an outcome of the February 28, 1997 process. Nihat Ergün, a young AKP MP from Sakarya, has argued that "conservative democracy is the outcome of the transformation of political Islam in Turkey [with] two key factors: the February 28 process and the Copenhagen criteria."[29] The party gave up Islamism or shed its Islamic identity in order to be accepted by the establishments both inside and outside Turkey. Although its grass-roots supporters still include a sizeable number of Islamists, its party politics and government practices are not Islamic at all. The major conflicts between the grass roots and the elite of the party are in terms of identity and the political claims of transforming the center. The party has decided to define itself economically as liberal and politically as a conservative party of Turkey (not Turkish), to position itself as the main center-right party of Turkey.

### The three faces of conservatism: family, Ottomanism and piety

Erdoğan's conception of conservatism is informed by the three-fold popular understanding: family, Ottomanism and piety. He argues, for example, that "it is important that conservatism – as a political approach, which accords importance to history, social culture, and, in this context, religion

---

nothing to do with political Islam." Yıldız, "Muhafazakarlığın Yerlileştirilmesi ya da AKP'nin 'Yeni Muhafazakar Demokratlığı,'" *Karizma* (January–March 2004), 53–56. (3) The concept does not indicate what it seeks to "conserve" and for what reason. Those scholars who defended the utility of the concept sought to define it as a "synthesis" of local and universal, past and present, Turko-Islamic and European values; a way of re-bridging the center and periphery of Turkey. M. Hakan Yavuz, "Türk Muhafazakarlığı: Modern ve Müslüman," *Zaman*, January 10, 2004.

[29] My interview with Nihat Ergün in his office at parliament, July 9, 2004. Ergün wants to redefine conservative democracy in terms of bringing morality to the public sphere and preventing the destructive aspects of capitalism and state-led social engineering. Ergün argues that the power of the state must be confined by social norms and the rule of law in any given society. The state, for him, has to be tightly controlled by social forces.

as well – re-establishes itself in a democratic format."[30] He has turned conservatism into an engine of socio-political change. Conservatism in Turkey is more a social attitude than a political one. Political conservatism in this context seeks to perpetuate traditional value and authority structures; it is anti-individual yet in favor of economic and technological change. The AKP's conception of change, however, is filtered through tradition (read Islam) and the party regards community as the main agent of social control. Most of the party's provincial officials are steeped in the conservative morality of Islam. Islam as a grammar of morality and identity and the glue of community continues to provide a recognizable discursive framework within which daily life issues, the meaning of the good life, and a meta-narrative to understand the past and the present are discussed. Most importantly, Islam offers rich symbols and principles to discuss with other members of the community. Yet this Islam is situated within the larger socio-political context and is in constant interaction with the particularities of Turkish society.

The layers of local and religious identities do not necessarily inform the policies of the party but rather define the identity of its supporters. On the basis of interviews with 25 AKP officials and 63 party activists, I hereby attempt to unpack the concept of "conservative democracy" in terms of three mutually constitutive discourses of family values (of a patriarchical kind), Ottoman-history-based patriotism (love for the Muslim-Turkish nation), and piety (a source of morality).

The first critical element of a conservative party is its stress on the family as an institution and on a particular set of values surrounding the family. The stress on family is nothing new in Turkey; in most Eastern and Muslim cultures, family has been the main source of identity and values and people are defined largely in terms of their familial obligations and responsibilities. Being a family man is a major form of political capital in Turkish politics. This stress on the family goes along with the communitarian nature of Turkish society and its value structure. Moreover, the family is critical for the preservation and perpetuation of religious values. Family values in the context of Turkey could also be interpreted as religious values. The two main effects of this stress on the family are that it tends to provide less room for individualism and that it can hamper efforts to achieve gender equality. The AKP understands that individual freedom means the removal of state intervention and constraints from the formation of the community. This understanding does not include the empowerment of the individual to form a critical outlook, nor does it

---

[30] R. T. Erdoğan's speech in M. Hakan Yavuz (ed.), *The Emergence of a New Turkey: Democracy and Ak Parti* (Salt Lake City: University of Utah Press, 2006), p. 366.

create the necessary cultural and social environment for the construction of "difference." Instead of difference, a religious sense of "sameness" is constantly formulated. It also focuses on state–society relations but ignores society–individual relations.

Family is defined largely in terms of patriarchal values and is a male-dominated institution in which women play a subordinate role. Thus men, not women, enter into the public domain and make decisions.[31] Not surprisingly, there are no prominent women at the local and national levels of the AKP. Political activity is primarily defined as a male or male-dominated activity and the political spaces of the AKP tend to thus be male-dominated. The AKP is therefore conservative as far as family values and lack of individualism are concerned.

The second layer of this conservatism is a specific version of imagined Ottoman history as shaped by victory, glory and Turkification.[32] One of the key unifying factors among the leadership of the AKP is a powerful conviction that the Ottoman past holds the key to the future of Turkey. There is a deep feeling of nostalgia towards the Ottoman and even Seljuk periods. This reconstruction of Ottoman identity has been at work for the last three decades and has recently been articulated in art, literature, cuisine and politics. Islamic movements in Turkey have always emphasized the Ottoman legacy in order to offer an alternative source of shared identity. This stress on Ottomanism also shapes the party's understanding of Europe, over a south-eastern part of which the Ottoman Empire ruled for centuries. In today's Ottomanism, as with the AKP, Europe remains the "other" and even an enemy. Thus, at the grass-roots level there is an ambivalence towards the EU, as both the historical "other" and also as an increasingly pertinent space for opportunity and prosperity.

The last layer of this conservatism, represented by the AKP, is a sense of communalized piety. It stresses individualized religious claims but regards Islam as a community-building ethos. Both the AKP leadership and most of its grass-roots supporters are Sunni Muslims who stress communal prayers and support public displays of religion to build a social capital of trust and to smooth personal relations and exchanges. Thus,

---

[31] For a critical view of the AKP's gender policies, see E. Fuat Keyman, "Muhafazakar demokrasinin 'kadın'la imtihanı," *Radikal II*, May 16, 2004. For more on the gender politics of the AKP, see Edibe Sözen, "Gender Politics of the AKP," in Yavuz, *The Emergence of a New Turkey*, pp. 258–280.

[32] Judd King, "The Battle for the Ottoman Legacy: The Construction of a Neo-Ottoman Political Identity In Turkey" (Duke University, July 12, 2004). This paper examines the AKP's reconstruction of Ottoman history. I would like to thank Judd for allowing me to read his unpublished manuscript. The perennialist cult within the AKP is very powerful. Their main target is the secular foundational principles of the Republic.

Islamic religiosity becomes a marker for the party and builds a deep sense of loyalty and attachment. Some party leaders, such as Mehmet Aydın, minister of state, and Tayyar Altıkulaç (former head of the DRA), appreciate the religious wisdom of the past. The feeling they create is that time-honored truths, tested and refined in the long experience of social life, offer the most effective way to deal with the social, political and technological challenges of the world. Islam, for the AKP leadership, is the identity of the Turkish people and the source of their morality as well as the source of legitimacy of the Turkish state. There is a widely shared understanding among the party leadership that there is no morality without Islam and Islam is a *sine qua non* for a moral society. The thinking goes that if people pray and fulfill their religious duties, they are less likely to be corrupted and more likely to work for the interest of the community.

For the AKP leadership, Islam is a national bond, a source of identity and the main source of legitimacy. Yet, for a variety of reasons the party has been obliged to filter Islam out of political life. The party's vision of society is organic and unified by Islamic values and Turkey's imperial Ottoman history. It argues that the community has the right to define political institutions via democracy. This communitarian and majoritarian notion of democracy is in fact the main feature of the AKP. Islamic and family values and agents of socialization seek to mold and "discipline" citizen believers with a sense of communal duty. The AKP stresses the role of religion in the crafting of this "disciplined" citizen who is expected to perpetuate "enduring values." The party leadership's notion of freedom is "instrumental," that is, freedom is valued primarily as a means to ends – becoming rich or developing a religiously shaped public life. In other words, Erdoğan's notion of freedom is an instrument to allow people to pursue and satisfy their individual interests. The AKP thus seeks to promote a system in which individual choices are shaped by religio-communal values.

The AKP has framed questions of identity, such as the headscarf issue, in terms of human rights and a personal choice to wear or not to wear a particular type of attire – Islamic or not. In economic terms, the AKP is syncretic, rather than liberal. Its electoral base incorporates farmers, the new urban middle class and the new Anatolian bourgeoisie.[33] These diverse sectors of the population came together around a "democratic Islamic identity" to bring the AKP to power. The three layers of family, history and piety are the defining features of the party's conservatism. However, this conservatism is free of emancipatory and moral rhetorical

---

[33] Nur Vergin, "Siyaset İle Sosyolojinin Buluştuğu Nokta," *Türkiye Günlüğü*, 76 (2004), 5–9.

underpinnings. It is shaped by middle-class merchants whose primary interest is becoming rich and powerful. The activists of the AKP are new urban dwellers who are semi-urban and regularly move between rural and urban neighborhoods, and regional, hometown and Kurdish loyalties are very powerful within the party organization. This new urban class is still in the making and its value system is very much goal-oriented. Religion, morality and ethnicity are politicized for the goal of becoming successful in new urban centers. They have no problem with modernity or capitalism as long as they participate in the consumer culture. New market conditions allow them to buy and display their identities.

The moral language of the AKP is the language of human desires and the search for power; moral idioms are marshaled for success in the market. Thus, morality, for the party's elite, is a means and not an end in itself. Even Islam has become an instrument for success. The AKP's conservatism is moral-free (principle-free) and goal-oriented: to succeed and become powerful. It is an achievement-oriented and progress-based language of politics. If one examines the party's policies since 2002, its cognitive map is derived from the logic and hope of economic and technological forces. There is no place for deeper "moral" values of shared humanity, but rather there is faith in technology and the economy to shape the future. As far as the identity of the AKP is concerned, it is what it becomes in action. Its identity is made-in-action rather than judged by a set of abstractions. Its politics are about what works and the result of "getting things done." As a leader-centered, vertically structured party, it has a large membership and a set of culturally rooted mobilizing institutions and networks.

Contemporary Turkish society, which is often pragmatic rather than principled, consists of a number of separate and overlapping circles of groups and communities who live together by living apart. Social, cultural and economic cleavages are the sources of associationalism and separatism. Most of the successful civic institutions and practices are built by utilizing the religious idioms and practices for a better life.[34] People, whether in rural or urban areas, are not able to act together for a common good that transcends the immediate material interest of the family or neighborhood. The only social capital that facilitates cross-family or hometown-identity-based association has been the religious networks. Most of Turkey's provincial foundations and associations are formed around a religious idea or institution. Many Turks (and other ethnic groups in Turkey as well) live with their families and single-person households are few. Turkish businesses are mostly family-owned, with fewer

---

[34] Jenny B. White, *Islamist Mobilization in Turkey* (Seattle: University of Washington Press, 2003).

than twenty employees, under patriarchical control, with family loyalty being paramount; there is very little trust in government. These small shop owners and merchants are the principal supporters of Erdoğan, giving him a much larger percentage of votes than the rest of the population.

Politics for the AKP leadership is a mixture of the promotion of communal or personal interests and occasionally the alliance of ideals and principles. There is a constant tension between principles and interests and this tension has not been resolved in favor of the larger masses. Ideas and ideals have always turned into instruments for pursuing personal or communitarian interests. Thus, the centers of power in Turkey still consist of alliances of interests more than ideals. The AKP does not see society as an organic unit with diverse interests and ideals that require compromise and a shared understanding of politics and identity. It does not seek to create a shared code of ethics and identity through interactions but rather treats society as an amalgam of diverse communities and interests. Politics means the expansion of the living space of the dominant group at the expense of the weak. It is not necessarily about policies derived from principles but rather about the politics of communitarian interests. This conception of politics means the distribution and transfer of a party's resources to its own followers and supporters.

The AKP constituents and supporters consist of a set of informal networks and groups.[35] They normally socialize together because they come from the same town or region or belong to the same Sufi order. They work to help one another to advance politically and economically. Hometown identities and loyalties (*hemserilik* – being from same place; "regionalism") are the key building blocks of informal networks in the party. They function as networks of social mobility or for the advancement of one's interests. One of the key implications of these informal networks is the dominance of personalities or personalism. The most important ties and loyalties tend to be personal. *Torpil*, or a way of achieving one's goal through personal contacts, is the way for appointments and recruitments. These informal networks and personal contacts consolidate personalism in Turkish politics, where personalities are always more important than party programs or institutions. Personal ties within the AKP, therefore, precede ideological convictions. These informal groups "are like a cluster of bees round a queen bee. If the queen bee is damaged

---

[35] For more on informal networks see Guilain Denoeux, *Urban Unrest in the Middle East* (Albany: State University of New York, 1993); Francis Fukuyama, *Trust: The Social Virtues and the Creation of Prosperity* (New York: Free Press, 1996); Jan van Deth (ed.), *Social Capital and European Democracy* (London: Routledge, 1999).

they quickly find another to cluster around."[36] In the center-right parties, the leadership has played a more foundational role than ideology. Demirel or Erbakan have very much functioned as the "queen bee." The current "queen bee" is Erdoğan, who has successfully kept the cluster of bees around himself. People within the AKP compete relentlessly with one another to have access to Erdoğan's inner circle. His inner circle consists of Ömer Celik, Mucahit Aslan and Cüneyt Zapsu, all being highly obedient to him. Some claim that there is no critical mind or major thinker around Erdoğan. His team is small, provincial and exclusive. In short, personalism and informality are the major characteristics of Erdoğan's rule.

The AKP is wrapped in a number of contradictions. It seeks to "reform" the political system and state–society relations in Turkey while at the same time declaring its identity as a "conservative" democracy; it champions political participation and pluralism while at the same time not allowing much room for its own internal democracy; it identifies with decentralization and local governance as a solution to Turkey's overburdened bureaucracy while it seeks to centralize the AKP's own party structure and decision making. The party has eliminated almost all bottom-up channels and Erdoğan rules it with his all-male advisors.

### Leadership versus democracy

Writing about party politics Schattschneider notes: "The nominating process has become the crucial process of party control. The nature of the nominating procedure determines the nature of the party; he who can make the nominations is the owner of the party. This is therefore one of the best points from which to observe the distribution of power within the party."[37]

Erdoğan has said:

Much distance has been covered in Turkey towards establishing and institutionalizing democracy in its fullest sense, a democracy which incorporates pluralism and tolerance, not a self-styled democracy. The ideal is not to have a mechanical democracy that is reduced to elections and certain institutions, but an organic democracy that pervades the administrative, social and political fields. We refer to this – we coined a new term for it, and I'd like to underline it – we refer to this as deep democracy.[38]

---

[36] This analogy has been made in regard to politics in India. See B. D. Graham, "The Succession of Factional Systems in the Uttar Pradesh Congress Party, 1937–1966," in J. Swartz (ed.), *Local-Level Politics: Social and Cultural Perspectives* (Chicago: Aldine, 1968), p. 355.

[37] E. E. Schattschneider, *Party Government* (New York: Holt, 1942), p. 64.

[38] R. T. Erdoğan's speech "Conservative Democracy and the Globalization of Freedom," in M. Hakan Yavuz (ed.), *The Emergence of a New Turkey* (Salt Lake City: University of Utah Press, 2006), p. 336.

What is "democracy" for the AKP? Is it an instrument for arriving at the final destination, or a framework for defining the meanings of the good life? Although the party assumes that it represents the core values of "the nation" and defines its identity as the identity of Turkey, it has not developed a language to cope with, or understand, existing cultural differences. On the question of the Kurds, Alevis or life-style groups, for example, the party has no policy. Conservative democracy is based on its particularistic understanding of the Turkish nation as an ideal type, a Sunni/Hanafi/ethnic-Turk homogeneous entity, without cultural or class divisions, and it assumes unity with the state. One of the AKP's goals is to achieve this assumed unity between a homogeneous nation and the state as the guardian of religio-national values. Thus, democracy is not fully internalized, and it is still a majoritarian democracy with heavy authoritarian inclinations. Dengir Mir Fırat, the deputy chairman of the AKP, for example, wants to prove the democratic credentials of the AKP by arguing that "we represent the sector of the population who needs democracy more than any other sector."[39] However, he fails to develop any argument either for democracy or for the democratic credentials of his party. One wonders how will a party, which has tirelessly advocated the Copenhagen criteria on democracy, apply them to its own structures?

Ironically one of the party's biggest strengths also prevents it from actually "being and becoming" democratic. Erdoğan's charismatic personality is one of the main obstacles to the institutionalization of the party's identity and its democratization.[40] Mustafa Ünal, a keen observer of the Turkish parliament, argues that "the Party has no moral authority or leading personalities and the parliamentary group is having difficulty developing working relations with the government."[41] Some deputies of the AKP have complained that "they have no function in Parliament but to raise their hand to vote for the government's bills." One prominent deputy has said that "the only organ we use in the Parliament is our hand."[42] The AKP deputy, Turan Çömez, has criticized the party for its lack of intra-party democracy, having said: "We're not toy soldiers. We are expected to simply raise our hands for any bill sent by the government."[43] The rank and file of the party members do not have any opportunity to participate in party deliberations and manifest their preferences.

---

[39] Fırat's interview with Neşe Düzel, *Radikal*, January 12, 2004.

[40] Democracy, for Erdoğan, a decade ago, was a streetcar: "You ride it until you arrive at your destination, then you step off." Many of his critiques feel as if he has a "hidden agenda" to undermine the secular nature of the Republic, even if he fails to Islamicize it.

[41] Mustafa Ünal, "4.yılında AK Parti'nin ahvali," *Zaman*, August 18, 2004.

[42] This AKP deputy asked not to be named; October 12, 2004.

[43] *Milliyet*, December 9, 2005.

Dissent is not permitted and opposition is not institutionalized in the AKP; there is no chance of competition for leadership posts. When grass-roots participation is very limited, the leadership does not need to be responsive to the rank and file and change is likely to come only when there is a major defeat at the national elections.

There is not much internal party deliberation or collective debate over major policy issues within the AKP. Mehmet Sait Armağan, a parliamentarian of the AKP, resigned from the party, arguing that "the Party is not a shared space anymore to formulate reasonable and meaningful policies."[44] He also complained about the anti-democratic and authoritarian nature of Erdoğan as an obstacle to democratization. Among other things, since its establishment, the AKP has changed its bylaws several times to stress "party discipline."[45] Although it has presented itself as a model of "democratizing the party structure" in Turkey, power has eventually concentrated in the hands of Erdoğan and the experiment with the internal democratization of the party appears to have ended with his increasing popularity.[46] Due to the change in the bylaws of the AKP, Supreme Court of Appeals Chief Prosecutor Nuri Ok in 2005 asked the Constitutional Court to warn the AKP for its failure to amend several party bylaws that he argues are in breach of the Political Parties Law of Turkey. Ok told the AKP that its bylaws were anti-democratic by pointing out the extraordinary power of the party leader. He has said that "in democracies, one individual [the leader of the party, namely Erdoğan] cannot be given such extraordinary powers to select candidates for elections and have the last say in selecting top party boards."[47] In fact, with the new bylaws, Erdoğan has exerted near dictatorial control over key nominations in the party.

The AKP deputy, Çömez, was the first to level criticism, at a party group meeting about how the government was not explaining its policies to deputies. According to Çömez, there were hundreds of questions one needed to ask concerning what the government was doing and claimed that some privatization projects have been co-opted by nepotism and favoritism. He has implied that the Finance minister, Kemal Unakıtan, who has very close ties with Erdoğan, was acting in his own interests.

---

[44] For Mehmet Said Armağan's statement, see *Milliyet*, March 10, 2005.

[45] Önder Kutlu, "AKP'de demokrasi eksik," *Radikal*, October 20, 2003.

[46] There were a number of amendments to the bylaws of the AKP. When the Assembly of the Founding Members of the AKP met to grant Erdoğan supreme authority to run the party, it made eleven changes and this led to a major uproar. Erdoğan got the power to determine the vice chairmen of the party among the members of the MKYK. With these changes, the AKP ended both intra-party and local democracy by allowing party chairmen in provinces to appoint all party board members. Üzeyir Tekin, *AK Parti'nin Muhafazakar Demokrat Kimliği* (Ankara: Orient, 2003), pp. 78–79.

[47] "AKP'ye Tüzük Davası," *Radikal*, December 1, 2005.

Erdoğan, who was then on an official visit to Australia, called the AKP Disciplinary Board to investigate Çömez's statement. This decision of Erdoğan, one can argue, illustrates his authoritarian streak and lack of tolerance for intra-party democracy. Çömez's outburst was followed by that of the AKP deputy, Afyon Mahmut Koçak, who told deputies at the parliament's General Assembly that anti-democratic practices in Turkish parties made it almost impossible for one to engage in politics. To engage in politics, according to Koçak, one has to be fully subservient to the party leadership. "Politicians have to refrain from criticizing their deputies. The identities of the party and its leader are not separated. Being the leader's man remains the way to the top," Koçak has said.

Since the AKP was organized by a top-down approach and its identity is also imposed along the same lines, democratic participation and bottom-up policy-making are wishful thinking. Generally speaking, it is Erdoğan and his advisors who make the crucial decisions. Erdoğan has in many ways become the party, its identity and its unifying glue. As he becomes more popular outside his party, he is likely to gradually move away from the workings of the party and ignore the will of the party.[48] This trend might be reversed only if there is a major challenge within the party itself.

When the AKP parliamentarians and the party leadership met in a closed-door session at Kızılcıhamam, a mountain retreat eighty kilometers from Ankara in September 2004, to be briefed about the policies of the government, the meeting had a stormy start over intra-party democracy. Many of the party's 368 deputies complained that they had no access to government ministers and some deputies criticized the prime minister for his autocratic use of power and the lack of intra-party democracy. Ertuğrul Yalçınbayır, a deputy from Bursa province, said that "We are told to express our free opinions and we do; then, you chew us out. Why do some people get upset when we demand intra-party democracy? These issues cannot be solved by getting upset."[49] He protested against intra-party intimidation of deputies and called for election for the party positions rather than appointment by Erdoğan. When pro-Erdoğan deputies came to the prime minister's defense, Yalçınbayır stormed out of the meeting. One of the main problems of this authoritarian style of rule is that no one in the party leadership wants to take any responsibility. Thus,

---

[48] Almost all parties in Turkey are dominated by their leaders. For instance, Mustafa Kemal, İsmet İnönü, Bülent Ecevit were dominant in the CHP. Erbakan was the center of his number of parties. So it may not be fair to single out the AKP for its hegemonic leadership.

[49] "Milletvekilleri 'fırça' dan şikayet etti," *Milliyet*, September 28, 2004; *Zaman*, September 28, 2004.

nearly every decision is expected from Erdoğan and there is no tradition of delegating power to the party board.[50]

Moreover, the AKP came to power before it institutionalized its identity and organization. In Turkey, unlike in the United States, party offices and branches are spread out over all towns and provinces. These local party organizations are the main networks of mobilization of and communication with the grass-roots supporters. They are essential in the make-up of the party leadership. The AKP has ignored these local party organizations and one sees only a leader-based rather than an organization-based party. Erdoğan has concentrated all power in his hands and uses the media to become the party itself. The party organizations are almost all in crisis and they all complain about the lack of "influence," the gap between the government and the AKP's deputies, and the increasing level of local party organizations and bureaucracy. The problem starts when deputies have problems seeing the government ministers to get their issues solved; in turn, these deputies cannot visit and rally their local organizations and since these local organizations have very little connections with their deputies and little to show grass-roots supporters, they are also losing credibility and power.

The main problem of the party is the lack of coordination, the domination of a web of personal friends and a lack of trust.[51] The AKP realizes that, for example, without an open political commitment to the EU process it will not be allowed to govern the country. The party also

---

[50] The AKP parliamentarians are fully surrendered to the leader in order to maintain their positions in the next elections. They believe that they owe their position to the leader and they are obligated to carry out the orders of the leader. This prevents them from free thinking and free action.

[51] Turhan Çömez, an AKP Deputy of Balıkesir, made a number of allegations of corruption in AKP Group meetings. He made a number of specific charges against Finance minister Kemal Unakıtan. Erdoğan reacted to Çömez's speech by sending him to the committee of discipline but he later dropped the case. See *Milliyet*, December 8, 2005. Another AKP Deputy, Mahmut Koçak, a deputy of Afyon, taking the floor in parliament on December 7, 2005, criticized his own party. Koçak stated that inner-party democracy should function properly. He argued that "In-party opposition should be tolerated and encouraged. Otherwise the Party's administration body cannot be renewed themselves and personal interests replace those of the public which in turn leads to degeneration and nepotism. Today, in order to take any position in the Party or in the government, one has to work in harmony with the Party leader and avoid any criticism of Erdoğan. You need to be somebody's man in order to have a position. Party leaders' personalities are more prominent than the parties' programs." *The New Anatolian*, December 8, 2005. The AKP's Disciplinary Board dismissed Hatay deputy Fuat Geçen from the party for "insulting the party and its members through the media" on June 6, 2006. Geçen claimed his party had forgotten the anti-corruption promises it had made to the public before coming to power, accusing the party of hindering those who were waging a battle against corruption. Afyon deputy Mahmut Koçak, known for his harsh criticism of Erdoğan, was sent to the AKP Disciplinary Board for dismissal in June 2006.

knows that solid economic policies are crucial to maintain support at the grass-roots level. Erol Kaya, a prominent and experienced mayor of Pendik, argues that

The major problems of the AKP are: communication within the government and between the government and the parliamentary group and among and within party organizations. We all follow each other through newspapers. There is no proper communication network. The Party has no identity nor does it offer any form of identity; it is like a supermarket, you go there regularly and buy goods. The store doesn't give you an identity. The AKP needs to go beyond being a store. ... It is [just] a bundle of people and networks that seek to distribute economic goods.[52]

In the party, there is a combination of high-level elite pragmatism and grass-roots religious and ethnic pluralism. Ethnic identity, the role of Islam and attitudes toward the EU are three sources of cleavage inside the party. There are four major groups within the party: pro-EU liberals, Kurds, Turkish nationalists and Islamists of the National Outlook Movement.[53] Turkish politics is driven by value orientation and the elite plays an important role in the articulation of alternative images of a good society. In the last four elections (1995, 1999, 2002 and 2007), the main ethnic groups (Turks and Kurds)[54] and religious values (secularists vs. Islamists) have played important roles in the voters' electoral choice. Due to the increasing polarization of ethnic identity, elections are also treated as an ethnic census by the nationalist Kurdish groups. Identity and protest voting are becoming very important. Increasing frustration with centrist parties has pushed voters to vote for "alternative" or anti-establishment parties.

The two major ideological groups within the AKP are *Turkish*-Islamic and *Islamic*-Turkish. The debate is between the primacy of political brotherhood (nationalism) and the primacy of Islamic brotherhood. The nationalists within the party offer an ethnocentric definition of Turkish national identity and stress loyalty and service to the Turkish state as the highest goal and regard Islam as the second most important component of national culture. Unlike the secularist Turkish nationalists, they do not glorify the pre-Islamic tradition but stress the "magnificent" Ottoman

---

[52] Interview with Kaya (Pendik), January 6, 2005.
[53] According to Pollmark's study of the AKP parliamentarians, Kurdish is the second tongue with 14.6% of the MPs. 0.5% speak Zaza, 2.4% Arabic, 1.4% Georgian.[54] When they were asked which institution is the most powerful in terms of determining the future of the country, they overwhelmingly said the Turkish military. "Ak Partili vekillerin profile," *Yeni Safak*, March 5, 2005.
[54] The Kurdish nationalist party DTP represent a direct challenge to both national identity and the state ideology of Kemalism. Its electoral support is concentrated in the Kurdish-populated provinces. The party has no appeal to Turkish voters.

past. Yet, just like the secularist Turkish nationalists, they regard the state as a sacred institution. The Islamist component of the AKP stresses first Islam and then the nation. For this group, national identity is defined by Islamic values and the Ottoman tradition. They stress service to the community, not the state, as the ultimate value. They are skeptical of the state because of the limited religious rights and the state ideology of Kemalism. This group also does not separate the private and public sphere and uses religion to make political claims, such as rallying around the headscarf issue and religious education. It stresses the state's role in providing religious education and religion-based citizenship. The first group opposes any concessions to the Kurds; the second group defends national unity by recognizing Kurdish cultural rights, and seeks to redefine nationhood with Islamic values. As far as foreign policy is concerned, the *Turkish*-Islamic group wants to develop closer ties with the Central Asian Turkic republics, and adopts a critical attitude towards the EU and US hegemony in the world. The *Islamic*-Turkish group supports closer relations with Muslim countries instead, opposes the US presence in the Middle East, and supports closer ties with the EU, to carve a larger space for religious rights and freedoms within the framework of the European Convention of Human Rights. Yet they are also very critical of the Westernization/Europeanization of Turkey.

### Electorate and regional party identity

We are a new party and just like an uncooked *asure* [a traditional dessert made from various kinds of dry fruits, nuts and beans] our movement also consists of diverse people from different origins [and] ideologies.[55]

What are the social bases of support for the AKP? Is it a religio-cultural division defined by value orientation? How does religious, ethnic and economic inequality interact in the social base of the AKP? The voting behavior of the AKP followers reflects their identity more than the identity of the party. Although the AKP sought to become a "catch-all" party of the center right, the issue of Islamic life-style is very important for the core supporters of the AKP.

Social conservatism and economic liberalism are the two principal features of the AKP. The new middle class must guide Turkey's search for identity and this new group is likely to provide the cornerstone of a politically strong and economically prosperous Turkey. Before I examine the main characteristics of this new class, it might be useful to disaggregate

---

[55] Mehmet Dülger's comments in *Milliyet*, September 17, 2004.

it into four major groupings: (1) provincial nobility with conservative leanings; (2) small and medium size businessmen and industrialists; (3) shopkeepers; and (4) master craftsmen, semi-industrialist farmers, and owners of construction firms. These sectors are socially conservative and economically liberal and occasionally share the same overriding political consciousness about the orientation of the country. This hybrid class coalition brings social conservatives and political liberals together to shape the future of Turkey. These groups are composed of a new urban class, a sector which has been marginalized because of the effects of globalization, and the rural population. The shantytowns that voted for the AKP want more welfare programs to address their bleak economic situation; the rural areas seek more state subsidies and protection from global competition; and the new rich seek less state control and more liberal policies. Thus, this coalition of classes is difficult to keep together. The glue so far among these three groups has been their resistance to the exclusionary policies of the establishment and their sharing of the same grammar of dissent: Islam. The party became the voice of the periphery which intends to transform the political landscape of Turkey. This social base is not anti-state but rather developmentalist; not ideological but pragmatic; yet socially conservative. Even though the AKP has failed to develop a clear discourse of politics, people have voted for it by focusing on the life-style of its leadership. Instead of discourse, habits shaped the votes of the mainly ordinary Muslim electorate. According to Ergun Yıldırım, a sociologist, for the voter "It is not important what Erdoğan is saying but rather how he says it, what he does, where he goes, what type of holidays he celebrates, and how he interacts with his family."[56]

The new urban class is still juxtaposed between rural and urban life-styles and is not yet fully integrated into the economic development of Turkey. This large sector is neither pre-modern nor modern but rather in transition and seeks to shape the process of modernity in terms of its own practices. This syncreticism of tradition and modernity is reflected in life-styles, in taste in music, food and furniture and in worldviews. With new opportunity spaces, this new group is allowed to articulate its own life-style and worldviews by utilizing restaurants, coffeeshops and entertainment places. This new urban class is also conservative in stressing the role of family, neighborhood and religion. It sees politics not as a domain of loyalty but rather as a way of claim-making and articulating one's rights and needs.

---

[56] Ergun Yıldırım (Ahmet Harputlu), "Bir politik durum olarak müslüman democrat," *Bilgi ve Düşünce*, No. 5 (February 2003), 15.

*Single Party Victory Elections*

| Party | % Vote | Number of MPs |
|-------|--------|---------------|
| 1950 DP | 53.3 | 408 |
| 1954 DP | 56.6 | 490 |
| 1957 DP | 47.3 | 419 |
| 1965 AP | 52.9 | 240 |
| 1969 AP | 46.5 | 256 |
| 1983 ANAP | 45.1 | 212 |
| 1987 ANAP | 36.3 | 292 |
| 2002 AKP | 34.4 | 363 |
| 2007 AKP | 46.5 | 341 |

*Source:* DIE Election Results.

The major outcome of Özal's reform policies was the emergence of this middle-class culture. Understanding the feelings, identity and socialization of these industrialists, men of commerce and professionals is the key to understanding the workings of the AKP. The AKP-allied associations are used to filter these new middle-class tastes and life-styles down to the masses. A growing commercialization of symbols and life-styles has made this possible. The morality and values of this new middle class have been the subject of condemnation or admiration for many people who see this new emerging class as distorters or co-opters of globalization (the EU process) against the privileges of the Kemalist elite who have failed over the years to transform and democratize the country. The main characteristics of this new class are efficiency, industriousness and political liberalism. Özal's revolution opened the door for new businessmen into the economy and because of this they gradually became a significant political force.

Although Erdoğan argued at his first party congress that the AKP is not a "coalition" of diverse groups or a "syncretic" party but rather a "unified whole," he failed to provide a coherent identity or define the unifying glue of his party. At this congress, Erdoğan argued that this whole is based on the "enduring values of the nation" (*millet*) and that the party seeks to balance these national values with universal values and also bring these "enduring values" (*kadim değerler*) to the forefront of Turkish politics.[57] Erdoğan defines this movement as a way of "bringing the center and the periphery together"; creating a new transmission "belt between the nation and the state"; creating a new "synergy between the Republic and

---

[57] Erdoğan or people around him never define these values.

democracy."[58] In foreign policy, he always stresses "dialogue" and not a "clash of civilizations."

A close examination of the AKP indicates that it is a coalition of classes (economically marginalized sectors of the population and the rising new bourgeoisie) and communities, if not ideologies, of Sunni Turks and the politically excluded Kurds. The trendsetter of the party is not the largest sector of the electorate but rather the rising and economically able new bourgeoisie and the intellectuals of municipalities. These two groups are the engines of social and political change in Turkey.

The AKP's electorate has its own identity and the boundary between the identity of the party administration and its supporters is still a major challenge. According to a GENAR survey, the supporters of the AKP define their political identity in the following way: 27% Islamist, 15% rightist, 14% democrat, 10% conservative, 10% social democrat, 6% nationalist, 3% Kemalist, 3% nationalist-conservative, and 10% not sure.[59] There is a major difference between the way in which the electorate defines itself and the way the party wants to define itself and its supporters. Studies such as the above survey ignore the increasing role of the bourgeoisie and the new class of intellectuals in the constitution of the AKP policies.

During the elections, among other things, although the AKP declared its commitment to the EU, half of its electorate was against eventual membership. Moreover, over half of the party voters were either below or at the poverty line and they expected the party to pursue more social policies through state intervention, yet the party continues to support the free market economy. This large segment of the population still expects parliament to change pro-market policies for more welfare-oriented ones.

In Sunni-Turkish-dominated central and eastern Anatolia, the center-right voters are conservative on social and cultural issues and this conservatism is reflected in the political domain in terms of "supporting a powerful state that defends tradition and the sacred."[60] This sector of the population attributes a semi-mythical place to the state and expects the

---

[58] Ahmet Taşgetiren, "Ak Parti Misyonu," *Yeni Şafak*, October 13, 2003. Fehmi Koru, a leading conspiracy theorist of Turkey (*Hürriyet*, May 6, 2006), has indicated the ways in which the AKP could become just like any other center-right party if it "transforms itself from people's party to leader's party, sacrifices internal party democracy to party discipline, ignores national will over some foreign policy calculations." "Ak Parti ye karşı AKP," *Yeni Şafak*, October 13, 2003. Indeed, during my fieldwork in Turkey, many provincial party organizations were complaining that the AKP is searching for its identity and legitimacy not in the parliament or inside Turkey but rather outside in the Copenhagen criteria and also in close ties to the USA.

[59] Ali Bulaç, "Muhafazakarlığın Referansları," *Zaman*, August 28, 2003.

[60] Naci Bostancı, "AKP merkez sağın neresinde?," *Zaman*, August 23, 2004.

state to be more assertive and for political parties to agree with the state. Thus, the social bases of free-market economics and political liberalism in Turkey are weak and a state-centric culture is still dominant, even though it is under transformation. How does the AKP close this gap between its electorate and its desire to pursue a free-market economy and introduce a number of liberal discourses? This tension is indicative of the central role of cultural issues in politics. The center-left parties' strong Kemalist and secular position has almost forced a large sector of the population to identify with the center right. In other words, cultural issues are still dominant in the electoral cleavages of Turkey. Second, the leaders of the center-right parties are more at peace with Turko-Islamic values and live the way in which most Turks live, especially religious Turks.

There is a close affinity between the life-style of the leaders and the electoral support they receive. Demirel, Özal and Erdoğan have not been civic leaders who have sought to empower the people, but because their life-styles accorded with those of a large sector of the population they were supported by the conservative masses. Erdoğan is an ordinary person and reflects the cultural code of Turkey. The AKP emerged as most powerful in the Sunni-Turkish-populated central and eastern Anatolian provinces where nationalism is as powerful as Islam, and the two usually work hand-in-hand. Since the party's main bastion of support is rooted in the Sunni-Turkish provinces, its policies towards the Kurds and Alevis are necessarily a source of tension and even a potential faultline. Yet the party emerged as the second most powerful force in south-east Anatolia where the Kurdish population is dominant. Thus, the building blocks of the AKP's communitarian identities are Sunni Turks and Kurds. These ethnic identities coincide as an Islamic identity with a shared language of oppositional identity. Islamic identity becomes a surrogate identity for Kurdish claims and Kurds use this Islamic identity to penetrate the system and use it for their own political purposes. The dense and exclusionary Islamic networks of the Refah Party still dominate the distribution of key party positions and bureaucratic appointments. The AKP is a party consisting of a small community of ex-Islamists. The leadership of the AKP sees Turkish nationalism as they see Kurdish nationalism – as an ethnic identity and a source of tension in Turkey.

What is the regional identity of the AKP in south-east Turkey? What is the relationship between the AKP and the DTP (Democratic Society Party) (previously DEHAP) in this part of the country? The DTP seeks to differentiate itself from all other parties in the region as the only representative of Kurdish aspirations and uses all means to challenge the legality of state authority. It is not an anti-system but an anti-state party. The Kurdish-AKP electorate presents itself as an *in-between* space between the state and the DTP, and maintains an equal distance from both actors.[61] The DTP stresses its marginality and its history of persecution at the hands of the state. Both the DTP and the Kurdish-AKP understand the state to be synonymous with the Turkish military. Since the AKP government appoints all civil servants, including the governors and police chiefs, the only force outside its appointments is the military. Thus, the military, for the Kurdish-AKP, represents the state and oppression, in opposition to which the AKP presents itself as the friend of Kurdish rights. Moreover, this Kurdish-AKP alliance has its own supporters in Ankara, and many local Kurdish-AKP organizations understand the prime minister's policy of "being against racism" as "being against Turkish nationalism." In other words, Erdoğan uses all available means to appeal to the Kurdish agenda by criticizing Turkish nationalism and presenting his party as the party of the excluded. The Kurds see the AKP as an anti-Kemalist and historically oppressed party – just like themselves. The AKP does not treat the DTP as its rival and does not compete with it. It seeks to get the support of ex-center-right supporters. In other words, it is the only available space for non-DTP supporters to organize themselves against the "system."

The politics of the Kurdish region are shaped by the interplay between four actors: (1) Sufi and tribal networks; (2) the state bureaucracy; (3) the PKK and DTP; and (4) the Kurdish Hizbullah. When Sufi orders and tribal networks send representatives to Ankara, the MP's first task is to generate investment for his province and make sure this money is distributed along his Sufi or tribal network base. Thus, the local bourgeoisie has been created from state bids and largesse, creating a close connection between the tribal networks and the political parties. Second, the elected representative seeks to influence the appointment of state employees in the region and the maintenance of the old order. Third, he uses all available means to control the local party organization in order to be nominated in the next election. The social base of the AKP is different from that of the DTP. The latter has fewer ties with Sufi orders and tribal networks. The traditional Sufi networks supported accommodation with the state and also functioned as the repository of Kurdish nationalism and Kurdish self-determination. The main support base of the DTP is the new urban youth who have lost their traditional networks and seek to form new

---

[61] As the state withdrew from the public domain, those previously organized associations rapidly filled these new opportunity spaces. In the case of the Kurds, the PKK moved to these opportunity spaces to articulate an ethnic and exclusionary Kurdish identity. When Kurdish nationalism became assertive and the state incapable of responding, the Turks, those who define themselves as Turks, reacted in sporadic ways rather than in an organized way.

networks of solidarity and identity through party connections. The DTP in the region has several overlapping roles: it is state, party and Kurdish civil society. It functions as a surrogate state through its municipal governments. Most civic and political activities in the region are carried out by DTP organizations. A closer examination of the AKP's regional organizations indicates that its regional identity is as Kurdish as that of the DTP. The only difference is that it is the party of the government, even though it is still in conflict with the state. Additionally, the AKP, unlike the DTP, is more conservative and has close ties with local Sufi and tribal networks. Moreover, AKP-dominated municipalities allow all types of religious and Kurdish symbols to be displayed as long as they are not overtly anti-state, and it is even tolerant towards Kurdish Hizbullah.[62] The newest development in the region in the last several years is the consolidation of the Zaza identity as having a close affinity with Islam.[63] This new Zaza-Islamic identity is closer to a Turkish than to a Kurdish identity. To conclude, Turkish identity as a supra-ethnic identity has been eroded during the AKP government. Just like the DTP, the AKP has treated Turkish identity as a specific ethnic identity on the same level as Kurdish identity, rather than treating it as an overarching constitutionally preferred identity.

For example, two days before his visit to the Kurdish-populated Diyarbakır and in response to pressures within his own party, Erdoğan told an in-party group that the most important domestic problem of Turkey "is the Kurdish question" and defended a solution within democracy.[64] This was the first time in the history of the republic for the prime minister to frame the issue of the "Kurdish question" as such. Moreover, Erdoğan decided to meet with a group of intellectuals and journalists about the Kurdish question. Although his new initiative was welcomed as courageous by Kurdish leaders both within his party and outside, like Leyla Zana, a prominent Kurdish ex-parliamentarian,[65] some of his supporters sharply criticized Erdoğan's new initiative as giving concessions to the Kurdish Workers' Party (PKK). Ahmet Tasgetiren, a columnist for the Istanbul daily *Yeni Şafak* and a main voice of the nationalist Turkish faction within the AKP, even accused the prime minister of being

---

[62] Ercan Citilioğlu, *Tahran Ankara Hattında Hizbullah* (Ankara: Umit, 2001); I. Bagasi, *Kendi Dilinden Hizbullah ve Mücadele Tarihinden kesitler* (Germany, 2004); Ruşen Çakır, *Derin Hizbullah/Islamcı Siddetin Geleceği* (Istanbul: Metis, 2001).

[63] Zazas are Zaza-speaking people whose language is considered a dialect of Kurdish. In recent years, there has been a process of assertion of a specific Zaza identity in opposition to the larger Kurdish identity.

[64] Adnan Keskin and Tolga Akiner, "Erdoğan: Kürt sorunu demokrasiyle çözülür," *Radikal*, August 11, 2005.

[65] *Radikal*, "Diyarbakır umutlu," August 12, 2005.

"misled" and of rewarding the terrorist organization PKK.[66] The AKP responded to Tasgetiren's criticisms by forcing him out of the newspaper and silencing him. Deniz Baykal, the head of the main opposition party, has sharply criticized Erdoğan's "framing" of the Kurdish question as danger-ous, and as a tacit recognition of the Kurdish demands through his use of the same political language ("democratic republic") as Öcalan.[67]

The AKP government has failed to develop a coherent policy on the Kurdish issue. The village guards system, a defense force of about 70,000 armed villagers, was established to defend Kurdish villages against PKK attacks and created as a buffer to resist PKK guerrillas. This system also seeks to provide alternative income, keep the loyalty of the Kurds and create a domestic network of intelligence against PKK activities. It is thus also very much a tactic by Ankara to sow division within the Kurdish community. The Turkish government has neither ended nor reformed these loose networks of localized and privatized security forces. It also has not developed a plan for those displaced Kurds who have been forcibly relocated from their villages and have had their homes destroyed, with the government arguing that these settlements were used by the PKK for strategic purposes. In the last two decades of the conflict, around four million Kurds have been relocated and displaced, and this internally displaced Kurdish population has been the major burden on some urban centers.[68] The government has evacuated and destroyed hundreds of villages, ostensibly to protect them from attack and from being used and taken over by the PKK.

The government's span of 1993–2002 was plagued by corruption scan-dals, the near total collapse of the justice system, an inability to deal with rising economic expectations, and increasing unemployment. Atatürk's founding myth that Turkey is a unified and Europeanized nation state looked shakier than ever as some religious and ethnic parties attempted to carve out their own political space. In these conditions the AKP became attractive to many middle-class Turks, who form its enduring support base. On certain issues, such as secularism, the Kurdish question and coping with unemployment, the party still lacks clarity. It does not have a clear definition of Turkish identity, nor a clear-cut policy on the Kurdish

---

[66] Zafer Özcan, "Tasgetiren: Tayyip Bey'i severim ama hatalarına aferin demem," in the weekly magazine *Aksiyon*, August 29, 2005.

[67] "Baykal: Başbakan'ın attığı adımla terör örgütüne nefes aldırıldı," *Milliyet*, August 21, 2005.

[68] Göç-der (Immigrants' Association for Social Cooperation and Culture), *The Research and Solution Report on the Socio-Economic and Socio-Cultural Conditions of the Kurdish Citizens Living in the Turkish Republic who are Forcibly Displaced due to Armed Conflict and Tension Politics* (2002).

question. As the party is mostly led by, and caters to, the upper-level "new-born" Muslim bourgeoisie, local and provincial party organizations are wary that marginalized AKP followers may begin to assert themselves, which would threaten to undermine its vision of a unified family under the paternal figure of Erdoğan. Erdoğan, in turn, has presented himself to the middle- and lower-middle-class population as a modern, pious, efficient alternative to the corruption-ridden center-right and center-left parties. However, both Erdoğan and key party leaders are not yet ready to disengage themselves from the Islamism that they imbibed at a younger age in the training camps and reading circles of Erbakan-led Islamic youth organizations. Thus, the party will continue to gauge the political climate in order to impose its cultural program.

The AKP has attracted a generation of rich Turks who live in European countries and are eager for cultural and economic links with Turkey. This desire has turned many of them into the AKP's most devoted sponsors, and has helped the AKP itself to evolve rapidly, despite its Islamic roots, into an ardent supporter of Turkey's EU membership.

### Conclusion

The AKP has two characteristics which distinguish it from other parties in Turkey. It is a party of social services (*hizmet partisi*), rather than being ideological; and it is extremely insecure vis-à-vis the state and the outside world, and seeks to overcome this sense of insecurity by freeing Turkish society from the state's ideology and removing all obstacles to private initiative. As such, it can be categorized as economically liberal and pro-market. Due to these two characteristics of being the party of social services and insecurity, it has no political blueprint for social transformation and reduces Islam into a set of "values indispensable to the nation." Its understanding of governance is shaped by a majoritarian democracy more than the rule of law.

The AKP is an *ad hoc* coalition of forces that came together in response to the oppression of the February 28 process. The insecurity of its leadership shapes its "liberal" policies to expand its base while it tries hard to keep its Islamic core. This coalition was composed of the emerging Anatolian bourgeoisie and the peripheral Islamic and some Kurdish forces. The emergence of these new actors has redefined state–society relations in Turkey and shaped the state ideology to shift from the secular nation-building ideology of Kemalism to a more multi-cultural understanding of nation, and of the state and its role in society. These new actors consist of the counter-elite, Anatolian bourgeoisie: new upwardly-mobile urban elites who benefited greatly from the income assigned to municipalities under the *Refah Partisi* (RP) in the 1990s; new politicians who were socialized in the networks of the National Outlook Movement and learned about politics at the municipal government levels; and new rural-urban upwardly-mobile villagers. The February 28 process helped them create a common front, and democracy allowed them to unify their political and economic capital to restructure the boundaries between state–society, public–private, secular–religious and modern–traditional. The most important transformation simultaneously brought about by the AKP is the introduction and use of human rights discourse in Turkey, itself largely brought about by the end of the Cold War and the EU accession talks.

Due to the closure of the previous Islamic parties by the Constitutional Court, the AKP feels insecure vis-à-vis the state and the legal system. This insecurity is the main shaper of the party's leadership personality and policies of the party. The AKP has been trying to overcome this deep insecurity by adopting the language of human rights discourse and this, in turn, has helped it ally with the liberal forces in Turkey such as the Association of Liberal Thinkers. Erdoğan and Gül, who were anti-EU and anti-West prior to the 1997 February coup, are now converts to the Europeanization of Turkey via the Copenhagen criteria. This serves as a tool for deflecting the charges of fundamentalism leveled by the secular Kemalist elite. In its sixth year in government, however, although it has made great progress in that realm, the AKP has yet to fully earn the confidence of the liberal forces inside and outside of Turkey, due to its instrumentalization of human rights discourse and its regularly harking back to its semi-fundamentalist Islamic roots to keep its grass roots mobilized.

But is the AKP an Islamic party? If not and if it wants to become one, is it possible for it to become one in the current social and political context in Turkey? Experts such as Graham Fuller argue that the AKP is an Islamic party, a successful experiment and an example to be emulated by other Muslim states. Other scholars have also tended to read the current experiment in Turkey as the successful political integration of an Islamic movement.[69] Although the AKP leadership denies its Islamic background and

---

[69] Graham E. Fuller, "Turkey's Strategic Model: Myths and Realities," *The Washington Quarterly*, 27:3 (Summer 2004), 51–64. Daniel Pipes has also argued that "The Justice and Development Party in Turkey is very different from the Taliban in its means, but not so different in its ends. If the Party gained full control over Turkey, it could be as dangerous as the Taliban were in Afghanistan." Washington Institute, Policy Watch, 746 (April 10, 2003), http://www.washingtoninstitute.org/watch/policywatch/policy-watch2003/746.htm.

claims to be a conservative democratic party, to all observers it is clear that the party emerged out of the ashes of the heavily Islamic RP and FP, which were closed by the Constitutional Court on charges of being forums and proponents of anti-secularism. Moreover, the majority of the AKP's deputies are observant Muslims in their daily lives. For instance, nearly all women associated with the AKP, who within the party organization are normally spouses rather than holding party positions, continue to wear headscarves, which have been banned at public offices, ceremonies and universities because of the alleged challenge they pose to the secular nature of Turkey.

As such, even if the administration of the party denies any connection with political Islam, can we still consider the party Islamic? Is it possible for an ex-Islamic movement to become a-Islamic or un-Islamic (à la European Christian Democratic parties of today)? Is the commitment of the members of the AKP to religious values in their personal lives enough to label the party Islamic? When does a movement or a party become or cease to be Islamic? One may read the party's denial as simply a compromise with the state. The AKP is free to govern the country as long as it stays within the framework of the constitution and ignores the many religious claims of its conservative constituency. Is the AKP a success story of an Islamic movement that has adapted to a host of new conditions or is it the story of the ability of the Turkish political system to transform and domesticate political Islam to the extent that it denies its Islamism, even its explicit Islamic roots?

As opposed to many who believe otherwise, it is very problematic to use Turkey as a model of Islamic democracy and the Turkish experiment is unlikely to be repeated in other Muslim countries. I say this because Turkey has still not definitely solved many significant problems regarding the integration of political Islam into its system by accepting it. Rather it has used extra-judicial means to transform political Islam to the point that the movement seeks refuge in the denial of its past and reacts very negatively when it is called Islamic or Muslim. A movement is defined as Islamic or a-Islamic in terms of its approach to the concept of *umma*, a political community that defines "us" (believers) versus "them" (unbelievers). The movement does not seek to transform the center of power and power relations from the perspective of the *umma* but rather seeks to assimilate and become the center itself.

I would argue that if an Islamic political movement sheds its Islamic ideology it is not Islamic anymore. A movement is Islamic if it is making political claims on the basis of Islam. In the case of Turkey, we see the process of post-Islamism or the shift from the politics of identity to the politics of service – *hizmet partisi*. Thus, the AKP is not a party of identity but rather a party that strives to provide better services for the people. It does not develop or articulate significant claims on the basis of Islam or identity. One sees the realization of liberal politics in Turkey in the sense that political movements are not engaged in the politics of identity, which tends to be conflict-ridden and confrontational, but rather in the politics of compromise and service. A new social and political contract is evolving in the case of Turkey on the basis of neo-liberal economic and political values. This could be seen as a process of normalization since it hints at the positive integration of the country into the macro trends taking place on a global scale. Going back to our main question, when and under what conditions does a movement cease to be Islamic, I would argue that it ceases to be Islamic if it fails to articulate any policy claim based on an Islamic identity, but only makes claims on the basis of public services.

Based on the actions of the AKP, it is possible to conclude that an Islamic political movement has helped to consolidate democracy by offering Turkey's marginalized groups an alternative venue for political participation. Yet this positive role is very much an outcome of expanding opportunity spaces and the constraining of military–legal institutions, made possible in large part through the actions and trendsetter role played by the new and rising Anatolian bourgeoisie who have refused to support confrontational politics. This democratic bargaining between the state and the AKP has forced the latter group to give up any search for governmental "hegemony" and to accept EU-oriented democratic norms. Turkey's Islamic groups, more than the secularists, have reluctantly supported this new democratic bargain because they have fully understood that this is the only way for them to come to power and stay there. The AKP is not a party of ideas but rather practices. It moves from practice to theory, not the other way around. It seeks to build up its identity through policy practices and it is thus not guided by abstract concepts.

EU norms have helped to domesticate and force the state and anti-system actors to change their perceptions and strategies and adopt EU norms as the point of reference for the creation of a new social contract in Turkey. After a possible accession date is given by the EU – likely 2012 – what the AKP will do is not very clear. Although some of the party's members are in the process of inventing some sort of post-EU platform, some other broad-based programs, which would appeal to the sectors of the population that have supported the party in the past, have yet to be articulated. There is still a major chance that Turkish voters will return to the identity-based parties they voted for in the past, having used the AKP "like a streetcar" to get to their desired destination (that is, EU membership and the cleansing of the political landscape of corrupt politicians), and then choosing to get off. I believe that this is the biggest question facing Turkish politics in the near future. In other words, has politics in Turkey really shifted from the politics of identity to the politics of issues, or is this simply a temporary development? Given the still unsolved issues such as the Kurdish and Armenian questions and the secular–religious divide, the politics of identity are likely still part and parcel of Turkish political identity.

# 4    *Kabadayı* and *mağdur*: Erdoğan and Gül

It is important to focus on the lives and roles of these two political leaders of the AKP since the life-spans of political leaders in Turkey have always been longer than their own political parties. While Turkey is a graveyard of political parties, political leaders rarely retire and hardly die. This is very much the outcome of the personality-centric aspect of Turkish political culture. Thus, political leaders are more significant than ideologies or party programs. Leaders are likely to be turned into a Sultan and they govern their own parties as their own domain. This de-institutionalized aspect of political parties encourages us to focus on key personalities, especially Erdoğan and Gül. Moreover, oppressed or marginalized masses tend to turn "victimized" political leaders into resistance heroes. It is very important to study the biographies of Erdoğan and Gül to understand not only their reconstruction in the social memory of Anatolian people but also the meaning of what they represent for ordinary people. Moreover, the social roots, socialization and ideological evolution of the two men might open new avenues to understand the social transformation of Turkey itself. Their life stories and changing ideological positions reflect the transformation of the Islamic movement and an evolving Turkey.

When I was going from Pendik to Kartal, I asked a taxi driver what he thinks about Erdoğan. He said "*Kasımpaşalı kabadayı olarak gitti, Etilerli olarak dönüyor*" (He went as a *kabadayı* of Kasımpaşa but returned as a man of Etiler). Kasımpaşa is a rough macho neighborhood populated by a mix of day laborers, gypsies, new immigrants from rural Anatolia and fishmongers. Etiler, on the other hand, is populated by a rich, secularist and urbanized elite who generally support the Kemalist establishment and look down on people in neighborhoods like Kasımpaşa as uneducated, religiously conservative and unrefined. Whether this description captures the whole story of Erdoğan's personal transformation is questionable, but it certainly helps us to understand the mood on the street in Turkey, where many people see Erdoğan either as a *kabadayı* or someone who is in the making to become a "white Turk." In the 2007 elections, during the many rallies one of the key posters was "welcome *mağdur* and *mazlum* Gül!" If

118

Erdoğan was the *"mazlum"* (wronged one) of the 2002 elections, Gül became the *mağdur* (victimized one) of the 2007 elections. Popular perception has always regarded Erdoğan as both a *kabadayı* and a *mazlum*, due to his social background and political oppression by the establishment; and due to the denial to him of the presidency by the Kemalist establishment, Gül has now become both *mağdur* and *mazlum*.

A *kabadayı* is an identity based on reputation, authority and honor. It is normally a male and respected authority figure in his neighborhood. His authority is not derived from his knowledge, kinship lineage or state power, but rather from the existing cultural code. A kabadayı is respected as a "protector" of the weak, needy and oppressed against a formal or an informal power structure. He also uses violence to impose informal settlements among the conflicting parties. A kabadayı has several key defining moral features: courage, mercy towards the needy, strength and self-confidence. It is an acquired identity that one builds in the course of time through engaging with neighborhood affairs. A kabadayı is a neighborhood disciplinarian by protecting the honor of the neighborhood and also by imposing order upon the restless youth. In short, reputation, authority and honor are the constituting elements of the kabadayı identity. He is expected to protect his reputation by protecting the common good of the neighborhood in order to maintain his authority. Both kabadayı and mağdur allow us to see the role of the symbols and social memory of the society. These two role models represent the political culture of "resistance" by stressing the role of the heroic leader who resists against all odds. These two "ideal types" are self-sacrificing and powerful but always on the side of justice; simultaneously harsh but fair. They are expected to lead the "resistance" and strive to establish a just order. Erdoğan, along with the treatment of Gül over the presidential elections in May 2007, represents this deep-rooted political consciousness of the Anatolian periphery in terms of his facial expressions, temper and body language.[1]

In addition to these two role models, there is also the model of Gazi Mustafa Kemal Atatürk. Leadership in Turkish politics is very much measured in relation to the leadership model of Atatürk. Atatürk gave people a destiny, whereas the politicians after him only promised happiness, while never fully delivering it. He embarked on a great mission and carried it out throughout his life, whereas other politicians were crippled by compromises and various patron–client relations. In other words, there

---

[1] Ergun Yıldırım and Hayrettin Özler, "A Sociological representation of the Justice and Development Party (AKP): Is it a political design or a political becoming?," *Turkish Studies*, 8 (March 2007), 5–24; Nur Vergin, "Siyaset ile Sosyolojinin Buluşduğu Nokta," *Türkiye Günlüğü*, 76 (2004), 5–9.

is a deeply internalized notion of Atatürk as the "father" of the Turks, and all politicians are very much measured against his cult of personality. Atatürk led the war of independence and implemented a great project of civilizational transformation of the country by the suppression of collective memory and cutting off its Islamic and Ottoman roots. He tried to build a great wall in the minds of people in the name of progressive Westernization to block out Islamic and Arab influences. Although this was not fully successful, his project of Westernization brought a sense of unity by defining a common enemy – the Islamic and Ottoman past and its institutions, to be feared at all times. But instead of keeping the feared Ottoman and Islamic past out, it fenced the Turks in. Atatürk built a mental wall to protect the Turks from their past and history. In that process, he sought to build a newly invented glorious past quite distinct from the Islamic age. Like many other dictators, he created a *tabula rasa* which could not be challenged by scholars and politicians. The immediate Ottoman past was by definition inferior and a source of backwardness. The break with history, the illusion of a *tabula rasa*, had a youthful idealism. The goal to create a new society free from religion and forged by sheer human will was an attractive idea. During the period of Atatürk (1922–1938) and especially after his death the guardians of his revolution thought they were modernizing and civilizing society. In fact, they were acting at the will of Atatürk to create a new Turk. The guardians believed in the divine aspiration of Atatürk. The major unifying glue of the guardians was their fear of imagined enemies at home,[2] hence their main fear was freedom of thought and self-expression. He promised prosperity and security without politics and this had a mass appeal in the early days of the Republic, whose population had experienced genocidal massacres in the Balkans, the Caucasus and even Anatolia.[3] The two leaders whom I examine in this chapter are the representatives of this suppressed memory that came to haunt the civilizational project.

### Recep Tayyip Erdoğan

Any discussion of contemporary Turkey must start with Erdoğan, since all important policy decisions are made by him.[4] Although he is the head

---

[2] Fatih Rıfkı Atay in *Zetindağı* (Istanbul: Remzi Kitapevi, 1943) examines the sources of these historical fears among the first generation of the Republican elite.

[3] Justin McCarthy, *Death and Exile: The Ethnic Cleansing of Ottoman Muslims, 1812–1922* (Princeton: Darwin Press, 1996).

[4] Turan Yılmaz, *Tayyip: Kasımpasa'dan Siyasetin Ön Saflarına* (Istanbul: Ümit, 2001).

of the AKP and Turkey is a multi-party system, Erdoğan commands such a large percentage of the popular vote that he makes other leaders or MPs in his party irrelevant. Erdoğan places loyalty above all other values, and some of the leadership of the party forged a very close and loyal personal relationship due to the political suppression during the February 28 process. Erdoğan's main weakness is his failure to realize that the AKP is no longer a resistance movement against the state, but the ruling party of a proudly democratic Turkey. Because of these conflicting signals, the AKP gives the air of a work in progress, in the midst of transforming itself from an ex-Islamic movement into a liberal party. Given the domestic and international constraints of Turkey, this transformation is not easy. In order to remain relevant and effective in the future, Erdoğan must continue adapting to the new environment inside and outside Turkey. In recent years, due to corruption in the government and tensions with some autonomous state institutions, Erdoğan has had a tendency to direct most of his frustration outward rather than inward, as well as attacking those who raise questions about his performance and the accumulating dossiers of corruption. Some of Erdoğan's frustration is understandable. He came to power with far more constraints placed on his government than he had ever imagined. He has to share the power with other unelected state institutions to continue the EU process, although none of this justifies the continuing corruption of the AKP.

Although I will begin with Erdoğan's Islamism, I will focus more on his political transformation, whether growth or degeneration, for subtlety or the possibilities of redemption. Erdoğan's personality is shaped by four institutions of socialization. These character-building environments are: the Kasımpaşa neighborhood; the religio-conservative Imam Hatip school system; the ethno-religious (MTTB) student union; and the National Outlook Movement of Erbakan. This chapter will examine the imprint of these socio-cultural environments in the constitution of Erdoğan's character and worldview. Moreover, his experience as mayor and his period of imprisonment inform his current policies as prime minister. In sum, one sees a man with a split identity, torn between his Islamic identity and the politics that he is obliged to pursue in order to stay in government. He has to play a dual role: one for his traditional Islamic supporters, and one for his secularist domestic and international audience. He has to call the fighters in Iraq "martyrs" and "terrorists." He would call Israel a "terrorist state" but still visit it due to pressure from the US. He is a man with diverse loyalties and a torn identity. He embodies the identity of Turkey: inner and outer identities are never the same and always in conflict.

### The personality of Erdoğan

Few prime ministers have had a greater impact on Turkish political life than Tayyip Erdoğan. Assuming office after a long and tortuous legal struggle, as well as exclusion by the establishment, Erdoğan presided over the key legislative process of the fulfillment of the Copenhagen criteria and the revolutionary legal changes that dramatically altered the balance of power between the military and the civilian government, and which created a new economic structure with foreign investment, which would permanently reshape the Turkish political landscape. He further deepened Turkey's ties with the EU and also sought to introduce a new political language.[5]

Erdoğan has always defied simple characterization.[6] He grew up in one of the poorest parts of Istanbul, and entered politics as the Islamist youth leader of the Milli Selamet Partisi (MSP) of Erbakan. He has always retained a religious conviction that Islam is the source of the identity of the Turkish social system, and that the Turkish state is too ideological and needs to be transformed. He believed that the government should have no role in the economy and that the market is the cure for the country's major problems. He acquired a fortune and rose to political prominence by

---

[5] Erdoğan's criticism of a European Court of Human Rights decision backing the headscarf ban reflected his mindset. He said, "I think it is wrong that those who have no connection to this field [of religion] make such a decision ... without consulting Islamic scholars." The semi-official Anatolian News Agency reported the prime minister's speech thus: "I am amazed by the last decision of the ECHR. I will obey the decision of the ECHR since it is a legal decision but I find it wrong as far as rights and liberties are concerned. Why am I critical of the decision? Why and how could a person violate the freedom of education, religion and consciousness by covering her hair? The Court says 'Faith should never by-pass the law [*İnanç hiçbir zaman yasanın önüne geçemez*].' My daughter has no such claim. She has a headscarf because it is a religious requirement. We have to respect this. The Court has no right to speak on this issue. The religious *ulema* should be the one to speak on the headscarf. You need to ask the religious scholars of Judaism, Christianity and Islam to find out whether this is a religious requirement or not. If they say it is a religious requirement, you must respect that. If they say no, then it is a different issue and it would become a political and ideological matter. If it is a religious requirement, one has to respect it. I say this is a religious requirement. I have been educated in this field [Islam]. I think that those who have nothing to do with Islamic doctrine and without consulting Muslim clergy should make a decision on the headscarf is wrong." *Milliyet*, November 17, 2005. In reaction to the opposition party's criticism, Erdoğan's spokesman sought to clarify his speech by saying that "The Prime Minister has been misunderstood." In Denmark, when a journalist asked Erdoğan at a workshop on Turkey, "I would like to know whether your religious beliefs come first before your commitment to human rights?" Erdogan's response was, "My sacred beliefs come before freedom of speech. We expect other people to respect our prophet Muhammad as much as we respect their prophets Jesus and Moses." This debate was taking place in the context of the Danish newspaper *Jyllands Posten*'s cartoon of Muhammad which depicts an aggressive image. *Milliyet*, November 17, 2005.

[6] Avni Özgürel, "Erdoğan'in sınırları," *Radikal*, June 21, 2006.

establishing close ties with Erbakan, and cultivated close ties with powerful conservative Islamic orders such as the Nakshibendi and Nurcu. A man of enormous energy, Erdoğan strikes many contemporaries as aggressive, vain and power-hungry. Yet he is beset by deep insecurities and as a prime minister is encircled by a group of third-rate advisors, who are subservient to him.

Erdoğan has emulated Süleyman Demirel in making the leadership of the AKP the primary center of power in Ankara and imposing his will on the party. However, he has not been successful in all intra-party struggles over foreign and some domestic policy issues. Erdoğan has flattered, threatened and maneuvered in an attempt to bend others to his will. He knows how to appeal to principle, politics and self-interest. He has counted noses and knows the minute details of party politics. He has also told people on different parts of the political spectrum what they wanted to hear. He can be nationalist in one meeting and pro-Kurdish in another; pro-farmers and pro-industrialist at the same time. As a result, Erdoğan has developed a reputation as a slick maneuverer who lacks fixed principles. In the end, he is trying very hard to run the country the way he is running the AKP – by imposing his will and dealing favors to individuals and punishing his critics. Yet, as prime minister, he faces a country beset by deep social fissures and almost irreconcilable policy differences.

## Life

Erdoğan was born in 1954 in Potamya (Güneysu) in Rize on the Black Sea and his family moved to Kasımpaşa in Istanbul when he was thirteen years old. He is the youngest of five children. His father was a religious and harsh man, a disciplinarian who was at times abusive. He worked as the captain of a ferry. He relates that his father once punished him for swearing by hanging him by his arms from the ceiling. His authority and harsh discipline shaped Erdoğan's early childhood. He was active in sports and played professional soccer for sixteen years, juggling this with school and political activism. For years he kept his playing a secret from his father, who did not approve.

Kasımpaşa, where his personality was first shaped, is a cosmopolitan and economically lower-middle-class district of Istanbul with its own neighborhood identity. The Kasımpaşa neighborhood was a formative influence on the young Erdoğan. Kasımpaşa is a rough, even infamous, area known for gangs and criminal behavior, yet Erdoğan speaks of it romantically. In this, he sounds like some successful Americans who grew up in New York City's Harlem or Lower East Side: "I was shaped by that mud, not like the poor kids of today who are surrounded by asphalt."[7] The Kasımpaşa neighborhood has a strong conservative moral ethos with a deep sense of solidarity among its poor dwellers. Its inhabitants have always been envious of the rich and powerful.[8] He received his religious education in the neighborhood summer school at the mosque.[9]

He went to an Imam Hatip school to study Islamic sciences along with the regular curriculum. The Imam Hatip schools were established under Article 4 of the Unification of Education Law no. 430 with the goal of training personnel to carry out religious services. In 1973, the objectives of these schools expanded, under Article 32 of the National Education Law no. 1739, to offer programs within the secondary school system that also prepared students for higher education. They were no longer simply vocational schools producing religious functionaries.

The story of the moving of these schools into the mainstream education system indicates the process of compromise between the religious and secular actors in the political system. The schools are built by public donations and are staffed by the Ministry of Education. Even though they are under the Ministry of Education, they presuppose and legitimate particular forms of authority, community and history. What is important to remember here is not the subject matter which is taught in these schools, but how it is taught by conservative teachers. The schools provide a "hidden" curriculum that includes extracurricular activities, student interaction and the role of the disciplinarian teacher.[10] In the schools, the atmosphere of the courses matters more than their content, and is significant in the molding of character. Socialization in these schools involves the inculcation of Islamic norms and values and behavior patterns. The teachers in the schools always criticize alternative life-styles and attack the country's Westernization project. Due to their Islamic character, the schools promote and encourage the Islamic life-style as the only moral way of living.

Erdoğan's political identity, which is very much influenced by his religious upbringing, is grounded in this school system. Religious parents want to pass on traditional/Islamic values by sending their children to

---

[7] Debrah Sontag, *New York Times*, May 11, 2003.

[8] Muhammed Pamuk, *Yasaklı Umut: Recep Tayyip Erdoğan* (Istanbul: Birey, 2001), 3rd edn, p. 21.

[9] Erdoğan's interview in *Vatan*, September 28, 1994.

[10] According to Roger Dale, a hidden curriculum refers to the unwritten body of shared understanding that shapes the conduct of the classroom. Dale, "Implications of the Rediscovery of the Hidden Curriculum for the Sociology of Teaching," in Denis Gleeson (ed.), *Identity and Structure: Issues in the Sociology of Education* (Driffield: Nafferton Books, 1977).

these schools. Erdoğan gives his religious education much credit for all that he is today. He argues that "the period of Imam Hatip school means everything to me. I obtained a frame, orientation, and all for my life ... Imam Hatip school gave myself to me."[11] In the Imam Hatip school, he learned how to recite poetry, especially religious and nationalist verses. He was an average student in high school and was admitted to Marmara University in Istanbul to study economics and commerce, graduating with a BA in business management in 1981. He has never learned a foreign language. In school, Erdoğan played soccer and participated in a professional league at the age of twenty-one. The sport taught him the value of team-work and the constant move to take new positions. In politics he also stresses the role of team-work, as long as he is the coach.

A third influence was his membership of *Milli Türk Talebe Birliği* (MTTB; the National Turkish Student Union). Although MTTB emerged as a secularist national student association, promoting top-down Kemalist reform policies, the organization changed its outlook and leadership in the late 1960s under the leadership of Rasim Cinisli and İsmail Kahraman (the latter would become the Minister of Culture in the Erbakan government). Ethno-religious (Islamo-Turkish) nationalism became the main ideology, with its own version of Ottoman history as the building core of Turkishness. Due to leftist challenges and the power of socialist ideas, conservative intellectuals built up Islam as an antidote to this challenge, and one sees the ideologization of Islam in the hands of Necip Fazıl, Nurettin Topcu and Osman Turan. Necip Fazıl became the ideologue of the MTTB in the 1970s. The organization became anti-communist, anti-Kemalist and anti-elite, and this ethno-religious and conservative student organization was a center of intellectual debate and provided a network of social mobility.[12] Erdoğan joined the MTTB in 1969 and participated in male-only activities.[13] In this Islamic youth organization, he was an activist rather than an ideologue. He was there because of his conservative upbringing rather than out of ideological conviction. This association helped him to expand his circle of friends and he learned the power of ideological brotherhood. After graduation, Erdoğan started working for the Istanbul public transport authority. During this period, he was involved in politics and even named his son after his political hero, Necmettin Erbakan. When his director asked him to shave his beard, he refused to do so on the basis of his religious

---

[11] Pamuk, *Yasaklı*, p. 22.
[12] M. Cağatay Okutan, *Bozkurt'tan Kuron'a Milli Türk Talebe Birliği (MTTB) 1916–1980* (Istanbul: Bilgi, 2004), pp. 133–204.
[13] Erdoğan's interview in *Vatan*, September 28, 1994.

convictions. After the 1980 military coup of September 12 he gave up football and left to work in the private sector, before serving his mandatory military service in 1982 as a commissioned officer.

The fourth major formative influence on Erdoğan was his work in the MSP as the head of the party youth branch in Istanbul until the September 12 military coup, and then in Erbakan's Refah Party.[14] He became the president of the Beyoğlu branch of the RP in 1984 when he was thirty-one years old. In the 1989 local elections, he was the RP mayoral candidate in the cosmopolitan Beyoğlu district of Istanbul. His campaign very much focused on all sectors of life. He narrowly lost the election and this contributed to his popularity within both the RP and Turkey. Due to his openness and his diverse election strategies and unquestioned loyalty to the leader, Erbakan, he became the RP nominee for Istanbul mayor in the 1994 election. As a result of the 1994 municipal elections, the RP became the voice of the periphery, paying close attention to the needs of average Turk. He gained his political skills within the RP. Due to his socialization and prevailing life-style, ordinary Turks were easily able to identify themselves with Erdoğan.[15]

Millions voted for Erdoğan because they saw him as one of them, having had first-hand experience of poverty. Moreover, they supported and identified with him since he succeeded in moving out of Kasımpaşa and changed his own destiny. As one of them, the people call him "our Tayyip" (*bizim Tayyip*). He became mayor of Istanbul at the age of 40 in 1994. By then he was an established businessmen with a distribution company, Ülker, a food producer. He has always been involved in business and making money has been one of the main objectives of his life. He was relatively successful in solving the chronic problems of the Istanbul municipality, from the distribution of clean water to transportation. While mayor of Istanbul, he developed an eye for a higher position in politics. He regularly visited Anatolia and delivered highly emotional speeches. One of these speeches, which he delivered in Siirt, would interrupt his political life.

As mayor of Istanbul, Erdoğan sought to consolidate the Islamic identity by retrieving the Ottoman memory through a number of initiatives.

---

[14] Recep Tayyip Erdoğan, *Bu Sarkı Burada Bitmez* (Istanbul: Nesil, 2001), p. 47.
[15] Serdar Turgut, "AKP Beyaz Türk İktidarını Yıktı," *Habertürk*, June 3, 2004; Ertuğrul Özkök, "Beyaz Türklerin Tasfiyesi mi," *Hürriyet*, April 21, 2006. Are we experiencing a revolution of the first generation rural-origin "strangers" in the cities? Did this revolution start the exclusion of the "white Turks"? As a result of Atatürkist reforms and urbanization, Turkish society experienced a major social mobility movement, and many rural-origin students made it to colleges and now play an important role in the governance of the country. The new head of the Central Bank, Durmuş Yılmaz, who comes from a traditional family background, was appointed by the AKP government and this led to a major debate over the exclusion of the "white Turks" by the "black Turks."

He not only refurbished the ruins of Ottoman architectural sites, but also turned the anniversary of the 1453 conquest of Constantinople into a major cultural event. His model was not the Republican taste and practice, but he rather reserved his respect for the Ottomans. For him, the Ottomans were an alternative memory and worldview to the Republic.

By stressing his piety and using religious language in public debate, Erdoğan became the "liberator" and a "banner" of the rising Islamic movement. Beneath the public display of religiosity and commitment to democracy runs an undercurrent of a hunger for ownership and authoritarianism, to "rule" rather than "govern" the party and the country. For Erdoğan, Islam is a source of identity, a network of social mobility and a form of spiritual capital that can be invested in the political domain. Despite the widely held view that Erdoğan is religious, he has implemented hardly any policies informed by an Islamic conception of justice. The major weakness of his administration is the widespread corruption around him and in his government. He has never managed to achieve a reconciliation with the Kemalists or the leftists, let alone to heal the secular versus Islamic division. He does not have the passion for the serious deliberation required to build consensus.

Erdoğan does not surround himself with experts; he prefers to surround himself with people who will follow orders and do what he wants of them. In this respect, he is the opposite of Necmettin Erbakan, who prefers to delegate responsibility whenever possible. Erdoğan has an ability to gather loyal people around him. He does not like rules, institutions and bureaucracy. In a Turkish context, he comes from a system long overburdened with rules, institutions and ponderous bureaucracy, and thus his attitude makes a good deal of sense. In many ways, he resembles everyone's favorite crusty, down-to-earth uncle, who cuts through all of the socially acceptable nonsense and speaks the plain truth.

### Erdoğan the politician

Erdoğan's political enemies were counting on public apathy, while his supporters were hoping that he would become a *cause célèbre* if he were imprisoned. Indeed, the Islamic groups, especially the followers of the NOM, did not forget Erdoğan in jail. Erdoğan was victimized by an alliance between the military and the secularist business association – a selfish machine that only cares about its own interests. The masses saw him as a victim of a corrupt political system and mobilized to vote for him. The people hoped that the electoral system would put an end to constant corruption and political injustice. The rise of Erdoğan is also about popular faith in the electoral system and the sense that the people are powerful enough to change the political landscape. In response to his increasing popularity and the intransigence of the establishment, Erdoğan cast himself as a moderate and openly criticized the policies of his former boss, Erbakan. Like Özal, he focused on two issues: economic development and the expansion of democracy. Privatization was Erdoğan's magic solution to address Turkey's economic and healthcare problems; the Copenhagen criteria became accepted as the political map to expand democracy and human rights. He supported Turkey's application for full membership of the EU. As Erdoğan backed away from his Islamic roots, even turning against them, he became more popular among the center-right voters. However, this did not overcome the deep skepticism of the establishment over Erdoğan's "real" intention to dismantle the basic principles of the Republic. The military never believed in Erdoğan's self-declared conversion to moderation and issued a number of warnings.

Erdoğan is the most popular and charismatic politician in contemporary Turkey.[16] Since many Turks live in a condition of habitual illegality (either their home or shop is built on state property and they do not usually pay proper taxes) and are also in conflict with the establishment over its own moral code and life-style, they easily identify with Erdoğan as an emblem of their own condition. Erdoğan speaks very little about democracy but a great deal about liberty. His understanding of liberty is very much defined in negative terms – removing impediments and interferences. By wishing to reduce the power and scope of the state as a necessary condition for freedom, he stresses the role of philanthropy and voluntary efforts to address the "ills" of the market economy. Peace and order, for Erdoğan, are an outcome of economic growth and this, in turn, presupposes an entrepreneurship that encourages people to take risks and improve their situation. Erdoğan ignores the effects of religious forces, economic realities and communitarian pressures on freedom. But a free market does not always produce economic growth and improved living standards without some positive action on the part of the state.

Erdoğan is popular because he gives equal weight to the material (technological) and the moral aspects of human life. He not only provides a clear point of destination for Turkey's future orientation, EU membership, but he also wants people to come to terms with their moral side and deeper spiritual feelings. He is as much reformist as conservative by stressing the moral and material aspects of life. He does not want to create a new identity or a new society, but like most conservatives he wants to "redefine" existing relations and identities in the market environment.

---

[16] For the most detailed interview about Erdoğan's life, see Fatma Aksu's interview in *Meydan*, September 26–October 14, 1994.

Erdoğan's paramount goal is party unity, without which he believes nothing can be achieved. He is the bridge between younger and older Islamists, rich and poor, modernists and traditionalists. He has been a mayor and an imprisoned activist, a jailed hero and is now the prime minister of Turkey. He is an embodiment of both the old Ottoman and the new Republican Turkey. Erdoğan, who succeeded Erbakan, is different, but in one critical aspect remains the same. Like Erbakan, he is an authoritarian leader and not especially fascinated by ideas. While Erbakan attained national status by identifying either with national or international issues and staying away from local issues, Erdoğan is deeply steeped in local politics and micro-management. He inhabits a world where new and old, secular and religious, modern and traditional can cohabit in the same space and time. In the case of Erbakan, the myth led the reality; yet he chose inclusion over confrontation and was always in search of a compromise.

He has been dominant in both the domestic and the foreign policy of Turkey. In many ways, it seems that there is no AKP or related movement but rather the hegemony and dominance of Erdoğan. Democratization and the human rights revolution are taking place very much outside the party. For instance, Erdoğan has criticized his MPs for presenting amendments to bills drafted by bureaucrats.[17] He wants "his" MPs to *vote*, not to discuss any bills prepared by the bureaucracy. This seems to indicate that neither democratic norms of debate nor processes are internalized by Erdoğan. He seems to see his authority above all legal means and does not tolerate any form of internal debate or dissent. The *New York Times* reporter and author, Stephen Kinzer, concluded from his meetings with Erdoğan that he has a "burning sense of his own authority. He sees himself personally, not his party or government, as the force driving Turkey today."[18] He sees himself as a man of destiny with a God-ordained mission to lead the country and has no taste for criticism. Moreover, there is a growing gap between the cabinet members of the party and the ordinary members of parliament. There are a number of differences between Erbakan and Erdoğan. In short, where Erbakan urged caution and religious nationalism, Erdoğan presses for change and seeks the de-politicization of Islam through conservative democracy. Erdoğan's strategy is based on action and communication, manifested by his energy and body language. In this post-ideological world, Erdoğan, not unlike Tony Blair and Bill Clinton, prefers inventive and tailor-made solutions to

[17] Cevdet Akçalı, "Başbakan Erdoğan'ın bir itirafı, Türkiye'de kanunları kim yapıyor?," *Yeni Şafak*, July 27, 2004.
[18] Stephen Kinzer, "Will Turkey Make It?" *New York Review*, July 15, 2004, p. 42.

big ideas and visions. He is a hard-core pragmatist; he is not a leader who espouses ideas but he relies rather on feelings and mass emotion in order to project and magnify his power. For Erdoğan, party politics is about loyalty and obedience to the leader. He is not always a team player but rather a leader who wants to dictate and be obeyed.

Some claim that Erdoğan is puritanical, rigid, authoritarian and judgmental, and even that power and wealth are his prime motivations. It may be true that he does not tolerate dissent, avoids the company of his intellectual superiors and prefers to surround himself with sycophants. It is said that he is not introspective, and has an exaggerated need for approval. There is no doubt that he is able to attract followers who are intensely loyal to him. He prizes loyalty as a major virtue, and thus gives loyalty in return. He is a "man's man," comfortable in the company of men but not women. He is also a true performer, being at his best, his most charismatic, in front of a crowd. The crowd energizes and empowers him. Yet he needs a degree of distance, and closeness or intimacy threatens him. He also is humorless, at least about himself. He has sued a political cartoonist who portrayed him as a cat tangled up in a ball of yarn.

The reason for his inconsistency is that his personality structure is fragmented and poorly integrated. Using the language of computers and systems, his personality's internal connectivity is poor. He is a bundle of contradictions: charismatic but intellectually weak; popular but arrogant; in favor of market freedom but desiring religious community; populist yet authoritarian. Which is the true Erdoğan? Perhaps people tend to read their own political position back into his contradictory identities. His administrative philosophy is a mix of a liberal political economy that states that privatization is the solution to traditional Islamic social mores. He does not try to gather experts and bright people around him, with whom he could get to the heart of problems and come up with solutions. Instead, he is surrounded in politics by a small band of semi-intellectuals and half-baked businessmen, as well as loyal friends, who are munificent in their admiration of their leader.

### The political language of Erdoğan

Erdoğan's concept of politics lies behind his electoral success in November 2002 and in July 2007. As an activist of Islamic politics within the National Outlook Movement of Erbakan and then as mayor of Istanbul, Erdoğan has understood that politics is essentially local. At the local level, politics is not about big ideas or liberation ideologies but rather about rendering social services and providing what matters most to the population. Politics, for Erdoğan, is about serving and improving one's everyday life and a pragmatic instrument to articulate popular claims. On the basis of his experience in Istanbul, Erdoğan became aware that the main source of the AKP's legitimacy was based on meeting the needs of people and providing "justice to all." This makes him the most pragmatic leader in Turkish history but at the same time the least ideologically committed. The AKP's politics depends on local issues and the needs of Turkey. It is local-based politics on a national scale.

The meaning of nationalism is changing, shifting away from love of Atatürkism and the state, to love of the homeland. Erdoğan has no special sense of nationalism or of being a Turk. His primary identity is Islam, and he sees the world from a religious perspective. For instance, in his much criticized speech in Siirt he argued against divisions amongst Turkish citizens based on ethnicity and region, emphasizing instead the existence of ties that bond all together in Turkey. He went on to say: "When I was at the university, people used to say: 'You are from Rize and are a Laz.'" He repeated this when he asked his father about his identity, and his father responded that he too had asked his own father the same question, who had said: "When it is time to die, God will only ask us: 'Who is your God? Who is your Prophet? And what is your religion?' He will not ask: 'What is your ethnicity?' Thus, whenever someone inquires about your identity, you should simply reply: 'Thank God [*Elhamdulillah*] I am a Muslim!' That is enough."

For Erdoğan therefore the ultimate identity of an individual is Islam. He has very little cognitive understanding of the ideas of nation or nationalism. This does not mean that he is not patriotic, but it does signal that his worldview is shaped by his religious upbringing, which supersedes his ethnic or regional origins. In addition to this "religious bond" that keeps everyone in Turkey together, in the same speech he mentioned "citizenship" as the second bond. Politics – serving the people – is now confined to upholding the rule of law and the value systems shared by society. Breaking with religio-nationalist views, the AKP wants to distance itself from ethnic or state-centered Turkish nationalism by stressing multi-culturalism and recognizing the cultural rights of the Kurds and giving up the rigid nationalist position on Cyprus. In its party program, the AKP commits itself to "recognizing cultural differences within the principle of a democratic state."[19]

During his official visit to Moscow, Erdoğan encountered a Kurdish worker named Zulfikar Boran who was working there on the construction site of the Turkish Business Center. This was the first time that Erdoğan had aired his views on the Kurdish problem in public. Erdoğan's answers

---

[19] AKP Programme, 2:8.

reflect his position and mode of thinking on the Kurdish issue. His world-view on nationalism and the role of Islamic identity becomes clear.[20]

BORAN:     You need to solve the Kurdish problem.
ERDOĞAN:   I am married from Siirt.
BORAN:     Right. Kurds are one of the historic peoples of the world.
ERDOĞAN:   I know those things. I am married from Siirt, being able to get married from Siirt.
BORAN:     Right. I am not married and I want to get married as well. Kurds have a history going back ten thousand years.
ERDOĞAN:   How many years?
BORAN:     In other words, a known history that we are aware of ten thousand years. We have lived together with the Turks for the last thousand years.
ERDOĞAN:   How did you learn that ten thousand years of history?
BORAN:     Indeed, if you research you could learn. We lived together with Turks for the last thousand years. We want this problem to be solved; we do not want these sufferings to continue.
ERDOĞAN:   You should not believe that there is a problem; you should believe that there is no problem. There would be a problem only if you think that there is a problem. When you think there is no problem, the problem will disappear. We say that there is no such problem for us.
BORAN:     You came to power as a single-party government, but you could also lose it. You should not look at the problem this way. I am a working man but when I look at politics ... Ecevit and many others came to power and lost it. When you overlook the problems ...
ERDOĞAN:   I do not accept such a problem. I deny the existence of such a problem. Look! I am married from Siirt, I am a happy man, that's it. You should approach the problem from this perspective. As long as you approach the issue from this perspective, there won't be any problem.
BORAN:     Mister Prime Minister I know this by experience. I have Turkish friends. We live and work together like brothers indeed.
ERDOĞAN:   We have to say we are all from Turkey [*Turkiyeliyiz*].
BORAN:     Indeed. For Turkey we could sacrifice our life.
ERDOĞAN:   Yes. This is correct. Then you would say "I am a Kurd"; a Turk would say "I am a Turk ..."
BORAN:     It does not make any difference anyway.
ERDOĞAN:   However, you would say we are all brothers.

After this exchange, the Prime Minister hugged Boran and told him, "I love you for the sake of Allah."

This conversation helps us to decipher Erdoğan's lack of understanding of nationalism and ethnicity as independent motivating factors of political

---

[20] Mehmet Özgül, "Erdoğan ile Kurt İscisi Boran'ın tartismasi," *Özgür Politika*, December 27, 2002. http://www.ozgurpolitika.org/2002/12/27/hab18b.html

action. From Erdoğan's perspective, a nation is a religious community and the people of Turkey constitute a nation by sharing Islam. This perspective not only prevents Erdoğan from developing a working solution to the Kurdish question but also shows why his lack of Turkish nationalism has become a mobilizing reason for many Turkish nationalists to think that the AKP government is seeking to de-Turkify the nation.

For the AKP, secularism is defined as the freedom of religion from state intervention and the protection of religious rights. Secularism, for Erdoğan, is necessary for democracy but it should not define the boundaries of democracy.[21] Erdoğan's understanding of secularism is very similar to Süleyman Demirel's, who argued that secularism should not be interpreted as hostility to religion: the state could be secular, but not individuals. Erdoğan argues:

Before anything else, I'm a Muslim. As a Muslim, I try to comply with the requirements of my religion. I have a responsibility to God, who created me, and I try to fulfill that responsibility. But now I try very much to keep this away from my political life, to keep it private. [Poker-faced, he exhaled.] A political party cannot have a religion. Only individuals can. Otherwise, you'd be exploiting religion, and religion is so supreme that it cannot be exploited or be taken advantage of.[22]

Yet, the AKP has ignored the destructive potential of the market. Market forces in Turkey need some adjusting and tinkering but the AKP possesses neither the vision nor the policies to control many of the negative impacts of the market on society. The morality of the AKP derives from its pragmatism and is garbed with Islam and shaped by the discourse of human rights. The AKP seeks to redefine Atatürkism by redefining it within the framework of democracy.[23] Erdoğan's speech on November 10, 2004, at the Atatürk Language and History Higher Council seeks to deconstruct Atatürkism from its rigidity by reinterpreting the principles of Atatürkism not as fixed and universal truths but rather as conjectural precepts to modernize society.[24]

As you all know, Atatürk did not deliver or promise an ideology; neither had he imposed any ideology on people. Rationality is the basis of his worldview. His goal was to create a modern civilization through reason, rationality and realities of daily life. We know the fact that Mustafa Kemal Atatürk never cared or took rigid and fixed ideas seriously. Atatürk shared a worldview that was open to development

---

[21] Erdoğan, "Atatürk'ün dünya görüşünün temeli akılcılıktır," *Milliyet*, November 10, 2004, http://www.milliyet.com.tr/2004/11/10/son/sonsiy06.html.

[22] Deborah Sontag, "The Erdogan Experiment," *New York Times*, May 11, 2003.

[23] Erdoğan's speech, *Milliyet*, November 10, 2004.

[24] Erdoğan, "Atatürk'ün dünya görüşünün temeli akılcılıktır," *Milliyet*, November 10, 2004, http://www.milliyet.com.tr/2004/11/10/son/sonsiy06.html

and advancement and he trusted the guide of reason in the process of development. ...The founding principles of the Republic of Turkey are republicanism, national sovereignty, nation-state, and secularism.

Erdoğan has been trying hard to disavow the hardline Islamic views of his past and trying to recast himself as a pro-European conservative. The AKP's conception of secularism is very similar to that of Demirel or Ali Fuat Basgil, a prominent legal scholar, who written one of the most comprehensive studies on secularism.

In conclusion, Erdoğan is not a thinker but rather a pragmatic politician. This lack of introspectiveness may be responsible for his apparent lack of general vision. It is more common than most of us would like to admit that thoughtful people should hold contradictory views simultaneously. It takes tolerance of ambiguity to accept this. Rather than repress his conflicts completely, he may well disassociate them into these distinct sides of his personality, so that they are all given voice, but not simultaneously. He is a self-made man with a gift for re-manufacturing himself when the need arises. He is in constant evolution and change; he may well be unaware, at times, of what his views really are. He is always in tune with the popular will to figure out what his views ought to be.

One of the major weaknesses but perhaps also the strength of the AKP is that it has no clearly articulated party identity. The 2007 crisis and the new list of the AKP deputies, which is more heterogeneous than the previous group, delayed the development of a new AKP corporate identity. Now the only glue that keeps the party together and provides its identity is Erdoğan. It is Erdoğan who could also develop a face-to-face, intimate and realistic dialogue between Turkey and Western Europe as well as the US. Moreover, he is the real leader of the AKP and dictates the deputies within the party. Yet, Erdoğan feels himself under siege from unelected officials, the judiciary and the media, despite his overwhelming power in parliament. He knows that the expectations of his core supporters are not fulfilled. He is torn between a sense of siege and frustration that he might lose the support of his base if he does not fulfill its demands. The supporters of the AKP are expecting Erdoğan's government to address major economic and political problems. As far as the economy is concerned, the biggest problem is unemployment and the worsening distribution of income. Politically, the supporters of the AKP demand that the government expand religious liberties so that the large numbers of conservative AKP supporters can practice their faith. In more concrete terms, they expect a favorable solution to the problem of the headscarf and the Imam Hatip schools in the second term. Erdoğan is forced to balance liberalism and the founding principles of the Republic. On April 25, 2006, he outlined his vision to the AKP party group:

The AK Party government has undertaken very important projects and taken very important decisions which in the future will be seen as a silent revolution. But the most important of them was to protect both the *republican principles* and *democracy* together through maintaining the necessary conditions for the economic and spiritual development of the people and through removing the political, economic and social obstacles that restrict basic rights and freedoms, which are stipulated as the task and purpose of the state in our Constitution, in ways that are not compatible with the social state, the rule of law and principles of fairness.[25]

One of the major changes in the Republican grammar of politics is to protect republican principles of secularism and nationalism through the democratic process. Erdoğan argues that the AKP is "aware that Republican principles cannot be protected through limiting democracy but through protecting Republican principles and democracy together."[26]

## Abdullah Gül: the second man

*Öz yurdunda garipsin, öz vatanında parya!*
You are a stranger in your own country, a pariah in your homeland! (Necip Fazıl)

In order to understand Abdullah Gül, a man of action, one has to know the intellectual roots of his cognitive map (*zihniyet*) that lead his actions in politics. While the youthful Gül's public philosophy about the role of state, nation, religion, secularism and the West originally derived from the writings of Necip Fazıl Kısakürek, a leading anti-leftist and Islamist ideologue, the mature Gül, as a politician, is very pragmatic and his actions are more shaped by the prevailing economic and political forces, especially the military interventions in 1997 and also in 2007 against his nomination as president.

He was the first to rebel against the Erbakan-dominated leadership of the Fazilet Party and the first prime minister of the AKP government, and the eleventh president of the Republic of Turkey, a position which used to guard the Kemalist doctrine in Turkey. His nomination to the presidency by Erdoğan in April 2007 caused a major uproar and even an e-memorandum by the Turkish military. Why did he cause such uproar? Was he a real threat to the secularism of the country? The resistance to his nomination by the universities, judiciary, secular sector of civil society and military created a constitutional crisis and led to the early elections in July 2007.

---

[25] Erdoğan speech, *The New Anatolian*, April 26, 2006.
[26] Erdoğan speech, *The New Anatolian*, April 26, 2006.

What did his nomination represent for the Islamic supporters of the AKP? Due to his nomination to the presidency, Gül has been closely scrutinized by the media and his opponents. He unfortunately preferred the easy way out by denying almost all his controversial statements, even some defensible ones. This, in turn, undermined public confidence in him and his new pro-EU position. For instance, on March 8, 1995, Abdullah Gül, then a member of parliament, presented his views about Turkish membership of the EU. He says:

In Turkey's relations with the EU, everything is one-sided. Whenever European interests are concerned, Turkey yields and makes all kinds of concessions. In short, this policy of surrender is the outcome of a rigid policy of becoming a member of the EU regardless of the cost to Turkish national interests. As long as the government continues with this mode of thinking, Turkey will never be allowed to enter into the house of the European rich but will rather be asked to stay in the dog house [*bahcedeki kulube*] in the garden. Turkey's entry into the EU is an imaginary tale. Turkey will never be allowed to join the EU and Turkey cannot become a member because the EU is a union of Christians.[27]

Gül later as Foreign minister had a different language and vision from the previous statement. He supported Turkey's full integration into the EU. His main slogan was "How can we catch up with Europe and preserve our cultural values and identity?" Although many people read the discrepancy in these statements as "evidence" of *takiyye*, it would be more productive to see it as a reflection of Gül's transformation. Unlike Erdoğan, he is an educated and fairly learned man, with a good command of English. He is sincere, and his understanding of the nature of the state is different from Erdoğan's. For Gül, the Turkish state is the manifestation of a collective consciousness and the ultimate source of security. Unlike Erdoğan, he has a broad civilizational outlook.

Gül was born on October 29, 1950 in Kayseri, attended high school in this city and went to Istanbul University to study economics. He received his PhD from there, spent two years in London and Exeter, and became an assistant professor at Sakarya University. His two years in London were transformative: he culturally became more conscious and also appreciated the modernity. This was his period of consciousness formation as a result of constant comparisons between Turkey and Britain. He gave up his academic position in 1981 to become an advisor at the Islamic Development Bank, where he worked until 1991. His years in Jeddah as an advisor at the Islamic Development Bank sharpened his consciousness. At the Bank, he became deeply aware of the problems in the Muslim

---

[27] Emin Cölaşan, "Bay Gül'ün Dünü ve Bugünü," *Hürriyet*, November 23, 2006.

world, and was always uneasy about the prevailing socio-political conditions. He gave up his position to become a member of parliament for the province of Kayseri in the 1991 election. Erbakan made Gül the Deputy Chairman of International Affairs of the Refah Party. He was the window of his party to the outside world. He participated in many conferences and represented Turkey on different platforms. In the 1995 election, he was re-elected and became the Minister of State in the 54th government, headed by Erbakan. He was also spokesman of the government. He was re-elected in 1999 from the Fazilet Party and then in 2002 as an MP of the AKP. Gül's political life also summarizes the evolution of the new actors of transformation in Anatolia.

### Gül's intellectual hero: Necip Fazıl Kısakürek

Gül's father Ahmet Hamdi first worked as preacher in the mosque of Gülük, a small town. After his military service, he worked for the Air Defense Factory and retired from there. Gül has a brother and a sister. His father was also in politics and became a candidate for the parliament in the *Milli Selamet Partisi* (MSP) of Erbakan in 1973, but was not elected. Gül's first direct political experience was when he was involved in the election campaign of Recai Kutan in Kayseri in 1974.

His family background is religious and conservative. When he was in high school, Gül read the works of Necip Fazıl Kısakürek, Nurettin Topcu and Sezai Karakoç, the most important Islamic (Turkish) intellectuals of that period. According to Gül, "The most important intellectual who had a major impact on my worldview was Necip Fazıl Kısakürek. He was not only an intellectual but also an activist and fighter against all forms of oppression."[28] Gül's ideals are shaped by his ideological connection with the Greater Eastern Movement (*Büyük Doğu Hareketi*) of Kısakürek, who sought to synthesize Islamism, Turkish nationalism and conservatism.[29]

In order to understand Gül's ideals, which constitute his self-identity, one has to examine the towering impact of Kısakürek, who due to his vulgar criticism of the Westernization project was closely allied with Islamism. Yet, by stressing Turkish nationalism and the Ottoman legacy, Kısakürek played an important role in the nationalization of Islam. Being concurrently an Islamist and a Turkish nationalist, Kısakürek was also considered the "number one enemy of the leftist movement" in Turkey. Thus, he was the intellectual engineer to formulate an anti-communist Islamic–nationalist movement, which is closely allied with the Islamic and

[28] Interview with Abdullah Gül, August 8, 2005 (Ankara).
[29] Interview with Abdullah Gül, August 8, 2005 (Ankara).

nationalist parties. He became the poster-boy in the 1950s and 60s against Westernization, the hegemony of the CHP and the leftist movement. His political rhetoric was infused with religious and Ottoman symbols and references. He articulated his ideas in his periodical *Büyük Doğu* (1943–1975) with the purpose of creating a new political philosophy or a public theology that was steeped in Islam and Ottoman history to retrieve and construct a new memory and mission for the 'nation'-state. At the core of Kısakürek's writings was the idea that the nation must understand its historical experience and national mission in Islamic terms. Gül and many young Islamists easily internalized the ideas of Kısakürek, since they had grown up in conservative and pious Muslim families. For them, Kısakürek's philosophy was the most important cognitive map with a greater meaning than mere biological existence. Kısakürek's ideas allowed the youth of the 1970s to imbue their nation with a transcendent meaning. A new right-wing political movement was thus created around the writings of Kısakürek. One of the reasons that Kısakürek's ideas turned into action with a mass following had to do with the constellation of ideas and practices that provided a sense of belonging together as Muslim Turks, and of being different from internal (leftist and Kemalist) and external (Western and Russian) enemies.

After the 1960 military coup, Turkey experienced a wave of leftist movements and leftist intellectual debate. As a reaction to this "un-Godly" leftist ideology, one of the well-organized anti-leftist organizations was the MTTB, the student movement already mentioned, which was closely aligned with Kısakürek. Kısakürek disseminated his ideas through the student networks of the MTTP in Anatolia. It was Gül, a young MTTB member, who organized Kısakürek's visits to Kayseri to give a number of lectures. In addition, Gül led the subscription campaign for *Büyük Doğu* in Kayseri and got many new people involved in the movement. Gül's high school and college years were very much punctuated by Kısakürek's writings. Kısakürek's ideology had three pillars. (1) Turkish-Muslim society had lost its "ties" with the past by losing its "language," morality and historical memory as a result of Westernization policies. (2) The Kemalist reforms deliberately sought to "destroy" the inner spiritual power of the Turkish nation. (3) This project of de-Islamization could be reversed with the rise of new "ruling elite" (*yönetici sınıf*) who shared a Turkish-Islamic cognitive map (*zihniyet*) of revival. In other words, by giving the youth a mission to restore memory and an Islamo-Turkish identity, Kısakürek mixed nationalism with Islam and offered an emotional attachment to political activity.

In the 1960s, Kısakürek became the leading anti-leftist polemicist. In the early 1970s, Kısakürek closely allied himself with the National

Outlook Movement of Erbakan, but withdrew his support when Erbakan formed a coalition government with the center-left CHP of Bülent Ecevit. He then flirted with the MHP of Alpaslan Türkeş, who led the nationalist movement. Due to his radical criticism of the Kemalist status quo, Kısakürek spent most of his time either in the courts or under police questioning and in jail. He was the "oppressed one" (*mazlum*) of Anatolia and his struggle had a major impact in conservative Anatolian cities such as Kayseri. Moreover, Kısakürek wrote a number of books of popular history to create an alternative memory to the Kemalist education system's history. He helped to create a new generation of semi-historians who invented a new history to criticize the Westernization project. Moreover, his conspiracy theories played an important role in the creation of a "hidden history" and he tried to decipher the "intentions" of the enemies of Islam, the Ottoman Empire and the Republic of Turkey to demonstrate injustices perpetrated against the Turkish-Muslim nation. In these books, he developed a Turkish-Muslim self that is always anti-communist, nationalistic and self-sacrificing. For Kısakürek, the task of the Turkish nation is to defend Islam and become its "sword" against the West. Thus, Kısakürek was also very anti-Salafi and critical of Arab understandings of Islam. He attacked Seyyid Qutb and Mawdudi in his writings. Gül, as one of his close followers, shared some, if not all, of the ideas of Kısakürek. After graduating from high school, he moved to Istanbul and entered the University of Istanbul where he developed deeper ties with the *Büyük Doğu* movement and joined the MTTB.[30] Gül never became the creator of ideas or the producer of new policies but rather remained a consumer of ideas and policies. This very much reflects his cautious and conservative character. He was a nationalist, an Islamist and yet partially pro-European. In short, he always remained a man with "part-time identities and ideologies," with the goal of maintaining his power through domestic and international connections with the minimum risk. The fear of making mistakes molded his personality as one loath to take any major initiatives. During his period as prime minister and Foreign minister, Gül hardly initiated a policy or came up with new ideas.

While at Istanbul University during the heyday of ideological polarization, Gül was an active member of the MTTB. One of their main activities was to participate in commemorating the Dardanelles War. They would do this every year by visiting the cemeteries in the Dardanelles. People who are shaped by a Turkish-Islamic worldview tend to stress the Dardanelles War more than the War of Independence. In Istanbul, Gül

---

[30] M. Çağatay Okutan, *Bozkut'tan Kuran'a Milli Türk Talebe Birliği (MTTB) 1916–1980* (Istanbul: Bilgi Universitesi Yayınları, 2004), p. 205.

read the writings of Erol Güngör, Idris Küçükömer and Cemil Meric in order to familiarize himself with the discourse of the Islamic and Turkish right. As a graduate assistant at Istanbul University, he worked under Nevzat Yalcıntaş and Sebahattin Zaimgil, two leading Islamo-Turkish opinion makers. While he was working on his dissertation, Gül went to London from 1976 to 1978 to study languages with a generous scholarship from a conservative foundation (the National Culture Foundation). He wrote his dissertation on "The Development of Economic Relations Between Turkey and Muslim Countries." His advisor was Nevzat Yalçıntaş, the father of the Turkish-Islamic Synthesis, an ideological cocktail to mold the youth and population around the military coup of 1980. A close examination of his PhD thesis reveals his dry mode of writing and distance from any conceptual thinking.

Being a close follower of Kısakürek, Gül regards the Kemalist reforms as a problem for rather than a solution of Turkey's most important problems, such as the role of religion in the public sphere and the Kurdish question. He is more a pan-Islamist than an ethnic Turkish nationalist, and regards Islam as the most important glue of national existence. Thus, he considers Islam and the Ottoman legacy as the shared identity of the people of Turkey, and regards the Kurdish problem as a reaction to state-invented Turkish nationalism. From his perspective, if the Turkish state gives up the policy of Turkish nationalism and adopts a Muslim-first identity policy, the Kurdish problem will be solved. Gül argues:

I was born in Kayseri and my friend is born in Van. These are outside our own will. We need to approach the Kurdish problem from the perspective of shared faith ... When we fought in different fields of Trablusgarp [Libya] or in Dardanelles, no one asked our ethnicity. No one even thought to think in terms of ethnicity since it was not part of Islamic morality. We came from this historical background ... The Republic of Turkey with its authoritarian single party system purposed policies that not only destroyed the Kurdish-origin citizens but also Turks as well ... The state still writes on the Cukurca Mountain that "Happy is the one who declares himself to be a Turk." Still these types of slogans are written at the center of Diyarbakir. Unfortunately, Turkish nationalism revealed itself as racist fanaticism ...The source of discrimination in Turkey has never been ethnicity but rather being Muslim.[31]

Gül concludes that "the common glue of this country has been Islamic brotherhood and the solution to the problem is also this shared faith." When Gül was asked about this speech on a national television program by Fikret Bila, a columnist of *Milliyet*, he vehemently denied saying these things. However, since it was published after the interview, his denial

---

[31] Mehmet Metiner, *Yemyesil Seriat Bembeyaz Demokrasi* (Istanbul: Doğan Kitap, 2004), pp. 481–482.

made his situation worse. He might have done better if he had defended his own words since his statement is sociologically correct. However, Gül has preferred an easy way out by denying his past.[32] The last statement of Gül about the state's writing on the walls and mountains that "happy is the one who declares himself to be a Turk" raised a sharp reaction in the military. In a military e-memorandum, just after Gül's nomination, it said "Those who have a problem with the sayings of Atatürk will remain the enemy of the nation."

### Gül as divider of the *Fazilet Partisi* (Virtue Party) (FP)

With the neo-liberal economic policies of Özal, a number of Anatolian cities became experimental sites of Muslim modernity, which regarded Islam and modernity as mutually inclusive and used economic forces to create a thicker civil society that was rooted in a new synthesis between interests and identity. Kayseri, a center of manufacturing that ranges from cables to textile to furniture, with a population of one million, benefited a great deal from Özal's economic policies, and has the first advanced entrepreneurial class that wanted to transform the political landscape of the country. This new entrepreneurial class, which also played a critical role in the split of the *Fazilet Partisi* (FP) of Recai Kutan, has become the new agent of Turkey's transformation and the basis of the AKP's support. Gül has represented Kayseri in parliament since 1991 and was fully aware of this deep transformation in Anatolia, and allied himself with this new economic elite. This new class did not want to have a confrontation with the state, nor did it support the anti-EU policies of the RP and FP. They wanted growth-oriented economic policies, with the supportive role of the state, lower tariffs and open borders for trade, and became supporters of Turkey's EU vocation for a number of instrumental reasons. This class wanted to infiltrate rather than overthrow the political system by support-ing the RP and FP. When the Muslim bourgeoisie came to the conclusion that the FP was an obstacle to their vision of a new Turkey, they supported the splitting of the FP.

Gül played a central role in the division and the transformation of the Islamic movement by becoming the leader of the new bourgeoisie in Anatolia. He represented a break with the National Outlook Movement by supporting the EU and closer ties with the US in the Middle East with the support of MÜSİAD. The new bourgeoisie was fully aware that their economic well-being requires better relations with the state and a

---

[32] Emin Cölaşan, "Inkar size yakışır mı Abdullah bey," *Hürriyet*, May 3, 2007.

pro-EU policy. According to Mehmet Bekaroğlu, the split within the FP became clear at the TÜSİAD convention in 2000. Bekaroğlu argues that:

The MÜSİAD convention in 2000 became the display of the muscles of the "reformers" [*yenilikçiler*] who concentrated around Gül. Even though Recai Kutan, the leader of *Fazilet*, asked to address the convention before he had to go to another engagement, he was denied. He had to leave. The former and present leadership of MÜSİAD sharply criticized Erbakan and the administration of *Fazilet Partisi*. Those who addressed the convention were Tayyip Erdoğan and Abdullah Gül, who presented their vision and policies.[33]

Indeed, the Tenth Convention of MÜSİAD planted the seeds of the split of the FP by criticizing the policies of the FP and its "over-worn" leadership. The former and new leaders of TÜSİAD crafted a careful argument against the policies of the FP and the need for a new leadership and policies that are not confrontational with the state. At the convention, Gül's group was mobilized against Recai Kutan. The convention became a testing ground for the power struggle over the leadership of the FP.[34] Erdoğan sharply attacked the party leadership. This convention, in hindsight, was a turning point in the division of the Islamic movement in Turkey. The Anatolian bourgeoisie openly allied itself with Gül and his colleagues against the old establishment of Erbakan.

Gül very much represented the goals of the Anatolian Muslims. He always searched for an external legitimacy in order to protect new actors against what he considered to be oppressive state policies. He fully agreed with the IMF policies of Kemal Derviş and implemented them religiously: the same policies, many argue, which resulted in the destruction of the farmers and the rural sector of the population. The economic policies of Derviş aimed to remove agricultural subsidies and support a new form of the state outside "production of economic activity." Gül was the key architect in the economic policies of the government. Without any rural roots and coming from one of the key trade centers (Kayseri), he stressed the role of finance in the economy more than growth. For Gül, the stock market and monetary and fiscal policies are more important than production or employment. His economic policies helped to create a fragmented population in cities where people live together by living apart. This fragmented nature of Turkish cities may well become a hotbed of extreme nationalism in the future. Gül became more and more critical of state subsidies in the rural areas and never developed a working relationship with rural Turkey.

---

[33] Mehmet Bekaroğlu, *"Adil Düzen"den "Dünya gercekleri"ne: Siyasetin Sonu* (Ankara: Elips, 2007), p. 223.
[34] *Hürriyet*, April 9, 2000.

## Conclusion

The new Turkey is evolving out of contradictions between what Turkey was and what Turkey wants to become. This evolving sense of identity is reflected in the policies of the Erdoğan–Gül government. The Turkey that is led and shaped by the AKP leadership is a fusion of the Ottoman legacy, social responsibility and the Kemalist desire to become European. Both Erdoğan and Gül believe in Turkey's Western "calling." According to them, Turkey should join the EU, as they see this Western orientation as self-strengthening, and not a cultural imitation. They both represent the syncretic character of the country; they are at home neither in present Turkey, nor in the Ottoman past. They see the future as an opportunity to recreate a new Turkey that is both Muslim and European.

# 5    Modes of secularism

Modern Turkish history could be viewed as a "conflict between two Turkeys," that is, a division between secularists and Islamic groups.[1] In the case of Turkey, secularism, commonly known as *laiklik*, is the identity of "progressive" people, the state project of modernization, a model of creating an enlightened Islam, and also a strategy of criminalizing religious opposition. It is therefore important to study secularism and Islamism as mutually constitutive and interactive concepts, since secularism is a way of redefining the meaning and the role of religion in society. Secularism thus becomes a "political settlement" of controlling and reconstituting Islam in accordance with the needs of the state and the political elites who have historically controlled the Turkish state. However, the economic and political opportunity spaces that have greatly expanded in recent decades have caused the constitutionally protected settlement to undergo renewal, revision and even rejection. Thus, the emergence of a new Turkey depends on the nature of this new settlement between religion and politics that must be negotiated through democratic processes. In this chapter, I examine the key debate over the realignment of the boundary between religion and politics by focusing on the AKP's understanding of secularism within the framework of the Kemalist legacy and changed market conditions. First I examine the contemporary theoretical debate by focusing on the analytical and causal connections between secularism, democracy and Islam. The second part of this

---

[1] For secularization, see Steve Bruce, *God is Dead: Secularization in the West* (Oxford: Blackwell, 2002); Steve Bruce (ed.), *Religion and Modernization: Sociologists and Historians Debate the Secularization Thesis* (New York: Oxford University Press, 1992); David Martin, *A General Theory of Secularization* (Oxford: Basil Blackwell, 1978). For desecularism, see Rajeev Bhargava (ed.), *Secularism and its Critics* (New Delhi: Oxford University Press, 1998); Nikki Keddie, "Secularism and its Discontents," *Daedalus*, 132 (Summer 2003), 14–30. See also Pippa Norris and Ronald Inglehart, *Sacred and Secular: Religion and Politics Worldwide* (Cambridge: Cambridge University Press, 2005); Jose Casanova, *Public Religions in the Modern World* (Chicago: University of Chicago Press, 1994), pp. 11–39; Wolfhart Pannenberg, "How to Think About Secularism," *First Things*, 64 (June/July 1996), 27–32.

144

chapter analyzes the sources of the branching of Kemalist secularism into three competing forms of secularism as a result of shifting state-society relations. The last section analyzes the AKP's version of secularism in terms of crucial religious education and headscarf issues.

## Patterns of secularism

Political development literature, which is based almost exclusively on European experiences, assumed the removal of religion from politics and societal life through the process of secularization as part of an inevitable and linear historical progression that is seen as being positive and progressive.[2] It is important to study secularization in a wider context, despite its Western origins, since the term is now entrenched in the study of contemporary Islamic movements. Many followers of Islamic movements, or those who consider themselves as "conscious" Muslims, equate secularization with Westernization, and for that reason particularly reject secularism as a form of internal colonization and the loss of religion.[3] A more useful way of studying the relationship between religion and politics is not to examine secularization as an inevitable end product of modernity, but rather as a non-linear and essentially unfixed process with ebbs and flows. In short, secularization and Islamization are not mutually exclusive processes and can work together; changes can take place in both directions. For instance, in the case of Turkey, there are various ways in which Islamic ideas and practices are infused into state institutions and policies as a result of expanding and shrinking opportunity spaces in the market and the public sphere.

In the case of the West, there are two major versions of secularism: the Anglo-American and the French Republican interpretations.[4] T. Jeremy Gunn's comparison between French and Anglo-American secularism captures this predicament:

Unlike France, where "*laïcité*" might have the connotation of the state protecting itself from the excesses of religion, the term "religious freedom" in the United States would be more likely to have the connotation of religion being protected

---

[2] Owen Chadwick, *The Secularization of the European Mind in the 19th Century* (Cambridge: Cambridge University Press, 1975).

[3] Ali Bulaç, *Çağdaş Kavramlar ve Düzenler* (Istanbul: Iz Yayıncılık, 1998).

[4] Charles Taylor, "Modes of Secularism," in Rajeev Bhargava (ed.), *Secularism and its Critics* (Delhi: Oxford University Press, 1998); Wilfred M. McClay, "Two Concepts of Secularism," *Wilson Quarterly*, 24 (Summer 2000), 63–64; Ahmet T. Kuru, "Reinterpretation of Secularism in Turkey: The Case of the Justice and Development Party," in M. Hakan Yavuz (ed.), *The Emergence of a New Turkey: Democracy and the AK Parti* (Salt Lake City: University of Utah Press, 2006), pp. 136–159.

from the excesses of the state. Thus Americans are more likely to be predisposed to have suspicions about state laws regulating religion while the French are more likely to be suspicious of an absence of regulation of religious activity. At least this is the theory.[5]

The American version is more religion-friendly and seeks freedom of religion from state control, whereas the French model stresses the role of the state and the freedom of the political sphere from the influence of religion. Between these two extremes, there are a number of particularized patterns of relations between religion and politics. In short, the particular conditions of each society determine its understanding and practices of secularism. Secularism can thus mean anti-clericalism, or state neutrality, or the rejection of religious idioms and symbols in the public sphere.

In this chapter, I develop a third mode of understanding secularism: the control of religious institutions and expression, as represented by the Turkish case. This third mode of secularism represents the *control of religion* by the state. In this case, the state develops a number of institutions to control religious symbols, language, leadership and networks. By controlling religion, the state seeks to achieve three goals. It seeks to create its own version of an enlightened Islam that would promote the modernization project of the state. It uses Islam as a repository for building national identity and setting the external boundaries of the political community. It also employs Islam to provide legitimacy for its governance and to prevent opposition groups from using religion against the state. In the case of Turkish secularism, *control* of religion more than *freedom of* or *from* religion is the dominant mode of understanding. Historically Turkish secularism was shaped by the Ottoman legacy of the control of Islam by state institutions, the politicization of Islam in the nineteenth century onwards, and the French revolutionary Jacobin understanding of politics, religion and society. In other words, there has been a mutually shaped symbiotic relationship between exclusivist and politicized understandings of Islam and the exclusivist and rationalist mode of understanding secularism. Thus, religious and secular fundamentalism mutually shaped each other. However, with the thickening of civil society and the evolving role of new middle classes in Turkey, one sees the evolution of more inclusive understandings of Islam and secularism. Not only Islam but also concepts and notions of secularism are undergoing major transformations. For instance, in response to the dominant version of secularism, the more religious and traditional sectors of society insist on interpreting secularism

---

[5] T. Jeremy Gunn, "Under God but Not the Scarf: The Founding Myths of Religious Freedom in the United States and *Laïcité* in France," *Journal of Church and State*, 46 (Winter 2004), 9.

as freedom *of* (or *for*) religion, whereas some militant Kemalist and left-wing sectors conceptualize secularism as freedom *from* religion.

Indeed, in the West, different understandings of secularism are informing theoretical debate as well. According to Bhikhu Parekh, a leading political theorist:

> The secularist thesis can take several forms, of which two are the most common. In its weaker version it separates *state* and *religion* and maintains that the state should not enforce, institutionalize or formally endorse a religion … and should in general retain an attitude of strict indifference to religion. In its stronger version it also separates *politics* and *religion* and maintains that political debate and deliberation should be conducted in terms of secular reasons alone.[6]

Diverse patterns of religion–politics are rooted in all historical contexts. However, one can identify four critical socio-historical factors in the evolution of these patterns of relations between religion and politics: (1) the role of religion in the establishment of the modern nation-state; (2) whether there is religious monopoly or religious diversity in terms of competing faiths; (3) whether the dominant understanding of religion and secularism is inclusive or exclusive; (4) the role of the state's economic structure as it relates to a diversified class structure, and especially the role of the bourgeoisie. The Kemalist modernization project was carried out *against* religious institutions and practices, whereas the American Revolution was carried out *with* religious institutions to free the people and prevent state intervention in religious affairs. Moreover, in the American case, there have always been competing religious institutions and practices, whereas in both France and Turkey one religion has traditionally had a total *monopoly* over the meaning and role of the sacred. Thus, doctrinal differences (inclusive and exclusive understandings of religious traditions) and competing religious institutions (religious pluralism) shape the form and content of secularism in each society. The line between religion and politics can therefore be drawn with reference to inclusive and exclusive understandings of religion and secularism in each society.

In this connection, Alfred Stepan's main conclusion is the following:

> [V]irtually no Western European democracy now has a rigid or hostile separation of church and state. Indeed, most have arrived at a democratically negotiated

---

[6] Bhikhu Parekh, *Rethinking Multiculturalism: Cultural Diversity and Political Theory* (Cambridge, MA: Harvard University Press, 2000), p. 322. Parekh recognizes the role of religion in democratic politics. He differs from John Rawls. The main source in Rawls is his *Political Liberalism* (New York: Columbia University Press, 1996). The debate between Wolterstorff and Audi is in their jointly authored *Religion in the Political Sphere* (Lanham, MD: Rowman and Littlefield, 1997).

freedom of religion from state interference and all of them allow religious groups freedom, not only of private worship, but to organize groups in civil society. ... The "lesson" from Western Europe, therefore, lies *not* in church–state separation but in the constant political construction and reconstruction of the "twin tolerations." Indeed, it is only in the context of the "twin tolerations" that the concept of "separation of church and state" has a place in the modern vocabulary of a West European democracy.[7]

By "twin toleration" Stepan means the ongoing debate between the state and religion over the boundary between the two on the basis of their mutual respect towards each other's autonomous domain. This does not mean a strict separation but rather an ongoing cooperation between the two as long as they respect each other's autonomous spheres. On the basis of Stepan's argument, one could conclude that twin toleration requires an inclusive secularism and a pluralist understanding of religion. In other words, militant secularism, which is rationalist in orientation and focuses on a scientific understanding of the world without any reference to God or a theistic normative order, represents an antidote to any form of compromise. This form of secularism is hostile to religion and atheistic in form and does not tolerate any form of religious symbol in the public sphere. On the other hand, a more inclusive understanding of secularism, which does not try to eliminate religious symbols and norms from the public sphere, seeks to accommodate a diversity of religious perspectives. Moreover, inclusive secularism would use religious values to support the existing social and political order. It does not exclude any framework of understanding, whether religiously rooted or not. When the first form of secularism becomes dominant with its goal of cleansing religion from the public sphere and denies any role to religion in terms of informing the meaning of the good life for citizens, it inadvertently promotes the politicization and assertiveness of religion, especially in countries like India and Turkey. In short, there are inclusive and exclusive forms of secularisms and the exclusive one produces what one may call secular fundamentalism.

However, in order to have "twin toleration" between religion and politics, one needs an inclusive and pluralist understanding of religion. In many cases, this type of secularism is shaped by a type of religious argument. If the dominant understanding of religion is exclusivist and does not accommodate a secular understanding of life and politics, such an exclusive version of religion becomes "fundamentalist." Religious fundamentalists, who see religion as a comprehensive framework for life

---

[7] Alfred Stepan, *Arguing Comparative Politics* (New York: Oxford University Press, 2001), pp. 213–253.

and politics, are likely to radicalize secular groups' attitudes toward religion. Thus, while inclusive religions are more supportive of secularism, exclusive religions, on the contrary, are more hostile to any form of secularism.

Islam by doctrine and history is more political than the other two Abrahamic religions. Thus, the history of Islam and the consequent role of religion in Ottoman state-craft, and also the militant mission of the Turkish Republican Jacobins to create a modern secular nation-state, required a particular arrangement between Islam and politics. This arrangement stresses "control" more than separation or toleration. This does not mean that Islam is anti-secular. However, in order to create a space for secularism, the Kemalist elite had to reinterpret Islam through the establishment of the Directorate of Religious Affairs (DRA).

The reason one sees a more rigid understanding of secularism in Turkey has to do with the exclusive nature of orthodox Islam. When Mustafa Kemal established the modern Turkish Republic in 1923, his regime confronted three residual remnants of the Ottoman system: the loyalties of ordinary Muslims to the *ulema* and the caliphate, as the most important source of legitimacy and social order; the power and popularity of the Sufi orders, especially the Nakshibendi order; and the widespread presence of illiteracy and folk Islam in a population devastated by the recent war conditions. Mustafa Kemal, in such a setting, worked with prominent religious scholars to mobilize popular religious feelings against the occupation forces and the caliphate in Istanbul. When Mustafa Kemal established the state, he abolished the institution of the caliphate and established the DRA to gain full control over the mosques by placing them under direct state control. All religious functionaries became state employees and licensing for preaching and leading prayers required a religious education in state schools. Additionally, all religious foundations were placed under the supervision of the Directorate of Foundations, and all Sufi orders were banned. Thus, the purpose of the new regime was to tame Islam and employ it in the service of secular reforms and the consolidation of state power, especially in building a new national Turkish identity. The Turkish state, unlike the Egyptian state, did not encourage or form a coalition with Islamic groups. The subsequent Islamic violence in Egypt suggests that the state unleashed forces it could not control. The implicit assumption within Kemalist secularism was its deep suspicion of religion as the key cause of the country's social and economic problems. Thus, Kemalist institutions worked to diminish the social role of religion in society. Kemalists defined modernity as an alternative life-style free from religion, and in order to reduce the role of religion in society, the state defined Islamic activism as divisive, anti-national and anti-modern.

This stigmatization of Islam helped to define secularism in Turkey as modern, progressive, national and emancipatory. Yet, at the same time, the Kemalist Republic tried to stress different interpretations of Islam – progressive vs. orthodox, enlightened vs. conservative, national vs. transnational.

In Turkey, religion was gradually introduced into politics through democratization and social transformation. Islam provided a moral and emotive basis of political activism: raw material to reconstruct national identity while setting the boundary between the state and society.

### The Islamic critique of secularism and democracy

There is a fundamental conflict between secular liberalism and Islamic groups. Liberal theorists usually want to form a barrier between religion and politics *via* secularism, whereas Islamists regard such a barrier as an attack on Islam since secularism tends to seek to suppress religion. Moreover, secularists frame the concept of democracy with a universal human rights discourse that expresses the will of the people in certain prescribed ways, while Islamists treat democracy as a dangerous form of exercising the will of the people without any limits. The "twin toleration" between religion and politics is difficult, if not impossible, to achieve in Muslim societies.

It is clear that liberal democracy requires some form of political secularism to maintain its momentum.[8] In the case of the Muslim world, since the identity of the most appealing political actors is steeped in Islam, the main challenge is to find a form of secularism that would allow religious voices access to the political sphere without letting them dictate the outcomes.[9] Many political scientists conclude that liberal democracy

---

[8] Richard Rorty defines himself as a "militant secularist." "I think that the Enlightenment was right to suggest that religion is something that the human species would be better if it could outgrow." Richard Rorty, "The Moral Purposes of the University: An Exchange," *The Hedgehog Review: Critical Reflections on Contemporary Culture*, 2 (Fall 2000), 107; John Rawls, *Political Liberalism* (New York: Columbia University Press, 1996), p. 12. Sami Zubaida summarizes Gellner in *Islam, the People and the State: Political Ideas and Movements in the Middle East* (New York: I. B. Tauris, 1993), pp. xiv–xv. For a concise overview and critique of Gellner on this topic, see Dale Eickelman, "From Here to Modernity: Ernest Gellner on Nationalism and Islamic Fundamentalism," in John A. Hall, *The State of the Nation: Ernest Gellner and the Theory of Nationalism* (Cambridge: Cambridge University Press, 1998), pp. 258–271.

[9] Sami Selçuk, "Laiklik ve Demokrasi," *Türkiye Günlüğü*, 56 (Summer 1999), 45–49; Nur Vergin, "Din ve Devlet İlişkileri: Düşüncenin 'Bitmeyen Senfoni'si," *Türkiye Günlüğü* 72 (2003), 39–44; M. Hakan Yavuz, "The Case of Turkey," *Daedalus*, Vol. 132:3 (Summer 2003), 59–62.

presupposes secularism but they disagree about the content and form of
such secularism. Secularism is rooted in the European experience and was
forced on Muslim countries either by colonial or post-colonial modernist
state projects. Thus Islamic identity has been framed and articulated in
opposition to, and in relation to, European secularism.[10] Today, the main
paradox in most Muslim countries lies in the question of how one can
expand and enhance secularism in order to build a liberal democracy.
Since politics is about legitimacy, how can Muslim Turks generate legitimacy for secularism in Turkey? What are the social and intellectual roots
allowing the possibility of the "twin tolerations" in Turkey? The reason
the Turkish state regards religious politics as antithetical to democracy is
because there is a strong belief that secularism is the *sine qua non* for
democracy. In the case of Turkey, secularization has evolved along with
religious transformation (or ongoing Islamic reformation). One can also
argue that secularism in Turkey gained its legitimacy as a result of a
functioning democracy.

In Turkey, secularism is about regulating the relationship between
religion and political institutions. From the perspectives of politically
conscious Muslims, the kind of secularism practiced in Turkey is incom-
patible with Islam. There is a growing literature both in Turkey and the
Arab countries against the implementation and objectives of secularism.
Even if a more inclusive version of secularism were to be implemented, a
range of moral and religious objections would still persist. Many believers
are against the reinterpretation of Islam in a way that would give religious
legitimacy to secularism. Those who defend "the ideal way of life as the
only life worth living" have developed various theological arguments
against any form of secularism. Secularism is a European phenomenon
and it evolved out of the European experience where there was a dominant
Church. It represents a rebellion against the oppression of the Catholic
Church, a body that ignored the role of reason and science. Moreover,
Christianity distinguishes between the realms of man and God. In Islam,
there is no Church, no conflict between reason and revelation, and no
distinction between the spiritual and material. Thus, Western secularism
is alien to Muslim culture and experience and cannot be imposed on

---

[10] Marshall Hodgson, "Modernity and the Islamic Heritage," in Marshall Hodgson,
*Rethinking World History: Essays on Europe, Islam, and World History* (Cambridge:
Cambridge University Press, 1993), p. 220. Hodgson argues that modernization is
characterized by a series of ruptures in the Middle East. In the case of Turkey, secularism
as an ideology was imitated from Europe to catch up with the West. It created a split
society between the secular (Westernized) elite versus the religious masses. Vali Nasr,
"Secularism: Lessons from the Muslim World," *Daedalus*, 132 (Summer 2003), 68.

Muslim societies.[11] Those who reject secularism *in toto* argue that any attempt to reinterpret Islam to open an intellectual space for secularism constitutes heresy or innovation (*bida*). This line of thinking regards those intellectuals who defend secularism as either *kafir* (unbelievers) or enemies of Islam. Moreover, Islamists argue that Islam is not a religion confined to the mosque but rather a comprehensive and universal worldview governing every aspect of life, including the economy, politics and the legal system. Thus, Islam is not reducible to the private domain. However, these views are challenged by some Muslim scholars who argue that Islam is a universal religion and that it is holistic and general; whereas politics is particular and limited in its concerns and objectives.[12] For instance, Fazlur Rahman, who treats Islamic principles as a source of moral guidance, criticizes political Islamists for employing "the slogan that 'in Islam religion and politics are inseparable' which is employed to dupe the common man into accepting that, instead of politics of the state serving the long range objectives of Islam, Islam should come to serve the immediate and myopic objectives of party politics."[13]

Since Turkish society is devoutly religious and since there are powerful religious currents in the country, the state controls the use and interpretation of Islam and marginalizes some radical interpretations. The Kemalists argue that, given the history of the Ottoman state and the claims of Islamic groups in Turkey, the state cannot maintain impartiality vis-à-vis the role of Islam. They argue that since Christianity is based on the principle of "Render unto Caesar the things that are Caesar's and unto God the things that are God's" and since Islamic classical law does not recognize these realms as separate and seeks to control all domains of human activity, it requires a form of secularism that stresses control of religion more than separation.

Ernest Gellner argues that Christianity recognizes the separation of the temporal and divine realms, whereas Islam stresses the fusion of religious and secular domains.[14] Moreover, Peter Berger argues that the existence of the Church and its bureaucracy in Christianity facilitated the diverse development of Church and State and that this eventually helped to

[11]  Kevin Dwyer, *Arab Voices: The Human Rights Debate in the Middle East* (Berkeley: University of California Press, 1991), p. 63; Alexander Flores, "Secularism, Integralism, and Political Islam: The Egyptian Debate," in Joel Benning and Joe Stork (eds.), *Political Islam: Essays from Middle East Report* (Berkeley: University of California Press, 1997), p. 91.

[12]  Asma Afsaruddin, "The Islamic State: Genealogy, Myths and Facts," *Journal of Church and State*, 48 (Winter 2006), 153–173.

[13]  Cited in Dale Eickelman and James Piscatori, *Muslim Politics* (Princeton: Princeton University Press, 1996), p. 53.

[14]  Ernest Gellner, *Muslim Society* (Cambridge: Cambridge University Press, 1981), p. 2.

separate the religious from the temporal world.[15] Since there is no Church in Islam, a separate institutionalization of religion did not take place. Religious activities and symbols are not concentrated in and regulated by a single institution but rather diffused in all sectors of society. However, empirical evidence challenges this essentialist reading of Islam and Christianity. There are various religio-political patterns of relationships that exist in Islam and Christianity as far as the political sphere is concerned. For instance, the Caesaro-Papism of the Eastern Orthodox Churches favors the fusion rather than the separation of the religious and secular domains. The case of the Anglican Church in the United Kingdom also challenges the single Christian and Islamic model of the state–religion relationship. And for all practical purposes, religious affairs became sharply demarcated from the political domain from the Abbasid period (750–1258) on.[16] Yet in the case of the Ottoman Empire a separate religious institution was formed to control religious activities and to also create a state-centric Islam. This institutionalization of Islam prevented the autonomy of religion and Islam always remained under the control of the state. This tradition of institutional control continued under the Republican regime with the establishment of the DRA. This institutionalization might also explain the relative success of secularism in Turkey.[17]

## Three modes of secularism in Turkey

In recent years, there has been a growing diversification and difference of opinion in Turkey with regard to the meaning and role of secularism. This diversification is the outcome of the socio-political transformation that the country has recently undergone. At least three positions have emerged within the secularist camp. They are: a rigid Kemalist version of militant secularism which stresses the "freedom from" religion; the conservative Turkish-Muslim understanding of secularism as the control of religion; and the liberal conception of secularism that stresses the separation of politics from religion (freedom of religion) – this third version is defended by Istanbul-based big business elites, some politicians and the Alevi community.

---

[15] Peter Berger, *The Sacred Canopy: Elements of a Sociological Theory of Religion* (New York: Anchor Brooks, 1969), pp. 110–24.

[16] Ira Lapidus, "The Separation of State and Religion in the Development of Early Islamic Society," *International Journal of Middle East Studies*, 6 (1975), 363–385.

[17] Şerif Mardin also explains the relative success of secularism in terms of this state institutionalism in the Ottoman Empire. See Mardin, "Religion and Secularism in Turkey," in Ali Kazancigil and Ergun Özbudun (eds.), *Atatürk: Founder of a Modern State* (Hamden: Archon Books, 1981), pp. 193–196.

The first mode of understanding of secularism, which is also known as militant secularism, treats secularism as a comprehensive way of life. The militant secularists, also known as *laikciler*, regard themselves as children of the Enlightenment, self-declared Europeans who deny the role of Islam and Ottoman history in the formation of Turkish identity. This mode, which stresses civilizational shift via secularism, has several characteristics: (a) secularism is defined as "Turkey's philosophy of life"[18] to reach the level of European countries and fully assimilate into European culture; (b) there is an inevitable evolution from traditional backward (Islamic) societies to developed modern (read secular) societies, and secularism is the instrument of this modernization; (c) secularism provides the identity and compass of the state for modernizing society; and (d) Islam by nature is a political religion and thus Turkish secularism with its strongly anti-religious attitude is different from those societies where Christianity is dominant.[19] This approach insists on aggressive public policies to "cleanse the public sphere" from any form of religious influence and reluctantly supports state control over religious education and institutions to protect secularism against religious politics. Such a discourse is based on the Enlightenment notion that the authority of law lies in reason as opposed to religious texts or tradition. Modernity is, in short, defined in terms of the freedom of reason, or freedom from religion, in which reason becomes the safeguard for moral and political conduct.

In recent decades, some state institutions, especially the judiciary in response to the increasing Islamic challenges in the public sphere, have adopted a more militant interpretation of secularism in order to "cleanse Islam from the public sphere." The decisions of the Turkish Constitutional Court (TCC) on the headscarf ban and the closure of the RP reflect the view of militant secularism and also a shift from a dominant understanding of secularism as control of religion to freedom from religion. The TCC's understanding of religion is based on an uncompromising confidence in progress and a rationalistic understanding of the world. This purposive reading of law has induced the TCC to use law as an instrument to create a modern, progressive and dynamic society in which reason would be the guiding principle and religion would be totally irrelevant in social and political life. This judicial activism is grounded in the ideas of social engineering that played an important role in the formation of the Kemalist Republic. Unlike the TCC's strict approach, Kemalism, however, is pragmatic in so far as it stresses the "felt needs" of Turkish society and the "principles of the times" as guiding principles for social life. The

[18] The TCC's rulings on the Refah Party case on January 16, 1997, no. 1998/1.
[19] The TCC's rulings on the Headscarf case on March 7, 1989; no. 1989/12.

TCC has severely limited the influence of social forces that wanted to curtail "modernizing interventions" by the state.

The militant secularists deny Islam any constitutive role in the reconfiguration of national identity and the construction of a moral language in the public sphere. They seek an Islam-free political language. In recent years, it is not the military but rather the court system that has become the major guardian of Kemalist secularism. This forced secularism did not lead to the removal of God from the public debate but rather to the flourishing of Islam. The dominant popular culture is much steeped in Islamic ideals and concepts. Most Turks are religious and belief in God is deeper than in most European countries. Yet, the official public culture seeks to impose its own version of militant secularism. For instance, the TCC declares that:

"Secularism" is a civilized way of life which tears down the dogmatism of the Middle Ages and constitutes the cornerstone of rationalism, science, improving the concept of freedom and of democracy, becoming one nation, independence, national sovereignty and the ideal of humanity. Contemporary science has emerged and developed as a result of the collapse of the scholastic way of thinking. Although it is defined as separation of state and religious affairs in a narrow sense and interpreted in different manners, the opinion that secularism is, in fact, the final phase of the philosophical and organizational evolution of societies is also being shared in theory. Secularism is the contemporary regulator of political, social and cultural life based on national sovereignty, democracy, freedom and science. It is the principle which provides individuals with the opportunity for free expression and individuality and ensures freedom of religion and faith, thereby requiring the separation of politics–religion and faith. In religious communities, religious ideas and evaluations prevail over political organizations and regulations are also based on religion. In a secular order, however, religion is depoliticized and no longer serves as a tool of government. It is restored to its original and respectable place and left to the conscience of individuals. Application of secular law to civil affairs and religious rules to religious affairs is one of the principles upon which contemporary democracies are built. Public affairs cannot be regulated according to religious rules which cannot be the basis for regulations.[20]

In short, judicial discourse in Turkey has been shaped by a rationalistic and modernist understanding of religion. The TCC has failed to differentiate Islam as a faith from Islam as an ideology, and has reduced Islam to a counter-ideology against the modernization of the Republic. In the same ruling the Court argues that:

The application of the principle of secularism in Turkey is not similar to those western countries. It is natural that the principle of secularism is shaped by the conditions prevailing in each country and by the characteristics of each religion.

[20] The TCC's decision to close the Refah Party.

The consistencies or inconsistencies between such conditions and characteristics may lead to different interpretations and applications by affecting the concept of secularism. Although it has been conventionally defined as separation of religion and governmental affairs, the differences between Islam and Christianity have led to disparate conditions and consequences in Turkey and in western countries. The principle of secularism cannot be expected to be adopted in the same sense and at the same level in countries which have totally dissimilar religions, histories and religious approaches. This is the natural outcome of the difference between conditions and rules. Moreover, secularism has taken different shapes within the West which shares the same religion. The concept of secularism is interpreted differently in various countries and it has been construed by different groups in a unique manner in different periods as a result of their own way of thinking and political preferences. Secularism is not only a philosophical concept but it has also become a legal institution defined by laws. It is influenced by the religious, social and political conditions of every country where it is implemented. Bearing a special importance for Turkey because of its different historical evolution, secularism is a principle which is adopted and protected by the Constitution.

This dominant, and often rather oppressive, militant secularist ideology is defended by the TCC, along with other branches of the judiciary and the military, which state that "religion controls the inner aspect of the individual, while secularism controls the outward aspect of the individual."[21] This sharp division between inner and outer, defining religion as anti-science and anti-reason, and attempting to confine religion to the personal sphere without any social implications, is both problematic and divisive.

The distinction between the private and the public, which is at the center of modern nation-state formation and law, informs Western liberal discourse, which argues that a free citizen has a right to private belief which is "protected" (and defined) by law. In the case of Turkey, due to the stresses of modernization on society, the law has expanded the meaning of the public to some private spheres to "domesticate and control" the private belief of its citizens. Thus, this discourse leaves no public role for religion. The Turkish judicial discourse is based on the Kemalist principles of creating a homogeneous nation and a secular state and society free from any religious influence. The judiciary closely allied itself with the military, the guardians of Kemalist ideology, to protect and perpetuate Kemalism as a public philosophy. The major weakness of the judiciary's discourse in Turkey has been its inability to comprehend non-rational elements of Islam and its constant and dogmatic attempts to engineer a society in accordance with traditional Kemalist teachings. Such legal

[21] Erik Zürcher, *The European Union, Turkey, and Islam* (Amsterdam: Amsterdam University Press, 2004), p. 94.

decisions are at the center of the current societal polarization between a secular and an Islamic identity.[22] This heavy-handed form of secularism has led many Islamic groups to believe that secularism systematically violates the basic tenets of Islam. Some even argue that the right to freedom of religion cannot be reduced to the practice of rituals. They believe that the TCC and the European Courts are imposing a Christian understanding of religion on Islam by insisting that religious observance takes place in limited time and space. Thus, many Muslims see secularism as inimical to their religious beliefs and practices. They argue that Islam calls for religiously informed citizens to take an active part in political processes and that they are also required to bring their religious opinions to the public sphere. In short, from the perspective of religious Muslims, the Kemalist interpretation of secularism by its very nature violates their right to religious freedom.

The second mode of the understanding of secularism is more deeply rooted in the sociology of Turkish society and the political philosophy of the Ottoman and the Turkish state systems. This socio-political mode of understanding is defended by the center and religious-right parties in Turkey, which treats secularization as a process, not a project, demonstrating a flexible settlement between religion and politics that can be modified according to the needs of society through democratic negotiation. This version is based on four assumptions: (a) Islam is the source of Turkish identity and morality and it should have the primary role in society but not in the state; (b) Islamic morality and networks are beneficial for social order and economic activity; (c) the state should provide religious (Sunni-Hanafi-Maturidi) education in public schools and the DRA should maintain its activities in accordance with the needs of the state; and (d) pan-Islamic solidarity should be utilized in foreign policy and Turkey should join the EU not to assimilate but rather to reinvigorate Islamic civilization elsewhere. For Muslims, or those who support the center-right parties in Turkey, Islam is the soul of the country and an essential element of Turkish identity and should be respected and utilized. History, memory and the special vocation of Turkey cannot be separated from the history of Islam and the Ottomans. Those who promote and defend this secularist version see themselves as the children of the Seljuk and Ottoman legacies, trying to reconcile Islam and science, and sharing a deep sense of memory and mission. Thus, the debate is over the soul of Turkey and what constitutes the Turkish nation. Indeed, this is not a

---

[22] The 1921 and 1924 Constitutions recognized Islam as the religion of the state. This clause was removed in a 1928 amendment and secularism became one of the unamendable articles of the Constitution with the Law 3115 of February 1937 as the founding principle of the Republic.

religious conflict but rather a political one: about the nature of the identity and the deeply political role of Turkey.

Amongst the center-right parties, there is a shared sense that the public sphere is naked as a result of the decline of moral values and the hegemonic position of the pursuit of personal and private interests. People constantly complain that values have gone out of politics, civic life and the professions. Although there is a major conflict of interests and a struggle for power, the deeper conflict in this society is the conflict over values and identities on the one hand, and democracy and secularism on the other. The electoral victory of the AKP is linked to the search for a new value system and the triumph of democracy over militant secularism. This conflict over values should not lead to the tearing apart of the social fabric; it could force Turkey to develop a new social contract among institutions to deal with the diversity of values and also develop a more democratic understanding of secularism. In short, the Turkish-Muslim understanding of secularism is based on three major defining characteristics. (1) The state should get involved in and promote religious education and impose religious morality. (2) Islam, for Turkish-Muslim secularists, is an integral part of the Turkish identity and Islam should be integrated into the national identity and foreign policy as well. (3) The Turks are regarded as *seyfülislam* (the sword of Islam) even by many nationalist politicians.

The conflict between the first two understandings of secularism is deeper than it seems. It is between the claims of a religiously rooted communal ethical life, on the one hand, and those of the republican principles of a secular (religion-free) society in which science becomes the sole organizing principle, on the other. Thus, the debate over the relationship between religion and politics bitterly divides Turks. While some Islamic groups think that society has forgotten God by pointing a finger at moral collapse, others fear that both the government, especially the police force, and the public sphere have been taken over by pro-Islamic forces, such as the AKP and the Gülen community.

The third mode of secularism, promoted by some libertarians and some members of the Alevi community, asks for a new arrangement of the relationship between religion and politics in terms of a total separation of religion and politics. This approach stresses the freedom of *politics* more than the freedom of *religion*. Their main concern is to free politics from religious debates and to regard politics as a way of debating and deciding the shared moral rules in a society. They all agree on the removal of the state from religious affairs but some of them, especially the Alevi community, support the freedom of religion (Alevi doctrine) from politics and also from the hegemonic Sunni understanding of Islam. This position is promoted by a group of intellectuals under the Association of Liberal Society in Turkey.

Islam has been the principal source of morality and identity for the majority of the Turkish population. To push for the creation of political and public spheres that are free from any form of Islamic identity and morality is not easy and has acted as a source of constant tension. The TCC in its above decision sought to cleanse the political sphere of religious influences. However, despite these statements of the TCC, Turkey's public sphere and political landscape are radically changing, as is evident from there being an AKP government and from the formation of a new political language. In order to understand the connection between secularism and democracy, and Islam and democracy, the case of the AKP government, with its roots in Islamic activism, is very important.

## The AKP's secularism: neither "separation" nor "control"

The AKP stresses a democratically negotiated secularism. The state of mind of the AKP politicians is divided. They are forced to conform to the Kemalist doctrine of secularism while inwardly pursuing policies that undermine it. Thus, the major *taqiyya* (precautionary dissimulation) takes place in the public sphere by hiding one's own true beliefs and showing conformity with the Kemalist official secularism to avoid criminalization. This is reflected in a speech of Prime Minister Erdoğan, who redefines secularism thus:

Secularism, as the key guarantee of societal peace and democracy, is a concept with two dimensions. Secularism's first dimension is that the state should not be structured according to religious laws. This requires a standardized, unitary and undivided legal order. Secularism's second dimension is that the state should be neutral and keep an equal distance from all religious beliefs and should be the guarantor of individuals' freedom of religion and belief. It is explained in the second article of the Constitution defining the contents of secularism that secularism does not mean atheism; rather it means that each individual has a right to his own belief or sect; the right to freedom of religious practice and the right to equal treatment before the law regardless of faith. Therefore, due to these characteristics, secularism is the foundational and integrative principle of the Republic. The right decisions of Mustafa Kemal from the days of the National Liberation Movement and the concepts that reflect these decisions, which are also fully internalized by our nation and integrative concepts, must be jealously guarded. I believe that we must carefully avoid turning these integrative concepts [secularism] into a zone of "social discontent." For this reason it is necessary for us to protect the meaning as well as the spirit of the concepts.[23]

---

[23] *Radikal*, May 16, 2006.

Since all previous Islamic parties have been closed down on charges of anti-secularism, the AKP leadership is extremely careful when discussing and raising questions about secularism in practice. The contradiction is that Erdoğan has to defend Kemalist secularism while also criticizing it.

The foremost challenge facing the AKP is the constraints on religious practices put in place by the Kemalist state. These constraints make it almost impossible for the AKP to meet the lofty expectations of many of its supporters regarding religious freedoms and the recognition of the role of Islam in the public sphere. Although the AKP took a number of steps to improve civil and political freedoms and amended the constitution, it still today cannot fulfill the expectations of its electorate on the headscarf issue and also on the defense of the rights of the students of religious training (Imam Hatip) schools. The party thought it would be able to address the religious rights of its core constituency by moving closer to the EU and implementing EU demands. However, the decision of the European Court of Human Rights on the headscarf issue and European support for the Kemalist goal of leaving religion outside the public sphere has created a degree of skepticism towards the EU process and many AKP supporters have started to raise the question of the AKP's real goals and the reasons for its existence as an instrument to promote the Westernization of the country at the expense of traditional Islamic values. In other words, one might see conservative democracy as a way of opening up the conservative values of Turkish society to a democratic and legal debate. The AKP's unquestioned commitment to the EU process is ironically both the means by which it manages to be effective and also the main obstacle to its taking any step towards a possible normalization of state–religion relations.

The debate between the AKP and the Kemalist establishment is not about secularism versus Islamic theocracy but rather about the meaning and role of secularism. Like most of the center-right parties, the AKP insists that secularism is not a comprehensive public policy that aims to shape everyday life or an identity for its citizens. On the contrary, it is a constitutional principle designed to protect religious freedom and practice against the state. This reading of secularism ignores the content and expansionist claims of Islam and the Islamists' attempt to restrict public reasoning in defining religious norms. In the Turkish context, secularism is paradoxically both progressive and authoritarian. The Kemalist establishment sector consists of a number of competing groups ranging from those who interpret the six principles of Kemalism (nationalism, secularism, populism, etatism, revolutionism, and republicanism) as "sacred" to those who regard the Kemalist project as an instrument to achieve the higher goal of attaining the level of universal civilization: creating a liberal democratic and economically developed society.

Bülent Arınç, the speaker of parliament, formulated a more controversial understanding of secularism within the AKP leadership. He criticized the implementation of secularism in a speech in parliament in 2006. Büyükanıt, the Chief of General Staff, regards Arınç's speech as a challenge to the secular nature of the Republic. Arınç argued that:

All discussions stem from different interpretations of the principle of secularism. Different implementations have been seen and debates have been made in every period regarding the public sphere as a result of these different interpretations. The public sphere is the one in which citizens can discuss their common concerns equally and freely. Therefore, it is a sphere in which each individual's rights are protected without discrimination and each enjoys these rights and feels free. To safeguard the security of the public sphere and to ensure that rights apply to all equally are the fundamental duties of the state. Public interest should be defined not as the interest of the state but as that of the people. The state is not the owner but the guardian of the public sphere. This guardianship involves providing equality, and the fair distribution and reception of services by every individual. Protectionism of the state enters the stage immediately when freedom and rights tilt toward one group or a section; and the state should prevent such injustice. The state cannot prohibit or delimit the rights which are valid for everyone, against a particular section of the population. Thus, as a starting point, it is imperative that differences in the interpretation of secularism should be put on the agenda.

The article on secularism which is the unamendable article of our constitution will exist forever. But it is necessary to eliminate the differences in interpretation on the basis of our social structure and current conditions ... Secularism should be perceived as a mechanism for social peace and compromise. Secularism requires the neutrality of the state vis-à-vis faith. To give the opportunity for faith to express itself and to provide freedom of worship are the basic functions of secularism. The state is a body that implements these functions and treats faiths with equal distance. The problem arises just at that stage. The state ought to guarantee the right of individuals to practice their religious beliefs; whereas it restricts the rights of some beliefs to live and the right of expression in the public zone. And it does it in the name of secularism and that is a big contradiction within the context of political science. This contradiction has been damaging domestic peace in Turkey for years and revealing problems that will never end. That is the contradiction that derives from differences of interpretation, and should be solved by intellectuals, politicians and academics together.[24]

---

[24] Bülent Arınç, "Address by Bülent Arınç, Speaker of the Grand National Assembly of Turkey at the Plenary Session Convened on Special Agenda on the Occasion of the 86th Anniversary of the Inauguration of the Grand National Assembly of Turkey, April 23, 2006." Arınç's speech caused a major uproar among the establishment and Büyükanıt delivered a sharp speech to Arınç arguing that the Islamists threaten the secular state. He asked, "Aren't there people in Turkey saying that secularism should be redefined?" (by covertly referring to Arınç). "Aren't those people occupying the highest seats of the state?

A close analysis of Arınç's speech reveals his conceptualization of the state, politics and secularism. For Arınç, the state must be an agent of serving the people and it should be rebuilt according to the political views of the majority. His understanding of democratic politics is not consensual but rather majoritarian, which would even bring about an "Islamic state" if the majority supported it. His understanding of secularism is even more problematic, since he defines secularism as "social compromise" or "neutrality of the state vis-à-vis faiths" and "allowing believers to express their religious views in the public sphere."

One wonders how this social compromise is to be achieved and whether it should aim to protect the rights of the minority or the majority. If the majority of the population are Muslims and politically organized Islamic groups are more assertive, does not it make more sense to build this compromise to protect minority views and life-styles? Again, by supporting the "neutrality of the state vis-à-vis faith," Arınç is ignoring the legacy of political Islam in Turkey and additionally he never defines what he means by "neutrality." Given his political activism carried out in political Islamic circles, his understanding of allowing believers to express their views in the public sphere would mean creating religious–political blocs in the country. Would that not undermine "social peace and compromise"?

In conclusion, Arınç and many politicians in the AKP refer to the US notion of secularism to criticize the Turkish version. However, this comparison is interesting but not helpful in trying to understand the Turkish case. Indeed, there is a major difference between the understanding and practice of secularism in the US and in Turkey.[25] Could a Muslim Turkey, under the influence of the Ottoman legacy, which experienced neither the Protestant Reformation nor the Industrial Revolution, experience the same form of secularism? When and under what conditions are there diverse understandings and practices of secularism? In the case of those societies where religion and tradition are dominant, the state tends to ally itself with secularism against the influences of religion. Especially if there is no institutionalized religious pluralism the state has no option but to provide institutional and ideological support to deepen secularism.

The decisions of the TCC conclude that democracy and modern life-styles require believers to abandon their beliefs. The leadership of the AKP disputes the decisions of the TCC since it argues that the political activities of religious people along with their use of religious networks in

Isn't the ideology of Atatürk, founder of the Republic, under attack?" If the answer to those questions was "yes," he argued, Islamist reactionaries do pose a threat. Büyükanıt's speech was on October 2, 2006.

25  Jose Casanova, *Public Religion in the Modern World* (Chicago: University of Chicago Press, 1994).

politics should not be constrained. The rhetoric of the AKP is very close to Robert Audi's argument that three principles constitute the definition of secular polity.[26] First, the principle of "toleration": the government has a responsibility to protect the religious liberties of its citizens; second, the principle of "equidistance": the state is expected to grant equal distance to all religions; and third, the principle of "neutrality": the state should not interfere in religious affairs nor should it support any religion.[27] There is a major conflict between the rhetoric and the practices of the AKP government. Although the rhetoric of the AKP is libertarian, its practices are deeply sectarian and intolerant towards different conceptualizations of Islam. One would expect the AKP government not to discriminate against any religious groups, including the Alevi minority. However, the AKP's definition of Islam is solely defined by Sunni–Hanefi teachings. Moreover, the AKP does not appreciate the significant difference between religious and secular reasoning. The AKP's libertarian rhetoric is disengaged from the realities of Turkey, where the historical legacy of the Ottoman state and a politicized version of Islam require a different settlement between religion and politics. A close examination of the AKP's policies indicates that the party wants religion to play an important role in policies and also favors only the Sunni–Hanefi version of Islam.

## The contested zones of secular policies

Under the AKP government, the main debate over secularism focused almost exclusively on religious education and the headscarf issue. Imam Hatip schools, established under Article 4 of the Unification of Education Law no. 430 and Article 32 of National Education Law no. 1739, were initially created by the state to train imams (mosque preachers).[28] They evolved into regular public schools with the additional goal of preparing children of conservative and religious families for higher education. By the 1990s, they were no longer just vocational schools with the purpose of training religious functionaries but rather religious hot-beds for preparing students for higher education, especially in law and political science. These schools, where both religion and the natural sciences were provided as part of the curriculum, were built by private donations and staffed by the Ministry of Education. Most conservative families sent their children

---

[26] Robert Audi, *Religious Commitment and Secular Reason* (Cambridge: Cambridge University Press, 2000), p. 26.

[27] R. Audi and N. Wolterstorff, *Religion in the Public Square* (Lanham, MD: Rowman and Littlefield, 1997), p. 38.

[28] Mehmet Ali Gökaçtı, *Türkiye'de Din Eğitimi ve İmam Hatipler* (Istanbul: İletişim, 2005).

to these schools.[29] Such schools, by virtue of their both open and hidden religious curriculum, promoted and encouraged an Islamic life-style. By the mid-1990s, Imam Hatip schools were defended by Erbakan as the "backyard" of the Islamization of society. In fact, the differentiation between the secular and the Imam Hatip schools created a major tension within the educational system and resulted in the hardening of two opposing versions of history, modernity and national identity. Until 1997, the graduates of these schools could take university examinations and then study to become lawyers, doctors or engineers. In order to arrest the Islamization of state and society, the military-led coup forced the Higher Education Council to screen the graduates of the Imam Hatip schools entering universities. Their access to universities was restricted and their grades were also lowered.

In May 2004 the AKP government passed a bill to remove all such restrictions imposed after the 1997 military coup. It sought to improve the situation of the Imam Hatip schools by allowing their graduates to enter universities without reducing the impact of their GPA (Grade Point Average) on entrance exams. The president vetoed the law by arguing that it violated the principle of secularism, which implied "the separation of the spheres of social life, education, family, economy and law from the rules of religion." As always, he made a sharp distinction between "religion" and "contemporariness and the necessities of life," on the one hand, and "religious knowledge" and "reason and science," on the other.[30] Due to the president's veto, together with criticism from TÜSİAD and the military, the AKP government decided not to pursue the case by not resubmitting the vetoed law to parliament.[31] Yet, in December 2005 the government opted to back-track by promoting a decree on higher education that would lift grade restrictions on university entry examinations for graduates of the religious training schools through regulation. The Higher Education Council lodged an objection to the decree and took the case to the Council of State. In February 2006, the Council suspended the regulation that would have allowed Imam Hatip graduates to obtain a regular high school diploma and to escape cuts at university entrance exams. Government initiatives aimed at facilitating university access for Imam Hatip graduates were found controversial and "anti-secular" by the academic authorities. As the battle over the Imam Hatip schools continues, their appeal has sharply diminished and the number of students went

---

[29] The curricula of these included compulsory elective courses in Qur'an Studies, Arabic, Islamic Law and Islamic Jurisprudence, Tawhid and Islamic Morality, Hadith and Sunna.
[30] Quoted by Kuru, "Reinterpretation of Secularism," p. 156 (see note 4 above).
[31] For the statement of the military, see *Milliyet*, June 6, 2004.

down from 511,502 in the academic year 1996–1997 to 84,898 in 2003–2004.

In December 2003 the government tried hard to repeal the February 28 process regulations that targeted Qur'anic seminaries (*Kuran Kurslan*). The new regulation included minor changes, such as allowing Qur'anic seminaries to open evening classes, reducing the enrolment requirement from 15 to 10, licensing seminaries to remain open for more than two-month-long sessions, and the relaxing of permission to open dormitories.[32] Again, due to fierce resistance from the secularist establishment, the government caved in.

### The headscarf battle

The secularists regard the veil and headscarf as threats to the principles of the Republic and its mission of creating "modern" citizens, secularism being the key principle of the modernization and nation-building project. The Republic defined "emancipation" in terms of unveiling and the full participation of women in public life. The modernization of the country is measured by women's attire and freedom. According to current state policies, women are not allowed to enter schools, universities and other public buildings wearing headscarves. Even the wives of ministers are excluded from government functions and formal state dinners if they wear headscarves. The ruling AKP, which has its roots in the Islamic movement, has made no secret of its desire to lift the ban on headscarves.

The Turkish courts have turned into a battleground between competing Islamist and secular ideologies as Turkey struggles to meet EU demands on human rights reforms. For the critics, the Turkish courts form the biggest obstacle on the long road to the EU – rigidly conservative, unaccountable, hostile to human rights and often corrupt. But to their supporters, the courts are on the front line in the daily battle to preserve the secular, unitary Turkish state from its many enemies, ranging from Islamists to Kurdish separatists. The court system in Turkey has been the civilian guardian of Kemalist ideology. The main function of the judiciary is to protect the regime and the nation against anti-republican movements.

Under the European Convention on Human Rights, in which an individual right to petition was accepted by Turkey in 1987, Leyla Şahin used her right to sue the Turkish state at the ECHR. On June 29, 2004, the ECHR issued its judgment in the Leyla Şahin vs. the Court of Turkey case, which was disappointing for Muslim women who face the choice of being

---

[32] Kuru, "Reinterpretation of Secularism," p. 158 (see note 4 above).

denied education or attending higher education in a manner that offends their conscience. After accepting the fact that the state interfered with her "right to manifest her religion," the ECHR agreed with the state-imposed restriction in the Turkish context where "the majority of the population, while professing a strong attachment to the rights of women and a secular way of life, adhered to the Islamic faith." The Court perceived that liberal and secular principles were still under threat. The Court argued that the headscarf ban was necessary in order to protect the principle of secularism and equality which guarantees democratic values, the inviolability of religion and the equality of citizens under the law. Moreover, the ban protects the rights and freedoms of others who do not want to be coerced to use religious attire in a largely Muslim country. The court also referred to the three previous decisions of Karaduman vs. Turkey, Dahlan vs. Switzerland and Bulut vs. Turkey. The secularists welcomed the decision of the Court as a "slap on the face" to the AKP.[33]

The Council of State, Turkey's highest administrative court, has been a target of criticism among pious Muslims for a series of decisions. For instance, on October 26, 2005, the Second Chamber of the Council of State upheld a ruling by the Ankara Administrative Court No. 6 that the Ankara governorate had been justified in refusing the teacher Aytaç Kilinç's promotion to the post of director of the Bayrak Nursery School at Gölbasi near Ankara, because she wore a headscarf on her way to and from school. In response, AKP politicians, including Erdoğan, had condemned this decision. The Council of State's decision was based on the grounds that the teacher "was setting a bad example for her students and violated the secular principles rooted in the Turkish constitution which prevents the state from showing a preference for a particular religion." AKP officials condemned the decision saying that jurisdiction "cannot tell teachers what to wear outside the school." In recent years, the courts have used their power to expand the ban to civil servants wearing the head-scarf in their private life.

The murder of Council of State Second Chamber Judge Mustafa Yücel Özbilgin, who ruled against the headscarf, and the wounding of four others by a terrorist on May 17, 2006 polarized society along secular and religious lines once again. To display public discontent, tens of thousands of people gathered at Anıtkabir, Atatürk's mausoleum, on a Thursday morning to voice their anger, along with some judges and professors from Ankara. The top judicial officials and the president,

---

[33] Neşe Düzel's interview with the head of YÖK, "Teziç: Üniversitelerde Basörtüsü Olmayacak," *Radikal*, July 26, 2004; Nuray Mert, "AIHM ve Turban Yasağı," *Radikal*, July 8, 2004; "Hedefleri Islam," *Milli Gazete*, June 30, 2004.

Sezer, gave the government's opposition to the headscarf ban as one of the reasons for the tragedy. The joint statement by the heads of high courts in Turkey said: "We consider the massacre attempt as having been made against the secular republic. Such attacks will not intimidate us. We would also like to note that those politicians and media organs that have incited people irresponsibly against recent judicial decisions are also responsible for the attack. We are determined more than ever to carry out our duties." The burial ceremony of Özbilgin turned into a secularist demonstration against the government. Tens of thousands took to the streets chanting secularist slogans such as "Turkey is secular and it will remain secular," "Down with Shariah," "Mullahs, go to Iran," and brandishing national flags and portraits of Atatürk. The angry crowd hurled plastic bottles at AKP ministers and called Erdoğan, out of town on a trip to southern Turkey, a "murderer." Many judges implicitly accused the government when the chairwoman of the Council of State described the murderous attack on the judges as being a result of "careless remarks by government officials" over headscarf rulings. The most damaging statement came from General Hilmi Özkök, who described public protests against the murder of Özbilgin and the wounding of four others as inspiring and admirable, saying that the public outpouring of support for the secular Turkish Republic should not be limited to a single day or event, and that the protests should gain momentum and increased participation. Erdoğan reacted to Özkök's comments by saying they were "irresponsible," and had the potential to "affect financial markets and internal stability." It is clear that the military tried to use the event to reassert its weakening influence over the political system. Özkök's statement aimed to stir up enough anti-AKP sentiment to spark early parliamentary elections.[34] After the arrest of the killer, it became clear that some right-wing religious group was behind the attack.

### Adultery and the AKP

In addition to nationalist groups, there is also a religiously conservative base of the AKP. This became clear during the adultery debate in 2004. Erdoğan wanted to criminalize adultery and again, due to adverse reaction from both within and outside the country, he had to drop the issue. During this debate Erdoğan said that Europe is "not a model of perfection for everything."[35] The AKP undermined its international and domestic legitimacy by proposing to criminalize adultery, which created a major debate both in Europe and in Turkey. In September 2004, parliament

---

[34] Vincent Boland, "Turkish Rift Widens after General's Call," *Financial Times*, May 22, 2006.
[35] "The Impossibility of Saying No," *The Economist*, September 18, 2004, 32.

convened to discuss a long-awaited new Penal Code. Women's groups mobilized against articles discriminating against women in the draft bill. They also insisted on introducing harsh punishment for "honor killings" and wanted to prevent "provocation" as a mitigating factor. Although not all the demands of these organizations were met, the final bill was much more progressive than the previous code. However, the fact that a group of AKP parliamentarians proposed to criminalize adultery angered these organizations and the Republican People's Party as well, and Turkey's secular media did not hesitate to use the adultery case to question the intentions of the AKP. For instance, Yalçın Doğan, a columnist for *Hürriyet*, argued that "adultery is one of the symbols of secularism [and the] understanding of this is a cultural issue."[36]

Until a decision of the Constitutional Court in 1996, the Penal Code contained an article that banned adultery. The Court, however, declared the article unconstitutional on the basis of the constitutional equality between men and women. Under the law, a woman could be punished for a single infraction, whereas a man had to be in a steady relationship with another woman in order for this to be considered as adultery. The court abolished this article, which was welcomed by many women's organizations and international bodies.

On September 14, 2004, a core group of religious AKP MPs decided to propose an amendment to criminalize adultery in the name of protecting "human dignity" and the "family." Erdoğan supported the proposal by arguing that "the family is a sacred institution for our party. The stronger the family, the stronger the nation. If the family is weakened, the nation is doomed to destruction." After criticism from the EU, Erdoğan argued that "the West is not perfect. If we take it as a model of perfection in everything, we would be denying ourselves and would perish." Indeed, this was the "real" Erdoğan with his deep convictions about Islamic patriarchical values. Women's groups in both Turkey and the EU reacted vehemently against this proposal. They argued that the proposal would encourage discrimination against women as well as honor killings. Since women tend to be dependent on their husbands, it is less likely for a woman to take her husband to court as compared to a man, who could easily use the article against his wife. Due to the reaction within Turkey and from the EU, the AKP gave up its proposal and, as has always been the case, it back-tracked on this controversial issue. The EU declarations on the proposal forced Erdoğan to visit Brussels and after listening to the comments of Guenter Verguen, then the EU commissioner for expansion,

---

[36] Yalçın Doğan, *Hürriyet*, September 21, 2004.

he telephoned the speaker of the Turkish parliament and asked him to pass the new code without criminalizing adultery.

What is the basis of the adultery debate? "Europeanization" vs. "Entering without changing." This dichotomy became very clear over the debate on adultery in Turkey. Erdoğan has said: "I am in favor of integration not assimilation." As far as assimilation is concerned, for him it requires forgetting the past and shedding one's identity. The adultery issue signifies the conflict between the AKP's two values: democracy and conservatism. These two values have not always been in accord in the Turkish context. The AKP committed itself to pursuing the Copenhagen democratization criteria and transforming its value structures in accord with the EU: embracing a process of Europeanization, or internalizing European values. This democratization requires a transformation of cultural values and everyday practices. Yet, the AKP's conservatism is the main obstacle to this value transformation. The party is conservative on issues of gender, sexuality, minority rights and family structure. The tension between conservatism and democracy is more likely to grow at the expense of the AKP. Moreover, one also sees a growing gap between the top and the bottom of the party, since the leadership and the elite are moving away from the popular expectations of its base and act more in harmony with the requirements of the EU. In other words, its identity (conservative) does not always facilitate its democratizing policies. The EU requirements are in conflict with the conservative value structure of the AKP. The grass roots of the party are less likely to support full-scale EU-guided democratization in Turkey.

## Conclusion

The conflict between secularism and Islamism still constitutes the fundamental framework of Turkish politics. In order to understand the Turkish version of secularism, one needs to differentiate secularization as an outcome of technological, economic and other forces that transform society from secularism as a conscious political ideology to determine a new way of secular life. It is this ideological secularism more than the process of secularization on which one needs to focus in order to understand the conflict over normative values in Turkish society.[37] The major characteristics of Turkish secularism are different from those in France or the

---

[37] Sami Selçuk, "Laiklik ve Demokrasi," *Türkiye Günlüğü*, 56 (Summer 1999), 45–49; Nur Vergin, "Din ve Devlet İlişkileri: Düşüncenin 'Bitmeyen Senfoni'si'," *Türkiye Günlüğü*, 72 (2003), 39–44; Semih Vaner, "Laiklik, Laikçilik ve Demokrasi," in İbrahim Ö. Kaboğlu, (ed.), *Laiklik ve Demokrasi* (Istanbul: İmge Kitabevi, 2001).

United States. The Turkish version does not aim at "separation" but rather control of religion and also its exclusion from the public sphere.

Under the AKP government, Turkish society has become embroiled in bitter conflict, largely between Kemalist secularists and Islamic groups. The disagreements are deep and both sides seek to "settle" the conflict either through the law or through majoritarian democracy. They disagree over the role of the state in education and religion, and about the definitions of secularism and freedom of expression. The conflict is about "first order principles" – fundamental beliefs about the role of religion and state. The AKP is more interested in imposing religio-communal moral values upon society and protecting religious liberties, but less focused on protecting personal liberties or reducing economic inequality. The leadership of the AKP stresses the power of majority opinion in restructuring political power. On the other hand, the Kemalists seek to use the law and state power to support their case rather than trying to change the majority opinion. The secularists and Islamic groups pose a security dilemma – each side feels threatened by the other and use extraordinary measures in defense of their own life-styles and values. Islamic activism and secularism are each considered a security problem by each side of the debate.

# 6    The Kurdish question and the AKP[1]

Turkey has the largest Kurdish population in the world. Estimates of the number of Kurds in Turkey in 2007 ranged from 8 million to 12 million. The Kurds of Turkey have made demands varying from full secession, to federalism, and, at a minimum, to the recognition of individual and cultural rights within the framework of the process of Turkey's entry into the European Union (EU).[2] Undoubtedly, the most extreme symptom of Kurdish nationalism in contemporary history has been the Kurdistan Workers' Party (PKK), which has led resistance and terrorist activities against the Turkish state as well as against moderate Kurds, which in turn has resulted in the Turkish armed forces' equally violent backlash against both PKK fighters and innocent Kurdish civilians. Turkish soldiers have battled the PKK in the south-east since 1984, a conflict that has caused an estimated 37,000 fatalities and hundreds of thousands of displaced people.

One cannot understand Turkish history over the last quarter-century without taking into full account the role played by Kurdish nationalism in general, and that of the PKK in particular. In a way, both the domestic and foreign policies of Turkey have been held hostage to the Kurdish problem for the past twenty-five years. In addition to causing human suffering, the PKK-led rebellion has defined the meaning and role of politics, redefined the boundaries between state and society, and has inadvertently empowered certain state institutions at the expense of others. It has also slowed down the democratization process of Turkey. Furthermore, the conflict has increased Turkey's defense spending at the expense of education and

---

[1] Some parts of this chapter have been published in M. Hakan Yavuz and Nihat Ali Özcan, "The Kurdish Question and Turkey's Justice and Development Party," *Middle East Policy*, 13:1 (Spring 2006), 102–119.

[2] Those who demand a federal solution are Melik Fırat and Şerafettin Elçi. They regard a federal structure as "the way of solving" the Kurdish question. The PKK-DTP wants a "democratic confederation" as a solution to the Kurdish problem. According to APF, on January 12, 2007 Öcalan urged Turkey to grant its Kurdish citizens "regional autonomy in order to resolve a 22-year conflict and avoid the kind of turmoil seen in Iraq."

healthcare. Among other things, the conflict has transformed the demographic structure of the country by means of large-scale population movements. Millions of Kurds, both willingly and by force, have left their homes in southern Turkey, relocating to major cities in western Anatolia.

The state has used almost all means to prevent "the communalization of the conflict" between the Turks and Kurds and has tried to separate the PKK from larger Kurdish issues.[3] Since the 1999 arrest of the PKK leader Abdullah Öcalan, the organization has shifted its strategies and, much to the chagrin of the Turkish military and Kemalists, "communalized" the Kurdish problem by using the new-found opportunity spaces of Turkey, much of it brought about by the EU Copenhagen criteria, which require the full implementation of democracy, the rule of law, human rights and the protection of ethnic minorities. On the basis of the Copenhagen criteria, the EU required Ankara to reform its legal system and provide minority rights for the Kurds. Subsequently, many Turkish politicians started to argue that "the way to the EU goes through Diyarbakir" – the largest Kurdish city in the world – and this, in turn, encouraged other Kurdish parties to develop organic ties with the PKK. Today, the legal pro-Kurdish Democratic Society Party (DTP), like the IRA's Sinn Fein, has the same constituency as the PKK and functions as its legal political wing. The EU process has neither facilitated the democratization process nor contained Kurdish claims. There is a major difference between the EU's view of the PKK as a "manifestation" of the political claims of the Kurds with demands for democratization, as opposed to Turkey's conviction that dealing with the PKK is a question of national security, sovereignty and territorial integrity.

During the campaign of June and July 2007, Turkish political parties did not develop any concrete proposals on how to tackle the Kurdish question. The Kurdish ethnic party DTP proved overly narrow in its aims, choosing to focus more on Kurdish issues and the redefinition of the state than on the socio-economic conditions of the citizens of the country. The election debates were dominated by fear-based nationalistic discourse. Indeed, this election was very important for the future of Turkey and its national unity. The failure to implement the death penalty pronounced on Abdullah Öcalan, the PKK leader, became the most visible way of addressing the most prominent issue of the country.

---

[3] Seyit Haşim Haşimi, "Kürt Meselesinde Ak Parti Sınavı," *Yeni Şafak*, 1 August 2005. This frank essay openly discusses the communalization of the conflict between the Turks and Kurds and examines its potential consequences.

Erdoğan and Devlet Bahceli of the MHP have continually argued about whose fault it is that PKK leader Öcalan was not hanged after his capture in 1999. This debate was started by Erdoğan, who was the first to argue that "You don't become nationalist by saying you are nationalist. They give you the head of a terrorist leader as a present. You put him in prison in Imrali [a prison island in the Sea of Marmara] and let the AKP pay the bill." Erdoğan was targeting the MHP since the party was in a coalition government when Öcalan was captured in 1999. The same government also abolished the death penalty in order to comply with EU criteria. Bahceli responded at a rally in Erzurum, eastern Anatolia: "Instead of accusing the MHP of not hanging him, if you cannot find rope, here is some rope, if you can hang the separatist leader, hang him." He shouted at a person behind him on stage, "Give it here," and the man quickly produced a rope, and gave it to Bahceli, who then threw it into the crowd. Erdoğan's answer was not slow in coming: "If you are so skillful [with the rope], if only people had sent you rope when you were in government, and you could have finished the job." The debate over the "rope" which was initiated by Erdoğan reflects his insecurity and is seen as a way of trying to outbid the nationalists in their discourse.

Today, Turkey is more polarized along ethnic lines than it was a decade ago and the Kurdish problem has shifted from the military sphere to the social and political spheres. It is not the Turkish state which is confronting the Kurds any longer, but the two societies – Turks and Kurds – that are confronting each other. There had been high expectations that the AKP government would address the Kurdish question and stop further social polarization among Turkey's two main ethnic groups. After five years in power, however, on the eve of further negotiations for Turkey's eventual entry into the EU, the AKP government has failed to develop any coherent policy on what is probably the most critical issue facing the country, suggesting that the government's only solution has been to sweep the issue under the rug of complacency. At the same time, due to legitimate Kurdish aspirations and illegal attacks on soft civilian targets by the PKK, the AKP has preferred to use the Kurdish question for its own benefit. It has used the Kurdish issue to critique the idea of secularism in Turkey as a "cause of division" between Turks and Kurds. The AKP has thus offered its solution, one of "Islam as social cement," to put an end to societal polarization. This chapter examines the Islamization of the Kurdish question and the reasons for the apparent inability of the AKP and the DTP to resolve the Kurdish question.

In 2002, the AKP came to power with a commitment to address the Kurdish issue, with an argument which could be summarized in the following way. *The Kurdish problem is not about nationalism but rather about forced secularism and its reaction to Turkish nationalism of the type enforced by Kemalist ideology. A stress on common Islamic ties and brotherhood will enhance the stature of the country [memleket] and also end the conflict.* The thesis of this chapter is that the AKP cannot develop or implement a coherent policy to address the Kurdish problem for four reasons. (1) Erdoğan's view of the Kurdish question is very different from that of the Kurdish actors, especially the PKK-influenced political parties (see Chapter 4);[4] (2) a major conflict exists between the state institutions and the AKP over the conceptualization of the Kurdish issue and the foundations of the Turkish Republic; (3) the Kurdish issue is one of the primary reasons causing the AKP to fear a split in the party which would thus undermine its support among ethnic Turks in the provinces in central and eastern Anatolia; and (4) the Kurdish issue has the potential of leading to a major confrontation with the military. The increasing PKK attacks on state institutions and the military have occasionally forced the AKP leadership to reluctantly confront the Kurdish problem.

Despite the 2007 electoral victory of the AKP in Kurdish regions and high expectations, the AKP has not only failed to develop a coherent policy towards the Kurdish question, but it has increased the conflict, with Turkish society today being more divided along ethnic lines than it was five years ago. Contrary to expectations, liberalization within the framework of the Copenhagen criteria has not led to the relaxation of hostilities and permanent peace, but instead to a retrenchment of ethnic boundaries, and to the rise of counter-Turkish nationalism.[5] As of 2007, there is a common feeling on the street, even among the Turkish elite, that all Kurds are terrorists, and in discussions PKK and Kurds are used interchangeably. In other words, democratization within the framework

---

[4] The PKK particularly does not want the AKP to develop a comprehensive policy since the PKK's main and only rival in the region appears to be the AKP. Especially after the local election in 2004, the pro-Kurdish DEHAP (Democratic People's Party) lost 6 of its stronghold cities to the AKP. In recent months, Abdullah Öcalan, the imprisoned leader of the PKK, has been more critical of the AKP government than of the military. He fears the Islamization of Kurdish identity at the expense of a separatist secular Kurdism in Turkey.

[5] The prosecutor at the Court of Appeal has recommended to the Court that the controversial 15-year jail sentence handed to Zana, Hatip Dicle, Orhan Doğan and Selim Sadak by the Ankara State Security Court be overturned. On June 9, 2004, the Court of Appeal annulled the verdict against Zana and three other Kurdish parliamentarians and ordered that they be retried in the criminal court due to a number of procedural problems in the first decision. On the same day, the first Kurdish broadcasting took place on the state television. Abdullah Gül met with the four ex-parliamentarians and asked them to work for Turkey's EU membership. These events mark a turning point in the rethinking of the Kurdish question in Turkey. Many nationalists regarded the Court's decision and Gül's meeting as surrendering to the EU.

of the Copenhagen criteria did not help to improve relations between Turks and Kurds; on the contrary, it polarized and radicalized their relations. This was an outcome of the PKK networks, in pursuit of a more assertive policy in terms of criticizing the Turkish state, which angered a large part of Turkish society and, in turn, led to the rise of Turkish nationalism. Five years later, the Turkish nationalist MHP made major gains and increased its vote from 8.34% in the 2002 elections to 14.28% in the 2007 elections and entered parliament with 71 seats. The Kurdish politicians failed to moderate Turkish nationalism. Instead, they competed over the leadership of the Kurdish nationalist movement.

Before I examine the policies of the AKP towards the Kurdish question, it is important to unpack two competing and reinforcing strands within Kurdish nationalism, and to examine the connection between religious and ethnic identity in addressing the Kurdish question. By analyzing the actors of secular and religious trends in Kurdish nationalism, I will provide the social and cultural context to understand the conflicting policies of the AKP. In the final section of the chapter, the concrete policy initiatives of the identity debate, the reduction of the 10% threshold, and broadcasting in Kurdish will be discussed.

### Islamic and secular strands of Kurdish nationalism

The Kurdish landscape in Turkey is divided by a number of economic, cultural and political fault-lines.[6] Although the Kurds of Turkey are not fully assimilated into the Turkish national ideology, they are well-integrated into the economic strata of Turkish life.

Although students of Kurdish nationalism, such as Robert Olson, Michael Gunter and Abbas Vali, under the influence of the classic work of Wadie Jwaideh, have stressed the secular nature of Kurdish nationalism, they have all ignored the constitutive role of Islam in the creation of

---

[6] Martin Van Bruinessen, *Agha, Shaikh and State: The Social and Political Structures of Kurdistan* (London: Zed Books, 1992); Bruinessen, *Mullas, Sufis and Heretics: The Role of Religion in Kurdish Society* (Istanbul: Isis, 2000); M. Hakan Yavuz and Michael M. Gunter, "The Kurdish Nation," *Current History*, 100 (January 2001), 33–39. For more on Turkey's Kurds, see M. Hakan Yavuz, "The Kurdish Ethno-Nationalism," in Maya Shatzmiller (ed.), *Nationalism and Minority Identities in Islamic Societies* (Toronto: McGill–Queen's University Press, 2005), pp. 156–185; Hakan Özoğlu, *Kurdish Notables and the Ottoman State: Evolving Identities* (Albany: State University of New York Press, 2004); Michael Gunter, *The Kurds and the Future of Turkey* (New York: St. Martin's Press, 1997); Robert Olson (ed.), *The Kurdish Nationalist Movement in the 1990s: Its Impact on Turkey and the Middle East* (Lexington, KY: University of Kentucky Press, 1996); Nihat Ali Özcan, *PKK Kürtistan İsci Partisi, tarihi, ideolojisi ve yöntemi* (Ankara: Asam, 1999); Mustafa Akyol, *Kürt Sorununu Yeniden Düşünmek: Yanlış Giden Neydi? Bundan Sonra Nereye?* (Istanbul: Doğan, 2006).

difference against the secularist Kemalist reforms.[7] Even Kurdish nationalist intellectuals, who all happen to be leftists, such as Hamit Bozaslan,
Gulistan Gurbey, Ferhad Ibrahim, and Mesut Yeğen, have regarded
Kurdish nationalism as inherently secular.[8] However, some scholars
such as McDowall and Bruinessen have identified the religio-ethnic origins of Kurdish nationalism.[9] There are three competing strands, secular,
traditional and Islamic, in the constitution of Kurdish nationalism.

The first and the most effective group is the secessionist PKK and its
political party outlets such as the Democracy Party (DEP), the People's
Democracy Party (HADEP), the Democratic People's Party (DEHAP)
and the Democratic Society Party (DTP).[10]

The main defining characteristics of the PKK-led movement are that it
is secular in orientation, anti-traditional and much supported by newly
urbanized and university-educated Kurds who do not have deep religious
and tribal ties. In the late 1980s, when the Turkish state armed some loyal
tribes against the PKK because of its tribal competition, some tribes
reluctantly became supporters of the PKK.[11] However, this secular strand
has been punctuated by regional, sectarian and class identities. This
strand engages in a dual rebellion both against the traditional structure
of Kurdish society and against the Kemalist state system. This group has
developed a number of shifting positions toward the state. The PKK
started with the idea of full independence, but then turned to favoring a
democratic, autonomous republic within Turkey, or at the least demands

---

[7]  Wadie Jwaideh, "The Kurdish Nationalist Movement: Its Origins and Development,"
    PhD dissertation, Syracuse University, 1960; Abbas Vali (ed.), *Essays on the Origins of
    Kurdish Nationalism* (Costa Mesa: Mazda Publishers, 2003).
[8]  Amir Hassanpour, *Nationalism and Language in Kurdistan, 1918–1985* (San Francisco:
    Mellen Research University, 1992). Hassanpour examines the evolution of Kurdish
    nationalism through the framework of social classes in terms of the gradual shift from
    feudal to bourgeois Kurdish nationalism.
[9]  David McDowall, *A Modern History of the Kurds* (London and New York: I. B. Tauris,
    1996).
[10] Interview with Mehmet Metiner, who resigned as the deputy chairman of HADEP on
    April 10, 2005, Istanbul. Ali Kemal Özcan, *Turkey's Kurds: A Theoretical Analysis of the
    PKK and Abdullah Öcalan* (London and New York: Routledge, 2006). Also see the
    interview with Resit Deli, deputy leader of the only-Kurdish HAK-PAR (the Rights and
    Freedoms Party) in *The New Anatolia*, January 1, 2006. Deli argues that: "Most Kurds are
    fed up with Abdullah Öcalan and the PKK, but they cannot say so openly because they are
    intimidated." In this interview, Deli calls for a federal solution and criticizes the DTP as
    the front of the PKK.
[11] Ahmet Kule, "Socialization Process of the Individuals who Join Terrorist Organizations in
    Turkey", unpublished PhD dissertion, City University of New York, 2007. Even though
    Abdullah Öcalan is the supreme and uncontested leader, Cemil Bayık and Murat Karayılan
    are very powerful. The PKK changed its name in April 2002 to KADEK, *Kongreya Azad' z
    Demokrasiya Kurdistan* (Kurdistan Democratic and Freedom Congress), and then to the
    *Kongra-Gel* (People's Congress).

for major constitutional changes (see Chapter 8). Short of outright secession, the goal of the PKK has been to (a) get the Turkish government to release its leader Öcalan from jail; (b) create a bi-national (Turkish– Kurdish) state by changing the constitution; (c) decentralize the administration of communities through local government reforms; and (d) prevent Turkish military incursions into Iraqi Kurdistan and enhance pan-Kurdism. In order to achieve these objectives, the PKK's strategies have shifted from a military confrontation that yielded only limited success to demanding constitutional changes in order to restructure the foundations of the Turkish Republic. This strategy is an attempt to use new political opportunity spaces, opened as a result of democratization, to "separate" Kurdish civil society and enhance Kurdish identity at the societal level.

In addition to controlling the ethnic Kurdish parties, the PKK controls at least five organizations: an armed militia mostly active in northern Iraq, called PKK/*Kongra-Gel*; a youth organization (Free Youth Organization); a women's organization (Free Women Organization); a student organization (Kurdistan Students' Association); and several media outlets such as three newspapers (*Yeni Özgur Politika* in Germany, *Gündem* and *Azadiya Welat* in Turkey); two news agencies (*Fırat* News Agency and *Dicle Haber Ajansı*); two satellite TV stations (*Ro TV* and *MMC TV*) and a radio station (*Radio Serhildan*).

The second group of Kurds, known as "occasional Kurds," are very much assimilated within Turkey and prefer to be active among national center-right and center-left parties. These ethnic Kurds function within legitimate opportunity spaces, use tribal ties to be elected to parliament and use state resources to maintain their support base. They have no major problems with the state, and their main goal is to define and refine their status in the national society of Turkey. Active in business and bureaucracy, these Kurds usually live in the major cities of western Turkey as well as maintaining ties with their Kurdish villages in the east.

### Kurdish Islamism

The third group of Kurds are best described as Muslim-Kurds, who stress Islamic values and normally identify with religion over ethnicity. Islam has been the "oppositional identity" of the Kurdish region since the centralization policies of the Ottoman state, and especially against the nation-building project of the Kemalist Republic. In the Kurdish regions of Turkey, Sufi Islam has acted as a surrogate of Kurdish identity, with ethnic Kurds preferring to conserve and perpetuate their Kurdish identity within these religio-tribal networks. In recent years, the Kurdish region has been functioning as a labor reservoir for the rest of the country and has remained an economic backwater since the neo-liberal economic politics of Özal. The lack of government investment and the decline in social services has further radicalized the Kurdish community against the state and helped them to closely identify with ethnic or religious social networks. While market forces turned large numbers of Kurds against the state, those who did well in the market became more integrated within Turkish society and less interested in the politics of Kurdish identity. Thus, market conditions simultaneously separate and integrate different sectors of Kurdish society. In the 2007 national elections, the Kurdish bourgeoisie aligned itself with the market-oriented AKP. Most AKP deputies are either merchants or businessmen from the region with some Nakshibendi and Nurcu connections.[12] Those who have suffered because of market forces demand a "Kurdish Islamic welfare state" to address their problems. In short, class lines shape religious loyalties in this part of the country.

Even though the most politicized Kurds belong to the Alevi sect, the majority of Kurds are Sunni (Safi'i) Muslims. Traditional Sufi networks, along with the neo-Sufi Nur movement and some modernist radical Islamic groups, are the dominant structures of solidarity and identity in the Kurdish regions. Nakshibendi Sufi orders comprise approximately fifty per cent and the Nurcus about twenty per cent of the population. The new emerging radical modernist Islamist groups are around fifteen–eighteen per cent of the Safi'i Kurds in Turkey.[13] Nakshibendi orders are the oldest networks of the region and they are still dominant among both Turks and Kurds. Broadly speaking, the Nur movement of Said Nursi is more concentrated in the cities and among the business elite who live outside the traditional Kurdish region. Among the radical Islamic groups there are various Islamic orientations, with different influences emanating from several sources. Kurdish Hizbullah is influenced by the writings of Seyyid Qutb and by the Iranian revolution and is prevalent in Batman, Diyarbakir, Sirnak and Hakkari and in the major cities.

Islam is the dominant identity among the majority of the Kurds. However, these Muslims feel Kurdish when confronted with the forced option of a Turkish identity. This Islamic strand in Kurdish nationalism repudiates the founding principles of secularism and nationalism of the Turkish Republic. One of Erdoğan's current associates, M. İhsan Arslan,

---

[12] The AKP's deputies from Diyarbakir are all merchants (Mehmet Mehdi Eker, Kubettin Arzu, M. İhsan Arslan, Abdurrahman Kurt, Osman Aslan and Ali İhsan Merdanoğlu).

[13] *Rapor: Güneydoğu'da Kürt Grupları* (Ankara: Emniyet Genel Müdürlüğü Terörle Mucadele Dairesi, March 2005).

a Kurdish Islamist deputy from Diyarbakir in the 2002 and 2007 elections, has said: "It is not a miracle to argue that the final confrontation between Islam and democracy [he defines democracy as a form of *küfür* (idolatry)] will take place in the Middle East." Arslan has also argued that "This regime [democracy] in Turkey made its population ignorant [*cahillestirme*], banned its religion, and even tried to reform and undermine Islam and force all of this on the people of Kurdistan as well. ... The employees of [Turkey's] Directorate of Religious Affairs are also involved in the project of undermining Islam."[14] This statement by Arslan demonstrates his attitude toward democracy, secularism and Turkish nationalism in general.

Aside from the PKK, Kurdish nationalism has worked within Islamic networks. Islamic Kurdish nationalism has evolved from two branches of Turkish/Kurdish Islamic Sufism: the Nakshibendi and Nurcu (follower of Said Nursi) networks. The supporters of this strand of Kurdish ethno-nationalism work with Turkish Islamic groups to oppose both secularism and hyper-Turkish nationalism.[15] Within this sector there are two major sub-groups. The first Kurdish Muslim groups are those who belong to traditional Nakshibendi and Nurcu movements and are supporters of the AKP. Although the Sufi networks were banned in 1925, they continued to function in the Kurdish region due to intertwined relationships between Sufi and tribal networks. Since the majority of the Kurds belong to the Safi'i school of Sunni Islam, they maintained their informal religious education centers (*medrese*) until the early 1980s. Menzil, a village of Adıyaman province, has the most popular Nakshibendi lodge in Turkey, with several hundred thousand Turkish and Kurdish followers, including Namık Kemal Zeybek and Muhsin Yazıcıoğlu, the chairman of the Greater Unity Party (BBP).[16] The Sufi leadership has always remained in the hands of

[14] On Islamic-Kurdism, see no author (ed.), *Kürt Soruşturması* (Ankara: Sor, 1992), pp. 261; 259; Mazlum-der (ed.), *Kurt Sorunu Forumu* (Ankara: Sor, 1993). These books reveal the Islamic position on the Kurdish question and the Kurdish Islamic attitude on the founding principles of the Turkish republic.

[15] The Nakshibendi Sufi order is the largest and most influential one in Turkey. The Nur movement is a faith movement established by Said Nursi. On the Kurdish Nurcu movement, see M. Sıddık Seyhanzade, *Nurculuğun Tarihçesi: Medeniyet-i Islamiyye* (Istanbul: Tenvir, 2003); Fulya Atacan, "A Kurdish Islamist Group in Modern Turkey: Shifting Identities," *Middle Eastern Studies*, 37:3 (July 2001), 111–144.

[16] Niyazi Usta, "Menzil Nakşiliği," *Demokrasi Platformu* 2:6 (Spring 2006), 21–44; A. Selahattin Kınacı, *Seyyid Muhammed Raşid Erol (K.S.A)'nın Hayatı* (Adıyaman: Menzil Yayınları, 1996); N. Fazıl Kuru, "Menzil Nakşiliği Merkez Cemaati Üzerine Sosyolojik Bir Araştırma," MA dissertation, University of Erciyes, Kayseri, 1999. When the PKK wanted the Menzil Nakshibendi order to support its cause of an independent Kurdistan, Muhammed Raşid Erol, then the Sheikh, refused this call and asked all his followers to "work for the unity and strength of the Turkish state."

Kurds, despite large numbers of Turkish followers. In recent elections, the Menzil *cemaat* (religious community), along with all Nakshibendi and Nur networks, voted for the AKP government.

Since the mid-1990s, with the emergence of the new Kurdish bourgeoisie and middle class, many Kurds have preferred to join the Nur movement of Said Nursi. This is organized around the writings of Nursi and reading-rooms, known as *dershanes*. With the current economic development, many Kurds are joining the modernist Nur movement, and they already constitute a major force in the Kurdish regions. However, in recent years as the community of Fethullah Gülen has been shedding its Turkish nationalism it is becoming more dominant among the Kurds. Also, there has always been an active Kurdish first Nur movement, known as *Med-Zehra*.

Parallel to the increase in the activity of the Nakshibendi and Nur movement-oriented organizations in the region was a similar increase in the number of Kurdish Hizbullah (KH) non-governmental organizations (NGOs) active there. KH NGOs that have been involved in social and economic development have emerged in Batman and Diyarbakir since 2004. The Mustazaflar Associations were founded in 2004 and are tied mainly to the KH and also some small-size businesses. The global dimension of Islam in the Kurdish region is perhaps best demonstrated by the arrival the KH in the 1980s. In light of the diverse Islamic orientations and influences mentioned above, there have been many cases of tension and violent clashes between different Kurdish Islamic groups, especially between the KH and traditional Sufi networks. These bloody clashes have largely given way to mutual suspicion, contempt and non-cooperation. The KH have targeted many prominent *Med-Zehra* leaders such as İzzettin Yıldırım, and a group of Kurdish businessmen.[17] In recent years, the KH have become the most organized and effective violence-prone organization among the rural and semi-urbanized Kurds. To sum

---

[17] So far the best document on the Kurdish Hizbullah was prepared by the Department of the Anti-Terror Unit of the Turkish Police: *Hizbullah Terör Örgütü* (Ankara: Emniyet Genel Müdürlüğü, 2001). See also Emrullah Uslu, "From Local Hizbullah to Global Terror: Militant Islam in Turkey," *Middle East Policy*, 14:1 (Spring 2007), 124–141; Human Rights Watch, "What Is Turkey's Hizbullah?", February 16, 2000; M. Hakan Yavuz, *Islamic Political Identity in Turkey* (New York: Oxford University Press, 2003), p. 176; *Milliyet*, January 20–23, 2000. The KH has two regular journals, *Gönülden Gönüle Damlalar* and *Inzar*. The KH also publishes *Mujde* in Basel, Switzerland. The KH-linked publishing houses, Davet Kitapevi in Elaziğ and Risale Kitapevi in Batman are very active. The KH benefited from the Copenhagen criteria and the absence of an anti-terror law allowed its non-governmental organization to form: *Insan Hakları ve Mustazaflarla Dayanışma Derneği* (Association for Human Rights and Solidarity with the Oppressed) in Diyarbakir.

up, the disunity of the Kurdish Islamists has been stressed and enhanced through the policies of the state. That is why it is improbable that the Kurdish Islamists will be able to unite under one leadership in order to care for their own divergent interests.

### Challenge to traditional religious authority: the Kurdish Hizbullah

The Kurdish Hizbullah (KH) was founded by Hüseyin Veziroğlu and his associates, who were active in the MSP of Necmettin Erbakan. After the successful Iranian Islamic Revolution of 1979 and the military coup of 1980 in Turkey, the leadership of the KH abandoned their hope of a democratic transformation of society and started to think "top-down" Islamic revolution through an Islamic Kurdish state. But as a result of ideological debate in the late 1980s, the KH realized the impossibility of getting an Islamic state due to the power of the Turkish military, and adopted a new strategy of the creation of an Islamic Kurdish community first and then an Islamic-Kurdish state. The leaders of the KH, such as Hüseyin Velioğlu and Fidan Güngör, sought to realize their goal through three stages: formation of political religious consciousness (*tebliğ*), community formation (*cemaat*), and armed struggle (*jihad*).

In order to achieve the first goal, the group stresses face-to-face "oral exchange," debating rather than reading, to politicize the religious consciousness of the Kurds. Since the dominant culture of the region is still based on oral culture and most of the members of the KH belong to several tribes, the KH prefers "face-to-face debate" over reading in order to indoctrinate its members.[18] This overlap between religious, tribal and ethnic identities helps to form powerful networks in different towns and cities. However, even though the centers of these debates are mostly family homes, the main channels of information and places of formal meetings take place in "book stores," which mainly function as reading rooms. Having oral culture as the dominant form of indoctrination within the context of book stores raises the interesting paradox of the relationship between oral and print culture and the shifting religious "authority" in Kurdish society. Since the KH is a major challenge to traditional Kurdish religious networks, its leadership needs the perception of being "scholars" who acquire religious knowledge through self-education as opposed to the

---

[18] There are several KH web-pages that provide discussion groups for KH members. The most important one is www.inzardergisi.com. The most visited web-site with controversial news is www. yesrip.com, which also broadcasts a radio program on the net.

traditional *medrese* education.[19] These book stores create the image of "scholarship and the power of the book" even though books are read by few and dissemination is through oral culture.

The connections between traditional Islamic authority, religious entrepreneurs and state policies are also important in the moderation of the movements. In Turkey, Kurdish religious entrepreneurs (the leadership of the KH) have been free to lead religious mobilization and frame the discourse as they want. In the case of Turkish Islamic movements, the traditional religious elite and authorities still condition the power of Turkish Islamic entrepreneurs. But the traditional religious elite has been fragmented and weakened in the Kurdish regions and has little power to exercise its traditional authority over these contemporary Kurdish Islamic groups. Even though the Islamic traditional elite was destroyed during the reforms of Mustafa Kemal, still neo-Sufi groups, especially the Nur movement, have played an important role in "in-group policing" of Turkish Islamic political activists. This in-group policing is more effective than party closure. New Islamist Kurdish political entrepreneurs easily flourish if traditional religious authorities are either fragmented or have different political interests from the rest of the community. The tension between traditional religious authority and contemporary religious entrepreneurs is very important for moderation and the state. Whenever traditional religious authority is weak, and their legitimacy is in dispute as is the case in the Kurdish cities, young Islamist Kurdish activists will lead the debate.

In recent years, the KH have built their own mesjids (small mosques). For instance, in the city of Batman, the Directorate of Religious Affairs controls eight mosques, the KH four. These mesjids fulfill a number of functions, including dispensing information about regional development, religious education for children, and social services for those in need. The leaders of these mesjids, known as *mele* (imam in Kırmancı Kurdish), not only lead regular prayers and teach Islam to children, but are also involved in the building of Muslim communities by addressing the social needs of the community. These *meles* are less educated in classical Islam but more in contemporary Islamic and Kurdish political issues. They are critical of the traditional *ulema*, asserting that they are co-opted by the state and not involved in community-building activities. Every Thursday evening there is a "conversation" in the mesjid and the *mele* usually debates the issues of the week with the people. The salaries of these *meles* are paid by the community and they are trained both in Arabic and Kurdish. They, unlike

---

[19] For more on the Kurdish Shafi'i *medrese* system, see Yavuz, *Islamic Political*, p. 231.

the state-appointed imams, know the local Kurdish culture and Islamic traditions and are also free from Turkish state influence.

In the face of the KH challenge, the PKK initiated a number of policies to maintain its power over religious Kurdish communities by establishing the Association of Imams of Kurdistan (*Kurdistan İmamlar Birliği*). This initiative led to a major confrontation between the KH and the PKK that resulted in the killing of 700 people between 1992 and 1995, mostly PKK members.[20] Although the KH originally distanced itself from PKK-type violence and focused on consciousness-raising educational activities, it eventually treated the violence as "redemptive" and as a "holy duty" against the "atheist PKK." Some of the prominent KH leaders, such as Fidan Güngör of the Menzil community, stressed intellectual jihad as a first stage and violence as a second stage of their struggle. For him, it was important to recruit a sufficient number of ideology-oriented followers, yet this view had been sharply criticized by Hüseyin Velioğlu of İlim Cevresi, who wanted the KH to be a revolutionary and activist movement rather than a text-based intellectual movement. As a result, he refused to work with Güngör, and that led to a major split in the KH. Velioğlu's branch stressed the redemptive quality of violence against the "atheist PKK." Veziroğlu stressed total confrontation with the PKK to open a space for its own activities, and he identified the PKK as the first enemy. Eventually, the İlim branch defeated the Menzil community and became the leading Islamic Kurdish movement, with its associated terror activities.

The KH is one of the most powerful local networks, with diverse associations in the Kurdish region, along with a membership of several thousand. On the basis of police arrests reports, most KH members have joined the organization through social bonds of family, tribe or religious networks. Family ties are the most effective recruitment networks within the KH, which functions as an extended family. Due to these family-based ties, the KH is more effective and much better informally organized than the PKK, and its recruitment process is a more "bottom-up" and self-selected process. In a close examination of several KH members in Turkey, I have come to the conclusion that the key "pull" factors of the self-recruitment of Kurdish youth are family ties, along with the dominant tribal culture of "shame." The young Kurds are taught at an early age how to avoid shame and acquire honor through a number of strategies of retaliation, self-defense and protecting one's tribal name, along with the virginity of the female members of the family. Any killing of a relative or

---

[20] S. Özeren and C. Van de Voorde, "Turkish Hizbullah: A Case Study of Radical Terrorism," *International Journal of Comparative and Applied Criminal Justice*, 30:1 (2006), 75–93.

brutalization by police raises the issue of the restoration of honor and this, in turn, leads to a cycle of violence.[21]

On January 17, 2000 the Turkish police initiated a series of systematic operations and raids against the KH with the goal of destroying the organization, which resulted in the killing of its leader and the arrest of over six thousand KH members. Yet it is still alive and very active in a number of social services. Under its new leader, Isa Altsoy, who lives in Germany, along with the new freedoms of organization, assembly and public speech, the KH retreated to its consciousness-raising (tebliğ) state. The KH now stresses more social participation with the goal of Kurdish Islamic community-building by organizing fund-raising activities, weddings and mass circumcision ceremonies in rural areas. In the urban centers, it provides popular education via the internet and also initiates small-size businesses such as selling office materials or opening food stores. Its main goal now is to create self-sustaining Islamic communities, which are constantly exposed to KH propaganda. These activities are carried out by the KH's associations, known as Mustazaflar (Persian for oppressed), which create dense networks of social relations shaped by the KH vision of Islam and tribal ties.[22]

These community-building activities spread to the electoral politics in the 2007 elections, and the KH voted for the AKP for three major reasons: "It is anti-Kemalist and the victim of the system just like us Kurds; the DTP's mayors failed to provided proper services and they are secularist and atheist; and the AKP people help to bring more freedom of organization and they help us if we need support."[23] In the 2007 elections, almost all meles in Batman asked their community to vote for the AKP candidates rather than "secularist" (this means anti-religious in the region) DTP candidates. Almost all KH networks worked for the victory of the AKP as a way of endorsing a new "milieu of openings" under the AKP government, and also voted against the secularist and leftist policies of the DTP municipalities. According to new police reports, the

---

[21]  Ismail Besikci examines the social impact of the guerrilla fight on Kurdish society. When a young Kurdish militia-man is killed by the Turkish security forces, he is called sehid (martyr) and mass prayers take place for him. People visit the family of the killed militia-man and express their solidarity and organize a major Kurdish mevlid (a poem written for the Prophet), along with a feast. Reading out a mevlid in Kurdish has a major impact on Kurdish society. These poems have had a major impact on the Islamization of Kurdish society. See Besikci, Kendini Kesfeden Ulus (Istanbul: Yurt Kitap Yayın, 1993), p. 79. For more on the socio-political environment of the recruitment of the PKK militias, see Ciyayı, Gerilla Anıları II (Istanbul: Aram, 2002); H. Uysal, Dağlarda Yaşamın Dili (Istanbul: Aram, 2001).

[22]  "Diyarbakir'daki Gizli Güç: Mustazaflar!," Sabah, April 20, 2006.

[23]  Interview with a KH sympathizer in Istanbul, August 10, 2007.

KH is the fastest growing organization in many villages. Over the Danish cartoon scandal, the leadership organized a huge demonstration of an estimated 120,000 people in Diyarbakir. In 2006, the largest gathering in Diyarbakir was organized by the KH to celebrate the birthday of the Prophet Muhammad. People read out from the Qur'an and sang Kurdish hymns (ilahi).

There is a new debate on KH web-sites over the establishment of an Islamic Kurdish party. This would indeed mark a new era in Kurdish nationalism, similar to the emergence of Hamas against the PLO in the fragmentation of Palestinian nationalism. Thus, while one sees the fragmentation of Kurdish nationalism along secular versus Islamist lines, one also sees a new realignment of Islamic forces in Turkey between the KH and the AKP. This raises hopes and fears for the long term evolution of Kurdish nationalism.

## The AKP's conflicting Kurdish policies

Without a clearly articulated policy, the AKP has had two strategies towards the Kurdish problem since the 2002 elections: to postpone the issue until the 2007 elections to avoid criticism from Turkish nationalist grass-roots groups and thus to avoid potential conflict with the military (and the threat of a coup); and to transfer the problem to the EU. So far the AKP has been successful in both strategies but not without increasing social cost. Both external and internal actors have been seeking to shape the AKP's policies. The EU has been calling on Turkey to restructure the Kemalist republic to open political spaces for the Kurds and other minority voices; to reduce the ten per cent threshold requirement that would open up the possibility of ethnic Kurdish representation in parliament; and to declare a general amnesty for PKK guerrillas and members. The issue has been the redefinition of sovereignty and the enhancement of local municipalities. Although the AKP has agreed to restructure the Republic and empower local municipalities, since it hopes to benefit from these constitutional changes more than the Kurds, it is adamant in not wishing to change the ten per cent threshold. The issue of a general amnesty for PKK members is also very unpopular among the AKP's grass-roots supporters. Yet, the AKP's main strategy is to de-militarize state and society. It measures its democratization successes in terms of rolling back the military presence in politics.

Aside from external (US and EU) pressures, the AKP's policies are formed in response to domestic pressures, especially as a reaction to the military and the PKK. As such, the AKP has developed a number of positions on the Kurdish question. Before it came to power, the party stressed its "opposition" to state ideology and to the use of the military in

Kurdish-populated regions. The common AKP theme in the ethnically Kurdish-dominated regions was: *We have suffered from this Kemalist ideological state and its associated military as much as you Kurds have. When we come to power, our first priority will be to redefine the state and deconstruct its Kemalist ideology.* As a result of its skillful positioning in the ideological marketplace, the AKP received a sizeable vote in the ethnic Kurdish regions, having portrayed itself as the party of opposition to the "system," while being "sensitive" to the Kurdish problem. Most of the AKP's votes from the Kurdish areas in the 2007 elections came from Islamic-oriented Kurdish villages, towns and cities. Those Kurds whose views were shaped by the traditional religious networks of the Nakshibendi and Nurcu groups, along with the radical Kurdish Hizbullah, supported the AKP as an "anti-system" party.

The major division in the 2002 and 2007 elections was between Kurdish and Islamic strategies. These two identities – ethnicity versus religion – have not been entirely mutually inclusive. Some Kurds, for example, preferred to stress only their ethnic Kurdish identity, through the DEHAP in 2002 and the DTP in 2007; whereas others have preferred to maintain their Kurdishness within the pro-Islam and anti-system AKP. Even though in the 2002 election the DEHAP was the sole party in the Kurdish cities and the AKP was the number two party, in the 2007 elections the AKP became the number one party in some Kurdish cities. For instance, in Diyarbakir province in the 2002 elections the DEHAP received the necessary votes to elect eight out of ten deputies, while in the 2007 elections the DTP only received enough votes to elect four deputies. Furthermore, the AKP won six deputies.[24] This vote was also a protest vote for the DTP. The AKP became the number one party in eight (Çermik, Çınar, Çüngüş, Dicle, Ergani, Eğil, Hani and Kulp) out of thirteen counties. In the small towns where the DTP mayors were participating in local governments, the AKP made dramatic increases. For instance, in those towns where the DTP mayors are in charge the AKP made the following gains.

|          | 2002   | 2007   |
|----------|--------|--------|
| Bilmil   | 4,749  | 14,165 |
| Ergani   | 6,598  | 19,189 |
| Silvan   | 2,073  | 8,904  |
| Kocaköy  | 583    | 1,743  |
| Kayapınar | 10,124 | 13,958 |

[24] Mehmet Mehdi Eker, Kutbettin Arzu, M. İhsan Arslan, Abdurrahman Kurt, Osman Aslan, Ali İhsan Merdanoğlu.

The AKP government's policy until 2007 was to ignore the Kurdish problem or to assume that there was no such problem to begin with. For the AKP leadership, the PKK was an issue which had been exaggerated by the military and some even claimed privately that *the military does not want the conflict to end in order to maintain their spending and role in Turkish politics.* Since the AKP leadership's conceptualization of nationhood was shaped by the National Outlook philosophy of Erbakan, they argue that the Kurdish problem has been created by the Kemalist principles of nationalism and secularism. The anti-military attitude of the AKP leadership in the February 28 process, which resulted in the criminalization of all Islamic movements, helped the PKK by distancing the government from the suggestions of the military.[25] In short, for the AKP, the Kurdish issue was partially created by the military and the best policy was to ignore it and stress Muslim brotherhood instead. This policy of "plausible denial," if you will, came to an end as a result of the resurgence of PKK attacks in May 2005. In addition, the leadership of the PKK, which has not seen any significant progress by the state towards their objectives, is thought to have met in northern Iraq and decided to spread their attacks on soft targets among different sectors of the population, in what some think is a strategy to create a wedge between ethnic Turks and Kurds.[26] It appears that through "demonstration effects" the PKK militants have learnt new tactics from the Iraq resistance, in terms of attacking military targets, mining roads and even carrying out suicide bombing. Moreover, the PKK is known to have had access to Iraqi military armaments. By May 2005 the Turkish security forces had suffered major losses in different parts of southern Anatolia at the hands of the PKK, which had also attacked some civilian targets in major urban centers, such as tourist centers and businesses.[27]

As such, both the Copenhagen criteria and the US-led invasion of Iraq have opened new opportunity spaces for the PKK and its associates to pursue a more integrated policy of resistance in terms of civil society networks, political activism, municipality-based participation and military attacks against Turkish state targets. This new integrated policy of Kurdish assertiveness has led to a major backlash within both Turkish

[25] The 1997 military coup is commonly known as the "February 28 process." The military mobilized the major business associations, media cartels, university rectors and the judiciary to its commands to engineer an anti-Refah Party (RP) drive to force the Necmettin Erbakan government to resign. The coup eventually introduced a system of controlling, monitoring and criminalizing all Islamic activism as a security threat.

[26] Mahsum Şafak, *PKK, Yeniden İnşa Kongre Belgeleri* (İstanbul: Çetin Yayınları, 2005).

[27] The PKK has targeted tourism centers in the following cities: Çeşme on July 10, 2005; Pendik/Istanbul on August 3, 2005; and Antalya on August 12, 2005.

society and state institutions. Hilmi Özkök, then the Chief of the General Staff, for example, openly called on the state to make the necessary legal changes to break down the infrastructure of PKK activism in Turkey.[28] Although Erdoğan had initially favored Özkök's views, he later changed his mind because of the "explanations" of his advisors and the grass-roots Islamic core of the party, which indicated that this new anti-terror law could also be used against Islamic groups. Thus, Islamic and Kurdish groups have pursued a major campaign against any possibility of passing an anti-terror law. When realizing that he could not respond to Özkök's calls for new legal changes, Erdoğan pursued a two-tier policy: ask the US to stop PKK activities in northern Iraq, and use pro-Kurdish language to disarm Öcalan's influence on the Kurdish parties.

### Erdoğan's views on the Kurdish question

Erdoğan does not appear to have a clear understanding of the power of nationalism and ethnic identity. He has constantly shifted his position from denial to the acceptance of the Kurdish issue. On April 13, 2005, he responded to a question in Oslo on the issue by saying:

There isn't a Kurdish problem in Turkey; it is a fictitious problem. We approach this issue within the framework of citizenship. We are at an equal distance to all ethnic groups that exist in Turkey. We do not make any distinction between [ethnic] groups such as Turks, Kurds, Laz, Georgian, and Abkhaz... Do only the Turks live in Turkey?! Beside them, there are at least close to thirty distinct ethnic groups living in the country.[29]

What he failed to emphasize was the sheer overwhelming numbers of ethnic Kurds in comparison to the numbers of other minorities in Turkey.

On August 11, 2005, Erdoğan visited Diyarbakir with the expectation that he would declare his government's new approach to the Kurdish problem, but his visit failed to produce a comprehensive diagnosis to the problem. Even though he reluctantly recognized the existence of the "Kurdish question," he failed to define the causes and content of the "question." Before his visit to Diyarbakir, the media raised expectations

---

[28] There is a major debate going on within Turkey. Some Islamist journalists have accused the Turkish military of placing these mines to force the government to pass the necessary legal framework. In other words, both the AKP government and its supporters do not give autonomy to Kurdish nationalism. They treat the issue as an external tool in the hands of Turkish secularists, the US and even Israel. See "PKK' nın derdi Kürtler değil," *Aksiyon*, No. 556 (August 1, 2005).

[29] Erdoğan's response to some questions about the Kurds and Kurdish nationalism after his speech at the Norwegian Institute of International Relations in Oslo; http://www.byegm. gov.tr/YAYINLARIMIZ/anadoluyahaberler-yeni/2005/nisan/ah_13_04–05.htm

that the government would declare its own solution to the problem. Moreover, since the social origins of the AKP, just like Kurdish nationalism, are rooted in opposition to the founding principles of the Republic, many observers expected a more nuanced and more pro-Kurdish attitude from the government. However, Erdoğan did what he is good at. When in Ankara, he spoke to the people in Diyarbakir; in Diyarbakir, he spoke for the establishment in Ankara; in Norway, he declared the Kurdish question as an "imagined" problem. He said: "All citizens of Turkey are united under the primary identity of being a citizen of the Republic; however, all Turks have sub-identities. No one should be offended by this. A Kurd can say I am a Kurd." State officials and some nationalists were furious and warned that any restructuring and empowering of national sub-entities could lead to the break-up of Turkey, like the former Yugoslavia.

In short, Erdoğan appears not to be committed to a given issue, constantly shifting positions instead, as would a skilled footballer. His goal seems to be simply the preservation of his power. As opposed to its own rhetoric, the AKP does not recognize "Turkish identity" as a supra-ethnic identity that would incorporate Kurdish, Bosniak and Albanian identities. At the same time, Kurdish nationalism rejects the definition of Turkish nationhood as a legal concept and defines the Turkish nation as it would define Kurdish nationhood. Erdoğan told a crowd in Diyarbakir:

There is no need to give a name to every problem. These are our shared collective problems. ... all problems are the problems of the citizens of Turkey no matter what their origin is, namely the problem of Kurds, Circassians, Laz or Abhaza. The sun heats everybody and the rain is God's grace for everybody. Thus I address those asking "What will happen to the Kurdish problem?": the Kurdish problem is my problem... We will solve all problems through democracy.[30]

Without defining the content of the Kurdish question, Erdoğan has argued to solve it within the principle of a "single flag, single state and single nation." His approach to and understanding of the Kurdish issue differs fundamentally from that of the Kurdish nationalists, especially the PKK. For Kurdish nationalists, the source of the problem is the historical injustices which the Kurds have endured. They argue that the Turks entered Anatolia in 1071 with the help of the Kurds against the Byzantine Empire; that the outcome of the major battle at Caldıran between the Ottoman and Persian states in 1514 was determined in favor of the Turks with the support of the Kurds; and that eventually, when Anatolia was occupied and partitioned by the European forces, the war of independence, under Atatürk's leadership, was won because of the Kurds.

---

[30] Erdoğan's speech; see "Son Dakika," *Milliyet*, August 12, 2005, www.milliyet.com.tr

Although Atatürk promised to create a bi-national Republic of Turks and Kurds, after the war he suppressed the Kurds instead and denied their national and cultural rights. He used all means to create a Turkish nation out of diverse Muslim ethnic groups. Thus, the main source of tension between Kurdish nationalism and the Republic is the way in which history is constructed and "nation" is defined. According to the jailed PKK leader, Öcalan, Turkey does not consist of a single (Turkish) nation but is composed of two nations: Turks and Kurds.

Öcalan's solution to the problem evolved from demanding full Kurdish independence using all possible means, including terrorist attacks on civilian populations, to a more moderate position. After his capture, he formulated his position in the following way: "democratic Republic, free motherland, democratic Middle East, unified motherland." By this slogan, he meant the "restructuring of Turkey according to the concept of bi-nationalism; the constitutional recognition of Kurdish political and cultural rights; education in Kurdish; and an apology from the Turkish state to the Kurds for historical injustices." This is the way Öcalan defines the Kurdish question, a view diametrically opposed to Erdoğan's. By stressing the idea of one "single nation," Erdoğan has restated the Republican principle which is also stressed in the preamble of the Turkish Constitution. The Kurdish question is a rebellion against the foundational principle of the Turkish nation-state. The PKK sees this principle as the source of a major contradiction and offers a solution, namely by recognizing the existence of the bi-national structure of Turkey. The PKK justifies the use of violence to unpack this contradiction. Erdoğan's emphasis on the "single nation" is in contradiction with Kurdish nationalist discourse. By stressing the "democratic Republic" theme, Öcalan is creating the conditions for ethnic democracy: political competition among ethnic groups or turning elections into a kind of ethnic census. This form of political competition tends to undermine the process of democratization and leads to the breakdown of political civility.

Erdoğan's apparent inability to understand ethnicity is likely to lead to the ethnification of the public sphere and to encourage ethnic groups to demand legal protection. During Erdoğan's Diyarbakir visit in 2005, ethnic Kurds had expected an economic and political package. However, Erdoğan does not grasp the origins and demands of the Kurdish problem because he has little sense of ethnic or civic nationalism. His dominant identity is Muslim and he thinks that Islamic identity will magically solve the Kurdish problem. On the other hand, Öcalan's discourse of a democratic Republic means creating a "free Kurdish area" within Turkey.

The prime minister's speech in Diyarbakir opened a debate over the "Turkish question" by avoiding the use of the phrase *Turkish* citizenship and only focusing on *citizenship* as a unifying bond of all the people who live in Turkey. In his speech, Erdoğan treated Turkish identity not as a supra-identity of all ethnic groups. Rather, he treated Turkishness just like a Kurdish, Laz or Bosniak identity. The legal aspect of Turkishness and the historical meaning of this concept were totally ignored and Erdoğan reduced it to ethnicity.[31]

On December 6, 2005, speaking at a conference titled "Turkey and the European Union: Opportunities and Obstacles for New Zealand" at the University of Canterbury in Christchurch, Erdoğan said: "In our country, ethnic components of the population are unified by shared Islamic bonds." Erdoğan also used the terms "Turkish origin" and "Kurdish origin" of Turkish citizens and mentioned that: "The Kurds have no difficulty [in Turkey]. Many Kurds occupy very prominent political positions and many are also businessmen. There is no Kurdish question but rather the problem of separatism, which exists in Turkey, and which has led and been used by the PKK/*Kongra-Gel* organizations." Erdoğan framed the Kurdish issue as "separatism" for the first time and identified Islam as the shared glue of Turkish and Kurdish citizens. This seems to show that he is either testing out his ideas or that he has no understanding of the ethnic problems in Turkey. He has shifted from a democratic to an "Islamic" solution to the Kurdish problem. But there are obvious non-Islamic ethnic and religious minorities in Turkey, such as Greeks, Armenians and Jews, all of whom under Turkish law, and to a large extent in practice, are fully fledged Turkish citizens. Perhaps the prime minister should explain how the Islamic bond is shared by these minorities, and does he consider the non-Islamic minorities equal to the majority?

In conclusion, one could argue that Erdoğan has no clear view about ethnicity or ethno-nationalism. Still, two things are very clear: (a) he does not regard "Turkish identity" or the "Turkish" nation as the national identity of the population of Turkey; and (b) he stresses Islamic identity, along with legal citizenship, as the national identity of Turkey. Could Islamic identity and legal citizenship solve the Kurdish problem? The Kurds have been Muslims and lived together with the Turks for centuries; they also have been citizens of Turkey since the establishment of the Republic. One can easily argue that ethnic Kurds do not want to be recognized just as Muslims or simply as Turkish citizens but rather demand the recognition of their Kurdish ethnic identity as co-equal to the Turkish identity.

---

[31] Fikret Bila, "Türk Sorunu," *Milliyet*, August 20, 2005; Ahmet Taşgetiren, "Pişmemiş Yemek," *Yeni Şafak*, August 15, 2005.

### "Turkishness" as a primary identity versus a sub-identity

Because of renewed PKK attacks on military and civilian targets – what some have broadly described as acts of "terrorism" – Erdoğan in 2002 decided to put forward some new ideas on the Kurdish question.[32] However, while attempting to describe his thoughts on the subject matter, he further distanced himself and his party both from the state institutions and from the PKK-led Kurdish actors. Erdoğan's understanding of "Turkishness" at one point has been different from the constitutional definition of nationhood. He has treated Turkish ethnic identity as the PKK has understood it, that is the same: Turkishness is an ethnic identity and not a political construct used to bring the diverse Muslim ethnic groups of the Republic together under a Turkish nation-state. Previously, Turkishness had been more of a state identity than an ethnic one. But Erdoğan has also declared that there is room for ethnic (Kurdish and Turkish) identities within the concept of citizenship. He has hesitated to call this citizenship Turkish, which is a bold declaration since historically Turkishness has been the only acceptable identity. (Indeed, as late as the 1980s, the very existence of the Kurds was denied by some elements within the Turkish state, with Kurds being described as "mountain Turks.") In an August 2005 speech in Ankara, Erdoğan stressed the existence of the Kurdish question and offered citizenship rather than "Turkish identity" as a supra-identity for both the Kurds and Turks.[33] When he was in Diyarbakir a few days later, however, he stressed the unitary nature of the Turkish state and single nationhood.[34] This gap between the two speeches indicates Erdoğan's lack of understanding of the Kurdish problem. In short, his understanding of the issue reflects his Islamic roots in Erbakan's National Outlook Movement. Erdoğan's differentiation of supra- and sub-national identities has not solved the

---

[32] The core group around Erdoğan are all integrated Kurds. They are Cüneyt Zapsu, who has been charged with a number of financial scandals (*Milliyet*, December 31, 2005), Ömer Çelik (who is sharply criticized by conservative groups due to his life-style and new-found wealth), and Mucahit Arslan (who is the son of İhsan Arslan). Inside the party, Dengir Mir Fırat and M. İhsan Arslan are the two most prominent Kurdish parliamentarians. In the cabinet, there are a number of Kurdish ministers. However, all these politicians are well integrated into Turkish society and have never been known to be involved in separatist activities.

[33] Mehmet Metiner, ex-Islamist Kurd, who differentiates "primary" versus "sub-identities" and suggests "constitutional citizenship" as a solution. See Mehmet Metiner, *Ideolojik Devletten Demokratik Devlete* (Istanbul: Beyan, 1999), p. 110. For Erdoğan's statement, see *Zaman*, August 11, 2005.

[34] *Zaman*, August 12, 2005; *Milliyet*, August 13, 2005.

problem, and in fact has further aggravated suspicions toward him. His conceptualization of the Kurdish problem in terms of "Muslim solidarity and brotherhood" has also not appeased nationalist and secularist Kurds – led by the PKK and the DTP – both of which have rejected his attempts to Islamize the identity debate. Moreover, there are also very conflicting views within the AKP parliamentary group. Erdoğan has started to favor a supra-identity over sub-identities, and the decentralization of the bureaucracy. Noble as they might be, Erdoğan's raw ideas appear to have created more problems than solutions. He has been sharply criticized by different state institutions, including almost all the opposition parties.

Turkey's National Security Council has been disturbed by the recent debate over "primary identities" versus "sub-identities." Erdoğan has been reluctant to use the phrase of Turkish nationhood, and identifies "citizenship" as the primary identity over ethnic or cultural identities; he also stresses Islam as the unifying identity of the people of Turkey. The National Security Policy Document of Turkey defines Kurdish, Bosniak, Albanian and Chechen identities as sub-ethnic identities under the state-centric Turkish identity. The military believes that the debate over primary identity versus sub-identity will erode national (Turkish) identity, that this stress on sub-identity will in turn "endanger the unitary structure of Turkey and harm its unity and integrity." While he was Deputy Chief of General Staff, General İlker Başbuğ is known to have said on the topic that "Those who live on Turkish territory and are bound to each other through ties of common aims are defined as the Turkish nation in a unitary state structure."[35] At the War Academy Command School in Istanbul in May 2003, General Yaşar Büyükanıt argued that

Both advocating a single culture in the name of world citizenship and universal culture, and trying to erode national identity through micro-nationalist movements which are supported by the separation of primary and sub-identities, is feeding the crisis of confidence in the international arena. We can foresee today that the political side of globalization can do more harm than good through eroding the concepts of nation-state and sovereignty.[36]

Although the military wants to stress territory and nationhood, and the state as an organic and integrated unit, the AKP disagrees with this and seeks to provide a more multicultural understanding of nationhood. It is

---

[35] Hilmi Özkök, "Yıllık Değerlendirme Konuşması on 20 April 2005," in *Genel Kurmnay Basın Bilgilendirme Toplantıları ve Basına Açık Ana Faaliyetleri* (Ankara: Genel Kurmay Genel Sekreterliği, 2005), p. 215.

[36] Yaşar Büyükanıt, "Küreşelleşme ve Uluslarası Güvenlik," *Birinci Uluslarası Sempozyum Bildirileri* (Ankara: Genel Kurmay Askeri Tarih ve Stratejik Etüt Baskanlığı Yayınları, 2003), p. 17.

clear that there is no shared language between the military and the government in the discussion of the Kurdish question.

Ahmet Necdet Sezer, when president, always criticized Erdoğan's conceptualization of Turkish identity,[37] but what is abundantly clear is that Erdoğan is not entirely sure of his own objectives. He claims to be capable of solving the Kurdish problem but he also rejects any legal changes that would work towards a solution, such as allowing ethnic Kurdish representation in parliament by reducing the ten per cent threshold law, as elaborated below.

### The ten per cent threshold and the DTP in the 2007 elections

In the 1982 constitution, the main goal of the military was to end the proportional representation of the parties.[38] It thus introduced a winner-take-all electoral system by establishing a ten per cent national threshold for party representation in parliament. In recent years, many people, especially Kurdish nationalists, have wanted to reduce the 10% threshold and introduce a radical version of proportional representation that many in the Turkish electorate are strongly against. The old proportional system, many argue, produced a plethora of small parties, unstable government majorities, short-lived revolving-door governments, and ceaseless horse-trading among party leaders, all of which institutionalized corruption and prevented the development of clear policies.

One of the major debates before the 2007 elections relating to the Kurdish question had to do with the 10% election threshold law. This threshold law, which all parties need to meet prior to sending representatives to the Turkish Parliament, had in essence deprived over 45% of the Turkish electorate from parliamentary representation in the 2002 national

---

[37] "Sezer'den yeni yıl mesajı," *Radikal,* January 1, 2006. Sezer argues that "According to our Constitution, the Republic of Turkey is an indispensable unity with its country and nation. Turkey has a unitary state structure. The unity is provided by a multi-cultural society with the principle of a national state. It is the most influential method of co-existence by preserving diversities. Acknowledging every citizen as a Turk does not mean the rejection of different ethnic identities. On the contrary, it provides equality among citizens."

[38] There are a number of problems in the Election Law. The law determines representation on the basis of demographic and also geographic representation. These two principles are in conflict and create injustice in terms of the representation of the population. For instance, in some provinces 8000 or 10,000 votes elect one seat; whereas this reaches to 90,000 in the Western provinces of the country. Although the law seeks to balance demographic and geographic representation, this balance has radically shifted toward geographic representation at the expense of the democratic principle.

elections, and is thus a barrier to the further democratization of Turkey.[39] After the 2002 elections, a group of DEHAP politicians launched a legal complaint to the European Court of Human Rights stating that the 10% threshold was undemocratic and that it was drafted with the intent of keeping the Kurdish party DEHAP out of parliament. The ECHR found Turkey right by arguing that the 10% vote threshold was accepted during a time of political instability to prevent parliamentary fragmentation, and thus it does not aim to deny representation to the Kurdish parties.[40]

Due to the closure case at the Constitutional Court, the DEHAP leadership closed the party, without awaiting the final verdict of the Court, and formed the new Kurdish Democratic Society Party (DTP).[41] This party, like previous Kurdish parties, remains an ethnic party and has failed to become a political force in Turkey. However, it is very popular among politically conscious Kurds who stress a separate identity and demand the redefinition of nationhood, along with constitutional changes. In its official declaration, the DTP has called on the government to remove "all restrictions on the Kurdish language" and for Kurdish to be "given the status of an official language along with Turkish in regions where Kurds live."[42]

After the ECHR's decision, the DTP decided to enter the 2007 elections with independent candidates to break the 10% national threshold for parliamentary representation.[43] These DTP candidates received a slightly smaller percentage of the popular vote than did their DEHAP predecessors in the 2002 election. Some Kurds did not vote for the DTP for three key reasons. The DTP has no economic policy to give hope to the youth or

---

[39] Sezer criticized the 10% threshold and asked parliament to rethink the Election Law. He argues that "The national will is the real source of national sovereignty. Political parties should be represented in parliament in proportion to the votes they win in elections. Nearly half of Turkish voters are not represented in parliament because of the electoral threshold. Today's election system contradicts the principle of justice in representation." *Radikal*, January 1, 2006.

[40] *Milliyet*, January 10, 2007.

[41] Before the Constitutional Court's decision about whether to close the party or not, on the order of Öcalan a group of DEHAP politicians formed the *Demokratik Toplum Partisi* (DTP) on November 9, 2005. The DEHAP closed itself and all DEHAP's 56 mayors and 852 municipal assembly members joined the new party in December 2005. *Vatan Gazetesi*, December 18, 2005.

[42] See "Turkey's Kurds Want Official Status for Language, Broader Rights," AFP, March 6, 2006.

[43] After the DTP's decision, the AKP, along with other parties in parliament, changed the election law to make Kurdish representation more difficult. Under the change the names of independent candidates will appear on the same ballot as those of political parties in the running, instead of on separate slips. This last-minute change, which was approved by President Sezer, is an attempt to obstruct voters in the mainly Kurdish south-east, where many are illiterate or do not speak Turkish, and are likely to have trouble picking their candidate's name from the long list of parties and other independents. Under the AKP government, the Kurds do not feel equal citizens of the Republic of Turkey.

the emerging Kurdish bourgeoisie. It has no policy for the regional development or distribution of the growing national "cake" of Turkey. People do not want to vote only on the basis of identity politics but rather demand better economic conditions. Moreover, the rhetoric of the DTP about the brotherhood of peoples, freedom and peace remains too abstract in the face of the immediate needs of the region; no one explains to the Kurds how these concepts would improve their daily life. The DTP mayors failed to implement these concepts and make a difference to the lives of their people. Finally, the secularist Kurdish leadership of the DTP is not close to the conservative, religious Kurdish masses, who are closer to the leadership of the AKP in terms of their moral values and piety.

Even though the AKP government did not propose any political solution to the Kurdish issue or put forward a regional economic development program, the Kurds voted for it. There are several reasons for the electoral victory of the AKP: the victimization of the party by the establishment; its distance from the policies of the military that favor intervention in northern Iraq; the AKP's promise to rewrite the constitution to give more rights to the Kurds; the new AKP initiatives in education and health care; and especially the Kurdish voters' preference for local over national names.

Many Kurds regard the AKP as an anti-Kemalist and anti-system party, which has been "suppressed" by the same enemy as they have been. The e-memorandum of the military created a sense of unity between the Kurds and the AKP: they both confront the same oppressive military and the Kemalist state. Moreover, many people liked the counter-memorandum of the AKP leadership against the military. When terrorist attacks were increased two months before the elections, the AKP presented this through its "local rumor channels" such as the coffee-houses as the work of the "hawks" within the military to militarize the region and even intervene in northern Iraq. Moreover, the AKP deputies in the Kurdish region carried out a vocal campaign against the military threat to intervene in the affairs of northern Iraq.

Many religious Kurds believe that the AKP has a "hidden agenda" to transform the Kemalist state through a new civic constitution. The AKP had a "Kurdish first" election platform in the region, and the people regarded this as a way of de-Kemalizing the state and constructing a bi-national state with the decentralization of power under a new "civic constitution" that the AKP promised to create. The number one candidate in the AKP electoral list was Kutbettin Arzu, the chairman of the Chamber of Trade and Industry and well liked by every group in Diyarbakir. The AKP deputies all have businesses in the region and also have close relations with the government. Contrary to the AKP, the DTP candidates were not local people with deep roots in the region. The DTP candidates were "professional" politicians, ideologues and activists without any business connections with the region. Rather they were Kurdish political activists who had a mission to "liberate" the Kurds from the Kemalist state, while the people themselves were more interested in improvements in their life. Moreover, the DTP municipalities had done a poor job and failed to improve the life-standards of the people. The people want tangible improvements in their life rather than intangible ideological rhetoric.

Is this the beginning of a new Kurdish politics in terms of supporting a center-right party rather than only a Kurdish-based party? Does this represent a change in the political landscape of Kurdish politics? Did many Kurds vote for the continuation of the AKP's policies or did they vote with the expectation of a new policy? The DTP was certainly taken aback by the AKP's strength in historic Kurdish areas of Turkey. The electoral shift in the province of Diyarbakir is very important in understanding the evolution of Kurdish nationalism, since this province is at the heart of historic Kurdish politics and also contains the largest Kurdish population. Although the DTP sent four deputies to parliament, the AKP garnered the major victory. Ahmet Türk, the co-chairman of the DTP, admitted, "AKP's victory destroyed our calculations." Indeed, the Kurdish ethnic party (the DTP) lost 40,000 votes compared to its DEHAP predecessor in the 2002 elections, declining from 240,000 to 200,000 votes. On the other hand, the AKP's vote increased from 67,000 in the 2002 elections to 190,000 in the 2007 elections. The CHP (Republican People's Party) was the biggest loser as its vote declined from 25,000 in the 2002 elections to just 9,000 in 2007. The MHP (Nationalist Action Party) received 11,000 votes in 2007.

On the Kurdish political landscape, different voices are emerging. Ayşel Tuğluk (the co-chair along with Ahmet Türk of the DTP) is calling upon the Kurds to understand the fear of Sèvres (the 1920 Peace Treaty of Sèvres, signed by the Turkish government, but not ratified by parliament, whereby north-east Turkey became an independent Armenian Republic, and the south-east (Kurdistan) was granted a plebiscite for independence) among the Turks and to develop a new reconciliation,[44] whereas Leyla Zana called for the division of Turkey along new federal lines.[45] One wonders whether the vote for the AKP in the region is a vote for the current AKP policies (if there are any) on the Kurdish question, or a vote with the

[44] Aysel Tuğluk, "Sevr Travması ve Kürtlerin Empatisi," *Radikal*, June 14, 2007.
[45] "Pro-Kurdish Politician Zana: Time To Divide Turkey into States," *Today's Zaman*, July 21, 2007.

expectation that the AKP will deliver a new Republic along the lines of a new civic constitution that might get rid of Kemalism and also open the door to a bi-national state solution. It is known, for example, that the AKP is not comfortable with the Kemalist state ideology and wants to transform it without openly saying so. The "unspoken project" of the AKP is to transform Turkey from a rigid nation-state into a new community of ethnic identities held together by their Muslim identity. Thus, the party supports the ethnic and cultural rights of the Kurds and other minorities within the framework of conservative (religious) values. In short, the AKP does not accept the Kemalist solution to diversity as homogenization (nation-building) but rather seeks to recognize diversity. It has a different notion of political community, similar to that of the Ottoman millet system.

## Kurdish broadcasting and *Roj TV*

Setting apart the 10% barrier to genuine Kurdish representation, the government has taken a number of positive steps by liberalizing Kurdish broadcasting from private TV and radio stations. Due to pressures from the EU membership process, Turkey had already changed its laws and as of 2004 had allowed limited broadcasts in Kurdish and other minority languages, and state TV had been airing programs in two Kurdish dialects for half an hour each week. However, as late as December 2005, private TV stations and radio stations were not allowed to broadcast in Kurdish. But then the Supreme Board of Radio and Television (RTÜK) decided to allow those "stations that have completed their applications" to be able to begin broadcasting in Kurdish by the end of January 2006. Although this decision still does not allow Kurdish-only broadcasting – Kurdish broadcasting actually being limited to a mere forty-five minutes a day – it is still a major step for Turkey, where until 1991 speaking one's mother tongue in public could result in ethnic Kurds paying fines or serving prison sentences. The two television channels in Diyarbakir – *Gün TV* and *Söz TV* – and a radio station in Şanlıurfa, *Medya FM*, have started to broadcast in Kurdish but are limited to forty-five minutes a day. In June 2006, RTÜK lifted the limit of forty-five minutes daily and four hours per week imposed on Kurdish-language broadcasts of cultural shows on TV. According to the decision those television stations that have permission to broadcast in Kurdish can now run movies and concerts beyond the time allocated, but the limitation still stands for news programs and discussion shows.

There are at least three TV channels that broadcast via satellite including *Roj TV*, *Mezopotamya* and *MCM*. *MCM* broadcasts video clips around the clock, and *Mezopotamya* is an art and culture channel. *Roj TV* is a prime-time channel, which also broadcasts news and political discussions.

The pro-PKK *Roj* ("Sun" in Kurdish) satellite television station that broadcasts from Denmark has been a major source of problems for the AKP government. *Roj TV* is a staunch supporter of the PKK, which is labeled a terrorist organization by the EU, and Turkey has long been calling on the Danish authorities to close it down. In late 2005, Erdoğan even refused to attend a news conference in Copenhagen because a *Roj TV* reporter was present. While the AKP government tried unsuccessfully to force the closure of *Roj*, which it claimed to be a mouthpiece for the outlawed PKK, a total of fifty-six Kurdish mayors of the DTP from southern Anatolia appealed to the Danish government, urging it not to do so, arguing in a petition to the Danish prime minister in December 2005 that: "For a truly democratic life to flourish in Turkey, *Roj TV* should not be silenced." These Kurdish mayors argued that rather than banning *Roj TV*, "Turkey should embrace it and give it a legal identity." *Roj TV*, just like *Kurdistan TV*, *Zaghros TV*, and *Kurdsat*, promotes Kurdish identity by stressing Kurdish political consciousness and by defining the Turks as the "other" of Kurdish identity.

### Iraq and the Kurdish question

The impact of the Iraq war on the Kurdish question has been profound. While many Kurds in Turkey look to Kurdish self-governance in Iraq for inspiration, the Turkish state, and most Turks, see it as an example of what the future could bring: a collapsed central state and brewing ethnic civil war. Most Turks view US policy towards the PKK as a double standard on Washington's part. The US is involved in a global war against terrorist groups and networks, yet it has done very little to stop PKK activities in northern Iraq. CENTCOM has agreed to plan an offensive against the PKK but has shown no willingness to implement it or to allow Turkey to cleanse the area of PKK fighters and their networks. US inaction is the major source of increasing frustration in the AKP government and Ankara believes that Washington is deliberately using the PKK card to give the AKP an internal problem and to limit Turkey's influence in Iraq until the Kurds carve out their own state. Current relations between Ankara and Washington are characterized by mutual suspicion and lack of trust on the Turkish side. The Turks see Kurdish sovereignty in Iraq as a threat to the integrity of their state. They regard a fully autonomous Kurdish state in Iraq as a precursor to a stronger push for independence and more divisive civil strife among the Kurds of Turkey.[46]

---

[46] İlker Başbuğ, the Ground Forces Commander, warned the government and the public about the potential threat of Kurdish autonomy, *Milliyet*, September 24, 2007.

Similar fears are felt in Iran. Playing on these concerns, the Iranian ambassador to Turkey asserted that "the US will carve pieces from us for a Kurdish state." The Turkish government is not alone in its distaste for the idea of a Kurdish state.

Moreover, since the US occupation in 2003, Iraq has become the major regional arms bazaar, with mountains of explosives and other weaponry literally left lying on the ground by the Saddam Hussein regime. As a result, militant Islamists and PKK terrorists operating in Iraq have access to ample quantities of military-grade explosives, mortars and rocket-propelled grenades. The PKK has full access to Iraqi explosives and mines to use against the Turkish military and security forces. Thus, since the occupation of Iraq, PKK attacks have increased and the death toll has also increased. Since the 2002 AKP government, PKK attacks have been on the rise. In 2002, only six soldiers died in PKK terrorist attacks, while the figures for 2003, 2004, 2005 and 2006 were 21, 73, 97 and 123 respectively. In the first nine months of 2007, 213 soldiers were killed. The funerals of the soldiers have been turned into protest meetings against the government and policies of Erdoğan. Protesters call on the prime minister to send his own son to fight the PKK guerrillas. Thus mourners in the western town of Bergama, near the Aegean port city of Izmir, were angry at Erdoğan's comments in September 2006: "Military service isn't the place to lie down and unwind," when an ordinary person asked how he would respond to the recent killings of soldiers. He said "Military service has risks. It's not a holiday." The premier's remarks have caused outrage. The common banner carried in these funerals now says: "He didn't lie down," in reference to dead soldiers. Moreover, some angry women have been seen shouting "Send Bilal to the army," in reference to Erdoğan's son, who lives in the United States. The increase in military casualties has turned the burial ceremonies for the dead soldiers into anti-government demonstrations, which forces the AKP government to search for a solution.

### Conclusion

In spite of high expectations, the AKP government has failed to offer a framework for a solution to the Kurdish question. There are a number of reasons for this failure and for the AKP's lack of commitment to the problem. Neither the AKP nor the government have sought expert opinion about the problem and prefer to avoid open debate on the issue. Thus, the AKP has no integrated road map as to how to respond to the Kurdish question. The party has shied away from a public debate on the issue and has ignored the insecurity felt by both ethnic Turks and Kurds. By not addressing the problem, it has simultaneously failed to win the confidence both of the Kurds and of the state institutions. The AKP must create a national consensus on the way to addressing the problem in parliament and in its own party structure. Erdoğan's double-talk on the topic – in attempting to simultaneously appease the Kurdish vote and suppress Kurdish freedom – has not helped the AKP, but rather undermined his credibility among Kurds and Turks alike. It appears therefore that the AKP's Kurdish policy continues to be that of "no policy" or an active attempt to "forget the issue." Erdoğan also faces a dilemma. If the AKP, which is a party mainly based on the Turkish-Muslim electorate, were to focus on the Kurdish problem, it would open itself to further criticism from the nationalist MHP in parliament. Nor would this attempt necessarily enhance the AKP's image among its ethnic Turkish base, who are generally against additional Kurdish group rights.

Moreover, the recent erosion in the credibility of the government further complicates the debate over the solution. Erdoğan, with his small circle of largely inexperienced advisors, is less likely to bring a creative solution to the problem. The public has already been debating his lack of commitment to Turkish identity. Some even think that he has become a hostage to pro-Barzani forces within the AKP. Simultaneously, the government's lack of a policy, in conjunction with the existence of substantial numbers of PKK militants inside Turkey, will likely lead to increased attacks on both hard and soft targets. This, in turn, will lead both the public and the military to force the AKP government to prepare the necessary legal framework to fight against PKK terrorism, including a possible military incursion into northern Iraq to destroy PKK camps. However, some ethnic Kurdish deputies of the AKP have already raised their objection to any military incursion that might weaken the autonomy of the Barzani-led Iraqi Kurdish regional government.[47] While Kurdish cultural and political rights have been increased under EU pressure as a part of larger democratic reforms, many Kurds rightly feel that such reforms have not gone far enough. The EU, the key driver of these reforms, has asked the AKP-dominated government to develop a comprehensive plan, also covering security aspects, to cope with regional socio-economic demands.

---

[47] "AKP'den Aykırı Sesler Var," *Radikal*, October 13, 2007.

# 7    The foreign policy of the AKP

We regard Turkey's EU membership as the biggest democratization project after the proclamation of the Republic.[1]

We want to integrate with Europe, not assimilate.[2]

The EU is our obsession. Even though we all understand different things from the EU membership, this obsession is what unifies us.[3]

What guides the foreign policy of the AKP? Has the AKP government made any changes in the orientation of Turkey's traditional pro-Western foreign policy? What is the connection between identity and interest in the formation of the AKP's foreign policy? These are some questions which this chapter attempts to answer.[4] On the basis of speeches by Prime Minister Erdoğan and President Gül, then Foreign minister, one can identify three guiding principles of AKP foreign policy: the Europeanization of foreign policy as a way of maintaining the domestic and international legitimacy of the government; the policy of "zero-problem with the neighbors," that is, to create a peaceful environment in Turkey by developing trade and political

---

[1] Erdoğan, *Konuşmalar*, p. 35.
[2] On September 23, 2004 Erdoğan was quoted at the European Parliament as having said: "We are in favor of integration not assimilation."
[3] Interview with Handan Memiş, a teacher in Aydın province, March 5, 2005.
[4] In my analysis of the AKP foreign policy, I focused on the following statements of the policy makers. See, for example, "Turkish Foreign Policy in the 21st Century," Statement by Prime Minister Recep Tayyip Erdoğan at the Council on Foreign Relations, January 26, 2004; "Democracy in the Middle East, Pluralism in Europe: the Turkish View," address by Recep Tayyip Erdoğan, prime minister of Turkey, Harvard University, Kennedy School of Government, January 30, 2004; speech made by Turkish Foreign Minister Abdullah Gül at the 30th Session of the Islamic Conference of Foreign Ministers, Tehran, May 28, 2003; statement by Abdullah Gül, deputy prime minister and minister of foreign affairs of the Republic of Turkey on Turkey's role in the Middle East, World Economic Forum, Dead Sea, June 22, 2003; statement by deputy prime minister and minister of foreign affairs of the Republic of Turkey, Abdullah Gül, at the Regional Countries' Meeting on Iraq, Kuwait, February 14, 2004 (http://www.mfa.gov.tr); Ahmet Davutoğlu, "Türkiye Küresel Güçtür!" *Anlayış* (March 2004), 40–45; Ahmet Davutoğlu, "Türkiye Merkez Ülke Olmalı," *Radikal*, February 26, 2004.

ties with neighbors, especially with Muslim countries; and pursuing a policy that balances the anti-American feelings of its grass-roots supporters with its need for US support.

The policy-makers of the AKP consider Turkey to be not a "bridge," but rather a "pivotal" state in the region. A close examination of the writings of Ahmet Davutoğlu, the top foreign policy advisor of the government, and Foreign Minister Gül's statements indicates that they both stress Turkey's "Eastern" – read Islamic – identity, while at the same time stressing the government's determination to adopt mainstream Western values and principles in order to join the EU.[5] There is thus a deep duality at play between "Eastern identity" and "the Western values" that the government seeks to implement.

The foreign policy of Turkey under the current AKP government can be characterized as full of fragmented characteristics that are very much the reflection of the AKP's own syncretic origins.[6] Moreover, current Turkish foreign policy is the outcome of the clash of institutional interests between the state establishment and the AKP. Since each institution equates its interests with those of the nation, and given the deep ideological gap between the AKP and the establishment, there is currently no unified framework for articulating a truly national "national interest". This fragmentation is the major characteristic of the post-2002 governments. For instance, Turkey's dwindling policies vis-à-vis the Cyprus dispute and the rejection of the March 1, 2003 motion by the Turkish parliament, which would have permitted the use of Turkish territory by the US in its invasion of Iraq, cannot be examined without taking into account the conflicting institutional interests of the military and the AKP. In the case of the Iraq war, the military wanted the total failure and delegitimization of the AKP government by not actively involving itself in the decision-making process and expecting the AKP government to shoulder the full responsibility for the decision to engage in the 2003 Iraq war, whereas the AKP wanted to create a schism between the military and its staunch supporter, the Pentagon, by voting against the motion.

The main argument I seek to advance in this chapter is that the AKP uses foreign policy both to transform the country and expand its own

---

[5] Davutoğlu's assumption that Turkey is the center of the region and should play a pivotal role in leading and shaping regional issues is premature. Turkey's internal divisions, combined with the precarious economic situation and the deep suspicions between the military and the civilian government, make it difficult for the time being for Turkey to have an independent foreign policy.

[6] Erhan Doğan, "The Historical and Discursive Roots of the Justice and Development Party's EU Stance," *Turkish Studies*, 6:3 (September 2005), 421–437.

domestic legitimacy vis-à-vis the establishment.[7] The AKP is building alliances with major international actors to secure and protect itself against domestic pressure from the civilian–military Kemalist–secularist establishment. In that sense one can persuasively argue that the experience of the Erbakan government in 1996–1997, which resulted in the resignation of the government under military and judicial pressure, compounded by an intensive media campaign, still informs the actions and policies of the AKP leadership. The looming shadow of the February 28 process is vividly seen in the policies of the current government as it tries to simultaneously placate and neutralize the military–bureaucratic establishment and its allies in the political system. By affirming and seeking to implement EU requirements and norms of civilian democracy and civil liberties for accession, the AKP seeks to redefine and limit the autonomous role of the military and its allies in the judiciary and bureaucracy. The leadership of the AKP appears to imagine a Turkey not defined by its military capabilities and geo-strategic/geo-political positions but instead by its democratic identity and economic power.[8] However in order to reduce the power of the military and Turkey's dependence on the US, it is vital to address Turkey's internal (Kurdish and Islamic identity claims) and external (Cyprus and the Kurdish issues) security issues by liberalizing the domestic and international political landscape and improving the economic and social integration of these sectors of society. To achieve those aims, the goal of the AKP is to remove from the security realm the identity claims and contestation of the Kurds and Islamic groups, which proved unsolvable through purely coercive means through the 1990s. In addressing its domestic and external problems, the AKP leadership has sought to improve Turkey's international standing as a model democratic and economically powerful state in the region, imitating the European model of Kantian soft-power. In addition, the EU process is being surprisingly championed by a political party of Islamic background, which seeks to enshrine civilian control over the military and freedom of thought and religion by, ironically, championing the liberal democratic basis of Westernization that the Kemalist Westernizers often chose to ignore. Not surprisingly, therefore, the first priority of the AKP government has been Turkey's impending membership of the EU.[9]

---

[7] M. Hakan Yavuz, *Islamic Political Identity in Turkey* (New York: Oxford University Press, 2005), p. 262.

[8] Saban Kardaş, "Türkiye AB Yolunda Reform dalgasını Sürdürmeli," *Zaman*, July 8, 2004.

[9] Bilal Şimsir, *AB, AKP ve Kıbrıs* (Ankara: Bilgi, 2003). This book lays out the Kemalist secular suspicions of the AKP government.

In the first part of this chapter, I will identify the two ideological parameters of Turkey's foreign policy by stressing first, the role of insecurity (the "Sèvres Syndrome"), which I argue is perpetuated through the memory of the disintegration of the Ottoman Empire, and second, the state's commitment to "Westernization" as a way of civilizational transformation.[10] In this section, I will also examine how three different identity-elite groups have developed diverse visions of foreign policy. I will also focus on the role of identity in the definition of national interests. In the second part of the chapter, I will analyze the AKP's policies toward the EU (and the Cyprus issue); the USA (the Iraqi crisis); and its relations with Israel and Arab countries to illustrate its perception of "national interest."

## I.      Foreign policy parameters and layers of identity

The psychology of Turkey's Republican ideology was based on the idea of protecting and defending the "last remaining Ottoman territory" against separatist and centrifugal forces. After the defeat and expulsion of foreign forces under the leadership of Mustafa Kemal Atatürk, this fear of disintegration has shaped the definition of friends and foes of the Republic, including the attitude towards opposition parties. Given the ideological orientation of the founding elite, the security identity of the Turkish state cannot be divorced from Kemalism. The insecurity of the Turkish state is very much the product of a Kemalism that determines the construction of the "self" and the "other." Kemalism as a nation-building project and modernizing ideology labeled all identity-based challenges to its homogenizing project as "enemies." This, in turn, shrank the political arena and hindered the development of democracy. In recent times, this deeply rooted psychology centered around fears of disintegration has been reactivated with the Kurdish demands for autonomy, several European countries' pressure on Turkey to recognize the Armenian claims of "genocide,"

---

[10] The Treaty of Sèvres, signed in 1920 between the allies and the Ottoman government, partitioned eastern Anatolia among diverse groups and provided only a fragment of north-east Anatolia to the Turks. Article 62 of the Treaty referred to the need for "local autonomy for the predominantly Kurdish areas" and Article 64 looked forward to the possibility that "the Kurdish people" might be granted "independence." This Treaty left deep scars on the collective memory of the Turks, and is known as the "Sèvres Syndrome." The fear of partition by the European powers was at the center of the Republican policies to suppress Kurdish identity claims. The treaty can be found online at: http://www.lib.byu.edu/~rdh/wwi/versa/sevres1.html My study is theoretically informed by the Copenhagen School (CS) of security studies. Security, for the CS, is not a concept with a fixed meaning, and thus it cannot be objectively defined. See B. Buzan et al., *Security: A New Framework for Analysis* (Boulder: Lynne Rienner, 1998).

and calls for concessions on Cyprus. These demands have not only hardened Turkish nationalism, but have also undermined the legitimacy of a government that has purported to be able to find a solution to those perennial issues. The first parameter of Turkish foreign policy is the protection of the state and of the territorial integrity of Turkey, and the second parameter is an extension of its domestic politics: the "Westernization" (read "secularism") of Turkey through its external relations.

Within the context of the state's commitment to the strident secularism of Mustafa Kemal, the AKP's Islamic roots are the main source of skepticism both inside and outside of Turkey. These roots became a symbol of illegitimacy in the eyes of the establishment, and the party has used its foreign policy as a tool to disassociate itself from its roots or charges of Islamism, and as an attempt to enhance its domestic and international legitimacy. To achieve this, among other things, the party has indexed itself to the Copenhagen criteria. Moreover, the party leadership thinks that the good governance and independence of the civilian government requires external support, especially American endorsement. Thus, the new government is extremely careful to balance the anti-American feelings of its grass-roots supporters and its need for US support. Even though shortly after the beginning of the US invasion of Iraq Turkish public opinion remained overwhelmingly against both the US use of Turkish territory and the demand that Turkish troops should be sent to Iraq, the AKP government concluded that cooperation with the US was inevitable and that it would be obliged to implement US demands. The AKP was not free to pursue an identity-based foreign policy because of the shadow cast by the February 28 process that resulted in the resignation of the Erbakan government. The government's reluctant cooperation with the US reflected both pragmatism and the use of foreign policy to enhance its legitimacy vis-à-vis the military and business establishments. In effect, the new AKP government wanted to place itself as the subcontractor for the US rather than the military. The government sought to outbid the military by not providing any opportunity for the armed forces to enforce their role in domestic or foreign policy. In this context, one cannot fully grasp the nature of Turkish–US relations if one ignores the ongoing government–military rivalry within Turkey. This case illustrates that the AKP's foreign policy is shaped more by the search for domestic and international legitimacy than by Islamic identity.

### The identity layers of Turkey and its foreign policy visions

Since identity is usually a matter of interaction between different sectors of society, it is not always easy to establish a causal link between identity and foreign policy.[11] Identities are not given but rather developed and transformed in interaction. The ongoing interaction between the AKP government and international institutions, for example, has changed the identity and attitude of the party. One layer of identity is stressed in certain situations depending on the identity of the "other" – that of other states or organizations. Alexander Wendt argues that a "world in which identities and interests are learned and sustained by inter-subjectively grounded practice, by what states think and do, is one in which 'anarchy is what states make of it.'"[12] These inter-subjective meanings evolve as a result of interactively constructed collective meanings. The identity of the state in Turkey shifted from a pan-Islamically oriented foreign policy under the Ottoman Sultan Abdülhamid II (1876–1909) to a national orientation under Mustafa Kemal (1922–1938), which presupposed an entirely new set of roles and expectations. Identities are significant because they help to define interests.[13] These interests, in turn, have shaped Turkey's conduct in the Balkans and Central Asia. Therefore, some fluctuations in Turkey's foreign policy are largely related to the identity debates among institutions in Turkey.[14] As long as this identity and interest transformation is not fully understood, one may not, for instance, fully grasp Turkey's role in Central Asia, the Middle East and the Balkans.[15]

I would argue that Turkish state identity has been constituted as a result of two processes: seismic international events that have directly affected Turkey's perception of its "self"; and the domestic transformation of elite politics. Moreover, the historical legacy of the Ottoman state and the "culture of insecurity" have constituted the two most fundamental constraints in the evolution of state identity in Turkey. However, in addition to the "self" of the Turkish state, which has been defined as secular and westernized, there is also the "self" of the Turkish nation, a "self" more

---

[11] İrfan Çiftçi, "Avrupa'nın 'Öteki'si Olarak Türk İmgesi: Olduğu gibi Görünemeyen, Göründüğü Gibi Olamayan Korkunun Efendileri: Türkler," *Istanbul Bilgi Universitesi Bilgi ve Bellek*, 3 (2006), 61–92.

[12] A. Wendt, "Levels of Analysis vs. Agents and Structures: Part III," *Review of International Studies*, 18 (1992), 183.

[13] A. Wendt, "Anarchy is what States Make of it: the Social Construction of Power Politics," *International Organization*, 46:2 (1992), 391–425.

[14] M. Hakan Yavuz, "Turkic Identity and Foreign Policy in Flux: the Rise of Neo-Ottomanism," *Critique*, 12 (1998), 19–42.

[15] Emmanuel Adler argues that the transformation of identities and interests may be the "constructivist dependent variable." Adler, "Seizing the Middle Ground: Constructivism in World Politics," *European Journal of International Relations*, 3 (1997), 344.

dynamic and open to change than the official discourse of the state, one which has long been held hostage by Kemalist ideology. To overcome this deep identity crisis between the state and nation, the AKP has stressed Turkey's Islamic and European layers of identity.

Identity is a fluid matter of our minds picturing the way the world and our social interactions are organized in relation to other social groups. Political elites usually seek to mobilize or construct identities to promote specific interests. Therefore, identity becomes an instrument for the pursuit of interests. At the same time, the causal arrow between interests and identity can also run from identity to interest. For instance, Turkey utilizes religious, linguistic and other cultural affinities to enhance its interest in Central Asia. At the same time, Turkish national interest is defined by how elites and populations view their identity. The national identity of Turkey has veered towards three mostly constructed and dominant layers of religion, ethnicity and supra-nationality: Islamic, Turkic and European. These three dimensions shape elite perceptions of interest and preferences but cannot explain specific policy choices.

The three layers of Turkey's national identity indicate contextual, relational and multiple features of identity. Due to its multiple national identities, the Turkish state invokes different layers of identity in response to specific policy issues. In the crises in Bosnia and Kosovo, for example, the state stressed its Ottoman and Islamic identity; whereas in Central Asia, it stresses its Turkic identity. In order to understand contemporary Turkish foreign policy, it is important to unpack the identity debate and analyze the competing identity-based elite factions that have an impact in the making of Turkey's foreign policies. These layers of identity are open to internal and external changes. There are three major identity-driven elite factions in Turkey:

(1) The "Kemalist" elite have traditionally supported Turkey's full integration into the EU as well as close ties with the US. In terms of their ideology, they have professed to view their ties with Europe and the EU as more of a "civilizational" pull. A Kemalist foreign policy for Turkey has therefore entailed the realization of a civilizational shift, which has, among other things, involved Turkey's participation in as many European organizations as possible. Kemalism has tended to treat the "Turkic world" as an opportunity arena in order to elevate Turkey's geo-strategic importance in the eyes of Europe and the international system, and has presented Turkey as a "secular state model" for Muslim states. In recent years, the adherents of Kemalism have been divided among nationalist hardliners, known as *ulusalcılar*, and liberal moderates. This will be examined in detail later.

(2) The burgeoning "Islamist" elite view the existing economic and political system imposed by the domestic Kemalists as their rival.[16] They
have subordinated ethnic–national identity to a religious and civilizational one (*umma*), and have supported close ties with Muslim countries in the Middle East and Central Asia. After their transformation
in the wake of the February 28 process, members of this group are not
inherently anti-Western and support Turkey's entry into the EU with
one important caveat: they reject the model of the Europeanization
(as Westernization) of the country. This view towards the Arab world
and Central Asia is colored by the idea of Islamic solidarity and
Islamic civilization. They endeavor to present Turkey as a pivotal
and a central element in Islamic civilization and want it to become a
"protector" in the Balkans and the former Soviet Union. They seek
cooperation with Muslim countries to form a core Islamic bloc. At the
same time, however, the Islamic elite's view is Turkic-centric in the
sense of seeing Turkey as the "leader" of the Islamic world and
seeking to activate or jumpstart the ideal of a revitalized and integrated Islamic civilization and bloc, through the active agency of the
Islamic world's most economically, politically and military advanced
country, Turkey. Most ministers, advisors and parliamentarians of
the AKP stress Islam as their core identity and define national interests within an Islamic framework.[17] As the grass-roots supporters of
the AKP share the views of the Islamist elite, they are very skeptical of
the EU project. The leadership of the AKP believes that Turkey in
general and the AKP in particular represent Islamic civilization. A
major new permutation – and both a possible benefit and a source of
contradiction – is that the party wants to promote a modern and
reformist Islamic identity by emulating many successful European
ideas and values.

(3) The "nationalist" elite include groups who support cultural and
political cooperation, and even integration, among Turkic states.
This group includes some ultra-nationalists, who disagree with
Turkey's full integration into the EU. This group seeks to form a
Turkic – but not necessarily Islamic – world under the cultural and
political leadership of Turkey.

---

[16] For an excellent analysis of the role of new Islamic bourgeoisie, see "Islamic Calvinists:
Change and Conservatism in Central Anatolia," European Stability Initiative (Berlin,
September 19, 2005). This paper demonstrates the role of economic activity in the
re-imagination of Islam.

[17] See: Ahmet Davutoğlu, *Sratejik Derinlik: Türkiye'nin uluslararası konumu* (Istanbul: Küre
Yayınları, 2001); *Küresel Bunalım* (Istanbul: Küre Yayınları, 2002). Also see: Derya
Sazak's interview with Davutoğlu, "Sohbet Odası," *Milliyet*, January 13, 2003.

The Kemalist Europhile elite have traditionally dominated the foreign policy of Turkey, due to a form of "dual-track government" in which the elected government must be subordinated to the prescribed Kemalist program of secularism and national homogenization as defined and enforced by the military–civilian bureaucracy.[18] This bureaucracy has played a significant role in the making and implementation of foreign policy. As Turkey becomes more democratic, foreign policy is also defined by the identity of the elected representatives.[19] Since the AKP has deep Islamic roots and the identity of its electoral base is more Islamic than nationalist, it is important to examine the Islamic discourses concerning Europe and Turkey's Europeanization process.

The main argument of the AKP leadership in relations with the EU and the US is to draw on the specter of the "clash of civilizations" to suggest that the West must support a successful Muslim Turkey because it would be the biggest antidote to the Huntington/Bin Laden thesis. The secular elite, however, especially the military, is very suspicious of Turkey being portrayed as an "Islamic model" either by the Americans or by the AKP leadership.[20] In April 2005, General Hilmi Özkök, then the Chief of the General Staff, strongly criticized those who seek to portray Turkey as a model for the Islamic world. Indeed, no Muslim country sees Turkey as a model *of* democracy or a model *for* Islamic life. Özkök, for instance, openly raised the flag of an "Islamic threat" as a danger to the Kemalist order.[21] He told a group of officers in Istanbul that "Turkey is not a Muslim state but a secular and democratic country."[22] Prime Minister Erdoğan always talks about an "alliance of civilizations" and claims that Turkey could bring about such an alliance. However, many people

---

[18] Yavuz, *Islamic Political Identity*, p. 255.

[19] This development was first predicted by M. Hakan Yavuz and Mujeeb R. Khan, "A Bridge between East and West: Duality and the Development of Turkish Foreign Policy Toward the Arab-Israeli Conflict," *Arab Studies Quarterly*, 14:4 (Fall 1992), 69–95.

[20] Graham Fuller, "Turkey's Strategic Model: Myths and Realities," *The Washington Quarterly*, 27:3 (Summer 2004), 51–64. Foreign minister Gül in Jordan in June 2003: "The Turkish experience might serve as a source of inspiration for some other countries. This experience is about an effort to achieve democracy, civil rights and liberties, respect for the rule of law, civil society and gender equality. Our Turkish experience proves that national and spiritual values can be in perfect harmony with contemporary standards of life. We believe that integration with the world is not possible without harmonizing our values and traditions with modernity. The alternative to this way is isolation and desperation." Hüseyin Bağcı and Saban Kardaş, "Post-September 11 Impact: The Strategic Importance of Turkey Revisited," in Idris Bal (ed.), *Turkish Foreign Policy in Post-Cold War Era* (Boca Raton: Brown Walker Press, 2004), pp. 421–455.

[21] Ahmet Tasgetiren, "Kippa Takmak," *Yeni Şafak*, May 2, 2005; Nuray Mert, "Islam Ülkesi," *Radikal*, April 26, 2006.

[22] Özkök said "Turkey is neither an Islamic state nor an Islamic country." (*Türkiye bir İslam devleti de, bir İslam ülkesi de değildir.*)

wonder whether Turkey seeks to play this role as a Western or an Islamic country. The secularists want Turkey to be the representative of the West, improve the human rights situation and offer the Turkish secular model to the Muslim world; whereas the AKP wants to be the representative of the Muslim world in an effort to improve the image of Islam and Muslims in the West.

## II.      The Copenhagen criteria: the AKP's lodestar of domestic transformation

There are two different discourses in Turkey regarding the country's membership of the EU.[23] Secular nationalists are increasingly critical of the EU. They defend the old notion of national sovereignty and anti-imperialist, and anti-globalist traits. In early 2004, a new anti-EU coalition was formed. This politically weak but vocal group strongly opposes Turkey's integration into the EU and insists on keeping its "national sovereignty." This coalition consists of "Kemalist-left" organizations led by the ex-Maoist Turkish Workers' Party (TİP) of Doğu Perincek and some ultra-nationalist factions of the MHP (Nationalist Action Party). This has resulted in a coalition network, known as "Red Apple," the Turkish dream of unifying all Turkic nations against colonialism, which includes retired generals, police officers, and right-wing intellectuals and some academics.[24] This loosely formed network has close ties with the Eurasian Movement that has been promoted by the Russian Alexander Dugin. This secular nationalist front is also anti-American. The prominent members of this coalition are: *Büyük Hukukcular Birliği* (Greater Jurists Union), *Kuvayi Milliye Hareketi* (Nationalist Forces Front), and *Vatansever Kuvvetler Birliği* (Patriotic Forces Union) which has over 150 branches throughout Turkey. It also includes *Devrimci İşçi Sendikaları* (Revolutionary Labor Union). These groups insist on one of the key principles of Kemalism, that "sovereignty belongs unconditionally and unreservedly to the nation," a statement which still hangs on the end wall of the plenary chamber in the Turkish parliament in Ankara. At the same time, this group insists on the "indivisibility of the Turkish nation" and is critical of multi-cultural pressures to redefine Turkish

---

[23] M. Hakan Yavuz, "Islam and Europeanization in Turkish-Muslim Socio-Political Movements," in Peter J. Katzenstein and Timothy A. Byrnes (eds.), *Religion in an Expanding Europe* (Cambridge: Cambridge University Press, 2006), pp. 225–255; Hasan Kösebalaban, "Turkey's EU Membership: A Clash of Security Cultures," *Middle East Policy*, 9:2 (2002), 130–46.

[24] Onur Atalay, *Kızıl Elma Koalisyonu: Ulusalcılar, Milliyetçiler, Kemalistler* (Istanbul: Paradigma Yayinlari, 2006), pp. 73–94.

nationhood. They denounce European pressure in favor of Kurdish rights and reject the expansion of democratic liberties and civil society as being at the expense of the state-dominated Kemalist political culture.

The second group, known as the secular liberals, is less dogmatic in its orientation and defends the country's integration into the world; hence they are supportive of both globalization and the EU process. They stress the civilizational aspect of Kemalism and are receptive to the idea of redefining Turkish nationhood as a multicultural and legal polity. The liberal Kemalists see EU membership as the realization of the Westernization project, which aims to create a Europeanized society.[25] For them EU membership is about becoming European by giving up one's traditional Islamic identity and legacy. For the Europhile Kemalists, the EU project is about assimilation into European culture and freedom from traditional religious worldviews. Due to the hegemonic position of this discourse until the 1980s, Turkey's political Islamists like Necmettin Erbakan reacted negatively to Turkey's integration with European institutions, thus becoming labeled "Islamic Euroskeptics."

| Ideological Outlook | | |
|---|---|---|
| **Position on Europe** | *Kemalist* | *Islamic* |
| **Europhile** | **Kemalist and liberal Europhile** TÜSİAD, ANAP, DYP, CHP Goal: Assimilation | **Europhile and communitarian** Nur community, the AKP Goal: Integration/Co-existence |
| **Euroskeptic** | **Kemalist nationalist Euroskeptic** TİP, MHP Goal: absolute sovereignty | **Islamic Euroskeptic** Haydar Baş, SP Goal: Islamic and anti-Europe |

As a result of neo-liberal economic policies and the February 28 process, a major transformation took place within the Islamic political movement in Turkey and two diametrically different positions developed. Today, there are broadly two Islamic mind-sets – "Euroskeptic" and "Europhile" – reflecting the wider division in Turkey with regard to policies and reforms related to EU membership or the Europeanization process. The Euroskeptic position argues that political reforms have made Turkey and Islamic culture vulnerable to European influence, if not

---

[25] M. Hakan Yavuz and Mujeeb R. Khan, "Turkey and Europe: Will East Meet West?," *Current History*, 103:676 (November 2004), 389–393.

manipulation.[26] This position argues that it is important for Turkey to have more political liberties but without "compromising" its Islamic identity. Also, they argue, Europe is not honest and sincere in its human rights discourse; according to the Islamic Euroskeptic mindset, human rights in the EU are for Christians and Jews, not for Muslims. They frequently remind the public about the EU's reluctance to intervene to prevent or halt the Bosnian genocide, the EHCR's controversial decision on the RP's closure and its illiberal decision to support the headscarf ban as not a violation of fundamental individual rights.[27] This defensive mindset argues that Europe has a double standard when it comes to dealing with Muslim issues; hence reforms in the EU towards increased pluralism are not innocent, there is a hidden agenda.

With the formation of new opportunity spaces in Turkey during the 1980s, the EU was cognitively reconstructed as a framework of protection against the oppressive Kemalist state, and as a forum for goods and ideas, to achieve economic and intellectual development. As a result, today, Islamic groups do not talk about "becoming" European but rather *entering* or *integrating into* the EU as Muslims, Turks and Kurds without giving up their particular identities. For most Islamists, Europe and the EU are understood largely in terms of economics, security and human rights rather than in civilizational or cultural or identity terms. The EU is attractive for these groups to the extent that it can curb the state's strict control over the activities of Islamic communities and open new opportunities in Turkey and abroad, for their cause or members.

The second approach, that of the Europhile Islamic mindset, is mostly less skeptical about the policies related to fulfilling the Copenhagen criteria, which are seen as essentials in any economic and democratic transformation. Cultural concerns articulated by the skeptics are construed by the Europhile elite as not well-founded. "We should not have anything to fear if we are confident about our values and culture; why bother about European influence, but think rather about a possible Turkish Islamic influence in Europe; the free market of ideas and associational life will benefit Muslims," they argue.[28] These Muslim groups are

[26] For detailed statements of the anti-EU radical Islamist arguments, see Kenan Alpay (ed.), *Avrupa Birliği ve Müslümanlar* (Istanbul: Özgür-der, 2002). In 2002, seventy-five pro-EU groups and associations, including liberal and Islamic foundations, formed the *Avrupa Hareketi 2002* (Movement for Europe 2002).

[27] On the impact of the Bosnian genocide on Turkish public opinion and national identity see Mujeeb R. Khan, "Bosnia-Herzegovina and the Crisis of the Post-Cold War International System," *East European Politics and Societies* (Fall 1995).

[28] Lastly, some communities, especially those of Fethullah Gülen's followers, have advocated integration with the host country by creating their own "Islamic" parallel society. Gülen advises his followers to settle where they "migrate," buy houses, establish

thus in favor of Turkey's European orientation and they see Europe as a new arena where one can earn a good living, and have a safe haven from persecution. They do not see Muslim and European identities as mutually exclusive. In fact, some intellectuals and leaders of Turkish Islamic movements – Erbakan, Sevket Eygi, Sevki Yılmaz, Saadettin Kaplan, among others – have frequently used Germany and Switzerland as places for escaping from state oppression in Turkey, especially after military coups. Over the years, details of meetings, talks and messages have often been transmitted to Turkey from this temporary exile.

However, some conservative Muslims who were Europhile are becoming more critical of what is perceived as European double standards. Especially after the December 18, 2004 decision, some of the religious people who supported Turkey's EU membership became disenchanted and skeptical about the EU's intentions on admitting Turkey as a member. The religious groups have argued that though the EU appears to care about religious and ethnic minorities, none of the EU progress reports have mentioned the closures of and bans on the Imam Hatip Islamic training schools in Turkey, the headscarf ban or any other issues that Islamic groups regard intrinsically as infringements of their religious freedoms. Thus, the EU has adopted a quite authoritarian top-down secular position, accepting the dissolution of the democratically elected *Refah Partisi* (RP), approving the decision of the Turkish military to fire religiously observant military officials,[29] and endorsing the decision of Turkish universities to refuse to issue certificates to students who choose to wear headscarfs on their identification photos.[30] With its legal decisions, the European Court of Human Rights has removed the possibility of a presence for Islamism in the public sphere. Despite these negative attitudes, the large bulk of Turkey's conservative Muslim population continue to support Erdoğan's EU orientation for a number of reasons. They believe that even if Turkey does not become a full member, the EU process offers a framework for addressing civilian–military relations, expanding human rights, promoting economic stability, and realizing the rule of law. In some ways, it is the traveling towards EU membership that counts more than the actual arrival at full membership.

permanent residence and find decent full-time jobs. The idea is to become a part of the public culture, of course without losing their Islamic identity, in order to represent Islam in these societies.

[29]  Kalaç vs. Turkey (App. No. 20704/02, judgment, 23 June 1997).
[30]  Karaduman vs. Turkey (App. No. 16278/90, inadmissibility decision, 3 May 1993).

*The Islamization of European identity versus the
Europeanization of Islam*

The discursive shift away from viewing the EU as being the foe of political Islamic identity to being its friend is the outcome of a number of factors.[31] Many people construe this shift as a survivalist need under a variety of military, legal and economic pressures to form an alliance with liberal groups. Indeed, one of the key factors that made Erdoğan distance himself from Islamism was the 1997 "soft coup." Erbakan and his friends wanted to maintain their control over Islamic movements by establishing the *Fazilet Partisi* (FP). However, the closure of the FP opened an unexpected space for a younger and more reformist generation of Islamist politicians to secede from the old guard and formulate their own more liberal and democratic Islam, or religion-free Islamism. The decision of the court opened new political spaces for the emergence of a new leadership after the erosion of Erbakan's position. Erdoğan certainly wants to avoid the fate of his predecessor. However, it would be a great mistake to explain this transformation only in terms of "fear" of the establishment. The most significant factor in this transformation of the Islamic political movement is the increasing role of the burgeoning merchant class. After the February 28 process and the politicization of the judicial system, Islamic groups began to regard EU institutions and norms as a source of protection against the state and a natural ally in the transformation of the state's ideology. In order to receive the necessary support from the EU, they had in turn to shed their old ideology and internalize the global discourse of human rights. This configuration of domestic and international factors gave Islamic groups the ability to craft a more democratic and liberal reading of Islam.

There are three major reasons for the AKP's widespread support of the EU process. One is its search for a political identity. Due to its Islamic roots, the AKP wants to project a new form of conservative democratic identity by identifying itself with the European norms of the Christian Democratic parties. While the Turkish Islam-inspired political parties initially regarded the EU (then the Common Market) as an attempt to undermine Turkey's Muslim identity and sovereignty, by the 1999 and 2002 elections Islamic parties regarded the EU not as an enemy but rather the ally of democratization and economic development. Consolidating democracy and raising the level of human rights protection in Turkey was linked to the Copenhagen criteria for admission to the EU. These

---

[31] Saban Taniyici, "The Transformation of Political Islam in Turkey: Islamists' Welfare Party's Pro-EU Turn," *Party Politics*, 9:4 (2003), 463–483.

reforms, both constitutional and legislative, created new legal opportunity spaces for the redefinition of state and society, Islam and secularism, and public and private relations.

Second, the AKP is more pro-EU than other political parties have been because it defines itself against the military and seeks to use the EU process to reduce the power of the military within the political system and dilute the Kemalist/secular overtones of the Turkish political system through expanding the scope of democratic politics and civil liberties. In the transformation of political Islam, political factors such as the Kemalist ideology of the Turkish state and the EU's attitude played an important role. The policy of the state institutions rejecting any deviation from the militantly secular nature of the state and the establishment's readiness to politically use the courts against Islamic parties forced the Islamic parties to act within the strict parameters of the secular system. For instance, in its party program, the AKP argues that

The National Security Council, which provides an exchange of views between the Armed Forces and the political powers in the areas of security and defense, shall be restructured in accordance with the standards of the European Union, taking into consideration examples in democratic countries.

Erdoğan and the people around him realized that the democratization and institutionalization of human rights required full international, especially EU, support. His jail experience and court cases helped him to realize not only the power of secular institutions but also the need for democracy to protect freedom of thought and expression. The AKP has no well-articulated project for the transformation of the political landscape but relies on the Copenhagen criteria as a compass for change. The AKP needs the EU's support in order to expand its political space and implement democratic control. However, this support has been conditional on the preservation of secularism and democratic rule in Turkey. The EU does not tolerate the use of Islam in politics or any discussion of the implementation of religious law, a position which has forced Turkey's Islamists to talk a secular language. Thus, the AKP has been successful in framing religious and local issues in terms of a broader European and universal language of human rights and political liberalism.

Third, the AKP needs external support to overcome Turkey's domestic constraints. In other words, the improvement of human rights, solving conflicts between religious rights in the public and private sphere, and economic development are very much linked to the EU process. The emerging bourgeoisie in Turkey has defended the EU as a way of expanding Turkey's economic opportunities, but the EU process is a convenient way to carry out domestic transformation as well. Given its Islamic background, the AKP seeks to overcome suspicions by treating EU membership as the "natural result of the modernization process."

### The AKP's conception of Europe: "becoming" versus "entering"

The Kemalist Republican People's Party (CHP) sees the EU as a process of assimilation into European culture(s) which will solve the Islamic issue once and for all. In their 1999 article, Buzan and Diez argue that Turkey's EU membership is important in undermining and preventing the Islamization of the country and that European identity through EU membership would suppress Islamic identity.[32] As of 2006, the AKP, a party with Islamic roots and close ties to many Islamic groups, has become the most ardent EU supporter in Turkey, and the leadership of the party evidently does not see its Islamic identity as being in opposition to the European process. Contrary to Buzan and Diez, they regard the process as a way of extending liberties and rights against authoritarian secularism. The EU is expected to provide legal protection for diverse ethnic and religious groups, although it is too early to see whether these rights would or would not fully extend to Islamic groups. The AKP outlines three ways in which Turkish membership will be beneficial to the EU. First, Turkey's inclusion will enhance the EU's ties with the Muslim world, will demonstrate the cooperation of diverse civilizations, and will free the EU from charges of exclusiveness and of being a Christian club in opposition to the Muslim world. Turkish membership will facilitate the further integration of Muslim communities into their host European states. Second, Turkey will enhance the EU's military might and security identity. Turkey will promote EU policy in the greater Middle East and this will help the EU to become a global power vis-à-vis the US. Third, Turkey's membership will enhance the EU's role in the Caucasus, the Balkans and the Islamic parts of the former Soviet Union.

Unlike the secularist Kemalists who still dominate the foreign policy bureaucracy of Turkey, Erdoğan wants to *join* or *enter* the EU as the representative of a country and culture sharing liberal and democratic rather than purely religious or cultural norms with the rest of Europe. This is the most important difference between the AKP and the CHP over EU membership. One of Erdoğan's common phrases whenever he is making an argument for Turkish membership is: "If the EU is not (to be) a Christian club then it has to accept Turkey. With the accession of

---

[32] Barry Buzan and Thomas Diez, "Turkey and the European Union: Where to from Here," *Survival*, 41:1 (1999), 41–57.

Turkey as the representative of a different civilization, the EU will become the space for the merging of civilizations."[33]

Erdoğan wants to highlight and transform Islamic identity by entering into Europe as a representative of "Islamic civilization." As such, one could argue that interaction with the EU is going to sharpen but also liberalize the Islamic consciousness in Turkey.[34] The AKP regards Turkey's Islamic and European identities as complementary rather than contradictory. It wants to stress Turkey as a European gate to the Muslim world or Muslim gate to Europe. Turkey has tried to organize a number of conferences between the EU and the Organization of the Islamic Conference (OIC) in Istanbul. The AKP government was very successful in getting the OIC to elect its Turkish candidate as the Secretary General of the organization.

Turkey's European orientation raises a number of questions. Is Turkey a Muslim country or a secular country with a Muslim population? Does Turkey need to join the EU to confirm the Kemalist project? Could Turkey remain a modern and secular state without joining the EU? Will Turkey's interaction with the EU heighten its Islamic political consciousness? Most of Turkey embraces both its Muslim and European identities. People do not see these two layers of identity in conflict, but rather in a symbiotic relationship, especially the latter as necessary for the existence of the former. Owen Matthews and Lorien Holland argue that:

Most importantly, Erdoğan's dramatic reforms of freedom of speech, along with a systematic dismantling of the apparatus of Turkey's old police state, are moving Turkey ever closer to EU membership – signaling that it's OK to be a Muslim *and* a European, too.[35]

The party has made the EU process the main goal of its domestic and foreign policy and mentioned the EU seventeen times in its party program. For instance:

Taking as a basis the principles pertaining to the democratization of the Copenhagen Criteria which constitute the minimum standards to which members of the European Union must conform, the necessary amendments to our national judicial system will be carried out in the shortest possible time.[36]

---

[33] Vincent Boland, "Eastern Premise," *Financial Times*, December 3, 2004.

[34] Mehmet Aydın, "Turkey and the European Union: A Cultural Perspective," in *Turkey and the EU: Looking Beyond Prejudice* (Maastricht: Maastricht School of Management, 2004), pp. 56–66. The proceedings of this symposium have a number of very interesting essays.

[35] Owen Matthews and Lorien Holland, "Islam's Happy Faces," *Newsweek*, Dec. 27–Jan. 3, 2005.

[36] http://www.AKParti.org.tr/programeng3.asp

The likelihood of EU membership, though highly conditional, is now open-ended, given the December 2004 EU–Turkey agreement, which in all probability will give Turkey some sort of EU membership by 2012. The EU Council has declared that the "objective of negotiations is access." The objective is qualified under the pressure of some member countries by adding that these negotiations are an open-ended process, whose outcome cannot be guaranteed beforehand. Moreover, it has opened the door for a possible "special relationship" by indicating "the candidate state concerned is fully anchored in the European structure through the strongest possible bond." This special relationship option was introduced in response to pressure from Angela Merkel, the leader of the German Christian Democrats, and Valéry Giscard d'Estaing, the former president of France. In Germany, the conservative parties CDU (Christian Democratic Union) and CSU (Christian Social Union) strongly oppose full EU membership for Turkey. Merkel said, "I don't believe that Turkey can become a member of the union in the foreseeable future. Negotiating a privileged partnership is a way to keep close ties between Turkey and the EU."[37]

Furthermore, during the French referendum debate on the EU Constitution, a group of twenty-five French deputies published an opinion piece in the French daily *Le Figaro* in May 2005 critical of Turkey. The piece, entitled "How could we accept those who say: Our minarets are our bayonets," urged the French public to reject Turkey's EU membership in favor of a "special partnership" arrangement. The title refers to a poem publicly recited seven years ago by Erdoğan, before he became prime minister and disavowed a number of his earlier views. In order to de-link the constitutional debate from unpopular Turkish membership of the EU, Jacques Chirac of France agreed to submit Turkish membership to a national referendum. Both the French and the Dutch rejected the European constitution for a number of reasons, such as increasing centralization, the implementation of neo-liberal economic policies, increasing worry over immigrants diluting European national identities and especially the possibility of Turkish membership. A French poll said "35 per cent of those who voted 'no' did so to oppose Turkey's entry into the EU." After the comments in the European press, many Turks have begun to

---

[37] Angela Merkel, *Deutsche Welle*, February 16, 2004. In the same speech Merkel also argued that "Christian Democrats have no desire to close the door on Turkey … and the CDU does not see the EU as a club of Christians. … Turkey does not fit into the EU because it is 'culturally different'." By culture Merkel means Islam. In her interview she said: "Much will depend on what path Turkey chooses for itself. … [I]t's not about religion. But it does play a role that Islam had not experienced the Enlightenment." *Süddeutsche Zeitung* (Munich), December 16, 2004 (translation by FBIS).

wonder whether their European dream is worth the effort, and also at the depth of bigotry harbored in many EU countries.

There are a number of European countries that would eventually oppose the Turkish bid, with Austria and France having always been the most vocal opponents. Public opinion polls taken throughout the EU usually show a majority of Europeans opposing Turkish membership. A May–June 2005 survey by Eurobarometer showed that 52% of EU citizens are against Turkish membership, with 35% supporting Turkey's bid. According to the polls, 80% of Austrians are against Turkish membership and only 10% support it. In France and Germany, opposition was 70–74%. Those against Turkish membership list four reasons: Europe is a civilizational project and Turkish values are unfit; Turkey is geographically not part of Europe, with only 3% of Turkey located in Europe; with Turkey's membership the EU will be sharing borders with countries that generate insecurity such as Iran, Iraq and Syria; the Turkish economy is not ready to join the EU and, with very high unemployment, it is possible that joining will result in a major migration of Turks to EU countries. Finland supports Turkish membership, with 75% for and 16% against. Great Britain's government is a supporter, by favoring "a wider as opposed to a more deeply integrated EU."

Turkish membership raises a number of questions about European identity itself. Is it economic, cultural, rights-based or geographical? A close examination indicates three tightly layered building blocks of EU identity. It is an economic union and has stressed its common economic interests vis-à-vis the US and China. It is a value-based community built on social and cultural backgrounds that draw the borders of "non-European" states. It is based on citizenship and a "rights-based" union with respect to political citizenship. These three blocks emphasize shifts in relation to changing challenges and concerns. Turkish membership is more an issue of "cultural background" and challenges the key component of the European cultural identity. Indeed, there is a major concern that Turkish membership will cast into question the content of this European identity.

### The impacts of the EU journey

The decision taken by the EU Council in December 2004 to open accession talks in October 2005 was very important. After coming to power, the AKP government accelerated the policies of the previous Ecevit government by implementing the requirements of the Copenhagen political criteria and amending the constitution: abolishing the death penalty, reducing the role of the military in the National Security Council, bringing the military budget under civilian control, allowing broadcasts in the Kurdish dialects of Zaza and Kırmancı, supporting the UN plan to unify the divided island of Cyprus, and further improving relations with Greece. Almost all of these domestic changes and foreign policy initiatives were introduced and implemented not because of policy or planning by the AKP but rather as requirements for EU membership. The AKP has tried to expand its socio-political base by framing its policies in the language of the EU.

The EU process is the most significant catalyst in the change of state policies on the Kurdish question. In October 2001, the constitutional amendments in Articles 26 and 28 removed the prohibition on the use of local languages and allowed broadcasting in those languages as well. Broadcasting in Kurdish was the cornerstone reform in a third democratization package in August 2002. The government carried out a number of reforms such as liberalization of the legal system to broadcast in Kurdish, and the right to learn and study Kurdish with the seventh package in July 2003 – though the actual implementation of such reforms has been slow. Still, in March 2004, Kurdish language courses were opened in Batman, Şanlıurfa and Van. Turkish television even started to broadcast in Kurdish, along with Bosnian, Arabic and Circassian in June 2004. Moreover, the Civil Registry Law was amended in 2003 to allow parents to give their children Kurdish names, a fundamental right which had been denied for decades. And the AKP government introduced the "Return to Village and Rehabilitation Project" to facilitate the return of displaced Kurds to their villages. One of the fundamental debates in Turkey today is how to redefine nationhood to include the Kurds and other ethnic groups.[38]

These changes have helped to consolidate democracy in Turkey without necessarily deepening democratic roots and transforming the political culture. Nevertheless Turkey in many ways is more liberal, open and democratic than it was a decade ago. However, the structural problems of the role of civil society, the submissiveness of parliament, the authoritarianism of political party leaders, and the weaknesses of the courts remain. For instance, almost all legal changes are still prepared by the bureaucracy and "legalized" by parliament, so that the role of parliament in the drafting of bills has been minimal. The AKP parliamentarians vote for every legal change as long as they are presented as a requirement of the EU or by the party leader Erdoğan. This unquestioned commitment to

---

[38] Dilek Kurban, "Confronting Equality: The Need for Constitutional Protection of Minorities in Turkey's Path to the European Union," *Columbia Human Rights Law Review*, 151:35 (2003), 151–214.

the EU process guides most domestic changes. Yet, the EU process has had little impact on intra-party democracy.

As a reward for Turkey's abiding by European political norms, the EU has offered protection and legitimacy for the AKP vis-à-vis the military–civilian establishment. It has also provided financial support and the prospect of membership to support the AKP initiatives. Before Erdoğan was elected to parliament, many EU officials publicly met with him, providing the legitimacy he needed to gain power in Turkey.[39] Erdoğan knows that the EU, or democracy in general, is not simply a streetcar that you get off when you arrive at your destination (gaining political power). As mayor of Istanbul, Erdoğan had previously compared democracy to that streetcar that could help you to arrive at the destination and then be discarded. He now understands that his political power was gained through democracy and this very democracy provides him EU protection and continued support. As prime minister he has become more liberal and open to diverse ideas. The EU project has not only expanded the legitimacy of the AKP government but, more importantly, it has provided an unambiguous compass for social and political change. The EU orientation, in turn, has helped Erdoğan to move beyond Erbakan's National Outlook Movement and carve out a broader and more inclusive political spectrum. This orientation has enhanced the AKP's claims to represent the "center-right" of Turkish politics and helped it to overcome charges of Islamism.

In the 1990s, domestic forces which wanted to transform state–society relations closely allied themselves with the forces of globalization and worked together to create a new rights-based legal system. In recent years, especially after the invasion of Iraq in 2003, these forces have been cross-cutting and this confuses the political leadership and raises a number of questions about the representation and the future of peripheral domestic forces. Although the peripheral and marginalized sectors of the population had hoped to increase their share in the economy and politics by becoming integrated into the globalization processes, they are not satisfied with the outcome. The distribution of income in Turkey and

---

[39] Despite these changes there is a powerful resistance to Turkey's membership in different European countries. These circles are against Turkey's membership by arguing that its size, underdeveloped regions and high unemployment could require massive financial support for farmers, the education system and transportation. There is fear of labor disruption and also fear of Islam and "otherness." It is a major challenge for Europe to incorporate a country which has not shared the experience of the Renaissance and the Enlightenment – which provide the basis of the European identity. However, many European politicians know well that saying "no" to Turkey would lead the country to turn inwards, and that many Muslims would likely read "no" as a sign of religious discrimination.

the EU has worsened and the gap between the haves and have-nots has widened. For instance, contrary to the expectations that the EU would open more spaces for religious freedoms, the European Court of Human Rights has banned the headscarf. Globalization benefits those who welcome its many consequences and those who seek to integrate out rather than integrate in. The same globalization process weakens and excludes those politicians who resist against its consequences; they are regarded as "provincial" or without global imagination, while those who surrender to the globalization process are reduced to its "subcontractors."

There is a major resistance to some of the reforms which the EU requires. This resistance includes circles on the secular nationalist right and on the nationalist left, in both the civilian and the military establishments. In their view, the EU has used the Copenhagen criteria to create new "minority" problems such as the Armenian and the Kurdish questions. This, in turn, has weakened the legitimacy of the EU process in Turkey, raised the security needs of the country and contributed to an increased wave of nationalism. Among other things, although some secular nationalists would have preferred to develop closer ties with the Turkic republics of Central Asia, some nationalist Islamists are also opposed to Turkey's complete integration with the EU. Secularist Kemalists, such as the military and civilian bureaucracy, do not like sharing power with elected officials and international institutions. They want to maintain the sovereignty of Turkey in the international system. Many Turks are deeply skeptical about the intentions of EU politicians and fear that the EU may destroy the territorial integrity of Turkey and the country's culture and tradition. In short, the EU is a source of attraction and repulsion at the same time.

### Gordian knot: the Cyprus problem

The Republic of Cyprus was established by the Zurich and London agreements in 1959 and 1960.[40] As a result of these treaties, Turkey became the guarantor of the status quo in the island, along with Greece and Britain; unification of the island with Greece was prohibited. The Turkish Cypriots became the co-founders of the new state and the treaties allowed Turkey to maintain a small number of Turkish troops on the island.[41] The

---

[40] David Hannay, *Cyprus: The Search for a Solution* (New York: I. B. Tauris, 2005). For the international treaties that founded the Republic of Cyprus, see http://www.cyprus-conflict.net/Treaties%20-1959-60.htm

[41] M. Hakan Yavuz, "Cyprus and International Politics," *The Cyprus Review*, 4:2 (Fall 1992), 135–143.

Greek Cypriot side did not like the bi-communal aspect of the Cyprus constitution and used all possible means to reduce the rights of Turkish Cypriots. The debate over the sharing of power between the two communities degenerated into inter-communal violence by the end of 1963 and early 1964. The UN sent a peacekeeping force to protect the Turkish minority against armed Greek militias. The argument then goes that in 1974 the right-wing military government in Athens engineered a coup in Cyprus to annex the island and this was followed by the Turkish invasion of the island to protect Turkish Cypriots against extremist Greek nationalists. The military operation and the subsequent Turkish occupation of northern Cyprus led to transfers of population on both sides of the island, with most of the Greek Cypriots living in the north going to the southern part of the island, while the Turkish Cypriots in the south went in the opposite direction. Northern Cyprus was proclaimed the Turkish Federated State of Cyprus in 1975. It became the "Turkish Republic of Northern Cyprus" in 1983, and has been recognized only by Turkey.

The island has thus been divided and there have been a number of UN initiatives to solve the problem. The military and bureaucratic establishment in Turkey pursued a policy of getting the international community to recognize the Turkish partition of the island, but the application of the Greek Cypriot side to join the EU has created a linkage between Turkey's EU aspirations and the Cyprus problem. The Europeanization of the Cyprus problem appeared as a result of the end of the Cold War, the Greek Cypriot membership application, and Turkey's desire to join the EU. The Turkish position on the Cyprus issue was dictated by the military–bureaucratic establishment's wish to use the "problem" as a mean of distancing Turkey from globalization processes and "prove" the establishment's nationalist credentials.

The Cyprus issue has been used by the state establishment to maintain the securitization of Turkish foreign policy and to display its nationalism to public opinion. Those who are against solving the Cyprus issue are that part of the establishment who are also very skeptical of the AKP government. The AKP needs the EU to balance the power of the state establishment, and the Cyprus problem has become a battleground between the establishment and the new government. The AKP's main goal is to de-securitize the domestic and foreign policies of Turkey through the EU process and to implement its liberalizing agenda. The major mistake of the leader of the Turkish Cypriots, Rauf Denktaş, was to ally himself with the anti-AKP coalition to fight against the unification of the island. Erdoğan and Gül's foreign policy decisions have been very much guided by their profound desire to undermine the domestic civilian–military bureaucratic alliance.

The AKP leadership did not voice a reaction to the EU Council decision in 2003 when the first clear linkage between Turkish membership and the resolution of the Cyprus dispute was made. The AKP in fact wanted to find a solution to the Cyprus dispute to differentiate itself from the establishment and Denktaş. The AKP leadership linked its political future to the EU membership process. Since the AKP recognized that the EU process was the "only way" of undermining the hegemony of Kemalist discourse and power, it insisted on the resolution of the Cyprus issue in order to remove major obstacles from the membership process. For the AKP, the EU process will complement and even balance Turkey's skewed relations and heavy dependence on the US. The government regards the EU as a balance to terminate or at least minimize cozy ties between the military and the US.

For Erdoğan, Cyprus was a symbol of the old-guard, status-quo-oriented foreign ministry's power over the future of the country, and a symbol of Turkish intransigence. He did not believe in enduring rivalry but in enduring cooperation. He conceptualized the Cyprus problem as a way of defeating the Kemalist establishment. During his six-year government, Erdoğan took the initiative of pressing for cordial relations with Greece, and was the first Turkish prime minister to visit the Turkish minority in Greece. He sought to solve the Cyprus problem within the framework of the UN and the EU.

Unification talks between the Turkish and Greek Cypriots started on February 10, 2004 in New York and an agreement was reached on a three-step plan. According to the plan, the leaders of the Turkish and Greek Cypriots would negotiate under the terms of the Kofi Annan plan and craft a final text by March 22, 2004. If the two sides failed to reach an agreement, Greece and Turkey would enter the negotiations for an additional week to produce a finalized text by March 29, 2004. Finally, in the case of persistent deadlock, Annan would arbitrate and exercise his discretion to fill all remaining gaps in order to produce a finalized text to be submitted to two separate referenda on April 21, 2004.[42] Only if both sides voted in favor of the plan would the "United Cyprus Republic" become an EU member on May 1, 2004. The Turks voted for the plan but the Greeks voted against, with the result that only the Greek Cypriot part of the island joined the EU. The AKP fully supported the "yes" vote for the UN plan.

By saying "yes" the Turkish side gained the upper hand over the Greek Cypriot leader Tassos Papadopoulos, who had led the "no" campaign to

---

[42] http://www.tcea.org.uk/Annan-Plan-For-Cyprus-Settlement.htm

the UN plan in the April 2004 referendum.[43] With a EU Council decision on December 17, 2004, Turkey was given eight more months to solve the Cyprus problem by making more concessions to the Greek side by recognizing Papadopoulos as the president of Cyprus. Given the functioning statehood of the Turkish Cypriot state in the eyes of Turkey during the last twenty years, this was a difficult concession to make. The Greek Cypriot side had no reason to make any concessions on the island since it was fully recognized by the EU. Neither the EU nor the US tried to put any pressure on the Greek side to come to terms with the Turkish side. Cyprus would be a historic loss for the AKP government if it decided to sign an agreement with the Greek side.

In July 2005, Turkey signed a protocol extending its customs accord with Brussels to the ten newest members of the bloc, including Cyprus, but it said that its signature did not amount to recognition of the Cypriot government. Turkey refused to open its ports and airports to traffic from the Greek Cypriot government-controlled territory and said that this would only happen if international restrictions imposed on the Turkish Republic of Northern Cyprus, which is only recognized by Ankara, were lifted. This refusal was utilized by the anti-Turkish camp in the EU to slow down Turkish membership at the EU summit in December 2006, at which the leaders of the EU endorsed the decision to freeze the opening of eight out of thirty-five chapters of negotiations with Turkey. Even so, the EU's official explanation for "slowing down" the membership process was that it was Turkey's fault, because the AKP government refused to open its ports to Greek Cypriot vessels. The Cyprus issue is being used by anti-Turkish European leaders to prevent Turkish membership.

The Greek Cypriot political parties seek a more active role for the EU in any talks, while Turkey is implacably opposed to any undermining of the authority of the United Nations. The Cyprus issue is being used by the Euroskeptics in Ankara to challenge the sincerity of the EU and as proof of the Erdoğan government's inability to defend the rights of Turkish Cypriots. Right-wing groups claim that the Erdoğan government is selling out Cyprus in order to show how obedient Turkey is to the EU. Aside from the Cyprus issue, nationalist Kemalists have now joined Islamic groups who are also increasingly skeptical of Turkey's application and the capacity of EU institutions to address the religious freedoms of the

---

[43] The Greek Cypriots voted against the referendum for four reasons: the Annan plan did not resolve the future of the Turkish settlers who moved to Cyprus after the 1974 military operation; the settlement gave the Turkish Cypriots a disproportionately large amount of seats in parliament; the settlement did not de-militarize the island and allowed the presence of 600 Turkish troops; and the right of return clause was unjust by allowing only 20% of Greek Cypriots to return to the Turkish zone over a twenty-five year period.

Turks impartially. There is an increasing sense of disappointment over the EU's commitment to the rights of those Muslims who hoped to expand freedom of religion by getting closer to the EU.[44]

Erdoğan used a large amount of political capital to defy the Turkish nationalists and the state establishment by advocating that all Turkish Cypriots should accept the Annan Plan and settle the long-standing dispute. The failure of the Annan plan was a major setback for the AKP, but it also garnered Erdoğan political credit within the EU. Even though the dispute is not resolved, it is now expected not to damage Turkey's case for EU membership.

### The fading of EU euphoria

Although Erdoğan has tied his political future to EU membership, EU euphoria has been fading since the decision of December 2004 to offer the opening of membership negotiations to Turkey in October 2005. When the French national assembly adopted a change in its constitution, also known as the "Turkish article," to hold a referendum over future expansion of the EU, this was a major blow to Turkish Europhiles, indicating that many Europeans were not serious about Turkey's membership. With the election to the French presidency of Nicolas Sarkozy, one of the most ardent European politicians against Turkey's membership, who has been arguing that "Turkey has no place inside the European Union,"[45] skepticism and anger has increased amongst the Turkish public. According to the latest (July 2007) Pew Research Center survey, just 27% of Turks have a favorable opinion of the EU, compared to 58% in 2004. In June 2007, in order to overcome this worsening public image of the EU and also bolster the pro-EU AKP's election chances, Angela Merkel, along with the EU

---

[44] Senem Aydın Düzgit, *Seeking Kant in the EU's Relations with Turkey* (Ankara: TESEV, 2006).

[45] George Parker, "France in Threat to Turkey's EU hopes," *Financial Times*, July 22, 2007. Sarkozy reiterated his position in the following interview:

TNI:   Do you think that Turkey, if it meets the conditions set by the EU, has a place in Europe?

NS:    Whether Turkey meets the conditions for entry or not does not solve the problem. On this matter, I have always been clear: I do not think Turkey has a right to join the European Union because it is not European. But just because Turkey should not become a member of Europe does not mean that it should be shunned by Europe. Who could seriously argue that the closeness of links between Turkey and Europe, which are the fruit of a long common history and a sincere friendship, should be destroyed if Turkey did not enter the EU? Turkey is a great country that shares a number of our interests and our values. Therefore we must strengthen our ties with the country through a "privileged partnership."

Commission, hoped to open three more "negotiating chapters" – out of thirty-five in total – with Turkey a month before the national elections in two new policy areas: statistics and financial control. However, French opposition to Turkish membership has delayed the third chapter, economic and monetary policy. Nicolas Sarkozy wants to open a new debate on whether Turkey is a European country or not. Sarkozy believes that Turkey is not a European country because it is Muslim.

There is a major nationalist backlash against a European "racist attitude towards Turkey's membership" in major urban centers in Turkey. The current wave of nationalism, which is a mixed-breed secular and religious ideology, has two goals: the preservation of national sovereignty (the Kemalist regime), and the protection of the state and national unity. This new form of nationalism is very much a reaction to the EU's mishandling of Turkish membership, along with the Cyprus question, the European accusation against the Turks of an Armenian genocide, the US occupation of Iraq, and renewed PKK attacks in Turkey. This new nationalism is popularized and turned into an action through a number of civil society associations, such as the Kemalist Thought Association (ADD) and the Association for Supporting Modern Life (CYDD). Quite surprisingly, as the AKP has begun to lose faith in the EU process, this corresponds to a stronger interest and involvement in the Middle East. The AKP government's decision to conduct direct talks with Palestine's Hamas, Erdoğan's participation in an Arab League summit, his Syria policy, and his criticism of several Western policies towards the region are examples of his search for a new policy.

*Deteriorating Turkish–American relations*

Turkey's ties with the US have been the backbone of Turkish foreign policy since the beginning of the Cold War. Although Gül, then Foreign minister, has defined these ties as "above and beyond everything else," one wonders what this description actually means. US policy towards Iraq and Turkey's refusal to accede to American demands have brought these

But we should go further and offer to the countries in the Mediterranean the establishment of a "Mediterranean Union," in which Turkey would be a natural pivot. This Union would work closely with the EU. It could organize periodic meetings between its chiefs of states similar to the model of the G8. There could be a Mediterranean Council, like the European Council. The foundations of this area of solidarity and cooperation would be a common immigration policy, commercial and economic development, the promotion of the rule of law, the protection of the environment and the promotion of co-development, with, for example, the creation of a Mediterranean investment bank based on the model of the European version. (Retrieved from: http://washingtonrealist.blogspot.com/2007/04/sarkozy-turkey-and-eu.html)

relations to their lowest point since the end of World War II. The difference between Turkey and the US is also the outcome of clashing understandings of political events. For instance, leading AKP parliamentarians considered the Fallujah operations as "genocide," the prime minister has called Israel's military operations against Palestinians acts of "state terrorism," Turkey and Russia have much the same view over Black Sea security, and Erdoğan has stated that there is "no genocide" in Sudanese Darfur, since "Islam does not recognize racism." Thus the sources that shape the AKP's worldview are still steeped in political Islamism and the advisors of the party have an essentially Muslim national worldview.[46]

A number of reasons explain Turkey's reluctance to get involved in the Iraq war on the side of the US coalition. Most importantly, before the 1991 Gulf War, Turkey had close political and economic relations with Iraq, and Turkey lost substantial income when the Kirkuk–Yumurtalık pipeline was shut down in the 1991 war. In spite of promises, Washington did not compensate Turkey's major pipeline income and loss of trade. Moreover, the 1991 war had major impacts on the Turkish economy, especially on tourism and trade, and Turkey worried that a new Iraq war would undermine Turkey's economic recovery under the IMF-sponsored program. The shadow of the 1991 war was not only confined to the economic domain, but also created a number of political crises. For instance, president Özal's unquestioned loyalty to US policies gave rise to a number of negative reactions, among which was the resignation of the Turkish Chief of General Staff, Necip Torumtay. As the personalized mode of Özal's policy continued, it caused other reactions. The foreign and defense ministers also resigned in protest against Özal's pro-American policies, and there is evidence that Özal lost a good amount of support from the Turkish public. Given the disastrous fall-out and unfulfilled promises from the 1991 American invasion of the region, Ankara was thus less than enthusiastic about supporting the US in 2003.

In addition, the new AKP government had pan-Islamic concerns and thus did not want to get involved on the side of the US and a rag-tag alliance of mostly Christian coalition forces against a Muslim country. Most of the AKP deputies are inexperienced in the foreign policy domain and come from former Islamic networks. Furthermore, Turkey's pro-Islam media and the AKP government were very concerned about

---

[46] An undisclosed AKP report entitled "The Turkey Project" argues that "Our party believes that Turkey should fill the power vacuum in the Middle East created by the fall of the Ottoman Empire. Turkey has to become a major intervening actor in the Middle East and the surrounding area. We believe that Turkey cannot solve its bilateral and domestic problems without becoming an imperial power in the Middle East. There is also no other way to bring peace and stability to the region."

anti-Turkish regional sentiment if Turkey were to participate in a war on the side of the US. The AKP government wanted to create a more positive image in the Muslim Arab world by distancing itself from the American war plans. Among other things, when asked to join the US-led invasion, Gül's government was busy with the Cyprus issue and the EU accession debate. It was far more focused on these two issues and did not have much time or will to dwell on the US–Iraq confrontation.

However, what has mostly been ignored by analysts and the international media is that the most important factor which determined Ankara's policy towards the US-led war plans was the perennial Kurdish question. Ankara had supported the US-led war against Iraq in 1991 by joining the coalition and closing the pipelines and as a result created a major Kurdish political consciousness. In 1991 (and after) the US encouraged a Kurdish rebellion against Saddam's rule, which resulted in a major military response from the Saddam government and one million ethnic Kurds taking refuge along the Turkish border and across the border in Iran. The international community reacted to this humanitarian crisis by creating a safe haven for the refugees and imposed a no-fly zone through the use of daily monitoring and/or bombing sorties by US and British airplanes based in Incirlik in Turkey. Turkey supported the creation of "safe-havens" and allowed the Incirlik military base to be used for this purpose. Successive Turkish governments' *de facto* backing of a US policy of "divide and rule" planted the seeds of the current near division of Iraq into three separate regions. Although both the US and Turkey have expressed their commitment to the territorial integrity of Iraq, the country seems to be falling apart along three fault lines. After the withdrawal of Saddam's forces from northern Iraq in October 1991, a self-governing Kurdistan Regional Government was created with the support of the US and Turkey in 1992. This political experiment with the Kurdish parties, the Patriotic Union of Kurdistan and the Kurdish Democratic Party, planted the seeds of Kurdish statehood. Although these two parties hardly worked together and had major military conflicts, self-governance consolidated Kurdish separatist political consciousness. Ankara closely followed the rise of the Iraqi Kurdish nationalist movement with its goal of full independence. What has alarmed Turkey has been the encouragement which its own Kurdish minority and its militant wing, led by the Kurdish Workers' Party (PKK), would gain from a successful experiment with Kurdish nationalism and self-rule in Iraq. Since 1991, with the agreement of Iraq, Turkey has a number of military posts in northern Iraq to monitor PKK activities. From Ankara's point of view, the growing Kurdish independence movement has been a major national security concern. Turkey does not want the Kurdish regional government to become a model for the Kurds in Turkey or a base for pan-Kurdish secessionist nationalism. In order to contain this secessionist nationalism, Ankara has worked closely with Iran and Syria, both of which are struggling with similar sentiments of autonomy and increased cultural rights on the part of their own Kurdish minorities. Turkey has therefore not wanted the Iraq war to consolidate or give an opportunity for the breakup of Iraq and the formation of a Kurdish independent state in northern Iraq.

After the March 2003 parliamentary motion denying free passage to US troops from Turkey to northern Iraq, the Kurds became the main "strategic partner" in the US war effort. In other words, US–Iraqi Kurdish relations have developed at the expense of Turkey. Since Turkey did not allow the opening of the northern frontier, the US became more dependent on the Kurdish militias in northern Iraq. As of 2007, Ankara has had no leverage over US policy in Iraq, and US dependence on the Kurds has made the Kurds an indispensable security force in northern Iraq. In addition, the US has used the Kurdish militia, the *peshmerge*, who are much better organized and better trained than the Iraqi armed forces, in operations in the Sunni-dominated zones of Iraq. Today Iraq's Kurdish factions have a clear policy: consolidate the Kurdish federal ethnic entity in Iraq; incorporate the oil-rich Kirkuk province into the Kurdish autonomous region and set up Kirkuk as the regional capital; formulate and maintain the Kurdish militias outside the control of the Iraqi army; and insist that the Kurdish region has the constitutional right to secede from Iraq as a first step toward independence by 2010 or shortly thereafter.[47] In response to these Kurdish aspirations, Ankara developed its own policy, commonly known as "red-lines," of defending and protecting the status quo: maintaining the Kirkuk–Mosul oilfields in the hands of the central Iraqi government; rejecting any ethnicity-based federalism in Iraq; and defending the rights of the Turkmen minority of Iraq, nearly all of whom live in northern Iraq, especially in and around Kirkuk. Turkey's "red-lines" policy was largely developed for domestic consumption, and in reality the AKP government's attempt to develop an Iraqi policy has failed miserably. For instance, foreign minister Gül deputed the campaign

---

[47] A draft constitution adopted by the two Kurdish parties in 2002 has sought to expand the territorial domain by incorporating the oil-rich region of Kirkuk, envisaging the city of Kirkuk as its capital, and demanding the maintenance of separate Kurdish military units (*peshmerge*) outside the control of Iraq's central government. The Kurds of Iraq have made known their desire to secede from the 2002 constitution. Ankara's fears have gradually built up as the Kurds have increased their self-rule and desire for independence from Iraq. Turkey fears that the KRG will become a safe haven for the PKK and a core for more irredentist Kurdish nationalism at the expense of Ankara. Ankara worries about the possibility of international support for the creation of an independent Kurdistan and about this threatening Turkey's national unity and territorial integrity.

Gül favors the democratic process and supports a larger role for parliament in the making of foreign policy, while Erdoğan wants to run it by himself. This style of politics has not helped the emergence of a new vision in foreign policy. However, Gül does not want to take risks and would like to delay and avoid any decision if there is potential risk involved. Erdoğan likes to face reality head on and take the full responsibility for outcomes. Gül, for instance, did not take responsibility for the March 1st motion since Erdoğan was going to replace him. Gül preferred that the decision for Turkey to join the Iraq war should be taken on Erdoğan's watch rather than on his.

Those coming from the National Outlook Movement mobilized around Gül and believed that Turkey could avoid entanglement in the Iraq war by not cooperating with the US. Although the no-war option was never viable, the associates of Gül tried to convince the people that the war could not be engaged in without Turkey. He worked very hard to avert the war by mobilizing the regional countries and the EU, but eventually his policy failed because the US did not want him to succeed and made up its mind to invade Iraq. Moreover, the intellectuals and public opinion formers of the AKP analyzed the US policy from an Islamic perspective and asked the government not to pursue short term interests, but to act on principles of Islamic solidarity instead. Internal party divisions played a critical role in the voting process, with most of the Islamists and the Kurdish parliamentarians voting against the motion.

### The constant reversal of policy

By rejecting the March 1, 2003 motion, Turkey lost the $6bn war compensation package and $24bn in cheap long-term loans which the US had dangled over the head of the government as incentives for allowing the use of Turkish territory to invade Iraq. The financial incentive was important given Turkish policy-makers' memory of the considerable economic costs of the 1991 Gulf War. However, the new and inexperienced government acted under extremely complex circumstances: widespread public opposition in Turkey to an impending war in Iraq, the ambivalence of the military, and the uncertainty over whether a second UN Security Council resolution mandating the Iraq war would be passed. Most importantly, the rejection of the motion plunged US–Turkey relations to their lowest ebb since the 1974 arms embargo on Turkey. Yet, the same event changed the perception of Turkey both in the Muslim world and in Europe. The Turkish position on the war greatly improved the public image of and confidence in the government in the Arab capitals. In addition, by staying away from the bloody war in Iraq and not getting involved in a conflict with Iraqi Kurdish forces, Turkey improved its standing in Iraq as well. The no-war policy of Turkey added a positive impetus to EU–Turkey relations. The fact that, despite its previous mistakes, the Turkish government took an independent and democratic decision concerning the war, while at the same time showing restraint in northern Iraq, sent positive signals, particularly to those Western European countries historically skeptical of Turkey's EU membership but also opposed to the war in Iraq.

The biggest consequence for US–Turkish relations of the March 1 vote was that the US was forced to ally itself with Iraqi Kurdish militias. The Kurds welcomed the US troops and provided all forms of logistical support in and around the Sunni areas. Moreover, some US officials started to accept lavish gifts from the Kurdish leadership in Iraq, which created a major conflict of interests on the part of the American troops. Instead of demanding that the Kurdish leader Masud Barzani travel to Baghdad for meetings with the Interim Governing Council, Paul Bremer gladly flew to Barzani's headquarters at a former resort on the Salahuddin Massif and was treated as the "colonial governor of Iraq." Many Shia, Turkmen and Sunni leaders felt uneasy and started to wonder whether American objectives in Iraq included fostering an independent Kurdish state. Another factor that led to the worsening of relations was the lack of any understanding of Turkey at the Central Command Center (CENTCOM) in charge of the Iraq operation. Turkish–US military relations have always been arranged through the European Command (EUCOM), and the CENTCOM officials treated Turkey as though it was just another Arab country with no democratic experience. CENTCOM compromised its mission, employing local favor and fear tactics by relying on the Kurdish militias for intelligence. Turkish–US relations were seriously strained when on July 4, 2003 the US troops in Suleymaniyah arrested a Turkish Special Forces unit with Bremer's approval. Turkey has stationed troops in Iraq since 1994, and by relying on the Kurdish militias, who have always wanted the Turkish troops to leave the area, the US military took up an aggressive attitude against the Turkish military unit by hand-cuffing and hooding the Turkish troops. The unit was held in Baghdad for three days, which was justified by US officials claiming that the Turkish unit was in possession of over $100,000 in sniper equipment, over fifteen kilograms of plastic explosive, and a map of Kirkuk detailing where the mayor of the city lived, apparently believing that the Turkish unit was trying to assassinate the mayor. The Turkish foreign ministry completely rejected these claims. However, no event has damaged relations as much as this incident, which turned the Turkish public against the US occupation of Iraq. The heavy use of force against the Turkmen minority in Talafer further undermined the US position inside Turkey, with suspicions beginning to dominate the relationship.

The March 1, 2003 decision was thus important for a number of reasons: it demonstrated the role of parliament in the making of foreign policy; the principled orientation of the country to stay out of this war, regardless of the promises of the US; Turkish state institutions were very skeptical of the outcome of the war and were also pleased with the decision of parliament.[49] However, a group surrounding the prime minister read the decision of parliament to stay out of the war as a "mistake" and tried to correct it.[50] The most concrete step on the part of this pro-war camp was parliament's decision of October 2003 to send 10,000 Turkish troops to Iraq to support the US war effort. This time 358 to 183 voted for the deployment. Under pressure from the Kurds, the Iraqi Governing Council announced that it did not want the Turkish troops. The Kurds rejected the offer and pressured the US not to allow Turkish troops to enter Iraq.

After the parliamentary elections in Iraq, Erdoğan described the results as illegitimate and raised a number of questions about the future of Iraq. But after reaction from the US, the government gradually shifted its position in line with Washington's. Turkey considered the Iraqi resistance as a "terrorist" movement; organized a conference for the regional states in Istanbul to support Iraq's new Jaafari government; and Erdoğan visited Israel.[51] All of this indicates the lack of policy of the AKP and a constant balancing act of relations with the US and domestic forces. Relations with Washington further deteriorated in 2004 when the chairman of parliament's Human Rights Committee described the US actions in Fallujah as "genocide." Erdoğan called Iraqi insurgents "martyrs" and members of his party described US offensives in different cities as reminiscent of "the Mongols of 1258." The most negative reports about the US were detailed in *Yeni Şafak*, a newspaper favored by Erdoğan and according to some reports partly owned by him.

After months of hesitation, only in May 2005 did Turkey agree in principle to allow the US expanded use of the strategic Incirlik air base as a major hub for non-lethal cargo deliveries to Iraq and Afghanistan. Turkey needs the US because the Turkish economy is heavily dependent on the IMF and the World Bank credits. Moreover, Turkey needs US

---

[49] General Özkök's statement, *Milliyet*, August 26, 2004.

[50] Recep Tayyip Erdoğan, "My Country is Your Faithful Ally and Friend," *The Wall Street Journal*, March 31, 2003.

[51] Prime Minister Ibrahim Jaafari made his first official visit to Turkey. He and the ministers of finance, industry, oil, electricity and water held bilateral talks with their Turkish counterparts on May 19, 2005.

support (a) over the Eurasian pipeline projects, (b) in solving the Cyprus problem and (c) as an ally if the EU process of full membership is not realized.

There are also a number of divergent areas in US and Turkish foreign policy objectives. Turkey and Iran cannot stop cooperating as the US wants. Turkey does not support the nuclearization of Iran, but it has close economic ties with Iran. Iran is its major source of natural gas and a major trade partner. Moreover, Turkey and Iran share the same goal of containing Kurdish separatism and Iran does not threaten Turkish territorial integrity the way some American and Israeli neo-conservative designs in the region do. The US should not expect the full cooperation of Turkey in support of its policies. However, Turkey could and should work with the US in the Balkans and the Caucasus.

### Conclusion

Despite all of Turkey's efforts, the prospect for EU membership is gloomier than ever. Turkey has a large population with major fundamental economic problems. Many Europeans feel uneasy about a powerful Muslim presence in Europe and also about pushing European eastern borders out to Syria, Iran and Iraq. The AKP government in relation to these efforts no longer has any power to formulate a policy for Turkey. All it can do is try to implement the Copenhagen criteria. The government realizes that it must approve of the Brussels stance and do what is asked, for as long as Turkey keeps knocking on the doors of the EU, asking for membership. The government must also realize that Brussels at any time may impose decisions, such as a recognition of the Armenian genocide, on Turkey, even if these are not explicitly required by the Commission report. In short, the same external security umbrella against the civilian–military forces conditions the actions of the AKP. When it comes to the issue of EU membership, this is a government for the "implementation" of Brussels's decisions, not a government for "decision-making," since all major decisions are made by Brussels and the task of Ankara is to implement them. Moreover, in order to maintain the support of the secularist coalition of the businessmen, media and military, the AKP has to remain committed to the EU process.

In addition to an economic boom and increased democratization, the end of the Cold War has meant that Turkey has increasingly determined its national interest independently of the US. Consequently, the national interests of the two, especially in relation to Middle East policy, have increasingly diverged. There is no longer a shared sense of threat or commonality of overall interest in the relationship between the two states.

The US, still the hegemon of the global system, wants to have unfettered access to oil, do away with anti-American groups, promote the interests of Israel and prevent any Middle Eastern country from evolving into a regional hegemon to challenge US and/or Israeli domination in the region. The US thus wants to maintain or when necessary reshape the fragmentation of the Middle East. It does this directly by sheer force, or indirectly by buttressing its allies and clients or forcing regime change on its enemies.

Since 2003, US–Turkey relations have gradually deteriorated because of US support for the Kurdish regional government in Iraq and the US–Israeli strategy to use the "Kurds," including the PKK, against what it considers as the rogue regional countries of Iran and Syria. Thus, northern Iraq has been a protected zone for the PKK to engage in regular incursions into Turkey, which the Turkish government and many of its citizenry consider as acts of terrorism. The potential and eventual emergence of a Kurdish state or an autonomous Kurdistan within Iraq will cause major turbulence for Turkey, which has been grappling with the aspirations of its own Kurds for decades. The AKP government appears not to have a clear policy on Iraq or towards the US, because it is functioning under the shadow of Kemalist military interventions. At the moment it regards the US as a balancing force against the Turkish military. Turkey's domestic power struggle between the secularist establishment and the AKP thus directly extends to foreign policy as well. This internal factionalism in Turkey, as in the case of other Muslim countries, prevents a unified and sustained formulation of the national interests in terms of Western interventions in the region.

# 8    The political crisis and the 2007 elections

This chapter examines the sociopolitical causes, actors and consequences of the April 2007 political crisis and its impact on the July 2007 national election results in Turkey. The actors in the crisis were the AKP leadership, an assertive secular sector of civil society that organized a series of "republican meetings," a secularist judiciary, and the guardians of the Kemalist system: the military. Three important causes existed for what can be described as an "elite-centric crisis": *disagreement* over the founding principles of the Republic, *concerns* of the military, and *fear* of the secular sector of civil society. To understand the causes of the crisis, I will first examine the disagreement between the AKP and the Kemalist sector over the meaning and role of such foundational principles as secularism and nationalism by focusing on the 2007 presidential election. In the second part, I will explore the mobilization of secular civil society in April and May 2007 by examining the demands and identity of the participants. And since the military's e-memorandum of April 27, 2007 considered almost all criticism of the Kemalist version of secularism and nationalism as "hostile voices" of religious fanaticism (*irtica*) or "separatistist" Kurdish ethno-nationalism, it is important to analyze the role of Kurdish identity claims and the "expansion" of the Gülen movement to understand the military's interference in the presidential election process. The final section of the chapter will analyze the 2007 election results.

The fears and concerns of the Kemalists were rooted in their perceptions of secularism and nationalism as the cardinal principles of the Turkish Republic. The crisis emerged at the end of the seven-year term of president Ahmet Necdet Sezer in April 2007. In the view of the Kemalist establishment, Sezer had been crucial in the process of opposing the Islamization of the state, while at the same time the AKP leadership regarded Sezer as the main obstacle to the appointment of key bureaucrats, the decentralization of power and the further democratization and liberalization of the system. Many Kemalists feared that the nomination of Abdullah Gül to the presidency would lead to the Islamization of the state through the recruitment of Islam-oriented bureaucrats into the higher echelons of the state.

In addition to the fear of the Islamization of the state, the second most important concern was the developments in Kurdish politics. The Turkish military was afraid of potential developments in Iraq, such as an eventual emergence of an independent Kurdish state ("Kurdistan"), which could encompass Iraq's oil-rich region of Kirkuk. This possible development, the Turkish military feared, would undermine national unity and the territorial integrity of Turkey. The military thought that the AKP government was either not aware of such a long-term threat or wanted to solve the Kurdish issue by transforming the regime (nation-state) in Turkey. The military also feared losing its autonomy over its own recruitment, promotion and budget, and being penetrated by ideological divisions through the Copenhagen criteria, required for EU membership. Moreover, the military was wary of attempts to curtail the social and economic privileges its members had enjoyed for decades. With the appointment of Yaşar Büyükanıt as the Chief of the General Staff in 2006, the military had become more assertive in protecting its privileges and political role. Finally, the independence and assertiveness of some Islamic groups, especially the Fethullah Gülen community, within the bureaucracy and business was another source of fear among secularists.[1]

### The events leading to the presidential elections

With little consultation inside or outside his party, in spring 2007 Prime Minister Erdoğan nominated Gül, then the Foreign minister, to become the next president of the country – this having occurred twenty-four hours before voting was to take place in parliament. Secularists, generals, many universities and the courts mobilized to stop the process. When the center-right parties (DYP, the True Path Party of Mehmet Ağar and ANAP, the Motherland Party of Erkan Mumcu) and the secular leftist opposition party (CHP, The Republican People's Party of Deniz Baykal) boycotted the poll for president on April 26, the generals issued a powerful statement on the official website of the Turkish Armed Forces on April 27 that threatened to overthrow the government if necessary to protect the secular nature of the Republic:

---

[1] The Gülen community is pursuing a policy of co-optation of scholars and politicians through promotional "academic" conferences in different countries and also organizes regular "tours" to different countries to "buy" these scholars or politicians. The last two "co-opting" conferences took place in Arizona and London to promote the Gülen community. Moreover, the group offers very high honoraria to the participants.

The problem that [has] emerged in the presidential election process is focused on arguments over secularism. The Turkish armed forces maintain their sound determination to carry out their duties stemming from laws to protect the unchangeable characteristics of the Republic of Turkey. It has been observed that some circles have been carrying out endless efforts to disturb the fundamental values of the Republic of Turkey, especially secularism, and have increased their efforts recently. Those activities include requests for the redefinition of the fundamental values of the Republic and attempts to organize alternative celebrations instead of our national festivals symbolizing the unity and solidarity of our nation. Those who carry out the mentioned activities, which are an open challenge against the state, do not refrain from exploiting the holy religious feelings of our people, and they try to hide their real goals under the guise of religion. ... Those who are opposed to the Great Leader Mustafa Kemal Atatürk's understanding "How happy is the one who says 'I am a Turk'," are enemies of the Republic of Turkey and will remain so. The Turkish Armed Forces maintain their sound determination to carry out their duties stemming from laws to protect the unchangeable characteristics of the Republic of Turkey. Their loyalty to this determination is absolute.

This statement created a major political debate, one which polarized Turkish society between the military and the AKP sympathizers. The main opposition party took the first poll to the Constitutional Court on April 28. The Constitutional Court, under the influence of the April 27 military statement and the major mass rallies in Ankara and Istanbul, annulled parliament's vote for Gül on the technical grounds that it lacked a two-thirds majority for a quorum. There was no real precedent for a majority of three-fourths of the MPs to be in parliament. Erdoğan called the Court's decision "a bullet fired at the heart of democracy." In the face of such opposition, Gül withdrew his candidacy and Erdoğan called for early elections, proposing a number of constitutional changes intended to prepare the ground for the election of the president through direct popular vote. These changes further deepened the political crisis in Turkey and had the potential to create a series of constitutional crises after the July 22, 2007 national elections. Under the proposed constitutional changes, future presidents would be elected for a five-year term, renewable for another five, a change from the current single seven-year term. The proposal also reduced the tenure of parliament to four years and the quorum from 367 to 184. Parliament passed the constitutional changes, but president Sezer vetoed the package on May 25, 2007, for a number of reasons. When parliament voted for the package a second time, president Sezer sent it out for a referendum on the proposed amendment to elect the president by popular vote, and also applied to the Constitutional Court to annul the legislation. Meanwhile, the CHP on June 3, 2007 petitioned the Constitutional Court to cancel the reform package on the grounds that parliament was violating its own bylaws. The Court ruled against the applications of the CHP and Sezer and opened the way for a referendum, which took place in October 2007.[2]

The main impetus behind the crisis was the Kemalist establishment's animus towards the AKP and Erdoğan's style of managing the presidential election. They accused Erdoğan of confusing the AKP parliamentary group with the synergetic nature of Turkish society. They felt that the AKP had not tried to create new "bridges" to diverse sectors of the society. It rather had stressed the "bonding" nature of communitarian politics, with a tight circle of advisors. In short, the assertive secular groups, especially the Alevi minority, felt threatened by the unfolding social and political processes. The government had ignored the public policy of creating a sense of belonging and coexisting among diverse groups in the country. The presidential election became an avenue of mass mobilization both at the elite and popular levels.

Erdoğan may have overplayed his hand in nominating to the presidency his foreign minister, Gül, who stemmed from the National Outlook Movement of Erbakan. He ignored the secularist/Kemalist resistance and the significance of the presidency for the Kemalist establishment, that is, its function in maintaining the "purity of the regime." For the secularist establishment and civil society, the governing party is allowed to have Islamic roots, as is the case with the AKP government, and to govern the country under the watchful eyes of the president and the military. For the Kemalists, however, the presidency is not only "the house of Atatürk," but also the ultimate protector of their version of the secular character of the Turkish state. Erdoğan's attempt to nominate Gül as the next president of Turkey without societal consensus led to a gradual military intervention into politics to get rid of the AKP government.

The military, along with the secular judiciary and the university administrations, resisted Gül as the president for a number of reasons. The

---

[2] The referendum took place on October 21, 2007 and a majority voted for it. There was no intelligent public debate over the long-term implications of the referendum and it lacked any democratic content. Electing the president by popular vote will not necessarily bring more democracy but rather the potential of initiating a more repressive regime. Turkey, unlike the US or France, is a parliamentary system and the prime minister is the head of the elected government, while the president is the "head of state" and "guardian" of the constitution. The election of the president by popular vote will increase the office's political weight and the president could even claim more democratic legitimacy than the government. The president could claim to represent the "whole nation," in contrast to the government, which is made up of political parties. It is clear from other examples that an elected president is going to be much stronger than his predecessors. Moreover, in the case of Turkey, the office of presidency has been dominated by the Kemalist establishment as a counter-weight to the popular temptations of the government.

president in the Turkish system has considerable power in blocking laws and appointing high officials. S/he has the authority to appoint judges of the Constitutional Court and members of the Council of Higher Education, as well as university rectors, high judges and the general directorate of Turkish Radio and Television. The president is also commander-in-chief of the armed forces, presides over the National Security Council, and has authority to impose a state of emergency and even declare war if parliament is not in session. As the commander-in-chief, the president plays an important role in the promotion of generals and can drive out officers who challenge the ideological unity (Kemalism) and homogeneity of the military. During the tenure of president Sezer, the military developed a good working relationship with the political institutions. The military preferred to have someone who did not have any (non-Kemalist) ideological position but rather was committed to the Kemalist ethos of secularism and nation-building. On April 12, 2007, General Büyükanıt told a group of journalists that the military expected a new president to be "someone who truly respects the principles of the republic, not someone who pretends to do so." Due to the military's concerns, shared by the secular sector, Erdoğan hesitated to reveal the name of the presidential candidate until the last minute. The military did not want someone like Gül, who had been a critic of Kemalism and was steeped in Islamic ideology. Thus, an attempt by Erdoğan to control the presidency was seen as upsetting the checks and balances of the state and an attempt to change its secular character.

In response, a number of anti-AKP civil-society organizations joined forces and organized mass rallies, known as "*cumhuriyet mitingleri*" (republican meetings), in Ankara, Istanbul, Manisa, Canakkale, Izmir and Samsun. These rallies, which gathered over a million people, smashed the delicate equilibrium between the Kemalist military, the AKP government and diverse sectors of society.

### Republican meetings

The protesters mobilized because they believed: (1) there was an Islamic threat to their secular life-style; (2) the AKP government was too pro-Kurdish and was seeking to change the founding principles of the republic to accommodate Kurdish political demands; and (3) the government was disloyal to Turkish identity and interests and was a puppet of global forces. In short, the protesters regarded the AKP government as an "existential threat" to the Kemalist legacy of the nation-state structure.

The mass rallies reflected the lack of compromise on how to co-exist with "new actors and voices" in the public spaces. The pragmatic constellation of neo-liberal economic policies of Özal with the Islamic movement had been undermining the old social landscape and class dynamics, and had created new opportunity spaces for marginalized groups. The Anatolian bourgeoisie had used the opportunity spaces of the 1990s to insert its interests against the dominant class alliances between the metropolitan bourgeoisie (TÜSIAD) and the secular military establishment. Indeed, after the 2002 elections, TÜSIAD had adopted an anti-military position and stressed "good governance and transparency" over the secularism of the military. This social transformation has resulted in the political shift of power from secular to Islamic parties and the moderate Islamist AKP. However, the AKP's concept of politics had remained limited to the reduction of the role of the state, providing an institutional framework for the functioning of neo-liberal economic policies.

The four major mass rallies of early 2007 played an important role in the mobilization of major sectors of Turkish society. Although these rallies were all organized by retired military officers, illiberal Kemalist associations and secular women's groups, the majority of the protesters were the middle class, who responded to perceived threats to their life-style. This Kemalist middle class is very different from the traditional merchant class, which is more conservative and usually votes for the center-right parties.[3] The Kemalist middle class has emerged out of the service economy; it consists of self-employed lawyers, engineers, doctors and professionals in the computer, banking and insurance sectors of the economy. They stress individualism and personal self-realization. They also emphasize formality and the rule of law rather than the rule of ethnic, tribal or religion-based solidarity networks. The Kemalist middle class feels insecure about the orientation of the country under an Islamist party – albeit a moderate one – the AKP.[4]

There was a powerful fear shared by the demonstrators that their modern life-style was threatened. They especially referred to the new criteria for promotion and social mobility. For instance, Aydın, a school-teacher from Cine, said:

I was principal of a high school. When the AKP came to power, they removed me from the post of principal to teacher and appointed a teacher who had only three months experience in teaching and is an ex-staff member at the Directorate of Religious Affairs. Under the old system, in order to be a principal you were supposed to work for five years as a teacher, pass two exams on administrative regulations, and also participate in two summer orientation meetings. The AKP

---

[3] Sencer Ayata, "Meydanlardakiler 'yeni orta sınıf'tır," *Milliyet*, May 21–22, 2007; Yavuz's email exchange with Professor Ayata on May 22, 2007.

[4] Gündüz Aktan, "Korkmazcanlar," *Radikal*, April 24, 2007; Aktan, "Çıplak Gerçekler," *Radikal*, May 1, 2007.

changed this established rigor to staff schools with its own sympathizers who have Islamic inclinations instead. Although the Council of State (*Danıştay*) has ruled against the change of the regulation, Hüseyin Celik, the minister of education, who has written a number of articles about the Nur movement, filled almost all administrative positions with the followers of the Gülen community.

They stressed the long-term implications of conservative AKP policies that seek to Islamicize Turkish society incrementally. Insecurity was thus the glue unifying the demonstrators. They were nervous that AKP policies were transforming society and the state at the same time. Indeed, Erdoğan has failed to bridge the gap between Turkey's religious heartland and secular Turks, and his policies have deepened the feeling among seculadrists of being under an Islamist siege.

This was the first time in Turkish history that ordinary citizens and civil society had taken to the streets in such numbers to defend their life-style and the Kemalist character of the state and society. The common slogans were: "Turkey is secular and will remain secular!"; "No pass to headscarf in the Cankaya Palace!"; "We are all Turks!"; "Neither *seriat* (Islamic Law) nor military coup!"; "Look at us! Count! How many are we here?"

The demonstrators included many from the most modern, secular and pro-Western sectors of the country. However, there were a number of contradictions reflected in these demonstrations. There was a sense that the AKP was using the EU to counter the Kemalist establishment. These secular nationalist (primarily ethnic) Turks believe that the EU, along with the United States, only cares about its own national interests and not secularism or modernity in Turkey. While claiming to be in favor of secularism and liberalism, they often voice intolerant views concerning the rights of religious citizens and fail to appreciate the contradiction in defending Western-style freedoms while championing the right of unelected military officers to intervene in civilian politics. Moreover, the demonstrators believe that the United States wants to see the evolution of Islamic movements by using the case of Turkey as an experiment. Also, in these demonstrators' view the European and American governments believe it would be much easier to work with the AKP rather than with secular sectors of society, since the AKP leadership is dependent on Washington and the West for security from another "soft coup" launched by the Kemalist establishment.

## Concerns of the military: Kurdish secessionism and the Gülen community

In the April 2007 crisis, the military acted as an "opposition party." To understand the reaction of the military to the presidential election, one has to examine the critical configuration of internal and external forces. The military was very much concerned about Kurdish secessionism and the challenges of the Islamic movements, especially the Gülen community. Moreover, both the Kurdish and Islamist activists were invoking an EU-centric human rights discourse and the US occupation of Iraq to redefine the founding principles of the Republic. An analysis of this cognitive framework of the military is important to understand its policies and strategies against the Kurdish and Islamic challenges.

The military played a decisive role in the establishment of the Republic and the formation of Turkish identity.[5] The generals treat secularism as a solution to sectarian and ethnic-based social fragmentation and as a way of creating a national identity. The military is extremely sensitive about

---

[5] There is a contradiction built into the education system of the Turkish military officers. While they are indoctrinated to stay away from daily politics with a negative view of politicians, they are also asked to safeguard and if necessary sacrifice themselves for the founding principles of the Republic, i.e. the nation state and the secular political structure. In their education, two events are constantly drawn to the attention of the young cadets. When a group of ideologically oriented military officers took over the control of the government between 1908 and 1918, they destroyed the empire and ended the Ottoman state and also put at risk the survivability of the Turks as a group. Since these officers took the empire into World War I, which resulted in the defeat and the partition of the country, the military lost its credibility. A worse trauma was the first Balkan war. An ideological polarization among the military commanders in the field resulted in lack of discipline and disobedience of the orders of the commanders by young officers. The army was badly defeated and lost the Balkans. These events are constantly utilized in the war colleges in Turkey to focus on the danger of an ideological polarization within the military and especially a breakdown of the chain of command. These events left permanent marks on the institutional identity of the military. The military only overcame this with the military victories of Mustafa Kemal himself. He was the one who regained the prestige of and restored confidence in the military. The Turkish military seeks to remain outside "party politics."

The second event was the series of small military mutinies after 1950 against the DP government. The 1960 coup was carried out by 37 low-ranking officers who called themselves the Committee of National Unity, and resulted in the hanging of the prime minister and two prominent ministers. This coup also forced high-ranking officers into early retirement and purged senior officers. This was a time when the military chain of command was totally violated. After the coup, the military rigidly centralized around four-star generals and the chief of staff became the backbone of the military. The politicians agreed to this centralization in order to prevent the breakdown of the chain of command. This centralization around the chief of staff protects the civilian politicians against bloody coups by young officers. Thus, the chief of staff, in order to maintain the loyalty of the young officers, also expresses their concerns and prevents any statement outside his control. When Büyükanıt was the commander of the War College in Ankara (Kara Harp Okulu), he organized a conference to examine "The Lessons of the Balkan Wars and Their Contemporary Impacts," on April 26, 1995. The proceedings of this conference were published by the War College. For more on the impact of the Balkan wars on the Turkish military, see Selek Sabahattin, *Anadolu İhtilali* (Istanbul: Kastaş Yayınları, 1987), pp. 105–117. For the impact of the military coups on military discipline, see Doğan Akyaz, *Askeri Müdahalelerin Orduya Etkisi, Hiyerarşi Dışı Örgütlenmeden Emir Komuta Zincirine* (Istanbul: İletişim Yayınları, 2002).

secularism, since it treats it as the cardinal principle of the Republic's ethos of modern nation-building. In the light of the sectarian and ethnic violence in Iraq, the military has become even more sensitive to the principles of national identity and secularism. Moreover, under the legacy of the collapse of the Ottoman Empire, the military thinks that consociational multi-ethnic and multi-religious entities cannot survive and that they will always lead to constant outside interference in domestic affairs, eventually leading to the destruction of the state.[6] To avoid the potential break-up of the state, the military stresses unitary national integration and the maintenance of a homogeneous nation through secularism and Turkish nationalism. Its conception of modernity equates it to the process of secular nation-state building. İlker Basbuğ argues that "the gist of the reforms of Atatürk is to create a nation-state and Turkish nation. … Atatürk's understanding of a nation-state does not have an ethnic or religious base. His reforms represent a shift from a religion-based political community to a secular nation-state. Thus, secularism is the cornerstone of the founding principles of the Republic."[7] Any challenge to this ethos is regarded as a threat to the state. There have been two major challenges to the project of secular nation-building: Islamic and Kurdish activism, both identified as enemies of the Republic.

Atatürk never envisioned the military as the guardian of secularism and nation-building. The military appropriated this "sacred" mission during the military coup in 1961. It legally assigned the task of preserving secularism and nationalism to itself with article 35 of the Internal Service Law of 1961, which says that the "Turkish Armed Forces are responsible for guarding and defending the Turkish Republic as defined by the constitution." Since then the military has functioned as a quasi-political party against civilian governments, with its own vision of politics and its own grass-roots supporters. However, there is a tacit consensus in society that when the country is under threat, it is the task of the military to intervene

---

[6] İlker Basbuğ, the Ground Forces Commander, speaking at the beginning of the 2007–2008 academic year at the Turkish Military Academy in Ankara, warned the cadets about the new threats to the founding principles of the Turkish Republic. He identified the nation-state, unitary political structure and secularism as the founding principles of the Republic and asked the cadets to be vigilant in the protection of these principles. He said: "It is interesting to see that the country's nation-state structure is being targeted by both anti-secularists and ethnic nationalists." He went on to say that the Turkish Armed Forces would always stand with those who wanted to protect the nation-state and would thus defend secularism. He said that some groups were trying to change the "political structure" established by the Turkish Republic founder, Atatürk, into one based on religion or ethnic nationalism. In the same speech, in response to an ongoing debate by the AKP over a draft constitution, he argued that the principle of "secularism should not become a topic of discussion" (*Milliyet*, September 24, 2007).

[7] *Milliyet*, September 24, 2007.

and save it – that is, stage a *coup d'état*. Yet, the same public has never voted for a pro-military party after the coups. The military has carried out coups nearly once every ten years, in 1960, 1971, 1980 and 1997, either to eliminate or contain these challenges. It has been largely successful in containing them, though its often brutal methods (especially at the expense of the Kurdish minority) have led to a self-fulfilling prophecy, strengthening Kurdish nationalist and separatist demands.[8] Relations between the military and the Islamic political movement, the National Outlook Movement, founded by Necmettin Erbakan, have always been confrontational. The military was involved in two coups (in 1980 and 1997) against Erbakan's pro-Islamic parties. Since the AKP evolved out of the National Outlook Movement, the military has always been suspicious about the "intentions" of the party and its leadership – Erdoğan, Gül and Bülent Arınç, who were also active members of the Islamic movement.

When the AKP came to power in 2002, the Chief of the General Staff was Hilmi Özkök, a moderate and a democrat, who defended European standards of civilian–military relations. Yet most of his commanders were extremely suspicious of the AKP and its intentions. The government failed to utilize Özkök to develop closer ties with the military. The first interaction between the military and the government took place over the US decision to open a second front through Turkey into Iraq. The AKP blamed the military for parliament's decision not to allow American troops into Turkey or send Turkish troops to Iraq.[9] In other words, the AKP's key foreign and domestic policy has been to limit the power and influence of the military and it has measured its success in terms of the withdrawal of the military from policy areas. These policies had a negative effect on the military, with many mid-level officers having started to question Özkök's soft line towards the government.[10] In the perception of high-ranking officers, the AKP government shifted the blame for deteriorating relations between the Turkish military and the Pentagon by constantly complaining about the military's positions on Iraq, the Kurdish question and the Islamic Republic of Iran. In short, internal

---

[8] M. Hakan Yavuz and Nihat Ali Özcan, "The Kurdish Question and the JDP," *The Middle East Journal*, 13:1 (2006), 102–119; M. Hakan Yavuz and Michael M. Gunter, "The Kurdish Nation," *Current History* (January 2001), 33–39.

[9] See Saban Kardaş, "Turkey and the Iraqi Crisis: JDP between Identity and Interest," in M. Hakan Yavuz (ed.), *The Emergence of a New Turkey: Democracy and the AK Parti* (Salt Lake City: University of Utah Press, 2006), pp. 306–333. Fikret Bila, *Sivil Darbe Girişimi ve Ankara'da Irak Savaşları* (Ankara: Ümit Yayıncılık, 2003), pp. 42, 43.

[10] For the dissent against the soft policies of Özkök, see Mustafa Balbay, "Genç Subaylar tedirgin," *Cumhuriyet*, May 23, 2003. Özkök defended its policies by organizing a press conference; see "TSKda görüş ayrılığı yok," *Radikal*, April 14, 2004.

divisions in Turkish society have led the AKP government, like its Kemalist opponents in the past, to appeal to the US as an ally against its domestic foes and to search for legitimacy in Washington by opposing the military's role in the Turkish political system.[11]

### Kurdish secessionism

The deeper problem has been the lack of shared understanding of the sources and nature of the Kurdish problem. The AKP leadership has treated the Kurdish challenge as stemming from past Kemalist authoritarianism and even regarded the Kurds as an ideological ally against the rigid Kemalist ideology. Erdoğan, for example, has been accused by nationalist circles of having too many advisors of Kurdish background. The military, in turn, has defined the separatist Kurdish challenge in terms of territorial integrity, national unity and the homogeneous Kemalist nation-state model. Thus, strategies for containing the Kurdish challenge have varied.

The AKP government has also been accused of being reluctant to use military force (an "offensive policy") to deal with the PKK attacks. For instance, in 2006 Erdoğan told a group of journalists: "There is no reason to carry out an operation against the PKK if they are not attacking."[12] Basbuğ, the Commander of the Ground Troops, reacted to Erdoğan's statement by saying that "offensive operations against the PKK will continue until no terrorists are left."[13] In response to the military's aggressive posture, the AKP government tried to use the EU institutions and norms to rein in the armed forces.[14] Some close to the government voiced the opinion that "the military wants to maintain its power and budget by exaggerating [the threat] and constantly engaging in military operations against the PKK." The Kurdish question has become the most significant weapon with which the military and the AKP government delegitimize

---

[11] One of the key reasons many Islamist deputies, along with pro-Barzani deputies of the AKP, voted against the March 1 motion has to do with the possibility of the increased role of the military and the declaration of emergency law around the Turkish-Iraqi border. For instance, Ahmet Davutoğlu told CNN-Turk TV: "If we were to allow in US troops, we would have to declare an emergency situation in southeast Turkey. This could have created a problem in our relations with the EU" (February 16, 2004).

[12] Hasan Cemal, "Başbakan Erdoğan'dan Amerika yolunda Komutanlara Mesajlar: İrtica diye Bir Tehdit Yok," *Milliyet*, October 1, 2006.

[13] For the statements of İlker Başbuğ, see http://www.kkk.tsk.mil.tr/BasinHalklaIliskiler/BasinAciklama/DiyarbakirBasinAciklama.doc.

[14] İlhan Uzgel, "Dış Politikada AKP: Stratejik Konumdan Stratejik Modele," *Mülkiye*, 252 (2006), 69–84.

each other. In this sense, the US invasion and occupation of Iraq has dealt a heavy blow to the relations between the AKP and the military. Moreover, the US occupation has brought a huge arsenal to Iraq, to which the PKK had access via Kurdish *peshmergas* (militias), in addition to likely new tactics with which to fight the Turkish military.[15]

### The activities of the Gülen community

The worst crisis was caused by the reaction in the military and some secular sectors over the recruitment of followers of the moderate Islamist religious leader Fethullah Gülen into the national police and the Ministry of Education. In a series of interviews, a high-ranking military officer had this to say:

> The Islamization of society was completed by different Islamic groups and Sufi orders. Now we are seeing the Islamization of state institutions and bureaucracy. It is very similar to the Islamization of the bureaucracy in Pakistan, especially the education and the police force. They have not been able to penetrate the military. The group which leads this Islamization of the state is the Fethullah Gülen community. They use almost every means, even those which are un-Islamic, to achieve their goal of controlling the state. The AKP government, which lacks its own educated cadre, is very much dependent on Gülen's followers. Moreover, the university exams are now dominated by the graduates of these Gülen schools. They will dominate the bureaucracy.[16]

Indeed, criticism has been voiced by a number of Kemalist bureaucrats about the attempts of the Gülen community to use the police force against the military.[17] During my interviews in Ankara, a number of high-ranking military officers raised questions about the degree to which promotion in some ministries took place on the basis of religious-network-based solidarity. This alleged penetration by the Gülen community of the bureaucracy

---

[15] Foreign Minister Gül argued that the PKK received not only military support from Iraqi groups under US occupation but also training and new military tactics from the Iraqi resistance and some Kurdish *peshmergas*. *Hürriyet*, June 14, 2007.

[16] Interview in Ankara on April 12, 2007. Nihat Ali Özcan and I interviewed a total of 12 high-ranking security and civilian bureaucrats in April 2007. Some of the findings are published in "Political Crisis in Turkey: The Conflict of Political Languages," *Middle East Policy*, 14:3 (Fall 2007), 118–135. The interviews were conducted in a face-to-face format in Ankara. All interviewees agreed to be quoted, subject to anonymity.

[17] Rusen Cakir, http://ntvmsnbc.com/news/275733.asp; Ahmet Insel, "Neofeodal devlette ilerlerken," *Radikal II*, March 4, 2007. For more on the military vs. Turkish police force, see: http://www.tsk.mil.tr/10_ARSIV/10_1_Basin_Yayin_Faaliyetleri/10_1_7_Konusmalar/2006/harpakademilerikonusmasi_02102006.html

is a major source of concern for the military, and they do not want a similar process to take place within the military as well.[18]

In addition to these policy differences between the AKP government and the military, the new Chief of the General Staff, Yasar Büyükanıt, has defended the traditional activist role of the military within the political system and has not hesitated to resist the policies of the government. Before Büyükanıt was appointed as the Chief of Staff, there was a vicious – one could claim "racist" – campaign against him. He was first accused of not being a "Turk" but rather of Sabbatean/Jewish ancestry.[19] "When these accusations were spreading around websites," according to a military officer, "Büyükanıt became the target of the Gülen community via the Semdinli incident," in which Turkish special security forces were accused of bombing a bookstore owned by a former Kurdish activist in Semdinli (in Van) in 2005, among other events. Ferhat Sarıkaya, a prosecutor in the city of Van and with known close ties to the Gülen community, was called to investigate Yasar Büyükanıt, along with three generals, over allegations of abusing their positions and setting up an illegal group to foment unrest in the mainly Kurdish cities in order to thus thwart Turkey's bid to join the EU. The indictment accused a paramilitary group, which is claimed to have been set up by Büyükanıt, of the bombing of a bookstore in Semdinli, which resulted in one death and several injuries.[20] Some AKP deputies expressed suspicion of military hardliners' involvement in the incident and supported the Van prosecutor's indictment of Büyükanıt. For instance, Faruk Ünsal, the AKP deputy from Adiyaman, said: "The indictment prepared by the office of the Van prosecutor has done what we were unable to do." Another AKP deputy, Hasan Taşcı from Manisa, said: "What we left unfinished is now completed by the Van prosecutor. He did his job."[21]

The military believes that the Gülen community launched a major campaign through its media outlets and pro-Gülen police force against Büyükanıt to stop his appointment. Indeed, the Gülen community did not want Büyükanıt to be the next Chief of the General Staff because, when he was Commander of the Kuleli Military High School and the War College

---

[18] Cemil Cicek, the minister of Justice, became the main target of the Gülen community because of his support for the anti-terror law. For more on the reaction of the military, see *Cumhuriyet*, April 9, 2007; Ahmet Hakan, "Cemaat, ey cemaat," *Hürriyet*, April 2, 2007; Ahmet Hakan, "Cemaat diyor ki: O bakan bize düsman," *Hürriyet*, April 4, 2007.

[19] These accusations spread around the websites. See critical responses to these rumors: Mehmet Yılmaz, *Hürriyet*, March 6, 2006; Bekir Coskun, *Hürriyet*, March 7, 2006.

[20] See the full indictment, http://www.milliyet.com.tr/sabitimg/06/gazete/siyaset/semdinli_iddianame.pdf

[21] Mehmet Yılmaz, *Hürriyet*, March 7, 2007.

in Ankara, he had purged a number of students who had ties with the Gülen community. The anti-Büyükanıt campaign and negative reporting on the military have created an anti-Gülen mood within the military and some high-ranking generals have blamed the AKP government for using the Gülen community against the military. General Büyükanıt regarded the campaign against him as the work of the Gülen community within the police and the government. This, in turn, made him more confrontational, and he became suspicious of the Gülen community's alliance with the AKP government. The leading daily newspaper *Zaman*, which is owned by the Gülen community, and the weekly magazine *Nokta* sought to associate him with underground organizations of the "deep state," accused of fomenting instability in the country in the past. The government did not defend the military or challenge journalists who voiced such suspicions.

In addition to these domestic and personality factors, trouble with the EU also facilitated the military memorandum of April 27, 2007. Hereby, an opportunity was created for the military to assert itself. The key event was the European Council decision in December 2005 that dashed Turkey's hopes of joining the EU. Both the military and large sectors of Turkish society started to question the EU's sincerity over full membership. This created room for maneuver against the AKP government. The EU, in the eyes of most Turks, lost its credibility after the election of Nicolas Sarkozy as the president of France. The United States, deeply involved with its "democratization" projects in Iraq and Afghanistan, did not have much time for Turkish politics and anti-Americanism was running high in Turkey. Thus, the military was not very concerned about outside reaction to its memorandum, nor, indeed, was there significant reaction.

### The transformation of the AKP

These meetings, along with the April 2007 military ultimatum, had a number of major political consequences for the political landscape of Turkey. Gül withdrew his candidacy and became a *"mazlum"*[22] – one who has been "wronged"; early national elections were called; fragmentation among political parties was ended through one successful and one failed merger; and Erdoğan made a drastic change in the list of newly

---

[22] The etymological definition of *mazlum* means "oppressed," "tormented," or "wronged." A *mazlum* is someone who has been subject to a grave injustice. In Islam, the Prophet Muhammad's grandson Imam Hussein, the son of Ali, is the archetypal epitome of a *mazlum*.

nominated deputies by purging almost all Islamically oriented deputies,[23] along with any critical voices from the party such as Ertuğrul Yalçınbayır, known to be the "moral conscience of the AKP."[24] In a so-far unsuccessful attempt to appease Kemalist/secularist critics, Erdoğan nominated ex-leftists, three Alevi intellectuals from the Alevi community and some women to overcome charges that the AKP is a "party of the religio-political community."[25] Erdoğan excluded a significant number of AKP deputies from the National Outlook Movement of Erbakan in an effort to alter perceptions that the party was too conservative and to position it in the center of the political spectrum. Moreover, he did not renominate most of the deputies who had voted against the March 1, 2003 motion that would have allowed US troops to enter Iraq from Turkey.

Since the 1980 coup, the Turkish political spectrum has been divided and contested among charismatic personalities more than on ideological grounds. Speakers at the republic rallies and protest slogans have repeatedly called for secularist parties to unite against the "Islamist" AKP. Indeed, in response to these calls, the leaders of the two main center-right parties, the DYP and the ANAP, tried to merge as the *Demokrat Parti* (DP) (Democrat Party). This merger failed a month before the election and prevented not only their representation in parliament but also center-right voters from having a genuine option to vote. On May 24, 2007 the *Demokratik Sol Parti* (DSP) (Democratic Left Party) reached an agreement with the main opposition *Cumhuriyet Halk Partisi* (CHP) (Republican People's Party) to have a common list at the elections. These mergers were criticized by Erdoğan; he argued: "Putting forty rotten eggs together

---

[23] Many ex-parliamentarians such as AKP's Adana MP Abdullah Çalışkan claim their vote was due to the April 27 memorandum of the military and the meeting between Erdoğan and Büyükanıt on May 5, 2007, at the Dolmabahçe Palace. Former MP Ersönmez Yarbay of Ankara, who has always been in favor of democratic processes within the AKP, explains the major transformation of the list as a reflection of a region-based solidarity network (*Milliyet*, June 7, 2007).

[24] Yalçınbayır said "The AKP won the 2002 election with a platform that stressed three 'Ys': *Yoksulluk* (Poverty), *Yasaklar* (Restrictions), and *Yolsuzluk* (Corruption). Now we need to add five more 'Ys' to describe the party: *Yozlaşma*, *Yandaşlık* (Clientalism), *Yağcılık*, *Yiyicilik* (Bribery), *Yobazlık* (Religious Fanaticism)" (*Radikal*, June 8, 2007). According to Kenan Camurcu, a leading analyst of Islamic politics, "Erdoğan could not allow some 'native' politicians to criticize his policies, and he preferred to bring 'guests' such as Ertuğrul Günay into the party to give the impression that the party is inclusive. But he does not want to lose his authoritarian control" (interview with Camurcu, June 8, 2007).

[25] The AKP included a number of prominent leftist politicians such as Ertuğrul Günay, Zafer Üskül, Haluk Özdalga, Erdal Kalkan and Ayşenur Bahçekapılı; two prominent Alevi intellectuals Reha Çamuroğlu and Hüseyin Tuğcu; some singers and businessmen (Zafer Çağlayan, Osman Yağmurdereli); and wrestler Hamza Yerlikaya – as a way of becoming a party of the center.

does not make a good one." Indeed, this merger did not help the CHP and also destroyed the center-right parties in the national elections. After the elections, thirteen deputies resigned from the CHP and joined the DSP.

### An analysis of the 2007 elections

The configuration of forces in the republican meetings, the statement by the military, the decisions of the Constitutional Court and the merging of the leftist parties failed to prevent the takeover of the presidency by the AKP. However, the AKP used this crisis to challenge the forces of the status quo and emerged as the biggest party in the July 22, 2007 elections. After receiving 34.4% of the vote in the November 2002 elections (see Table 8.1), it increased its total to 46.5% in the July 2007 elections. This was an increase of 12% for its second term. That total gave the AKP 341 seats in the 550-member parliament. The secularist CHP and the nationalist MHP won 112 and 71 seats respectively. Up to 25 seats went to independent candidates, including 20 Kurdish representatives who merged under the pro-Kurdish *Demokratik Toplum Partisi* (DTP) (Democratic Society Party).

The CHP's election platform was based on the fear of the Islamization of the state and society. Its aggressive leadership asked people to vote for the CHP as a vote for the reforms of Mustafa Kemal. The CHP is currently headed by Deniz Baykal, a political science professor and a former foreign minister. Baykal has a very divisive personality with a personal goal of remaining the head of the CHP more than that of becoming prime minister. Baykal's party failed to create bridges with the new emerging economic actors in society. Its election platform was built on fear and the supposed threat to secularism. The result, however, was a vote against the military's interference in politics and especially the

Table 8.1

| Party | Votes | % | Seats | % |
|---|---|---|---|---|
| AKP 2007 | 15,641,382 | 46.5 | 341 | 61.5 |
| AKP 2002 | 10,804,458 | 34.4 | 365 | 66.4 |
| CHP 2007 | 6,974,598 | 20.9 | 112 | 20.2 |
| CHP 2002 | 6,096,488 | 19.4 | 177 | 32.2 |
| MHP 2007 | 4,842.024 | 14.3 | 71 | 13.5 |
| Independent | 1,713,769 | 5.7 | 27 | 4.9 |

politics of fear that was manipulated by the generals. Thus, the military received a rejection from the nation over its self-declared guardianship role. The people preferred that the army withdraw to its barracks according to the standards of the EU.

By receiving 14.3% of the vote, the MHP was the third party to enter parliament, with 71 seats. Although many expected the MHP to receive around 18% of the vote, it had to compete with the AKP in Anatolia. It remains the main Turkish nationalist party, although it has shifted from ethnic to civic Turkish nationalism. The party is led by Devlet Bahceli, an economist and a former deputy prime minister. In the 2002 election, the MHP failed to garner even 10% of the national vote. It has remained skeptical about Turkey's EU bid, accuses the AKP government of being too soft on separatist Kurdish guerrillas, and supports a military incursion into northern Iraq to crack down on PKK rebels based there. Interestingly, the MHP also has distanced itself from the military agenda and does not support military interference in politics. The MHP's electoral success is based on increased Turkish nationalism as a result of the Kurdish insurgency and the perceived EU mistreatment of Turkey. It has stressed Islam as an important factor of Turkish identity. Moreover, it has nominated as deputies several important intellectuals such as Gündüz Aktan and Osman Bölükbası.

That the AKP emerged once again as the leading party following the 2007 elections is no surprise. However, very few, including the AKP itself, expected such a landslide victory. This victory is a vote *for* the policies of the AKP and *against* the crisis created by the secular–military establishment over the presidency. The AKP was able to unite many disparate voters in its bid to retain control of the Turkish parliament. Some voted for democracy, others voted against the e-memorandum, yet others voted with the expectation of a new constitution, and yet still others voted in favor of EU membership. With interests and demographics ranging from business groups to shantytown dwellers, from devout Muslims to Armenians[26], liberals and conservatives all came together to vote for the same party. In short, the AKP electorate is not unified by a single identity, but rather a coalition of identities that attracted nearly half (46.5%) of the total votes.

There are two key reasons for the AKP's landslide electoral victory: *economic* and *political*. According to the public-opinion surveys, the most important factor, which determined people's decision to vote for the

---

[26] The Armenian Patriarch Mesrob II Mutafyan told *Der Spiegel* that the "Armenians will vote for the AKP," *Yeni Şafak*, June 4, 2007.

AKP, was the economy. For instance, when voters were asked to identify the most critical factor in their decision to vote, 78% identified the "economic situation and expectations," 14% indicated "democratization," and 11% "the threat to secularism" as an important factor in their decision.[27] In short, not democratization or the issue of secularism but rather economic factors were what shaped the decision of the majority of the people. As already noted, during the previous five years Turkey has achieved 7.5% average annual growth rates in its gross domestic product, record foreign investment that jumped from US$1.2 billion to US$20 billion per year, and a lowering of its inflation rate. The AKP-led social welfare networks also played an important role in reducing the negative consequences of the market economy. Moreover, the Turkish currency was reconfigured and has since maintained its value against the dollar and the euro. In short, the people cared about their daily life more than any supposed long-term ideological threat from the AKP. Thus, neither identity nor ideology, but rather services and improvements in daily existence were what determined the people's vote. The party had used municipalities to provide food, coal and especially healthcare through new reforms to millions of people. Under the new healthcare reform, people had access to private healthcare with the government's support. In other words, under the AKP, privatization of healthcare improved the situation at least in the short run. The AKP government also expanded the bureaucracy through new bureaucratic employment.

As far as *political* factors are concerned, there are at least five factors that shaped the election outcome: the AKP's assertive strategy against the military e-memorandum; the victimization of Gül during the presidential elections; the charismatic personality of Erdoğan; the more inclusive list of new AKP deputies; and the mobilization of Islamic networks and the framing of the issues in "local" language. The people did not only provide a "protest" vote, they also voted for the new "social contract." One of the key election commitments of the AKP was to devise a new constitution that would deepen democracy and civil society. This commitment took place both on the election platform and also as oral statements by the party leaders. Many people in the country felt that this was an opportunity to restructure the Republic in accordance with the needs of the EU. The electoral victory of the AKP in Kurdish-populated regions is closely related to this commitment of devising a new constitution.

After the e-memorandum of the military, the AKP pursued a multi-layered response by indirectly challenging the military intervention. It did

---

[27] Bekir Ağırdır, "Seçmenin röntgeni I," *Radikal*, July 25, 2007.

not shy away from issuing a sharp response to the military, while proposing the direct election of the presidency by the people. The AKP also launched a massive campaign to further educate the people about the statements of the military and convince the electorate that the AKP is not a threat but rather the hope of the people. Finally, the AKP proposed an early election to defeat military pressure. By using these stratagems, the AKP succeeded in transforming the conflict between the military and the AKP into the status quo versus democratic change, or the military versus democracy. Following the successful implementation of these policies the people overwhelmingly voted for the AKP and against the military-led campaign. While the military simply issued its statement and waited for the results of the July election, the AKP owed its victory to its well-organized grass-roots efforts to educate the people about the military's statements and to portray opposition to Gül's candidacy as a rebellion of Kemalist forces against the Islamic way of life. In other words, the AKP election campaign was very much based on Gül's candidacy as being the "election of a pious president." By framing the reaction to Gül as an attack on traditional Islamic piety, the AKP mobilized the Islamic networks throughout Anatolia, along with the Islamic media, to stir the masses against the opposition parties. Since the state machine was in the hands of the AKP, along with municipal governments, the AKP had an advantage over the military in reaching the people. The military e-memorandum rescued the AKP from hard questions in the election debate and the elections turned into a referendum over Kemalism versus democracy and respect for Turkey's Muslim heritage.

With the military "using" PKK resistance and terrorism and the need to intervene in northern Iraq as a burning question of national security the AKP was made to seem weak on national security. The AKP government responded with a clever policy by arguing for a powerful military response to the PKK threat but also stressing the negative timing and the possible results of this military confrontation. The AKP also hinted that the military was not defending the borders properly, stressing that there were more terrorists within the country than outside. In other words, the military used all its cards against the AKP and it miserably failed to achieve anything but the squandering of the last of its credibility within and outside the country. The debate over an incursion into Iraq under the pressure of the military, the CHP and the MHP was a major source of worry among many people, who feared that this would undermine stability in the country and also force it into an unknown tunnel with major potential pitfalls. The public remained very much opposed to any such incursion and eventually interpreted the increase in terrorist activities three months before the elections as a pretext for demonstrating "the lack of nationalistic qualities of the AKP" and also "the work of security forces" in the country. In other words, many Turks started to ask whether the military were deliberately pursuing a confrontational policy to undermine the AKP government. In the 2007 election, an overwhelming majority of Kurds preferred the AKP. This helped in the decline of the ethnic Kurdish DTP, previously DEHAP, whose votes decreased from 6.2% in 2002 to 4% in 2007. Many Kurds supported the policies of the AKP with the expectation that their situation would improve under another AKP government. They expect more cultural rights, the improvement of their economic situation and equitable treatment at the hands of the state.

The most crucial factor was Erdoğan's charisma as the supreme leader of the conservative masses. He was always viewed as one of them in terms of his body language, the model he presented and his over-all life-style. In addition, Gül became as significant as Erdoğan in the 2007 elections, since the AKP election platform was much built around the Kemalist campaign against his presidency. The impact of the presidential election worked in favor of the AKP. The AKP dramatized the *mazlum* (wronged one) and the *mağdur* (victimized one) and the exclusion of pious people from the public sphere by the "white Turks." The Kemalist establishment were framed as the "whites" and the supporters of the AKP as the "blacks" of Turkey, who had been marginalized by the system. This "framing" of the crisis was very successful among ordinary Turks. It mobilized Islamic networks, especially the Gülen community, which has an ongoing conflict with the military, in favor of the AKP. With the support of Islamic networks, the AKP organized a multiplicity of meetings and carried its message to every corner of the country.[28] For instance, it organized mass rallies in fifty-eight provinces during the 2007 election campaign, whereas the CHP had them in only twenty.

### Post-election anxiety: the new constitution

The electoral victories (parliamentary and presidential) of the AKP have increased societal anxiety and highlighted the deepening divide between the pro-Islam AKP and its secular–nationalist opponents, who fear that the political system in the country is facing an existential threat from Islamic groups, especially the Gülen movement. The military in particular is becoming very concerned.[29] With the poor showing of the CHP, which

---

[28] On the mobilization of the Gülen networks in Kurdish provinces, see Altan Tan's interview in *Milliyet*, July 30, 2007.

[29] Hilmi Özkök, a retired Chief of the General Staff, shared his concerns over a number of issues with Fikret Bila, *Milliyet*, October 1–5, 2007.

miserably failed to capitalize on the anxieties of secular Turks even after major public rallies, the military has less public ground to voice its opposition to AKP policies. The military, along with some secularists, feel more vulnerable than before and there is a deep sense of "siege" and a feeling of despair. This mood, in turn, may carry the seeds of new tensions if Erdoğan does not take such sensitivities and concerns into account. Given the MHP's and DTP's entries into parliament, the 2007 elections may ironically deepen polarization both in parliament and society. The minority nationalist groups may further their mobilization, while their siege mentality could even lead to some bloody events if the AKP does not take these concerns into account. The main concern of the secular groups has to do with the AKP's initiative to craft a new constitution. Through the constitutional debate the AKP seeks to redefine the founding principles of the Republic. This has already created a new divide between Islamic groups who want to undo the authoritarian aspects of the Kemalist system and the secular groups who want to protect it.

The AKP hired a group of constitutional law professors under the leadership of Ergun Özbudun, a professor of Bilkent University, who had prepared a number of draft constitutions for different organizations. The purpose of the AKP is to redefine the founding principles of the Republic with the support of the liberals in order not to be accused of being Islamic. The draft constitution reflects the wishes of Turkey's opinionated and liberal intellectuals. Some of these intellectuals, who argue for the establishment of the "Second Republic," have a controversial historical understanding of the evolution of the political system.[30] By the Second Republic they mean a completely de-Kemalized Turkey, with a new definition of secularism to open more spaces for religiously-based political arguments, supporting an arrangement in which much of central power is devolved to the provinces (as a way of meeting the political demands of the Kurdish minority), and a polity without any officially enforced ideology. In other words, they believe that the Republic should

---

[30] Mehmet Altan, one of the proponents of the Second Republic debate, defines the term thus: "The Republic which was founded in 1923 has no democratic and pluralist qualities; sovereignty belongs not to the people but to the bureaucracy and the military; and its understanding of a statist economic system turned into a 'robbery system.' Therefore, the Republic should be democratized and the political structure should go into a period of restructuring. This is the core of the notion behind the Second Republic. What does it suggest? It seeks to transform bureaucratic polity into a democratic system. This means reducing the role of the state in the economy, developing a transparent political and economic system, and giving more control to tax payers. It especially means the removal of the military's control over the regime, and restructuring the state into a productive and democratic regime, with the participation of all social groups" (*The Turkish Daily News*, September 28, 2007).

not side with any national or ideological position but rather maintain an equal distance from all preferences, opinions and religions. Some critics feel that the draft fails to realize that there are no deep liberal traditions in Turkey and those who are well-organized and ruthless are bound to emerge victorious. Thus, the prescription of those who favor the radical transformation of the Kemalist Republic might lead to greater division and instability. A close examination of the draft constitution indicates that it: celebrates a market economy and private ownership as high ideals; redefines Turkishness; has Kurdish taught as a second language in government schools; restructures the Constitutional Court, along with its duties; ends the autonomy of the military by subjecting the decisions of Supreme Military Council to legal review; and reduces the powers of the Turkish president. The AKP seeks to resolve the headscarf issue through constitutional change in the Higher Education Council.

The draft constitution has already caused a major debate and strong reaction in diverse sections of society. Many critics are suspicious that the AKP is seeking to redefine the Republic along multi-cultural lines. The proposed draft has a number of articles that would lead to the total decentralization of the state, open new avenues for the redefinition of the state as a bi-national (Kurdish and Turkish) polity, and also undermine the Kemalist version of the separation of state and religion. Some of the reaction reflected the peculiar Kemalist interpretation of Western liberalism. For instance, Mustafa Bumin, a former head of the Constitutional Court, has said that the draft seeks to ease the ban on the headscarf and that this, in turn, would put pressure on all women to adopt it on campuses.

These academics have good intentions but they don't know the reality of Turkey. This is a country where people get beaten up in the street for not observing the fast during Ramadan. If the constitution allows people to dress the way they want, then the headscarved students will prevent those who do not want to cover.[31]

The growing numbers of an increasingly influential middle class from Anatolia – more socially conservative than their metropolitan peers – have struggled for a long time to lift the ban in the name of freedom of education and freedom of choice. Although the European Court of Human Rights ruled in 2005 that the ban did not infringe the rights of a young woman to have an education or freedom of choice, the AKP government wants to lift the ban through constitutional change. The goal of the AKP is bigger than the lifting of the headscarf ban. The 1982 constitution aims to protect the founding principles of the state more than the rights of its citizens. Thus, it is a key obstacle to democratization and change.

---

[31] For Bumin's interview, see *Hürriyet*, September 17, 2007.

Indeed, Erdoğan and some of his liberal supporters regarded the 2007 election victory as an opportunity for the establishment of the "Second Republic," redefining secularism and national identity and de-Kemalizing the Turkish state. This, in turn, counter-mobilized the secular establishment in "criminalizing the ruling party" as a threat to secularism. After the constitutional amendments to allow the wearing of the headscarf in Turkish universities, Abdurrahman Yalçınkaya, the chief prosecutor of the High Court of Appeals, accused the AKP of fomenting "anti-secular activities" and becoming the "focal point for undermining secularism." In a 163-page indictment for the dissolution of the AKP, Yalçınkaya cited the government's efforts to lift a ban on wearing Islamic headscarves in universities, attempts to roll back restrictions on religious education, and 'anti-secular' comments by ruling party officials. The prosecutor asked the Constitutional Court to bar seventy-one people, including Erdoğan and Gül, from politics for five years. On March 31, 2008 the Constitutional Court, in which eight of the eleven judges were appointed by Ahmet Necdet Sezer, the former president who was a strong supporter of Turkey's Kemalist–secularist traditions, voted unanimously to hear the case. The governing party sharply criticized the threatened closure court case, arguing that it would undermine the political and economic reforms as part of Turkey's bid to join the EU.

Indeed, a week after the chief prosecutor's case, the AKP government pursued a dramatic middle-of-the night round-up of prominent opponents, such as the eighty-three-year-old Ilhan Selcuk, a columnist of the militant secularist daily *Cumhuriyet*, along with Kemal Alemdaroğlu, former president of Istanbul University and Doğu Perincek, the leader of the left-wing nationalist Workers' Party. They are all charged with being members of the "Ergenekon çetesi" gang, with plans for engaging in "illegal violent activities" to "overthrow the government."

On July 30, 2008, the Constitutional Court rejected the chief prosecutor's demand to permanently shut down the AKP and ban Erdoğan, Gül and seventy other leading AKP members from political office for a period of five years by charging the AKP with being the focal point for "anti-secular activities" and "seeking to turn the country into an Islamic state." However, the court agreed with the prosecutor's indictment that the AKP had shown signs of being "a focal point for anti-secular activity" and ruled the party be deprived of fifty per cent of the financial aid it receives from the state treasury. Even though the Court did not close down the party, its decision will deepen the anxiety among the anti-AKP Kemalist sector of society by legitimating their fear that the AKP is engaged in anti-secular activities. In fact, the Court has put the AKP and Erdoğan on probation. The decision is expected to have repercussions for the AKP's governance too. In the light of this decision, the ruling party will be forced to act more cautiously on sensitive issues such as the rights of religious Turks and ethnic minorities, and constitutional reforms to expand civil liberties in accordance with EU criteria. In short, Erdoğan has to stay away from controversial, divisive religious issues which deepen the fractures in society. The Court's decision leaves liberal Islamic groups and advocates of greater civilian control over the military–bureaucratic establishment and of expanded civil liberties in continued tension with more Kemalist–secular groups who want to maintain the status quo and the power of the old Republican establishment.

The case reflects the power struggle between the Kemalist–secular establishment and pro-Islam forces over the future of Turkey and the degree to which there should be a balance between Republicanism and democracy on the one hand, and secularism and Islam's role in politics and society on the other. The court case highlights the deep divisions in Turkey and the failed policies of the government to address the fears of the secular establishment. The AKP conception of "majoritarian" democracy, that is, determining decisions with majority rule, and the illiberal intolerance of many in the Kemalist establishment has not been productive for creating a shared political language and a degree of consensus within society. There is no shared language to address these divisive issues, and the evolution of two opposing political languages cannot be resolved within the electoral process but rather requires a deliberative democracy and the participatory public to create a new neutral language of the "political." Neither majoritarian democracy nor the politicization of the courts is going to create a shared language, but rather this will deepen the crisis in the country. The pro-Islam forces are trying to assert their life-style and language through a parliamentary majority, while the Kemalists are using the judiciary to curtail the power of the elected government.

### The fear of Islamic "majoritarianism"

A slow institutional and behavioral Islamization process has been going on in Turkey since the mid-1980s. This everyday Islamization or public religiosity is evolving together with the Islamic electoral victories in local and national governments. Thus, the process of Islamization is complex and has multiple dimensions. The key macro and micro factors and the tension between structure and agency must be examined together in order to understand the short and long term implications of the Islamization process. The main process of Islamization is taking place at the network level and these networks are also used for political mobilization and social mobility. In other words, in-group bonding is further enhanced at the expense of out-group bridging between different communities. Since 2002, the AKP has hired observant Muslims at every layer of bureaucracy, especially the ministry of education, which is now dominated by the followers of Fethullah Gülen. This shift in the political language and public spaces in terms of Islamization goes to the heart of the fear and mass mobilization in April and May 2007. Many people are worried about the long term implications of this Islamization at the societal and state levels. However, it would be a mistake to read this Islamization as purely negative. It has played an important role in the ongoing economic development of the country and, as a result, many Muslims have become more moderate. In other words, the Islamization process has also played a moderating role in society and in re-bridging state and society while recasting the notion of secularism. Yet, for secular Turks, these moderating influences are the first stage of the ultimate Islamization of the state in a potentially authoritarian direction. These changes are the outcome of several decades of economic and political transformations. A jewelry shop owner tells a *New York Times* reporter that: "In a very quiet, deep way, you can sense an Islamization ...They're not after rapid change. They're investing for 50 years ahead."[32]

The growing fear among the traditionally secular segments of society is that the AKP is seeking to transform modern life-styles by creating a new set of principles over the definition of a "good person and good way of life." The issue is complex and it is not about the AKP per se but rather about the formation of new modes and practices. When former president Sezer tried to stop the appointments of pro-Islam staff to key government positions, the government appointed them as "substitutes" (*vekil*), to overcome the presidential veto. Since the election of Abdullah Gül as president, most high positions in the bureaucracy have been staffed by pro-AKP officials. In recent years, as ironically has also been the trend in the US, there has been a major change in Turkey in the curriculum in terms of re-imposing "intelligent design" (more space for a religious perspective on creation and less for "evolution" and Darwin's "theory of natural selection").

There is some indication of the gradual Islamization of formerly Kemalist sectors of state and society. By gradual Islamization, I mean the permeation of Islamic ideas and values into institutions, life-styles, political language and the media. This subtle form of Islamization is something you do not voice or force but rather it is unconsciously

---

[32] The *New York Times*, June 1, 2007.

internalized and acted upon. It is Islamization by moral pressure, which creates an aura or atmosphere of a new normative system. In other words, people start to imitate Islamic forms of behaving through greetings, dress codes and praying, to reflect the belonging to a Muslim community, even if some of them do not believe in these forms. This is Islamization by imitation and public pressure. Şerif Mardin, a Turkish sociologist, has termed this *mahalle baskısı* or "neighborhood pressure," which has evolved out of this institutional Islamization and for critics may restrict personal freedoms.[33] *Mahalle baskısı* has permeated high schools, neighborhoods and even state institutions. New patterns of conduct and interactions, of greetings and dress codes, are introduced as "Islamic" and are thus legitimated to be followed by society.

Erdoğan's conception of plebiscite democracy, which is not only majoritarian but also communal, is the main source of contemporary fear in more secular sectors. His communalized democracy consists of two ideas: (1) those who share the same religion have common political and economic interests regardless of their ethnic origins; and (2) the interests of believing Muslims are different from the interests of followers of ethnic or ideological identity groups. By stressing Islamic solidarity and Muslim nationalism above ethnic nationalism, Erdoğan seeks to provide sanction (or license) for government action. He believes that religion and nation are unified as two aspects of the same coin and that politics is a vehicle for the realization of moral order and happiness.

Erdoğan could have adopted a language of compromise among opposing political forces rather than seeking to impose this majoritarianism, but rather he embraced the idea of a Turkey divided between a winning majority and a losing minority. Equally controversial has been the uncritical adoption of the idea that the unfettered free market can take over the functions of the state. This Reagan–Thatcher ideology of neo-liberalism reduces and calls into question the basic responsibilities of the state even in such critical areas as education, healthcare and the development of the poor regions of the country.

This market-based governance has been at the center of worsening inequality in Turkey and today there is a growing tension between market winners and losers. This new economic system has helped to popularize the selfishness and the competitive individualism of the market system. For critics, the profit motive has led to the official valorization of private interests over public ones. The frontlines of this tension are apparent in newspapers, pulpits, radio stations, coffee-shops and the sequestered

---

[33] See Şerif Mardin's interview in *Vatan*, May 15, 2007.

walks of private life. The new *"fanatiques"* are not religious per se but they are nationalist. In reaction to the market-based morality, a new counter-morality is evolving. In its counter-nationalistic moral language, state and nation become key themes, with marginalized sectors of the population encouraged to carve out spaces for themselves through political aspiration in favor of lives of public service with a sense of heroism. Good conduct is redefined in terms of self-sacrifice.

## Conclusion

Turkey is seeking to develop a shared and inclusive political language to redefine its future. The Turkish version of electoral "democratism" is under pressure to achieve the state and societal integration long sought during the republican period. The military wants to maintain the power structure of old Turkey (what it knows best) whereas the AKP government wants to dictate its own version of a new Turkey. The AKP seeks to discontinue the authoritarian nation-building project of Kemalism and instead recognize the multiculturalism of the country – though with Islamic undertones – including political and cultural rights for the Kurdish minority. The crisis is between these opposing visions of Turkey. The main challenges are the role of Islam in the public sphere and the definition of the Turkish "nation." The AKP is defending the radical restructuring of the country along multi-ethnic lines and with a greater role for Islam as the new glue for the Turkish nation or state. The military, along with the more secular sectors of society, fear the shadow of the multi-ethnic and multi-religious Ottoman legacy and the possibility of the fragmentation of the state.

The sweeping electoral victory of the AKP in 2007 was a milestone in Turkey's long and contentious transition to and consolidation of democracy. The democratic election and rule of a political party rooted in an Islamic socio-political reform movement represents both paradox and promise in the wake of the 9/11 global crisis. Historically, the Kemalist legitimation of authoritarian rule and the exclusion of the traditional Anatolian Sunni majority from the corridors of power were based upon a modernizing mission of making Turkey a part of European civilization. However, the great paradox of Turkish politics over the last few years has been that the champion of integration with the EU and the consolidation of secular liberal democracy has been the formerly Islamist AKP and the main opponents have been the ostensibly Westernizing Kemalists. The AKP realized that fulfilling the Copenhagen Criteria for EU accession provided the best guarantee for civilian control of the military, freedom of religion, and even a peaceful settlement of the Kurdish question.

However, critics have accused the AKP government of only tactical adherence to such goals as a way of wresting power from the Kemalist establishment.

But the transformations in Turkish society since the liberalizing economic and political reforms of Turgut Özal in the 1980s have been much deeper than that. The liberalization of the economy in key export oriented sectors has led to the emergence of a new traditionally complexioned Anatolian bourgeoisie, that in turn has been transformed through its encounter with the cultural, ideological and economic forces of globalization. Political scientists have noted that the attainment of a GDP per capita of $6,000 strongly correlates with the transition to democracy. This new Turkish Muslim counter-elite melds worldly ambition and success with the symbols and practices of both piety and modernity, which particularly infuriates many members of the old Kemalist elite. In a perverse reversal of the gender apartheid found in various Islamic regimes such as Saudi Arabia and Iran, ambitious female students who wear head-coverings are prevented from attending universities, and even the wives of the prime minister and other cabinet officials are barred from official state functions because their finely coutured ensembles include Hermès headscarves. But despite the present sharp polarization of Turkish society there is room for hope. A very significant number of both religious and non-religious Turks have come to appreciate that the solution to their current socio-political impasse lies in a form of liberal democracy and secularism that guarantees mutual toleration and freedom both of and from religion. Such critical social reflexivity in the public sphere is a result of the iterative practice of democracy and underscores why Western support for the derailment of Islamist democratic transitions in places such as Algeria and the Palestinian territories is so disastrous for defusing radicalism.

In this regard, the success of Turkey's democratic transition is also vital for the broader region because, as the former seat of the Ottoman Empire, the country has long been in the vanguard of the struggle to achieve independence and political and socio-economic development in the Muslim world. Indeed, many of the current tragedies and conflicts afflicting the Middle East have structural–systemic roots dating back to the dismantling of the Ottoman Muslim state following World War I. The conquests of the War's victors short-circuited the early promising era of Muslim parliamentary and liberal reform in the Ottoman State, Egypt and Iran. Since its defeat the civilizational core of the Islamic world, unlike peers such as China or India, has lacked a hegemonic state structure capable of deterring external interventions and undertaking social and industrial/technological development on a global scale.

# Conclusion: the end of dual sovereignty and the creole political language

The silent revolution of Turkey contains two fundamental changes. The AKP's second term electoral victory and the election of Abdullah Gül as the president of the Republic represent the end of dual sovereignty or "parallel governments" in Turkey because the power of the military has been reduced. In addition, there is the evolution of a new moral language of politics that is very much shaped by the global discourses of human rights. The meanings of state, national identity, secularism and political community are redefined as a result of four interrelated transformations. These transformations are economic (introduction of market conditions), ideological (Islamic values and ideas are contemporarized), social (urbanization, spread of higher education and higher degree of social mobility) and political (democratization of the state and thickening of civil society), and they account for this revolutionary change. The neo-liberal economic reforms of Turgut Özal and the EU-led political reforms entailed an ideological transformation, especially the reinterpretation of Islamic ideas and norms in accordance with the needs of the new bourgeoisie. The economic transformation affects all sectors of society, especially conservative and peripheral Islamic groups with values and norms different from those of the modern (secular) sector of society and the Kemalist establishment.[1] Turkey has been experiencing a dual and simultaneous process of integration and polarization. While the distance between the city and countryside, on one hand, and the state and a large sector of the conservative masses, on the other hand, is reduced with the democratic process, the most secular sector of society and the politicized Kurdish community feels alienated from the state. This deepening socio-political cleavage within society makes the task of building a national consensus

---

[1] The most comprehensive survey results indicate a remarkable increase of people "who defined their identity primarily as Muslim." It jumped from 36% in 1999 to 45% in 2006. Moreover, according to the same survey, 41% support a religious-based political party. Ali Çarkoğlu and Binnaz Toprak, *Religion, Society and Politics in a Changing Turkey* (Istanbul: TESEV, 2007).

more difficult, if not impossible. Turkey, unlike many Middle East countries, has experimented with economic and social transformations, along with ideological and political ones. The capitalist transformation has won the battle of public opinion against the Kemalist conception of modernization, the nation, secularism and the use of sovereignty. The gap over values and identities between the bourgeoisie and the rest of society has narrowed, and the bourgeoisie has emerged as the main agent of political change by adopting EU values and norms. With the neo-liberal economic policies of Özal and the EU reforms, the gravity of social and political power has shifted from the civilian and military bureaucracy to the bourgeoisie-led civil coalition. The new bourgeoisie plays the role of a transmission belt between the conservative (religious) sector of society and the changing political structure. Market ideas with religious values signify a new mode of thinking that shapes the cognitive map of the masses about the legitimacy of the existing order. The rising bourgeois class and traditional social forces are mutually shaping one another and this, in turn, is restructuring the political landscape of the country.

## Military-civilian ties: the end of dual sovereignty

During the formative period of Mustafa Kemal Atatürk, Kemalism was a framework for building the modern nation state of Turkey through popular networks. The mission of nation-building was guided by this Republican elite. In the 1950s, the military tried to gain legitimacy over electoral politics by defining itself as the "guardian" of Kemalism. This has been the key source of the military's power and the justification for its continued interventions in civilian politics. Thus, as Islamic tradition is for the AKP, so is Kemalism a sacred ideology for the military establishment. The military-guided civilian bureaucracy is today more committed to the preservation of Kemalism than the consolidation of democracy. Kemalism has become the new cult of the ruling elite. There are distinct political power (*siyasal ikdidar*) and state power (*devlet ikdidarı*) loci in Turkey, with the latter having derived its legitimacy by acting as the self-imposed "guardian" of Kemalism. These Kemalists do not necessarily fully "believe in Kemalism but they all belong to it" since it provides their source of legitimacy.

The founders of the Republic of Turkey, Mustafa Kemal and İsmet İnönü, were both generals. They made the military an important partner in establishing and safeguarding unity and a secular state with a reformist agenda and a European orientation. Thus, sovereignty in Turkey always has been divided between those who are elected and those who are appointed, such as the military establishment and the civilian bureaucracy.

The latter group has had more power to set the agenda of parliament and the functioning rules of democracy and has also determined whose voice is to be deemed legitimate or illegitimate. In previous governments, those who were appointed were never held accountable by the populace and derived their legitimacy simply by "preserving the Kemalist ideology." As the protectors of the state ideology, they protected their own power and position and, among other things, sought to keep the elected government within the boundaries of the state ideology through the manipulation and use of the media, military and judiciary. Their goal was to protect the state and its ideology from the populace and democratically elected politicians. This appointed group determined and formulated its own "defensive and protective task" of Kemalism. They, just like the *mollas* of the Council of Guardians in neighboring Iran, designated the boundaries of elected government. In Iran, appointed groups such as the Council of Guardians justify their duty in the name of Shi'a Islam. In Turkey the same was justified in the name of Mustafa Kemal and a process termed Westernization. This dual government came to an end with the constitutional changes in 2004. This change came with the support of domestic forces, especially the coalition that developed between Istanbul and the new Anatolian-based bourgeoisie.

The end of the military's power came about because of two interrelated events. With the 1997 soft coup, by implementing harsh policies against Muslim groups and the presence of Islamic symbols in the public sphere, the military lost its popular base of support – that of pious Sunni Muslims.[2] Moreover, the Copenhagen criteria called openly for the reduction of military power in the state's political structure. Turkey's Euroskeptic conservative Muslims became Europhiles almost overnight

---

[2] See Yavuz, *Islamic Political Identity*, p. 49. "The contradictory sources of the legitimacy of the Turkish military has very much been ignored by scholars of Turkey. The military sees itself as the modernizer of Turkish society and seeks to derive its legitimacy from its mission of modernizing the society (through the process of Europeanization) and creating a secular nation-state. This is while the masses see the military as the most sacred institution to protect the equally sacred values of the Turks: the state and religion. There is not much distrust and fear between the populace and the military. One of the reasons that facilitated the military to implement its modernizing policies has to do with its 'imagined' sacred roots among ordinary Turks. The military remains a very popular and trusted organization, even among those who don't seem to share its radical secularist agenda. The Turkish military, the guardians of secularism, is historically steeped in Islamic legitimization. The goal of the military is the *preservation of the state*. Since the Turks usually see the state as the necessary condition for the survival of Islam, they always justify any act for the preservation of the state as a sacred duty. For instance, every member of the Turkish army is called a '*mehmetcik*' (soldier of Muhammad). The armed forces are regarded as the *Peygamber Ocağı* (The Heart of the Prophet). Every soldier who is killed on duty is also regarded as a martyr (*sehid*); and those who are involved in military conflict are called *gazi*."

after the February 28, 1997 coup.[3] Many realized that domestic forces did not have the necessary resources and ability to end the military's power and recognized the Copenhagen criteria as the only way of rolling back the military's power and thereby allowing the opening of more political spaces for the consolidation of democracy, the rule of law and the protection of intrinsic freedoms. Today, because of this process, one sees the emergence of a democratic Turkey and the consequent expansion of political freedoms. Since 1999, the Turkish parliament has enacted seven major reform packages and a number of harmonization laws to fulfill the Copenhagen political criteria for EU membership.[4]

The Kemalist establishment's (that is, the military's) understanding of the state and society very much dominated the 1982 Constitution. The underlying philosophy of the Constitution was to restore the state's authority and to protect the state from society's ideological cleavages, rather than protecting civil rights and enhancing society vis-à-vis the state. The Constitution used every opportunity to restore the state's power. Rights and liberties were defined in restrictive terms. Moreover, the Constitution enhanced the power of the military by creating "reserved domains" and also provided strong exit guarantees to the military regime. Subsequently, the Constitution was amended seven times (in 1987, 1993, 1995, twice in 1999, 2002, 2004), with almost all amendments strengthening individual rights and limiting the power of the state in general and the military in particular.

Due to the EU requirements, the Turkish parliament passed nine reform packages, known as "harmonization laws." The major package on fundamental rights was passed in 2001 and changed the overall approach to fundamental rights by removing restrictions on personal liberty and security, privacy of individual life, secrecy of communication, freedom of residence and travel, freedom of expression, freedom of the press, and the right to a fair trial, and limited the death penalty to certain categories. For instance, by deleting the "language prohibited by law" in Article 26, which was included in the 1982 Constitution, against the use of Kurdish (the mother tongue spoken by millions of households in Turkey), it also allowed Kurdish broadcasting and relative liberty in the use of the language. In 2002, it amended Article 312 of the Penal Code that punished "inciting people to hostility" by speech and writing and limited it to

---

[3] Murat Yetkin, "Beni 28 Subat ABci yaptı," *Radikal*, June 5, 2005.
[4] Bertil Emrah Oder, "Enhancing the human face of constitutional reality in Turkey through accession partnership with the EU," in Bertil Duner (ed.), *Turkey: The Road Ahead?* (Stockholm: The Swedish Institute of International Affairs, 2002), pp. 72–104.

"creating a danger for public order." In 2003, the package eliminated "thought crimes." The most important amendment that aimed to strengthen civil society was passed in 2004 and was an entirely new law (No. 5231) on associations. This was Turkey's most advanced law on associations and removed almost all obstacles to establish, engage and develop financial connections within or outside the country. These were major steps in freeing civil society from the supervision of state authorities and allowing NGOs to develop their own agendas.

The most important legal changes took place in civil–military relations, however. Due to the cultural role of the military in Turkey as the founders and guardians of the Republic and the protectors of the modernization process, the military remains the most trusted institution. Moreover, the widespread corruption of civilian politicians, the military's up-to-date information networks and its perceived successes in the war against the PKK enhanced its prestige in the early 1990s. Thus, Turkish democracy has always functioned under the shadow of military power.

Even after all these changes, military–civilian relations are not fully compatible with those of EU member countries. Many analysts would argue that the major problem remains that of the civilian politicians rather than the military. Due to a peculiar socialization process and four military interventions (1960, 1971, 1980 and 1998), civilian politicians feel obliged to get the approval of the military before making major domestic or foreign policy decisions. During the first military take-over, the military took to itself important prerogatives that included the establishment of the National Security Council (NSC), thus allowing the military to guide and shape the policies of the civilian governments. The 1961 Constitution removed the Chief of the General Staff from the ministry of National Defense to the office of the prime minister. This changed the hierarchical status of the Chief of the General Staff. After the 1971 coup, the military created its own Supreme Military Administrative Court to free its decisions from civilian courts. State Security Courts were authorized to use military officers to try crimes against the security of the state. Moreover, the expenditures of the Turkish Armed Forces were excluded from judicial review by the Court of Accounts (*Sayıstay*). A major extension of prerogatives took place with the 1982 Constitution. The head of the coup – the Chief of the General Staff – became the president of the country with the constitutional referendum. Although the Constitution authorized parliament to elect the president, transitional article 1 made an exception to declare the head of the coup as the president for a seven-year term. General Evren's main task was to navigate the transition to civilian government and also to protect the 1982 Constitution. That Constitution enhanced the office of the president by establishing the State Supervision

Council, a body authorized to control the legality of the administration. The Constitution changed the composition of the NSC by increasing its military members and strengthening the decisions of the NSC over the cabinet. According to Article 118 of the Constitution:

The National Security Council shall be composed of the Prime Minister, the Chief of the General Staff, the Ministers of National Defense, Internal Affairs and Foreign Affairs, the Commanders of the Army, Navy and the Air Force and the General Commander of the Gendarmerie, under the chairmanship of the President ... The Council of Ministers shall give priority consideration to the decisions of the National Security Council concerning the measures that it deems necessary for the preservation of the existence and independence of the State, the integrity and indivisibility of the country and the peace and security of society.

The nine harmonization laws eliminated a number of military prerogatives. In 1999, the military judge in the State Security Court was removed. The 2001 reform made major changes to article 118, which organizes the NSC. The new changes altered the composition of the NSC by including the deputy prime minister and the minister of Justice and giving numerical weight to civilian members. Moreover, the function of the NSC was redefined: "The [NSC] submits to the Council of Ministers its views on the advisory decisions that have been taken and ensures the necessary coordination with regard to the formulation, determination and implementation of the national security policy of the State..." Thus, with this change the decisions of the NSC were weakened and the meetings of the NSC were limited to once in two months. A new law concerning the NSC (No. 4963), which went into force in August 2003, introduced a number of changes in the structure and functions of the NSC. The NSC is defined as an advisory body. The privilege of the exclusion of military expenditures from the judicial control of the Court of Accounts was eliminated with the seventh democratization package in 2004. With the sixth harmonization package in 2003, the representatives of the NSC on the Supervision Board of Cinema, Video and Music were removed. With the May 2004 constitutional amendment, the military representative in the Higher Educational Council (YÖK) was also removed.

Do these legal changes mean an end to military hegemony? Does the elimination of military prerogatives mean the democratization of politics? Due to the military role in the establishment of the Republic and the external security threats against the unity of the country, the military has been a "state within a state" for the purposes of guarding the secular nation state and the unity of the country. According to Çarkoğlu and Toprak's most detailed and comprehensive public survey, fifty-nine per cent of the public support the view that the military "can criticize the civilian government when necessary."[5] Since the source of power for the military is not legal but rather socio-historical, these legal changes will become more meaningful if there is a change in civilian–military culture. Yet, the role of guidance has now shifted from the military to the new bourgeoisie. The new agent of change in Turkey is no longer the military but the evolving bourgeoisie. The new class of intellectuals, who are funded by the bourgeoisie, and work outside the state institutions, play an important role in the process of redefining the political language of Turkey in accordance with the global discourses of human rights, democracy and market economy. In short, the people are no longer a subject but an object of their own destiny. They do not want to be defined by the state but seek to define the state instead. Turkey is searching for a new social contract outside a rigid Kemalist public philosophy. It is very important in this process to redefine the role of religion and the military. The recent decisions of the European Court of Human Rights has offered a framework for this new social contract in Turkish society by stressing the secular nature of the Republic in opposition to the possible Islamization of the state, while at the same time expanding political freedoms and individual rights.

### A new political language

The second major change that has taken place is a new conceptualization of Turkey's political terminology which includes, but is not limited to, the meanings of politics, the nation, secularism, ethics and the state. Ideas have played as important a role as the new emerging economic class in the making of a new Turkey. The new bourgeoisie has provided the necessary material support to put these ideas into practice. The evolution of political Islam is also the story of the support of this new class and its ability to carry its ideas into the political domain. This class first supported the *Refah Partisi* (RP), engineered a transformation within the party, and eventually came out in support of the Gül–Erdoğan ticket. As a result of the synergy between economy, politics and intellectuals, Turkey's political terminology has been redefined. The very meanings of nation, state, secularism, Westernization and security have been redefined in accordance with the new wave of globalization and, most importantly, the demands of the Copenhagen criteria. The most significant revolution, however, has taken place at the cognitive level. With EU institutional support, new interest groups want to guarantee their intrinsic freedoms and protect

---

[5] Çarkoğlu and Toprak, *Religion*, p. 102.

their new meanings. Another major change is taking place with respect to the definition of the state. The state used to have a semi-sacred meaning, and the Turkish nation and the Islamic faith existed to serve the state. This has changed and the state is regarded as a set of institutions to serve the people and to protect the value-structures of society.

The supporters of the AKP do not want the party to define itself in terms of the concerns and needs of the political center. They have redefined the core values of the social center and have demanded that the party restructure the political center. Politics in Turkey always has been treated as an instrument of propagating bureaucratic decisions to the people and not as an instrument of articulating societal claims and demands. Thus, political debates in Turkey have always focused on the protection and consolidation of state power, and the nation is defined as an extension of the state. A popular saying in Turkey goes: "May God protect the state and the nation" (*Allah devlete ve millete zeval vermesin*). For instance, opposition parties did not monitor state activities on the basis of societal interests but rather from the perspective of state interests. Although politics was presented as a conflict between the forces of modernity and religious fundamentalism, it was an elite-centered instrument managing the process of exclusion and inclusion into and out of the system. It was Adnan Menderes and Turgut Özal who first sought to redefine politics as an instrument of empowering the people vis-à-vis the state. They shifted from Kemalist vs. Islamist, center vs. periphery, progressive vs. traditional to free and not free politics, and to the balance between society and individual rights and the cultural rights of minorities. As a result of the dominance of market forces and the rise of the new bourgeoisie, Erdoğan has introduced "entrepreneurial politics" (*tüccar siyaseti*) by stressing the market as a model of politics and society. The integrating force of society, for Erdoğan, is the process of economic growth that is expected to improve living standards and help to create a new moral system.

### Entrepreneurial ethics

There has been a major shift from bureaucratic ethics to entrepreneurial ethics as a result of the marketization of Turkish society. Until recently, public morality had been set by the Kemalist doctrine that had evolved from the speeches of Mustafa Kemal, especially from *Nutuk*.[6] Here there is a sense of "first duty" to the state and nation. This first duty is carried

---

[6] Aysel Morin, "Crafting a Nation: The Mythic Construction of the New Turkish National Identity in Atatürk's Nutuk," unpublished PhD dissertation, University of Nebraska, 2004.

out through serving in the military. With military service, boys become "men" and the "sons of the nation." The love of country, national honor, independence, promoting the collective good and self-sacrifice are the key moral principles of the Kemalist public morality. A Turk is someone who loves her state and nation by sacrificing her interest for the good of the country. In the public discourse, nation always is equated with the military and military ethics are shared as the core ethics of the nation.

The second important building block of this public ethics has been the fight against internal (tribal, ethnic, sectarian and religious groups) and external (colonial European powers) enemies of the state and nation. The goal has also been to internalize European ways and practices to become civilized. Therefore, Kemalist morality is based on a binary opposition between backward versus progressive; private versus public; religious versus secular; the *umma* versus the nation. It sought to depict religious people as reactionary and the enemies of the secular, modern nation state. In Kemalist discourse, there are two competing visions of Europe. The first vision admires Europe, the second resents it. The first image of Europe is secular, modern and divorced from religious influences. This vision treats secularism as the way to Europeanization. The second image of Europe is colonialist, expansionist, Christian and greedy. The Kemalists neglected the cultivation of a liberal Islam and the religio-emotional basis of Turkish society. Their nationalist discourse helped to create a public culture of exclusion and even hatred of those who challenged the official definition of nation. The secular Kemalists were quite successful in establishing a series of institutions but they failed to provide a flexible normative (religious or philosophical) basis of governance. Kemalism never developed an individual-based mode of critical thinking or self-examination but rather asked people to "obey and follow" the order of the state in the name of progress. There was no room for an idea of an inner life or self-examination to form an activist citizen who was necessary for democratic culture. The elite or high purists of the Kemalist order thought that it was their responsibility to manage the moral, social and political contradictions in society.

The new ethics, however, is more communalized and less a public conception of ethics. At the core of this new entrepreneurial ethics is the notion of becoming rich and realizing one's potential rather than becoming a part of a greater collectivity. The new work ethic and the conceptualization of hard work is evolving as a result of structural changes in Turkish society. Islamic networks such as the Sufi orders and Nurcu *dershanes* play a crucial role in the re-formation of a capitalist system in concert with the new work ethics. Contemporary Islamic movements and networks in Turkey are not only transformatory but are also revolutionary in creating a new ethical system that is friendly towards capitalism. One here not only witnesses the internal transformation of Islam but also how this internal transformation helps to create a new sense of networks, social institutions and especially practices that are based on a new sense of discipline and salvation through *profit*. Islamic actors want to penetrate every aspect of life with the influence of religion to restructure and recreate the world.

When market forces are deepening and the welfare functions of the state are in decline, the religious networks are the only actors to provide much needed trust and information for the circulation of goods and ideas. Due to these structural changes of neo-liberalism, many believers are forced or encouraged to use their reason to create a new language instead of following old habits to deal with the new challenges. The key characteristic of the neo-liberal context was the institutionalization of the principle of competition among old and new economic forces, ideas, education systems, identities and especially moral orders. This competitive environment offered an opportunity for an Islamic life-style to compete with other life-styles and moral orders. From the perspective of the new moral language, being a nominal Muslim is not enough; one has to become a politically and socially conscious Muslim by utilizing one's reason to develop new Islamically-rooted moral principles in order to cope with new challenges.

The new entrepreneurial moral code stresses the significance of both saving and earning more, and dropping the traditional understanding of "being satisfied with less" and focusing on religious worship. Moreover, the new moral code requires businessmen to stress commonality with the rest of society in terms of life-style and taste in order to dissolve the existing division between the Istanbul-based rich and the rest of the society. A communalized and externally imposed morality, rather than an internally created ethics, is becoming more important. This new ethical code is based on the idea that change should be towards an individually internalized ethic – rather than a community-and-control base. This inner faith of individuals helps to reconfigure self-control-based ethics. The inner world of the individuals is going through a major transformation in terms of the rationalization of religious belief and the instrumentalization of ethics to create a "heaven" here and now.

## Re-imagining nationhood

On the issue of the redefinition of nationhood, Turkey has been confronted with another problem: the tension between pluralism and liberal democracy and the republican (Kemalist) notion of nationhood. In the Kemalist discourse, all those who are citizens of Turkey are Turks in both the ethnic and national sense. The state has used various means to create this imagined nation either by persuasion or by force. This has required the centralization of political power, especially as regards the education system.

Since the establishment of the Turkish Republic, the state-centric parties have all supported a centralized administration to cope with the issues of modernization, economic planning and nation-building. Only during the Özal period did Turkey experience a degree of decentralization; and with the neo-liberal economic policies and the EU process, a slow decentralization is now taking place in different sectors of the state, such as municipal governments, education, healthcare and economic planning. In the 2000s, in response to decentralization, along with the identity claims of the Kurds, the republican Kemalist discourse framed multicultural politics as a threat to national unity and sovereignty. Privatization of education is seen by many Kemalists as a process of the dissolution of the republican notion of nationhood. This is also a key reason as to why many Kemalists are against the EU process. They treat the EU process as a loss of national sovereignty and they seek to defend national identity and sovereignty against the forces of globalization and multiculturalism. Indeed, Kemalist republicanism, which stresses "universalism and citizenship," cannot acknowledge the recognition of minorities or their rights – especially that of the "other" – the Kurds. According to the Turkish military, the national unity and territorial integrity of Turkey depends on national indivisibility and uniformity. From the republican perspective, the Kurdish question thus haunts Turkey and its unity.

The EU process provides a framework of discussion about identity, sovereignty, nationhood, dignity and tolerance of differences. One also needs to see the headscarf issue from the same perspective of difference. Thus, today, one sees the convergence of some leftist and rightist forces over the issue of the uniformity of the nation and the loss of national sovereignty. Neither *laiklik* nor Kemalist nationalism are any longer agreed principles of the Republic; both have rather become contested territories to be fought over. From the Kemalist perspectives, the identity claims of Kurds, Alevis and Islamists are threats to the nation and must be contained and isolated in the private domain. The Kemalists must realize, however, that these identity claims have deep socio-economic roots and cannot be easily confined to domestic life. While Kemalism was an emancipatory ideology in the 1920s and 30s, it has over the decades taken an increasingly authoritarian form due to its own idiosyncratic insecurities in light of the new socio-political realities in Turkey. It is time to update and renew the social contract of Turkey. Turkish society has to rethink notions of nationhood, citizenship and the public sphere in order to overcome the current crisis.

It is possible to grant recognition to cultural groups and to the individual search for dignity within his or her own cultural framework, as long as this does not violate the shared sensibilities of human rights discourse and the legitimacy of the state. And to this or other ends, dialogue and persuasion are the only way to build a new consensus and social contract. Those who share Kurdish ethnic identity could be committed to being both Turkish (in a civic sense) and Kurdish (in an ethnic sense). If it becomes difficult to achieve a consensus on civic Turkish identity, one should re-examine the possibility of a "secular Muslim" identity as a societal glue, just like the role of Islam in Bosnia or in Malaysia (though that model would discriminate against the minority non-Muslims, such as Jews, Armenians and Turkey's relatively large agnostic community). However, given the process of secularization among the Kurdish elite, a secular Muslim identity is a difficult prospect. We thus have to develop a framework of the politics of recognition that entails the demand for the recognition and affirmation of Kurdish, Alevi and Islamic identity-based claims with the goal of restoring the self-respect and dignity of these respective identities.[7] This recognition should not lead to the fragmentation of national society and especially to the process of Lebanonization. One form or another of the European civil models (French civil nationalism or even Switzerland, for example) must be the objective. Will Kymlicka's suggestion has some relevance to the problems we face in Turkey.[8] He argues that there are two forms of communities to which individuals belong: the political (Turkish) community of fellow citizens and the cultural Kurdish (and other minority) community within which people can live their language, tradition and faith as long as they do not violate shared sensibilities and the rights of others. It is not that easy for many Turks to give up the republican principles of secularism, equality before the law and citizenship. Thus, one needs to develop in Turkey a republican pluralism and liberal tolerance, one which would allow for the recognition of ethnic and religious identities along with an affirmation of liberal individualism allowing citizens to cross over definitional boundaries and not be locked into ascriptive definitions of the "self." Only in this way can the Ottoman ideals of communal solidarity and mutual tolerance and the republican ideal of a united national citizenry equal before the law be finally reconciled.

---

[7] Charles Taylor, "The Politics of Recognition," in Amy Gutman, ed., *Multiculturalism* (Princeton: Princeton University Press, 1994), pp. 25–73.
[8] Will Kymlicka, *Liberalism, Community and Culture* (Oxford: Clarendon Press, 1989), p. 135.

## The creole political language

In Turkey, a new "creole" political language is emerging as a result of a number of underlying discursive weaknesses of the Kemalist version of secularism.[9] The conceptual battle between Islamism and secularism is not over. In recent years, democratization and economic development have resulted in a strengthening of Islamic power at the expense of secularism. Islamic groups have made these inroads through an accommodation and moderation of their position against the secularists by utilizing human rights discourse. The most important development is that the secularists, in turn, increasingly are using Islamic discourse to defend their secular identities and ideas. These developments have resulted in a major shift of language in Turkey to create a powerful Islamicly informed public language for legitimate political debate. Although secularism is still dominant in Turkey in the public spaces, Islam is becoming more hegemonic in society than before 1997. The rise of the Islamic language to a hegemonic position is an outcome of a thickening of civil society. Islamic groups are becoming more powerful in civil society and this phenomenon, in turn, has reflected itself in the political arena. It is too early to affirm the victory of the Islamic movements, even though they have penetrated all layers of civil society and some sections of the state with their hegemonic discourse. There is a major yet gradual blending of religious and secular languages and practices. A new form of political language is evolving. This new language is neither secular nor Islamist; it is syncretic and creole. The secular language still holds power over the military, the judiciary and higher education, but it is losing its hegemony in civil society. The state, in the language of Gramsci, does not rule by hegemony (the Kemalist political discourse of creating a secular nation state) any more, but rather is forced to employ Islamic language to maintain its legitimacy and domination.

Turkey is at a crucial crossroads with three reformulating structural trends: the emergence of a Muslim bourgeoisie, the expansion of the public sphere, and the new human rights consciousness. These pivotal changes will continue to transform the political language of the country radically. The July 22, 2007 elections were instrumental in determining the country's direction in the 21st century via more integration with the processes of globalization and Europeanization. However, the anti-Turkish policies of major European countries and the negative consequences of globalization are likely to create domestic opposition and tilt Turkey towards an inward

[9] Sheri Berman, "Islamism, Revolution and Civil Society," *Perspectives on Politics*, 1:2 (June 2003), 257–272.

looking country. Despite Turkey's impressive democratic progress in building civil society and enhancing individual liberties, the military remains a more trusted institution than any politicians or political party. The population still regards the military as the ultimate guardian of secularism and/or stability. Thus, the conflict over the new political language will be fought between different sectors of civilian and military groups and sympathizers. Furthermore, a consensus over a shared political language and the meaning of identity will not emerge if there is no agreement on the part of the military. Any form of working agreement for the consolidation of democracy must take the concerns of the military into account. At the same time, the military must accommodate itself to the new realities of Turkish politics. Given the suspicions of the military and the AKP about each other's intentions and the AKP's search for extra-legitimacy in Washington at the expense of Turkish national interests, it is difficult to imagine a peaceful consolidation of democracy if the military is not convinced and provided with some incentives to withdraw itself from the political sphere. The military will not endorse any consensus if the founding principles of the Republic – the Kemalist ideals of a secular nation state and the separation of mosque and state – are not respected. The AKP, along with other parties, should not provoke the military by raising any questions about such founding republican principles. At the same time, the processes of globalization will lead indirectly to the restructuring of the Turkish nation state by sharing sovereignty with other supranational institutions. The military and other nationalist groups reluctantly and gradually will accept the redefinition of the nation state and a new form of sovereignty.

The debate over secularism (the role of religion in the public sphere and the boundary between the private and the public), the politicization of the judiciary, and the tension between the military and civilian government are all outcomes of Turkey's structural problems. The most difficult challenge the country is facing today is the political claims of Kurdish nationalism. Turkey is in the middle of a major power struggle between the forces of multiculturalism and homogeneous nation-building. This power struggle is carried out over sensitive Kurdish and Islamic issues. The war against the PKK has been the most important weapon in the hands of the nationalist forces to question the legitimacy and loyalty of the governing AKP. The nationalist groups have orchestrated political and civil forces around the Kurdish question and against the AKP government, and they act as the main opposition power by criticizing the policies of the government. As a result of this rising Turkish nationalism, the parameters of the political domain have been redefined in terms of the security concerns of the state. The political domain easily could shrink and politics could be reduced to the mere management of the security of secularism and national unity. As of November 2007, the everyday language of politics has already become one of recrimination and loyalty, one's ethnic roots, and accusations of serving foreign governments.

With the rise of the new bourgeoisie, the conceptual landscape of the Turkish Republic is under transformation. This transformation is not simply the product of a failed modernity or the result of "new found religiosity." It is an outcome of the success of modernity and search for identity, social justice and especially a new moral order. This transformation entails two opposing trends: (1) The rising human rights consciousness and further desire to integrate with the processes of globalization; and (2) a radical rise of reactionary statist nationalism, especially after the latter part of 2004. This new form of Turkish nationalism, known as *ulusalcılar*, defines itself with the duty of "saving the homeland and the state" against the centrifugal forces of Kurdish ethnic and religious nationalisms. Thus, there are a number of structural reasons for the reconfiguration of religious and ethnic nationalism to create a more peaceful and democratic Turkey; and if these structural forces are not handled properly, it could lead either to the break-up of the country or to the further polarization of society along ethnic and religious lines.

The political crisis will wax and wane until the citizens of Turkey find a new shared political language to overcome their fears and build a new Turkey through democratic processes and liberal practices. One of the major challenges the military faces is its adaptation to this new Turkey. The newly emerging Turkey is based on three principles. It seeks to remove *secularism* as a source of tension and polarization in society by redefining the meaning and function of authoritarian secularism; it wants to redefine *political community* on the basis of the cosmopolitan Ottoman legacy rather than on the concept of ethnic nationalism to address the Kurdish issue. It also wants to have a *democratic* state, a thickened civil society, and a reduced public sector role in the economy and in the politics of national identity. The builders of this new multicultural and democratic Turkey are neither the military nor the bureaucratic elite. They are the Anatolian entrepreneurs, activist Kurds, neo-Islamic movements and the Alevi community. Whether successful or not, the present transitional period promises to be as momentous for the country as was the period between the demise of the Ottoman Empire and the rise of the Kemalist Republic.

# Bibliography

Adaleti Savunanlar Derneği (ASDER), *Ben Disiplinsiz Değilim* (Istanbul: ASDER, 2004).

Adler, Emmanuel, "Seizing the Middle Ground: Constructivism in World Politics," *European Journal of International Relations*, 3, 1997.

Afsaruddin, Asma, "The Islamic State: Genealogy, Myths and Facts," *Journal of Church and State* (2006).

Ağırdır, Bekir, "Seçmenin röntgeni," *Radikal*, July 25, 2007.

Ahmad, Feroz, *The Making of Modern Turkey* (New York: Routledge, 1993).

Akçalı, Cevdet, "Başbakan Erdoğan'ın bir itirafı, Türkiye'de kanunları kim yapıyor?" *Yeni Şafak*, July 27, 2004.

Akdoğan, Yalçın, *Muhafazakar Demokrasi* (Ankara: Ak Parti, 2003).

——, *Ak Parti ve Muhafazakar Demokrasi*, (Istanbul: Alfa, 2004).

Aktan, Gündüz, "Korkmazcanlar," *Radikal*, April 24, 2007.

——, "Çıplak Gercekler," *Radikal*, May 1, 2007.

Aktay, Yasin, "Siyasette İslamiliğin Sınırları ve İmkanları," *Tezkire*, 33, July-August 2003.

——, *Türk Dininin Sosyolojik İmkanı* (Istanbul: İletişim Yayınevi, 2006).

Akyol, Mustafa. *Kürt Sorununu Yeniden Düşünmek: Yanlış Giden Neydi? Bundan Sonra Nereye?* (Istanbul: Doğan, 2006).

Alatlı, Alev, "Pişmiş Aşa Su katmak," *Zaman*, April 4, 2004.

Alkan, Mehmet Ö., "Laik Bir İdeolojinin Doğusu ya da II. Meşrutiyet'te Türkçülüğün Toplumsal İdeolojisi: Yeni Hayat ve Yeni Felsefe Mecmuası," *Tarık Zafer Tunaya'ya Armağan* (Istanbul: Istanbul Barosu Yayını, 1992).

Alpay, Kenan (ed.), *Avrupa Birliği ve Müslümanlar* (Istanbul: Özgür-der, 2002).

Arai, Masami, "Jön Türk Dönemi Türk Milliyetçiliği," in Mehmet Ö. Alkan (ed.), *Tanzimat ve Meşrutiyet'in Birikimi: Cumhuriyet'e Devreden Düşünce Mirası* (Istanbul: İletişim, 2001).

Atacan, Fulya, "A Kurdish Islamist Group in Modern Turkey: Shifting Identities," *Middle Eastern Studies*, 37:3, July 2001.

——, "Explaining Religious Politics at the Crossroad: AKP-SP," *Turkish Studies*, 6:4, September 2005.

Atalay, Onur, *Kızıl Elma Koalisyonu: Ulusalcılar, Milliyetciler, Kemalistler* (Istanbul: Paradigma Yayınları, 2006).

Atay, Fatih Rıfkı, *Zetindağı* (Istanbul: Remzi Kitapevi, 1943).

Audi, Robert and Nicholas Wolterstorff, *Religion in the Public Square* (Lanham, MD: Rowman and Littlefield, 1997).

Audi, Robert, *Religious Commitment and Secular Reason* (Cambridge: Cambridge University Press, 2000).

Ayata, Sencer, "Meydanlardakiler 'yeni orta sınıf'tır," *Milliyet*, May 21–22, 2007.

Aydılı, Ersel, Nihat Ali Özcan and Doğan Akyaz, "The Turkish Military's March Toward Europe," *Foreign Affairs*, January-February 2006.

Aydın, Mehmet, "Turkey and the European Union: A Cultural Perspective," in *Turkey and the EU: Looking Beyond Prejudice* (Maastricht: Maastricht School of Management, 2004).

Ayubi, Nazih, *Political Islam: Religion and Politics in the Arab World* (New York: Routledge, 1991).

Bağcı, Hüseyin and Saban Kardaş, "Post- September 11 Impact: The Strategic Importance of Turkey Revisited," in Idris Bal (ed.), *Turkish Foreign Policy in Post-Cold War Era* (Boca Raton: BrownWalker Press, 2004).

Bağış, İ., *Kendi Dilinden Hizbullah ve Mücadele Tarihinden Kesitler* (unpublished book manuscript, 2004).

Balbay, Mustafa, "Genç Subaylar tedirgin," *Cumhuriyet*, May 23, 2003.

Bayat, Asef, "Revolution without Movement, Movement without Revolution: Comparing Islamic Activism in Iran and Egypt," *Comparative Studies in Society and History*, 40, January 1998.

Bayramoğlu, Ali, "AK Parti makineleri stop etti," *Radikal*, March 21, 2005.

Beinin, Joel and Joe Stork (eds.), *Political Islam: Essays From Middle East Report* (Berkeley and Los Angeles: University of California Press, 1997).

Bekaroğlu, Mehmet, *"Adil Düzen"den "Dünya gercekleri"ne: Siyasetin Sonu* (Ankara: Elips, 2007).

Berger, Peter, *The Sacred Canopy: Elements of a Sociological Theory of Religion* (New York: Anchor Brooks, 1969).

Berkes, Niyazi, *Teokrasi ve Laiklik* (Istanbul: Adam, 1997).

—, *The Development of Secularism in Turkey* (London: Routledge, 1999).

Berman, Sheri, "Islamism, Revolution and Civil Society," *Perspectives on Politics*, 1, June 2003.

Bermeo, Nancy, "Myths of Moderation: Confrontation and Conflict during Democratic Transitions," *Comparative Politics*, 29, April 1997.

Besikci, İsmail, *Kendini Kesfeden Ulus* (Istanbul: Yurt Kitap Yayın, 1993).

Bhargava, Rajeev (ed.), *Secularism and its Critics* (New Delhi: Oxford University Press, 1998).

Bianchi, Robert, *Interest Groups and Political Development in Turkey* (Princeton: Princeton University Press, 1984).

Bila, Fikret, *Sivil Darbe Girişimi ve Ankara'da Irak Savaşları* (Ankara: Ümit Yayıncılık, 2003).

—, "Türk sorunu," *Milliyet*, August 20, 2005.

Boland, Vincent, "Eastern Premise," *Financial Times*, December 3, 2004.

—, "Turkish Rift Widens after General's Call," *Financial Times*, May 22, 2006.

Bostancı, Naci, "AKP Merkez Sağın Neresinde?" *Zaman*, August 23, 2004.

Bowcott, N., "Islamic Party Wins in Turkey," *Guardian*, November 7, 2002.

Brown, L. Carl, *Religion and State: The Muslim Approach to Politics* (New York: Columbia University Press, 2000).

Bruce, Steve (ed.), *Religion and Modernization: Sociologists and Historians Debate the Secularization Thesis* (New York: Oxford University Press, 1992).

—, *God is Dead: Secularization in the West* (Oxford: Blackwell, 2002).

Bruinessen, Martin van, *Agha, Shaikh and State: The Social and Political Structures of Kurdistan* (London: Zed Books, 1992).

—, *Mullahs, Sufis and Heretics: The Role of Religion in Kurdish Society*, (Istanbul: Isis, 2000).

Buğra, Ayse, *State and Business in Modern Turkey: A Comparative Study* (Albany: State University of New York Press, 1994).

—, "Class, Culture, and State: An Analysis of Interest Representation by Two Turkish Business Associations," *International Journal of Middle East Studies* 30, 1998.

Bulaç, Ali, "Muhafazakarlığın Referansları," *Zaman*, August 28, 2003.

—, "Bilgi ve Hikmetten Servet ve Iktidara," *Bilgi ve Hikmet*, February 22, 2006, URL: http://www.bilgihikmet.com/

—, "AKP'deki Haciyatmazlar," *Bilgi ve Hikmet*, March 17, 2006, URL: http://www.bilgihikmet.com/

Büyükanıt, Yaşar, "Küreşelleşme ve Uluslarası Güvenlik," *Birinci Uluslarasi Sempozyum Bildirileri* (Ankara: Genel Kurmay Askeri Tarih ve Stratejik Etüt Başkanlığı Yayınları, 2003).

Buzan, Barry, et al., *Security: A New Framework for Analysis* (Boulder: Lynne Rienner, 1998).

Buzan, Barry and Thomas Diez, "Turkey and the European Union: Where to from Here," *Survival* 41, 1999.

Çakır, Ruşen, *Derin Hizbullah/İslamcı Siddetin Geleceği* (Istanbul: Metis, 2001).

—, and Irfan Bozan, *Sivil, Şeffaf ve Demokratik Bir Diyanet İşleri Başkanlığı Mümkün Mü?* (Istanbul: TESEV, 2005).

Camurcu, Kenan, *Ak Parti'nin Stratejik Meseleleri* (Istanbul: Şehir Yayınları, 2006).

Can, Eyup, "AK parti neyi Muhafaza Ediyor?" *Zaman*, August 27, 2004.

Carkoğlu, Ali, "Turkey's November 2002 Elections: A New Beginning," *MERIA e-Journal* 6:4, 2002.

Çarkoğlu, Ali and Binnaz Toprak, *Religion, Society and Politics in a Changing Turkey* (Istanbul: TESEV, 2007).

Casanova, Jose, *Public Religion in the Modern World* (Chicago: University of Chicago Press, 1994).

Cemal, Hasan, "Başbakan Erdoğan'dan Amerika yolunda Komutanlara Mesajlar: İrtica diye Bir Tehdit Yok," *Milliyet*, October 1, 2006.

Chadwick, Owen, *The Secularization of the European Mind in the 19th Century* (Cambridge: Cambridge University Press, 1975).

Ciftci, İrfan, "Avrupa'nın 'Öteki'si Olarak Türk İmgesi: Oldugu gibi Görünemeyen, Göründüğü Gibi Olamayan Korkunun Efendileri: Türkler," *İstanbul Bilgi Universitesi Bilgi ve Bellek*, 3 (2006).

Citilioğlu, Ercan, *Tarhan Ankara Hattında Hizbullah* (Ankara: Umit Yayıncılık, 2001).

Ciyayı, *Gerilla Anıları II* (Istanbul: Aram, 2002).

Cölaşan, Emin, "Bay Gül'un Dünü ve Bugünü," *Hürriyet*, November 23, 2006.

——, "İnkar size yakışır mı Abdullah bey," *Hürriyet*, May 3, 2007.

Coşkun, Ahmet Hakan, "Cemaat, ey cemaat," *Hürriyet*, April 2, 2007.

——, "Cemaat diyor ki: O bakan bize düşman," *Hürriyet*, April 4, 2007.

Dale, Roger, "Implications of the Rediscovery of the Hidden Curriculum for the Sociology of Teaching," in Denis Gleeson (ed.), *Identity and Structure: Issues in the Sociology of Education* (Nafferton, Driffield: Studies in Education, 1977).

Daver, Bülent, *Türkiye Cumhuriyetinde Layiklik* (Ankara: Son Havadis Marbaası, 1955).

Davutoğlu, Ahmet, *Sratejik Derinlik: Türkiye'nin uluslararası konumu* (Istanbul: Küre Yayınları, 2001).

——, "Türkiye Merkez Ülke Olmalı," *Radikal*, February 26, 2004.

——, "Türkiye Küresel Güçtür!," *Anlayış*, March 2004.

Denoeux, Guilain, *Urban Unrest in the Middle East* (Albany: State University of New York Press, 1993).

Department of Anti-Terror Unit of the Turkish Police, *Hizbullah Terör Örgütü* (Ankara: Emniyet genel Müdürlüğü, 2001).

Deringil, Selim, "From Ottoman to Turk; Self-Image and Social Engineering in Turkey," in D. Gladney (ed.), *Making Majorities: Constituting the Nation in Japan, Korea, China, Malaysia, Fiji, Turkey and the United States* (Stanford: Stanford University Press, 1998).

Deth, Jan van (ed.), *Social Capital and European Democracy* (London: Routledge, 1999).

Doğan, Akyaz, *Askeri Müdahalelerin Orduya Etkisi, Hiyerarşi Dışı Örgütlenmeden Emir Komuta Zincirine* (Istanbul: İletişim Yayınları, 2002).

Doğan, Erhan, "The Historical and Discursive Roots of the Justice and Development Party's EU Stance," *Turkish Studies*, 6, September 2005.

Dumont, Paul, "Hojas for the Revolution: The Religious Strategy of Mustafa Kemal Atatürk," *American Institute for the Study of Middle Eastern Civilization*, 1981.

Duran, Bünyamin, *Islam Toplumlarında Sosyo-Ekonomik Değişmeye Yönelik Tezler* (Istanbul: Osmanlı Araştırmaları Vakfı, 1995).

Düzgit, Senem Aydın, *Seeking Kant in the EU's Relations with Turkey* (Ankara: TESEV, 2006).

Dwyer, Kevin, *Arab Voices: The Human Rights Debate in the Middle East* (Berkeley: University of California Press, 1991).

Edip, Halide, "Dictatorship and Reform in Turkey," *The Yale Review*, 19, 1929.

Eickelman, Dale, "From Here to Modernity: Ernest Gellner on Nationalism and Islamic Fundamentalism," in John A. Hall (ed.), *The State of the Nation: Ernest Gellner and the Theory of Nationalism* (Cambridge: Cambridge University Press, 1998).

——, and James Piscatori, *Muslim Politics* (Princeton: Princeton University Press, 1996).

Emre, Süleyman Akif, *Siyasette 35 Yıl* (3 Volumes) (Ankara: Keşif Yayınları, 1991).

Erbakan, Necmettin, *Milli Görüş* (Istanbul: Dergah, 1975).

Erdoğan, Mustafa, "Fazilet Partisi'nin Kapatma Işığında Türkiye'nin Anayasa Mahkemesi Sorunu," *Liberal Düşünce*, 23 (Summer 2001).

——, "AİHM'nin RP Kararının Düşündürdükleri," *Liberal Düşünce*, 23 (Summer 2001).

Erdoğan, Recep T., *Bu Sarkı Burada Bitmez* (Istanbul: Nesil, 2001).

—, "My Country is Your Faithful Ally and Friend," *The Wall Street Journal*, March 31, 2003.

—, *Konuşmalar* (Ankara: AK Parti, 2004).

—, "Türkiye'nin İmkanları ve Kaynaklarıyla Türkiye'yi kaldıracağız," in *Konuşmalar* (Ankara: AK Parti, 2004).

Eroğlu, Cem, *Demokrat Parti: Tarihi ve Ideolojisi* (Ankara: Imge, 1998).

Esposito, John and François Burgat (eds.), *Modernizing Islam: Religion in the Public Sphere in Europe and the Middle East* (New Brunswick, NJ: Rutgers University Press, 2003).

Esposito, John and Azzam Tamimi, *Islam and Secularism in the Middle East* (London: C. Hurst, 2000).

Feyzioğlu, Turhan, "Türk Inkılabının Temel Taşı: Laiklik," in Ethem Ruhi Fığlalı (ed.), *Atatürkçü Düşüncesinde Din ve Laiklik* (Ankara: ATAM, 1999).

Findley, Carter Vaughn, *The Turks in World History* (New York: Oxford University Press, 2004).

Flores, Alexander, "Secularism, Integralism, and Political Islam: The Egyptian Debate," in Joel Benning and Joe Stork (eds.), *Political Islam: Essays from Middle East Report* (Berkeley: University of California Press, 1997).

Fukuyama, Francis, *Trust: The Social Virtues and the Creation of Prosperity* (New York: Free Press, 1996).

Fuller, Graham, "Turkey's Strategic Model: Myths and Realities," *The Washington Quarterly*, 27, Summer 2004.

—, "Freedom and Security: Necessary Conditions for Moderation," *American Journal of Islamic Social Sciences*, 22, Summer 2005.

Geertz, Clifford, *The Interpretation of Cultures: Selected Essays* (New York: Basic Books, 1973).

Gellner, Ernest, *Muslim Society* (Cambridge: Cambridge University Press, 1981).

Genç, Reşat, *Türkiye'yi Laikleştiren Yasalar 3 Mart 1924 Tarihli Meclis Müzakereleri ve Kararları* (Ankara: Atatürk Araştırma Merkezi, 2005).

Gökaçtı, Mehmet Ali, *Türkiye'de Din Eğitimi ve İmam Hatipler* (Istanbul: İletişim, 2005).

Gökalp, Ziya, *Türkçülüğün Esasları* (Istanbul: Toker Yayınevi 1999).

—, *Türkleşmek, İslamlaşmak, Muasırlaşmak* (Istanbul: Toker Yayınevi, 1999).

Goldberg, Ellis, "Smashing Idols and the State: The Protestant Ethic and Egyptian Sunni Radicalism," in Juan R. I. Cole (ed.), *Comparing Muslim Societies: Knowledge and the State in a World Civilization* (Ann Arbor: University of Michigan Press, 1992).

Göle, Nilüfer, *The Forbidden Modern: Civilization and Veiling* (Ann Arbor: University of Michigan Press, 1997).

Göle, Nilüfer and Ludwing Ammann (eds.), *Islam in Public: Turkey, Iran, and Europe* (Istanbul: Bilgi University, 2006).

Graham, B.D., "The Succession of Factional Systems in the Uttar Pradesh Congress Party, 1937–1966," in Marc J. Swartz (ed.), *Local-Level Politics: Social and Cultural Perspectives* (Chicago: Aldine, 1968).

Gül, Abdullah, "Fazilet Kongresi," *Milliyet*, May 17, 2000.

Gunn, T. Jeremy, "Under God but Not the Scarf: The Founding Myths of Religious Freedom in the United States and Laicité in France," *Journal of Church and State*, 46, Winter 2004.

Gunter, Michael, *The Kurds and the Future of Turkey* (New York: St. Martin's Press, 1997).

Günalp, Haldun, "Globalization and Political Islam: The Social Bases of Turkey's Welfare Party," *International Journal of Middle East Studies*, 33, 2001.

Hannay, David, *Cyprus: The Search for a Solution* (New York: I. B. Tauris, 2005).

Harvey, David, *A Brief History of Neoliberalism* (New York: Oxford University Press, 2005).

Hasimi, Seyit Haşim, "Kürt Meselesinde Ak Parti Sınavı," *Yeni Şafak*, August 1, 2005.

Hassanpour, Amir, *Nationalism and Language in Kurdistan, 1918–1985* (San Francisco: Mellen Research University, 1992).

Hefner, Robert W. (ed.), *Remaking Muslim Politics: Pluralism, Contestation, Democratization* (Princeton: Princeton University Press, 2005).

Hersh, Seymour, "Annals of National Security. Plan B," *The New Yorker*, June 1, 2004.

Hodgson, Marshall, "Modernity and the Islamic Heritage," in Marshall Hodgson (ed.), *Rethinking World History: Essays on Europe, Islam, and World History* (Cambridge: Cambridge University Press, 1993).

Imber, Colin, "The Ottoman Dynastic Myth," *Turcica*, 19, 1987.

İnalcık, Halil, "Turkey," in Robert E. Ward and Dankwart Rustow (eds.), *Political Modernization in Japan and Turkey* (Princeton: Princeton University Press, 1964).

—, "Islam in the Ottoman Empire," *Turcica*, 5–6, 1968–1970.

Irem, Nazım, "Turkish Conservative Modernism: Birth of a Nationalist Quest for Cultural Renewal," *International Journal of Middle East Studies*, 34, 2002.

Işık, Faik, *Recep Tayyip Erdoğan Davası, No. 1998/36 Esas* (Istanbul: Keskin, 1998).

Işık, Yüksel, *Siyasal İslam ve Sendikalar* (Ankara: Öteki Yayınevi, 1996).

Jwaideh, Wadie, "The Kurdish Nationalist Movement: Its Origins and Development" (PhD dissertation, Syracuse University, 1960).

Kadioğlu, Ayşe, "Civil Society, Islam and Democracy in Turkey: A Study of Three Islamic NGOs," *The Muslim World*, 95, January 2005.

Kafadar, Camal, *Between Two Worlds: The Construction of the Ottoman State* (Berkeley: University of California Press, 1995).

Kalyvas, Stathis N., "Commitment Problems in Emerging Democracies: The Case of Religious Parties," *Comparative Politics*, 22, July 2000.

—, "Religious Mobilization and Unsecular Politics," in T. Keselman and J. Buttigieg (eds.), *European Christian Democracy: Historical Legacies and Comparative Perspectives* (Notre Dame: University of Notre Dame Press, 2003).

Karakuş, Abdullah and Namik Durukan, "Erdoğan'a göre Kürt sorununun çözümü:'Tek devlet tek millet tek bayrak," *Milliyet*, August 13, 2005.

Karaman, "İlkeli mi Faydacı mı?" *Yeni Şafak*, March 21, 1999.

Kardaş, Şaban, "Human Rights and Democracy Promotion: The Case of Turkey-EU Relations," *Alternatives: Turkish Journal of International Relations*, 1:3, 2002.

Kavakcı, Merve Safa, *Basörtüsüz Demokrasi* (Istanbul: Timaş, 2004).

Kaya, Kamil, *Türkiye'de Din-Devlet İlişkileri ve Diyanet İşleri Başkanlığı* (Istanbul: no publisher, 1998).

Kazan, Sevket, *Refah Partisi Gerceği* (Ankara: Keşif Yayınları, 2002).

Keddie, Nikki, "Secularism and its Discontents," *Daedalus*, 132, Summer 2003.

Keskin, Adnan and Tolga Akiner, "Erdoğan: Kürt sorunu demokrasiyle çözülür," *Radikal*, August 11, 2005.

Keyman, E. Fuat, "Muhafazakar demokrasinin 'kadın'la imtihanı," *Radikal II*, May 16, 2004.

—, "Modernity, Secularism and Islam in Turkey," *Theory Culture & Society*, 24, March 2007.

—, and Ziya Oniş, "Helsinki, Copenhagen and Beyond: Challenges to the New Europe and the Turkish State," in Mehmet Uğur and Nergis Canefe (eds.), *Turkey and European Integration: Accession Prospects and Issues* (London: Routledge, 2004).

Khan, Mujeeb R., "Islamic and Western Worlds: The End of History or Clash of Civilizations," in Emran Qureshi and Michael A. Sells (eds)., *The New Crusades: Constructing the Muslim Enemy* (New York: Columbia University Press, 2003).

Kibaroğlu, Mustafa, "Clash of Interests Over Northern Iraq Drives Turkish–Israeli Alliance to a Crossroads," *The Middle East Journal*, 59, Spring 2005.

King, Judd, *The Battle for the Ottoman Legacy: The Construction of a Neo-Ottoman Political Identity In Turkey* (MA dissertation, Duke University, 2004).

Kinzer, Stephen, "Will Turkey Make It?" *New York Review*, July 15, 2004.

Koğacıoğlu, Dicle, "Dissolution of Political Parties by the Constitutional Court in Turkey: Judicial Delimitation of the Political Domain," *International Sociology*, 18, 2003.

—, "Progress, Unity, and Democracy: Dissolving Political Parties in Turkey," *Law & Society*, 38, 2004.

Koru, Fehmi, "Ak Parti ye karşı AKP," *Yeni Şafak*, October 13, 2003.

Köse, A. Cengizhan, *Yöresel Dayanışma Örgütlerinin Kentlileşme Sürecindeki Rolü* (MA dissertation, Konya Selcuk University, 1996).

Kösebalaban, Hasan, "Turkey's EU Membership: A Clash of Security Cultures," *Middle East Policy*, 9, 2002.

Kule, Ahmet, "Socialization Process of the Individuals who Join Terrorist Organizations in Turkey" (PhD dissertation, City University of New York, 2007).

Kurban, Dilek, "Confronting Equality: The Need for Constitutional Protection of Minorities in Turkey's Path to the European Union," *Columbia Human Rights Law Review*, 151, 2003.

Kuru, Ahmet T., "Reinterpretation of Secularism in Turkey: The Case of the Justice and Development Party," in M. Hakan Yavuz (ed.), *The Emergence of a New Turkey: Democracy and the AK Parti* (Salt Lake City: University of Utah Press, 2006).

Kurzman, Charles, "Bin Laden and Other Thoroughly Modern Muslims," *Contexts*, 1 2002.

Kushner, David, *The Rise of Turkish Nationalism, 1876–1908* (London: Cass, 1977).

Kutlu, Önder, "AKP'de demokrasi eksik," *Radikal*, October 20, 2003.

Laustsen, Carsten Bagge and Ole Waever, "In Defence of Religion: Sacred Referent Objects for Securitization," *Millennium: Journal of International Studies*, 29:3, 2000.

Lerner, Daniel, *The Passing of Traditional Society: Modernizing the Middle East* (New York: Free Press, 1964).

Lewis, Bernard, *The Emergence of Modern Turkey* (2nd edn, London: Oxford University Press, 1969).

Lowry, Heath W., *The Nature of the Early Ottoman State* (Albany: State University of New York Press, 2003).

Mahcupyan, Etyen, "Muhafazakar bir Tür Mekez mi?" *Zaman*, August 25, 2003.

Mainwaring, Scott and Timothy R. Scully (eds.), *Christian Democracy in Latin America: Electoral Competition and Regime Change* (Stanford: Stanford University Press, 2003).

Mango, Andrew, *Atatürk: The Biography of the Founder of Modern Turkey* (Woodstock, NY: Overlook Press, 2000).

Mardin, Şerif, *The Genesis of Young Ottoman Thought: A Study in the Modernization of Turkish Political Ideas* (Princeton: Princeton University Press, 1962).

—, "Ideology and Religion in the Turkish Revolution," *International Journal of Middle East Studies*, 2, 1971.

—, "Center and Periphery Relations: A Key to Turkish Politics?" *Daedalus*, 102, 1973.

—, "Religion and Secularism in Turkey," in Ali Kazancigil and Ergun Özbudun (eds.), *Atatürk: Founder of a Modern State* (Hamden: Archon Books, 1981).

—, *Jön Türklerinin Siyasi Fikirleri, 1895–1908* (1964; 2nd edn., Istanbul: İletişim, 1983).

—, *Religion and Social Change in Modern Turkey: The Case of Bediüzzaman Said Nursi* (Albany: State University of New York, 1989).

—, *Türkiye'de Din ve Siyaset* (Istanbul: İletişim, 1991).

—, "The Nakshibendi Order of Turkey," in Martin E. Marty (ed.), *Fundamentalism and Society* (Chicago: University of Chicago Press, 1993).

—, (ed.), *Cultural Transitions in the Middle East* (Leiden: E. J. Brill, 1994).

Maritain, Jacques, *Integral Humanism* (New York: Scribner's, 1938).

Martin, David, *A General Theory of Secularization* (Oxford: Basil Blackwell, 1978).

Matthews, Owen and Lorien Holland, "Islam's happy faces," *Newsweek*, Dec. 27–Jan. 3, 2005.

McCarthy, Justin, *Death and Exile: The Ethnic Cleansing of Ottoman Muslims, 1812–1922* (Princeton: Darwin Press, 1996).

McClay, Wilfred M., "Two Concepts of Secularism," *Wilson Quarterly*, 24, Summer 2000.

McDowall, David, *A Modern History of the Kurds* (London and New York: I. B. Tauris, 1996).

Mert, Nuray, *Hep Muhalif Olmak* (Istanbul: İletişim, 2001).

Metiner, Mehmet, *Ideolojik Devletten Demokratik Devlete* (Istanbul: Beyan, 1999).

Moe, Christian, "Refah Partisi (The Welfare Party) and Others v. Turkey," *The International Journal of Not-for-Profit Law* 6:1, 2003.

Morin, Aysel, "Crafting a Nation: The Mythic Construction of the New Turkish National Identity in Atatürk's Nutuk" (PhD dissertation, The University of Nebraska, 2004).

Nasr, Seyyed Vali Reza, *Mawdudi and the Making of Islamic Revivalism* (New York: Oxford University Press, 1996).

Nasr, Vali, "Secularism: Lessons from the Muslim World," *Daedalus*, 132, Summer 2003.

—, "The Rise of 'Muslim Democracy'," *Journal of Democracy*, 16:2, April 2005.

Norris, Pippa and Ronald Inglehart, *Sacred and Secular: Religion and Politics Worldwide* (Cambridge: Cambridge University Press, 2005).

Oder, Bertil Emrah, "Enhancing the Human Face of Constitutional Reality in Turkey through Accession Partnership with the EU," in Bertil Duner (ed.), *Turkey: The Road Ahead?* (Stockholm: The Swedish Institute of International Affairs, 2002).

Oğuzoğlu, Yusuf, *Osmanlı Devlet Anlayışı* (Istanbul: Eren, 2000).

Okutan, M. Çağatay, *Bozkut'tan Kuran'a Milli Türk Talebe Birliği (MTTB) 1916–1980* (Istanbul: Bilgi Universitesi Yayınları, 2004).

—, *Tek Parti Döneminde Azınlık Polikaları* (Istanbul: Bilgi Universitesi, 2004).

Olson, Robert (ed.), *The Kurdish Nationalist Movement in the 1990s: Its Impact on Turkey and the Middle East* (Lexington, KY: University of Kentucky Press, 1996).

Öniş, Ziya, "Turkish Modernization and Challenges for the New Europe," *Perceptions. Journal of International Affairs*, 9, 2004.

Ortaylı, İlber, *Imparatorluğun En Uzun Yüzyılı* (Istanbul: Hil Yayınları, 1995).

Özcan, Nihat Ali, *PKK Kürdistan İsci Partisi, tarihi, ideolojisi ve yöntemi* (Ankara: Asam, 1999).

Özdalga, Elisabeth et al., *Alevi Identity* (Istanbul: Swedish Research Institute in Istanbul, 1998).

Özdemir, Şennur, *MÜSİAD: Anadolu Sermayesinin Dönüşümü ve Türk Modernleşmesinin Derinleşmesi* (Ankara: Vadi, 2006).

Özeren, Süleyman and C. Van de Voorde, "Turkish Hizbullah: A Case Study of Radical Terrorism," *International Journal of Comparative and Applied Criminal Justice*, 30, 2006.

Özgül, Mehmet, "Erdoğan ile Kurt İşçisi Boran'in tartışması," *Özgür Politika*, 27 December 2002 (http://www.ozgurpolitika.org/2002/12/27/hab18b.html).

Özgürel, Avni, "Erdoğan'in sınırları," *Radikal*, June 21, 2006.

Özkök, Ertuğrul, "Beyaz Türklerin Tasfiyesi mi," *Hürriyet*, April 21, 2006.

Özkök, Hilmi, "Yıllık Değerlendirme Konuşması on 20 April 2005," in *Genel Kurmay Basını Bilgilendirme Toplantıları ve Basına Açık Ana Faaliyetleri* (Ankara: Genel Kurmay Genel Sekreterliği, 2005).

Özoğlu, Hakan, *Kurdish Notables and the Ottoman State: Evolving Identities* (Albany: SUNY Press, 2004).

Pamuk, Muhammed, *Yasaklı Umut: Recep Tayyip Erdoğan* (Istanbul: Birey, 2001).

Pannenberg, Wolfhart, "How to Think About Secularism," *First Things*, 64, June/July 1996.

Parekh, Bhikhu, *Rethinking Multiculturalism: Cultural Diversity and Political Theory* (Cambridge, MA: Harvard University Press, 2000).

Prusher, Ilene R., "New Turkish Leader Lifts US Hopes," *The Christian Science Monitor*, March 10, 2003.

Rawls, John, *Political Liberalism* (New York: Columbia University Press, 1996).

Reed, Howard A., "Revival of Islam in Secular Turkey," *The Middle East Journal*, 8, 1954.

Rorty, Richard, "The Moral Purposes of the University: An Exchange," *The Hedgehog Review: Critical Reflections on Contemporary Culture*, 2, Fall 2000.

Roy, Olivier, *The Failure of Political Islam*, translated by Carol Volk (Cambridge, MA: Harvard University Press, 1994).

—, *Globalized Islam: The Search for a New Ummah* (New York: Columbia University Press, 2004).

Sabahattin, Selek, *Anadolu İhtilali* (Istanbul: Kastaş Yayınları, 1987).

Şafak, Mahsum, *PKK, Yeniden İnşa Kongre Belgeleri* (Istanbul: Çetin Yayınları, 2005).

Salt, Jeremy, *A Fez of the Heart* (Washington, PA: Harvest Books, 1996).

Sancar, Mithat, *Devlet Aklı Kıskacında Hukuk Devleti* (Istanbul: Iletişim, 2000).

Sarıbaş, Sermin, "Türkiye'nin en Ünlü Komplo Teorisyenleri," *Hürriyet*, May 6, 2001.

Sarıbay, Ali Yaşar, *Türkiye'de Modernleşme Din ve Parti Politikası: "MSP Örnek Olayı"* (Istanbul: Alan Yayıncılık, 1985).

Sarınay, Yusuf, *Türk Milliyetçiliğinin Tarihi Gelişimi ve Türk Ocakları (1912–1931)* (Istanbul: Ötüken Neşriyat, 2004).

Sayarı, Binnaz, "Türkiye'de Dinin Denetim Islevi," *A. U. Siyasal Bilgiler Fakultesi Dergisi*, 33, March–June 1978.

Schattschneider, E. E., *Party Government* (New York: Holt, 1942).

Selçuk, Sami, "Laiklik ve Demokrasi," *Türkiye Günlüğü*, 56, Summer 1999.

Selim, Yavuz, *Gül'ün Adı* (Ankara: Kim Yayınları, 2002).

—, *Yol Ayrımı: Milli Görüş Hareketindeki Ayrışmanın Perde Arkası* (Ankara: Hiler, 2002).

Seyhanzade, M. Sıddık, *Nurculuğun Tarihçesi: Medeniyet-i Islamiyye* (Istanbul: Tenvir, 2003).

Shaw, Stanford J. and Ezel Kural Shaw, *History of the Ottoman Empire and Modern Turkey* (New York: Cambridge University Press, 1977).

Sigmund, Paul, "Maritain on Politics," in Deal Hudson and Matthew Mancini (eds.), *Understanding Maritain* (Macon: Mercer University Press, 1987).

Simsir, Bilal, *AB, AKP ve Kıbrıs* (Ankara: Bilgi, 2003).

Sivan, Emmanuel, "The Clash within Islam," *Survival*, 45: 1, Spring 2003.

Sontag, Deborah, "The Erdogan Experiment," *New York Times*, May 11, 2003.

Sözen, Edibe, "Gender Politics of the JDP," in M. Hakan Yavuz (ed.), *The Emergence of a New Turkey: Democracy and the AK Parti* (Salt Lake City: The University of Utah Press, 2006).

Stepan, Alfred, *Arguing Comparative Politics* (New York: Oxford University Press, 2001).

Taniyici, Saban, "The Transformation of Political Islam in Turkey: Islamists' Welfare Party's Pro-EU Turn," *Party Politics*, 9, 2003.

*Tanzimat I* (Istanbul: Devlet Basımevi, 1940).

Tarhanlı, İştar and Gözaydın, *Müslüman Toplum, "Laik" Devlet, Türkiye'de Diyanet İşleri Başkanlığı* (Istanbul: Afa, 1993).

Taylor, Charles, "Modes of Secularism," in Rajeev Bhargava (ed.), *Secularism and its Critics* (Delhi: Oxford University Press, 1988).

Tekin, Üzeyir, *AK Parti'nin Muhafazakar Demokrat Kimliği* (Ankara: Orient, 2003).

Topçuoğlu, Abdullah, *Akrabalık ve Hemşehrilik İlişkilerinni Toplumsal Sermaye Değeri* (Konya: Çizgi Kitabevi, 2003).

Toprak, Binnaz, *Islam and Political Development in Turkey* (Leiden: E. J. Brill, 1981).

Tuğluk, Aysel, "Sevr Travması ve Kürtlerin Empatisi," *Radikal*, June 14, 2007.

Tunaya, Tarık Zafer, *İslamcılık Akımı* (Istanbul: Simavi Yayınları, 1991).

Turgut, Serdar, "AKP Beyaz Türk İktidarını Yıktı," *Habetürk*, June 3, 2004.

Ünal, Mustafa, "4.yılında AK Parti'nin ahvali," *Zaman*, August 18, 2004.

Usta, Niyazi, "Menzil Nakşiliği," *Demokrasi Platformu*, 2, Spring 2006.

Utvik, Bjorn Olav, "The Modernizing Force of Islam," in John Esposito and François Burgat (eds.), *Modernizing Islam: Religion in the Public Sphere in Europe and the Middle East* (New Brunswick, NJ: Rutgers University Press, 2003).

—, "*Hizb al-Wasat* and the Potential for Change in Egyptian Islamism," *Critique: Critical Middle Eastern Studies*, 14:3, 2005.

Uysal, H., *Dağlarda Yasamın Dili* (Istanbul: Aram, 2001).

Uzgel, İlhan, "Dış Politikada AKP: Stratejik Konumdan Stratejik Modele," *Mülkiye*, 252, 2006.

Vali, Abbas (ed.), *Essays on the Origins of Kurdish Nationalism* (Costa Mesa: Mazda Publishers, 2003).

Vaner, Semih, "Laiklik, Laikçilik ve Demokrasi," in İbrahim Ö. Kaboğlu (ed.), *Laiklik ve Demokrasi* (Istanbul: İmge Kitabevi, 2001).

Vergin, Nur, "Din ve Devlet İlişkileri: Düşüncenin 'Bitmeyen Senfoni'si," *Türkiye Günlüğü*, 72, 2003.

—, "Siyaset ile Sosyolojinin Buluşduğu Nokda," *Türkiye Günlüğü*, 76, 2004.

Volkan, Vamik and Norman Itzkowitz, *The Immortal Atatürk* (Chicago: University of Chicago Press, 1984).

Waever, Ole, "Securitization and Desecuritization," in Ronnie D. Lipschutz (ed.), *On Security* (New York: Columbia University Press, 1995).

Waterbury, John, "Fortuitous By-Products," *Comparative Politics*, 29, April 1997.

Weber, Max, "Social Psychology of the World Religions," in H. H. Gerth and C. W. Mills (eds.), *From Max Weber: Essays in Sociology* (New York: Oxford University Press, 1958).

Weiker, Walter F., *The Turkish Revolution: 1960–1961* (Washington, DC: Brookings Institution, 1963).

Wendt, A., "Anarchy is what States Make of it: the Social Construction of Power Politics," *International Organization*, 46, 1992.

—, "Levels of Analysis vs. Agents and Structures: part III," *Review of International Studies*, 18, 1992.

White, Jenny B., *Islamist Mobilization in Turkey: A Study in Vernacular Politics* (Seattle: University of Washington Press, 2003).

Wolterstorff, Nicholas and Robert Audi, *Religion in the Public Square: The Place of Religious Convictions in Political Debate* (Lanham, MD: Rowman and Littlefield, 1997).

Wuthnow, Robert, *Meaning and Moral Order: Explorations in Cultural Analysis* (Berkeley: University of California Press, 1987).

Yavuz, M. Hakan, "Nationalism and Islam: Yusuf Akçura, 'Üç Tarz-i Siyaset'," *Oxford Journal of Islamic Studies*, 4, 1993.

—, "Political Islam and the Welfare Party in Turkey," *Comparative Politics*, 30, 1997.

—, "Turkic Identity and Foreign Policy in Flux: The Rise of neo-Ottomanism," *Critique*, 12, 1998.

—, "Cleansing Islam from the Public Sphere and the February 28 Process," *Journal of International Affairs*, 54, Fall 2000.

—, *Islamic Political Identity in Turkey* (New York: Oxford University Press, 2003).

—, "The Case of Turkey," *Daedalus*, 132, Summer 2003.

—, "Türk Muhafazakarlığı: Modern ve Müslüman," *Zaman*, January 10, 2004.

—, "AK parti ve sorunları," in *Uluslarası Muhafazakarlık ve Demokrasi Sempozyumu* (Istanbul: Alfa, 2004).

—, "Is there a Turkish Islam? The Emergence of Convergence and Consensus," *Journal of Muslim Minority Affairs*, 24:2, 2004.

—, "The Kurdish Ethno-Nationalism," in Maya Shatzmiller (ed.), *Nationalism and Minority Identities in Islamic Societies* (Toronto: McGill–Queen's University Press, 2005).

—, "Islam and Europeanization in Turkish-Muslim Socio-Political Movements," in Peter J. Katzenstein and Timothy A. Byrnes (eds.), *Religion in an Expanding Europe* (Cambridge: Cambridge University Press, 2006).

—, (ed.), *The Emergence of a New Turkey: Democracy and AK Parti* (Salt Lake City: The University of Utah Press, 2006).

—, and John Esposito (eds.), *Turkish Islam and the Secular State: The Gülen Movement* (Syracuse: Syracuse University Press, 2003).

—, and Mujeeb R. Khan, "'A Bridge between East and West': Duality and the Development of Turkish Foreign Policy toward the Arab-Israeli Conflict," *Arab Studies Quarterly*, 14, 1992.

—, and Mujeeb R. Khan, "Turkey and Europe: Will East Meet West?," *Current History*, 103, November 2004.

—, and Nihat Ali Özcan, "The Kurdish Question and the JDP," *The Middle East Journal*, 13, 2006.

Yenigun, Halil Ibrahim, "Islamism and Nationalism in Turkey: An Uneasy Relationship" (paper read at 2nd Annual Graduate Student Conference of the Department of Politics, March 28, 2005 at the University of Virginia, Charlottesville).

Yesilada, Birol A., "The Virtue Party," *Turkish Studies*, 3, 2002.

Yetkin, Murat, "Beni 28 Şubat AB'ci Yaptı," *Radikal*, June 5, 2005.

Yıldırım, Ergun (Ahmet Harputlu), "Bir politics durum olarak müslüman demo-crat," *Bilgi ve Düşünce*, 5, 2003.

Yıldırım, Ergun and Hayrettin Özler, "A Sociological Representation of the Justice and Development Party (AKP): Is it a Political Design or a Political Becoming?" *Turkish Studies*, 8, 2007.

Yıldız, Ahmet, "Muhafazakarlığın Yerlileştirilmesi ya da AKP'nin `Yeni Muhafazakar Demokratlığı," *Karizma*, January–March 2004.

—, "AK Partinin 'Yeni Muhafazakar Demokratlığı': Türkiye Siyasetinde Adlandırma Problemi," *Liberal Düşünce*, No. 34, Spring 2004.

Yıldız, İlhan, *Ahmet Hamdi Akseki ve Din Eğitimindeki Yeri* (PhD dissertation, Uludağ Universitesi, 1997).

Yılmaz, Turan, *Tayyip: Kasımpasa'dan Siyasetin Ön Saflarına* (Istanbul: Umit, 2001).

Zafer, Özcan, "Tasgetiren: Tayyip Bey'i severim ama hatalarına aferin demem," *Aksiyon*, 560, August 29, 2005.

Zubaida, Sami, *Islam, the People and the State: Political Ideas and Movements in the Middle East* (New York: I. B. Tauris, 1993).

Zürcher, Eric, *Turkey: A Modern History* (New York: I. B. Tauris, 1997).

—, *The European Union, Turkey, and Islam* (Amsterdam: Amsterdam University Press, 2004).

# Index

Abdulhamid II 18, 21, 207
Abdullah Cevdet 22, 24
Adalet ve Kalkınma Partisi *see* AKP
Adultery debate 167–169
Akdoğan, Yalçın 2, 88, 91
Akseki, Ahmet H. 23
AKP 15, 79, 80–95
  2002 elections 1, 16, 32, 71, 79, 80, 81,
    119, 175, 185, 186, 195, 197, 215,
    244, 254
  2007 electoral victory of 1, 2,
    118–119, 175, 179,
    184–186, 194–195, 197, 254–258, 279
  adoption of human rights and democracy
    58, 211, 213, 214, 215, 216, 223
  advisors of 99, 102, 123, 201, 209, 229,
    242, 249
  and Cyprus issue xiii, 205, 224–227, 230
  and "hidden agenda" 100, 159
  and initiative for a new constitution
    255–259
  and Kurdish question xii, 111, 171,
    172–180, 230, 248, 249, 266
  and military 203–207, 209, 210, 221,
    232–234, 237, 276, 268–272
  and the EU 3, 4, 15, 47, 61, 68, 160,
    203–205, 210, 213–218
  conservative revolution 59, 61, 87, 244
  conservative value structure of 84, 96, 97,
    245, 253
  constituents and supporters of 86, 98,
    134, 160
  foreign policy of 74, 202–238
  four major groups 104–105, 106
  "fundamentalist party" 1, 51, 92, 114
  government 79, 82, 84, 88, 89, 98,
    110–111, 116, 123, 160, 240, 242, 249,
    258, 265
  ideological gap between the AKP and the
    establishment 240
  ideological groups within 104, 107
  image of 84, 89, 104, 211, 234

  intra-party conflict 90, 100–102, 123
  intra-party democracy 100, 102
  Is the AKP an Islamic party? 114
  Islamic party 1–4, 48, 114
  Islamist party 93, 105, 109
  Kurdish policies of 185–201, 243,
    249, 265
  leadership 68, 81, 84, 88, 90, 91, 95, 96,
    98, 99, 101, 106, 109, 113–114, 143,
    239, 245, 248, 249
  meaning of 94
  ministers of 96
  moral idioms of 97, 264
  parliamentarians of 102–104, 168, 253
  policies of 51, 87, 94, 98, 102, 114, 133,
    255, 258
  principal features of 105
  regional identity of the AKP in Southeast
    Turkey 86, 97, 98, 105–111
  second term electoral victory of 254
  secularism 81, 112, 123, 134, 145,
    158–163, 206, 210, 216, 217, 259, 261
  sympathizers with 241, 245
  transformation of 72, 88, 89, 93, 109,
    113, 114, 251–260
Aktan, Gündüz 244, 255
Aktay, Yasin 2, 29, 53
Alevi 29, 32, 33, 100, 109, 153, 158, 163,
  242, 253, 277–280
Altıkulaç, Tayyar 96
ANAP 28, 37, 50, 61, 62, 80, 107, 212,
  240, 253
Anatolian bourgeoisie 14, 15, 29, 30, 43,
  49, 51–56, 76, 79, 86, 96, 108, 110,
  113, 116
  Muslim bourgeoisie xii, 11, 45, 47, 48,
    52–57, 60, 69, 76, 78, 141, 280
Ankara 28, 39, 63, 102, 110, 166, 172, 175,
  189, 192, 199, 211, 226, 229–231, 237,
  241–243
AP 3, 28, 37, 42, 50, 107
Arınç, Bülent 68, 72, 161, 162, 248

# CAMBRIDGE MIDDLE EAST STUDIES 28